Contents at a Glance

Introduction 1

Part I: Getting Started with Football 5
Chapter 1: America's Greatest Game 7
Chapter 2: Meet Me on the Gridiron 17
Chapter 3: Them's the Rules (And Regulations) 31

Part II: Go, Offense! 59
Chapter 4: The Quarterback, Football's MVP 61
Chapter 5: The Passing Game 77
Chapter 6: Hitting the Ground Running 91
Chapter 7: The Offensive Line at Work in the Trenches 111
Chapter 8: Examining Offensive Plays and Strategies 125

Part III: The Big D 151
Chapter 9: These Guys Are Huge: The Defensive Line 153
Chapter 10: The Secondary: Last Line of Defense 169
Chapter 11: Delving into Defensive Tactics and Strategies 187

Part IV: Meet the Rest of the Team 205
Chapter 12: Special Teams, Masters of the Kicking Game 207
Chapter 13: Coaches, General Managers, and Other Important Folks 229

Part V: Football for Everyone 241
Chapter 14: Armchair Quarterbacks and Other Fabulous Fans 243
Chapter 15: Youth Leagues and High School Football 253
Chapter 16: College Football — Where It All Started 263
Chapter 17: Taking a Look at the NFL (And Other Professional Leagues) 277
Chapter 18: Playing Fantasy Football 293

Part VI: The Part of Tens 301
Chapter 19: The Ten (Or So) Greatest Defensive Players of All Time 303
Chapter 20: More Than Ten Top Non-Quarterback Offensive Players 313

Chapter 21: The Ten Greatest Quarterbacks of All Time 323
Chapter 22: The Ten Greatest Coaches in the History of the Game 331
Appendix...341

Index 353

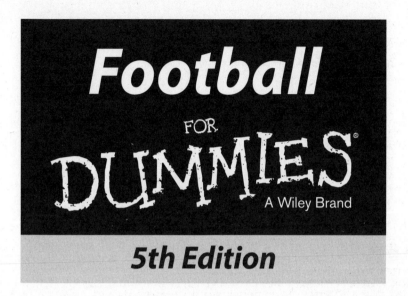

Football FOR DUMMIES®

A Wiley Brand

5th Edition

by Howie Long with John Czarnecki

Football For Dummies®, 5th Edition

Published by: **John Wiley & Sons, Inc.,** 111 River Street, Hoboken, NJ 07030-5774, www.wiley.com

Copyright © 2015 by John Wiley & Sons, Inc., Hoboken, New Jersey

Published simultaneously in Canada

For general information on our other products and services, please contact our Customer Care Department within the U.S. at 877-762-2974, outside the U.S. at 317-572-3993, or fax 317-572-4002. For technical support, please visit www.wiley.com/techsupport.

Wiley publishes in a variety of print and electronic formats and by print-on-demand. Some material included with standard print versions of this book may not be included in e-books or in print-on-demand. If this book refers to media such as a CD or DVD that is not included in the version you purchased, you may download this material at http://booksupport.wiley.com. For more information about Wiley products, visit www.wiley.com.

Library of Congress Control Number: 2015937670

ISBN 978-1-119-02263-3 (pbk); ISBN 978-1-119-02265-7 (ebk); ISBN 978-1-119-02264-0 (ebk)

Manufactured in the United States of America

10 9 8 7 6 5 4 3 2 1

Contents

Introduction 1

About This Book 2
Foolish Assumptions 2
Icons Used in This Book 3
Beyond the Book 4
Where to Go from Here 4

Part I: Getting Started with Football 5

Chapter 1: America's Greatest Game 7

Why Football Is the Best 8
Who's Playing Football 9
How Football Began 10
Camp defines the rules 10
Grange helps spread the popularity of pro ball 11
How the Football Season Is Set Up Today 13
How Television Helped Increase Football's Popularity 15
Why Millions Cheer Each Year for College Football 15
What Makes the Super Bowl Number One 16

Chapter 2: Meet Me on the Gridiron 17

The Big Picture: Stadiums 17
Getting Down to Business: The Field 18
Field dimensions 18
The marks on the field 19
The playing surface 21
Goalposts and other on-the-field equipment 23
Looking at That Funny-Shaped Ball 24
Meeting the Cast of Characters 25
What Football Uniforms Are All About 26
The jersey 26
Helmets and face masks 28
Pads 29
Shoes and cleats 29

Chapter 3: Them's the Rules (And Regulations) **31**

The Ins and Outs of the Game Clock 31
The Coin Toss and Kickoff 33
Downs Plus Yardage Equals Excitement 35
Scoring Points 36
    Touchdowns 36
    Extra points and two-point conversions 37
    Field goals 38
    Safeties 39
The Role of the Officials 39
    Referee 40
    Umpire 41
    Head linesman 41
    Line judge 41
    Back judge 42
    Field judge 42
    Side judge 43
Familiarizing Yourself with Referee Signals 43
Penalties and Other Violations 49
    Looking at 5-yard penalties 49
    Surveying 10-yard penalties 52
    Recognizing 15-yard penalties 54
    Identifying specific pass-play penalties 56
Disputing a Call: The Instant Replay Challenge System 57

Part II: Go, Offense! **59**

Chapter 4: The Quarterback, Football's MVP **61**

Taking a Look at the Quarterback's Job 61
Determining What a Quarterback Needs to Succeed 63
    Arm strength 64
    Accuracy 64
    Competitiveness 64
    Intelligence 65
    Mobility 65
    Release 66
    Size 67
    Vision 67
Quarterbacking Fundamentals 68
    Settling into the stance 69
    Dropping back 69
    Handing off 70
    Getting a grip 71

Reading a Defense 71
Calling Plays and Audibilizing.................................... 74
Acing Quarterback Math... 75

Chapter 5: The Passing Game **77**
Getting to Know the Passing Game 77
Recognizing the Role of Receivers 78
  Achieving the proper stance 80
  Lining up correctly 81
  Catching the ball 81
  Beating man-to-man coverage 81
Defining Important Passing Terms 83
Looking at Passing Patterns 85
Getting into the Shotgun Formation............................ 88

Chapter 6: Hitting the Ground Running......................**91**
An Overview of the Ground Game............................... 92
Meeting the Men Who Play the Ground Game.................... 93
  The halfback, a team's principal ball carrier 93
  The fullback, protector of the halfback 94
Recognizing that Running Backs Come in All Sizes and Shapes....... 94
Exploring Running Back Fundamentals 95
  The basic skills.. 96
  The job description 97
  The stances.. 99
  The number one priority 100
Lining Up: The Formations 102
Walking through the Basic Running Plays....................... 104

Chapter 7: The Offensive Line at Work in the Trenches **111**
Looking Down the Line 112
  Centers 113
  Guards 114
  Tackles 115
The Lineman Physique: Fat Guys Doing the Job 116
Understanding the Keys to Successful Offensive Line Play 117
  The proper stance 117
  A solid base 119
  Leverage.. 119
  Toughness... 120
  Repetition... 121
Uncovering a Lineman's Worst Offense: Penalties................ 121
Getting Acquainted with Blocking Terms........................ 122

Chapter 8: Examining Offensive Plays and Strategies **125**

Offense Begins with Players 126
Zeroing in on Specialized Pass Offenses 127
    West Coast offense 127
    Shotgun offense 128
Looking at Some Newfangled Offenses 130
    The wildcat 130
    The spread 131
    The pistol 131
Beating a Defense 131
    Battling a 3-4 front 132
    Running against a 4-3 front 133
    Defeating the four-across defense 134
    Beating press coverage 135
    Passing against a zone coverage 135
    Selecting an offense versus a zone blitz 137
    Throwing the post versus blitzing teams 138
    Wearing out a defense with the no-huddle offense 138
Gaining Better Field Position 139
    Throwing a field position pass 139
    Opting for possession passes 139
    Moving downfield with play-action passes 140
Surveying Offenses for Sticky Situations 140
    Deciding whether to gamble on fourth-and-1 140
    Making a first down on a fourth-down gamble 141
    Running a quarterback sneak 142
    Doing the two-minute drill 143
Scoring Offenses 144
    Making the best run play on the goal line 144
    Scoring inside the opponent's 10-yard line 145
    Going for two-point conversions 146
Disguising a Successful Play 148

Part III: The Big D *151*

Chapter 9: These Guys Are Huge: The Defensive Line **153**

Those Big Guys Called Linemen 154
    Looking closely at the D line 155
    Identifying types of defensive linemen 155
    Understanding what makes a good defensive lineman 157
    Delving into D-line lingo 158
    Unlocking the keys to a defensive lineman 160

Linebackers: The Leaders of the Defense..161
    Figuring out what linebackers do 162
    Dealing with the senses..163
    Naming all the linebackers 164
Defensive Alignments...165
Sacks, Tackles, and Other Defensive Gems.......................................166

Chapter 10: The Secondary: Last Line of Defense **169**
Presenting the Performers 170
    Cornerbacks 170
    Safeties 172
    Nickel and dime backs 174
Studying Secondary Tricks and Techniques..176
    Doing a bump and run...176
    Staying with a receiver..177
    Stemming around...177
Making a Mark: A Good Day in the Life of a Defensive Back..............178
The Problem of Pass Interference and Illegal Contact......................179
Examining the Two Types of Coverage (And Their Variations)...........180
    Man-to-man coverage..180
    Zone coverage...182
    Eight men in the box...182
    The Nickel 40 defense...183

Chapter 11: Delving into Defensive Tactics and Strategies........**187**
Choosing a Base Defense..187
Examining the Different Defenses...189
    4-3 front 189
    3-4 front 191
    3-4 eagle..193
    Dallas 4-3 194
    Flex..195
    Zone blitz 196
    46..198
    Over/under 4-3 200
    Cover two (and Tampa two)...201
Tackling Tricky Situations...203
    Stopping a superstar 203
    Stopping the two-point conversion 203
    Stuffing short yardage 204

Part IV: Meet the Rest of the Team 205

Chapter 12: Special Teams, Masters of the Kicking Game 207

Finding Out Who's Who on Special Teams 208
Understanding What's So Special about Special Teams.......................209
Placekicking...210
    Kicking off 210
    Returning the kickoff 215
    Kicking field goals and PATs 217
    Blocking field goals and PATs 219
Punting..222
    Setting up and kicking the ball..223
    Meeting the key performers on the punt team 223
    Reviewing punt rules...225
    Punting out of trouble 226
    Examining the dangerous art of punt returning 226

Chapter 13: Coaches, General Managers, and Other Important Folks 229

A Team's Fearless Leaders: The Coaches 230
    Discovering who does what on the coaching staff.........................230
    Exploring the different coaching styles and philosophies 233
    Looking into what coaches do when they're not yelling
        on the sidelines 236
The Team's Public Face: The Owners...238
An Owner's Eyes and Ears: General Managers 239
The People Responsible for Finding Talent: Scouts..............................239
Keeping Players Strong and Healthy: Trainers and Team Doctors.......240

Part V: Football for Everyone..................................... 241

Chapter 14: Armchair Quarterbacks and Other Fabulous Fans 243

Deciphering the Announcers' Slang...243
Following a Game on Television or Radio 244
    Watching a game on television 245
    Listening to a game on the radio 246
Attending a Game 247
    Picking the best seats..247
    Knowing what to focus on 248
    Enjoying the halftime show 249

Keeping Up with Your Favorite Teams 249
    The NFL Network and the NFL Redzone Channel 249
    Internet sports sites 250
    Fantasy football sites 251
    Twitter 251
    Mobile apps 252
Visiting the Football Halls of Fame 252

Chapter 15: Youth Leagues and High School Football............253

Determining When to Start Playing 253
Signing Up Your Kids for Youth Football 254
    Pop Warner and similar programs 254
    Punt, Pass & Kick 255
Realizing What Sets High School Football Apart 256
    Rule differences 257
    Style of play 257
    Player lineups 258
Making the Most of the High School Game 259
    Players 259
    Coaches 260
    Parents 260
Thinking Ahead to a College Football Career 261

Chapter 16: College Football — Where It All Started 263

Why People Love College Football 263
Big, Medium, and Small 265
    Big-time schools 266
    Small college powers 268
Examining College Conferences 268
The College Football Playoff 270
    The selection process 271
    The semifinals 271
    The national championship game 271
The Heisman and Other Trophies 272
All-American and Other All-Star Teams 274

Chapter 17: Taking a Look at the NFL (And Other Professional Leagues)...277

The Birth of Pro Football 278
Dividing the Ranks: The NFL Conferences 279
Getting to Know the Pro Football Schedule 280
    The regular-season games 280
    The playoffs 280
    The Super Bowl 281

Building a Team: It's More than Drawing Straws 282
    Drafting players out of school 283
    Trading to get who you want 284
    Going the free agent route 284
Status Is Everything: Determining Player Designations 285
The Business of Professional Football 287
    Show me the money: Player salaries 287
    The salary cap levels the playing field 288
    Collective bargaining agreements 289
    Big business and the television connection 289
Making the Players' Health a Priority 291
Peeking at Other Pro Leagues 291

Chapter 18: Playing Fantasy Football 293

Exploring How Fantasy Football Leagues Work 293
Figuring Out How to Play 294
    Starting a league 295
    Choosing a fantasy football site 295
    Drafting a team 296
    Filling out your roster 296
    Managing your team after the draft 297
    Figuring your point total and winning 297
Finding Information to Help Your Team 299
Considering Tips for Fantasy Football Success 299

Part VI: The Part of Tens 301

**Chapter 19: The Ten (Or So) Greatest Defensive Players
of All Time 303**

Doug Atkins 303
Dick Butkus 304
Kenny Easley 304
Joe Greene 305
Jack Ham and Ted Hendricks 306
Mike Haynes 306
Ken Houston 307
Sam Huff and Ray Nitschke 308
Deacon Jones and Merlin Olsen 308
Jack Lambert 309
Dick "Night Train" Lane 309
Bob Lilly 310
Gino Marchetti 311

Chapter 20: More Than Ten Top Non-Quarterback Offensive Players **313**

Jim Brown 313
Earl Campbell 314
Dave Casper 315
Mike Ditka and John Mackey 315
John Hannah 316
Don Hutson 317
Hugh McElhenny .317
Jim Parker 318
Walter Payton 318
Gale Sayers 319
Art Shell 320
Gene Upshaw 320

Chapter 21: The Ten Greatest Quarterbacks of All Time **323**

Terry Bradshaw 323
Tom Brady 324
John Elway 325
Otto Graham 325
Peyton Manning 326
Dan Marino 327
Joe Montana 327
Fran Tarkenton 328
Johnny Unitas 328
Steve Young 329

Chapter 22: The Ten Greatest Coaches in the History of the Game **331**

Paul Brown 331
Joe Gibbs 332
George Halas 333
Jimmy Johnson 334
Vince Lombardi 334
John Madden 335
Bill Parcells 336
Knute Rockne 337
Don Shula 338
Bill Walsh 339

Appendix **341**

Index **353**

Introduction

M illions of people across the United States are intrigued by football — all types and levels of it. These people may have friends or family who have made the football season a ritual, from the last weekend in August through the college bowl games in December until Super Bowl Sunday at the start of February. To be a part of that experience, you need to have a working knowledge of the game.

Football For Dummies, 5th Edition, serves to give you that knowledge and help you better facilitate interaction with your friends, family, or whoever you watch football with. For many people, on the surface, football seems to be a complicated game. Twenty-two players are on the field at one time, plus a number of officials. The intricacies of first down, second down, and third down, and everything from how many offensive linemen there are to what the quarterback really does or doesn't do all need to be explained and simplified. This book will help; that's why I decided to write it.

I think football is far less intimidating when you have a basic working knowledge of the game. After you break through that initial fear of being overwhelmed by football and what you don't understand, everything else about the game falls into place. You begin to see the game clearly, like when you wipe the early morning dew off your windshield — suddenly everything becomes crystal clear.

Today I know a lot more about the game as a whole than I did when I was a player. I played in high school and in college, plus I played for 13 seasons in the National Football League (NFL). But being a television analyst — 2015 will be my 22nd season working for FOX Sports — has forced me to learn even more about this game that I love.

As a player, I had a working knowledge of the passing game, of how a secondary works in coverages, and of the offensive and defensive line formations. I also had a working knowledge of general managers, scouts, and head coaches. But working as an analyst, I've been forced to cover the entire game. I no longer view football from a defensive lineman's perspective. Instead, I look at football as a whole. And I'm still learning every day. That never changes. I don't think you'll ever stop learning when it comes to football. It's the same for everyone — the players, the fans, the coaches, and the television experts. So don't feel alone out there.

About This Book

I wrote *Football For Dummies,* 5th Edition, to help you find out what you want to know about football. Therefore, I don't expect you to read every single page in order. Sure, you can read the book from front to back if you want, but if you'd rather skip around and just read about the topics that interest you, that's fine, too.

And I don't make you remember obscure facts from earlier chapters to make sense of later chapters. If you need to know something that I cover in an earlier chapter, I either define it again or refer you to the chapter that contains the information. Also, if you don't know certain football jargon, you can turn to the Appendix, which explains some of the most common terms. What could be simpler?

I also use diagrams — you know, those X and O things — to show you what I'm talking about when I describe lineups, formations, and plays. So you aren't left wondering what all those little symbols mean, here's a key to the diagrams used in this book:

O	Offensive player
X	Offensive center
◑	Offensive player with defender lined up on left shoulder
◐	Offensive player with defender lined up on right shoulder
▲	Defensive player
⟶	Path of offensive player
—|	Spot where offensive player stops to block or catch a pass
- - - - -	Pass
··········	Pitchout

Foolish Assumptions

Here's what I'm assuming about you: You're interested in football and want to get familiar with the sport, including its history, so you can watch games in person and on television, follow all the action, and enjoy football games to the hilt. You may not know much about football, but I know that you're no dummy either. You may, however, have burning questions like these:

- Is the ball really made of pigskin, or is that an inside joke?
- Why do you get six points for a touchdown but only three points for a field goal?
- Does it really matter how all those guys line up on the field?
- Does it really mean something when the officials do those funny signals with their arms, or are they just bored out there?

This book answers all these questions and more.

Icons Used in This Book

To help you navigate your way through this book, I place icons in the margins. These little pictures point you to a particular type of information. Here's a list of the icons in this book and what they mean:

A book about football wouldn't be the same without tales of the sport's greats. This icon flags stories about the game's greatest, most recognized players.

Being a commentator, I can't help but want to throw in my two cents once in a while. When I have my own tale to tell on a subject, I mark it with this icon.

When you see this icon, you know you're reading a piece of information that's especially important to remember. If you take away nothing else from this book but the paragraphs flagged with this icon, you'll have a solid understanding of football.

Look for this icon if you want to know all the helpful tidbits of info that can make you a more informed fan.

Beyond the Book

This book provides great information to help you learn about football, but you can find many more resources on Dummies.com:

✔ You can download the book's Cheat Sheet at `www.dummies.com/cheatsheet/football`. It's a handy resource to keep on your computer, tablet, or smartphone.

✔ You can read interesting companion articles that supplement the book's content at `www.dummies.com/extras/football`. I even include an extra top-ten list.

Where to Go from Here

So you're geared up and ready to play, metaphorically speaking. Where you go from here depends on the type of information you're looking for. If you want a primer on football starting at square one, head to Chapter 1. If you want to know about how a particular phase of the game — say, the offensive line or the kicking game — works, head to that specific chapter. And if you want to read about some of the greatest players in football history, head to Part VI. Wherever you start, enjoy the game!

Part I
Getting Started with Football

In this part . . .

- ✔ Get an overview of football's history, the players and personnel involved, and the roots of the world's greatest game

- ✔ Look at the field and equipment and the meanings behind the uniforms

- ✔ Review the rules of football and understand its ins and outs

Chapter 1

America's Greatest Game

In This Chapter

▶ Discovering why football is America's passion

▶ Looking back on football's progression throughout the years

▶ Figuring out how the modern football season works

▶ Recognizing what makes college games so much fun and the Super Bowl such a major event

*W*hen I was 14, a sophomore in high school, I moved out of Boston to live with my uncle. During my first weekend in Milford, Massachusetts, I saw my first high school football game. I had never seen anything like it. Before the game, an antique fire engine led a parade on the track around the football field while the crowd clapped and cheered. The players then thundered across a wooden bridge over a pond and burst through a banner to enter the stadium. I said to myself, "Wow, this game is for me."

I wasn't necessarily drawn to the game itself; I simply loved what came with the sport: *respect.* For me, football was an opportunity to belong to something, giving me confidence for the first time in my life. It was more of a personal thing than it was about playing football. It wasn't so much the football, but what football did for me. Football gave me a sense of self-worth, which I've carried with me throughout my life.

Sure, I experienced down periods when I first started playing, but I never thought about quitting. My first high school coach, Dick Corbin, was great to me and encouraged me to continue playing the game. Believe me, coaches are important. I've always had the support of football coaches, both on *and* off the field.

Football is responsible for everything that I've accomplished in my life. The discipline and hard work that made me a successful athlete have helped me in other areas of my life, allowing me to venture into new careers in movies and television.

Why Football Is the Best

Baseball may be America's pastime, but football is America's passion. Football is the only team sport in America that conjures up visions of Roman gladiators, pitting city versus city, state versus state — sometimes with a Civil War feel, like when the Jets play the Giants in New York or the Dallas Cowboys play the Washington Redskins.

Football is played in all weather conditions — snow, rain, and sleet — with temperatures on the playing field ranging from –30 to 120 degrees Fahrenheit. Whatever the conditions may be, the game goes on. And unlike other major sports, the football playoff system, in the National Football League (NFL) anyway, is a single-elimination tournament. In other words, the NFL has no playoff series; the playoffs are do-or-die, culminating in what has become the single biggest one-day sporting event in America: the Super Bowl.

Or, in simpler terms, anytime you stick 22 men in high-tech plastic helmets on a football field and have them continually run great distances at incredible speeds and slam into each other, people will watch.

Football has wedged itself into the American culture. In fact, in many small towns across the United States, the centerpiece is the Friday night high school football game. The NFL doesn't play on Fridays simply to protect this great part of Americana, in which football often gives schools and even towns a certain identity. For example, hard-core fans know that tiny Massillon, Ohio, is where the late, great Paul Brown of the Cleveland Browns began his coaching career. To this day, Massillon's high school has maintained a tremendous high school football tradition. With so many factions of the student body involved, plus their families, a strong core of fans is built. For many, this enthusiasm for football continues in college.

You may not think it now, but millions of people are familiar with the strategy of the game, and most of them pass it down through their families. A lot of fathers coach their sons, and on rare occasions, their daughters. Although the focus may have changed in today's society, at one time the only team that mattered in high school was the football team. The pace of the game — stoppage after every play with a huddle — is perfect for most fans because it allows them time to guess what the team will try next.

Football is *it* in the United States

Since 1985, Harris Interactive (a global market- ing research firm) has been conducting polls to determine which sport is the most popular in the United States. Pro football has been ranked number 1 in 30 straight polls. In 2014, 35 per- cent of Americans polled chose pro football as their favorite sport. Baseball came in second at 14 percent. Guess which sport came in third? That would be college football at 11 percent. Any way you slice it, football is unquestionably the most popular spectator sport in the United States.

On two particular holidays, sitting down and watching football has become an American tradition:

- ✔ **Thanksgiving Day** is reserved for a turkey dinner with the family, followed by a pro football game. The Detroit Lions started the tradition in 1934, and in 2014 they played in their 75th Thanksgiving Day game. There have been at least two pro football games on Thanksgiving Day every year since 1960. Since 2006, fans have enjoyed three games on that holiday.
- ✔ **New Year's Day** has long been the day for college football bowl games, which generally match up some of the nation's finest teams.

Who's Playing Football

Football is suited to all sizes of athletes. Larger athletes generally play on the offensive and defensive lines — what are called the *trenches*. Leaner athletes who are faster and quicker generally play the skill positions, such as quar- terback, running back, and receiver. But no matter how big or how talented you are, you must have inner courage to play football. This game requires strength and perseverance. If you don't believe you're tough enough to play, then you probably shouldn't try.

And if you're not up to the full-force-hitting variety of football, you can still enjoy the sport as a player. Touch football is totally different from tackle foot- ball. All you need are a ball and maybe six players, three per team. Anyone can play this game, and the players decide the rules and the size of the field at the start of the game. I've seen people playing touch football on the streets of New York City and in parks and front lawns all across America — the beauty of the game is that you can play anywhere.

Of all the team sports, football is the most violent and dangerous, with hockey a distant second. I played football for respect, and I believe that it builds character. Considering some of the problems in society today, football can give a youngster's life some structure and can also teach discipline. All the players who belong to a football team are in the struggle together, sharing in the joy and the pain of the sport. Every play can be such an adrenaline rush.

How Football Began

Just as many fans get caught up in the hype and hoopla of today's NFL, many others love the game for its sense of tradition. The game itself has endured for more than 140 years.

Games involving kicking a ball into a goal on a lined field have existed for more than 2,000 years. American football evolved from two particular games that were popular in other parts of the world: soccer (as it's known in the United States) and rugby. Both the Romans and the Spartans (remember that movie *Spartacus*? Now those guys were tough!) played some version of soccer. Soccer and rugby came to North America in the 19th century, and historians have noted that the first form of American football emerged on November 6, 1869, when teams from Princeton and Rutgers, two New Jersey universities, competed in a game of what was closer to rugby than football. Rutgers won that game 6–4.

The following sections introduce you to the contributions of two key individuals in the football world: Walter Camp and Harold "Red" Grange.

Camp defines the rules

Walter Camp, a sensational player at Yale University and a driving force behind many football rules, is known as the father of American football. Around 1876, when football was already being played in universities on the East Coast and in Canada, Camp helped write the game's first rules. In 1880, he authored rules that reduced the number of players per team from 15 to 11 (today's total) and replaced the rugby scrum with the center snap to put the ball in play. (In a *scrum,* players from both sides bunch tightly together, butting heads while the ball is thrown between them. The players then try to gain possession of the ball with their feet. Using your hands to gain possession is unique to American football — both rugby and soccer forbid it.)

Camp also championed the rule that a team needed to gain 5 yards in three plays in order to maintain possession. Today, teams must gain 10 yards in four plays. (Head to Chapter 3 for more information about these and other rules.)

Camp devised plays and formations and instituted referees. However, his biggest proposal was tackling, which was introduced in 1888. *Tackling* — the act of hitting players below the waist — made the game more violent. It also popularized an offensive strategy known as the *flying wedge,* where an entire team (ten players) would mass in front of one ball carrier in the form of a wedge. Football was almost banned in 1906 after a dozen and a half deaths (and many more serious injuries in the preceding season), but President Theodore Roosevelt saved the game by convincing college representatives to initiate stricter rules to make the game less brutal and dangerous.

Football has been cleaned up a great deal over the years and has come a long way from clothesline shots and quarterbacks taking late hits and direct blows to the head. But let's not kid one another: Football is a high-impact collision sport, and with collision comes pain and injury. Even with the rules being adjusted to protect today's quarterbacks, rarely does a Monday morning come without the news that at least one quarterback sustained a concussion. Players are bigger, faster, and stronger. Let me put it this way: You're driving down the road traveling at 35 miles per hour. Would you rather be met head-on by a car of similar size or by a truck? Well, that's the difference between 20 years ago and now. Only thing is, the truck's now going 45 miles per hour rather than 35.

Grange helps spread the popularity of pro ball

Americans started playing football in colleges and on club teams in the 1870s. Football became a source of identity for collegians and a regular Saturday afternoon activity by the turn of the century.

In the first 90 years of football, college football was far more popular than pro football; it was (and still is, at many schools) all about tradition and the many rivalries between colleges. Ninety years ago, having more than 50,000 fans attend a great college game wasn't unusual. During that same period, games in the NFL, which officially began in 1920, were fortunate to draw 5,000 fans.

Two days after the 1925 college season ended, Illinois All-American halfback Harold "Red" Grange (see Figure 1-1) signed a contract to play with the struggling Chicago Bears. On Thanksgiving Day of that year, 36,000 fans — the largest crowd in pro football history at that time — watched Grange and the Bears play the league's top team, the Chicago Cardinals, to a scoreless tie in Cubs Park (now called Wrigley Field, the home of the Chicago Cubs baseball team). The Bears went on to play a barnstorming tour, and in New York's Polo Grounds, more than 73,000 fans watched Grange — nicknamed "the Galloping Ghost" — compete against the New York Giants. Although Grange did attract new fans to the pro game, fewer than 30,000 fans attended championship games in the early 1930s.

Pro football emerged as an equal to college football after its games began being televised nationally in the 1960s, but it took decades for the NFL to supplant college football. And to this day, many colleges have as much fan support as some NFL franchises. Universities such as Nebraska, USC, and Notre Dame can claim more fans than, say, the Atlanta Falcons.

Figure 1-1: Harold "Red" Grange, known as "the Galloping Ghost," played for the Chicago Bears in 1925.

Photo credit: © New York Times Co./Getty Images

Football immortals

With every sport comes a list of immortals — those great players who nurtured the game and made it what it is today. Following are some of the early legends of American football:

✔ **John W. Heisman:** The annual award given to the nation's best college player — the Heisman Trophy — is named after this Brown University (and later University of Pennsylvania) player. Heisman was also a member of New York's Downtown Athletic Club, where the award was presented every December until the building was damaged in the September 11, 2001, terrorist attacks. Heisman was an early advocate of the forward pass.

✔ **Fritz Pollard:** Pollard starred for Brown University in 1915 and 1916 and was the first African American player to appear in the Rose Bowl. He's also considered the first African American football player to turn professional, the first to be selected to the college All-American team, and the first African American pro head coach (of the Akron Pros in 1921). In 1954, he became the first African American inducted into the College Football Hall of Fame.

✔ **Amos Alonzo Stagg:** Stagg was a famous University of Chicago coach who developed the "Statue of Liberty" play, in which a halfback takes the ball from the quarterback who has his hands raised as if to throw a forward pass. (I explain offensive positions in Part II.) He was also the first coach to put numbers on players' uniforms.

✔ **Jim Thorpe:** A Native American who won the decathlon and pentathlon in the 1912 Stockholm Olympics, Thorpe was an All-American at Carlisle (Pennsylvania) Indian School and was the first big-time American athlete to play pro football. He was paid the princely sum of $250 to play a game for the Canton Bulldogs in 1915. Today, Canton, Ohio, is the home of the Pro Football Hall of Fame.

✔ **Pop Warner:** The national tackle youth league (described in Chapter 15) is named after this famous coach, who developed the single-wing formation, which snaps the ball directly to the running back and has four linemen to one side of the center and two to the other side. Warner was the first to use the hidden ball trick, in which an offensive lineman slipped the ball under his jersey. The first "hunchback play" went for a touchdown against Harvard in 1902.

How the Football Season Is Set Up Today

Football as an organized sport has come a long way since the early years. Teams at every level play during a standard season and are governed by various football leagues, such as the NFL and NCAA (National Collegiate Athletic Association).

The heart of the football season is during the fall months. However, training camps, practices, and preseason games often begin in the summer, and playoffs and bowl games are staged after Christmas and into February. Here's how the season breaks down for each level of play:

- **High school football teams** usually play between eight and ten games in a season, starting after Labor Day. If teams have successful league seasons, they advance to regional or state playoff tournaments. Some schools in Texas play as many as 15 games if they advance to the state championship game. Most high school teams play in a regional league, although some travel 50 to 100 miles to play opponents. You can find out more about high school football in Chapter 15.

- **College football teams** play between 10 and 13 games, the majority in a specific conference — Pac-12, Big Ten, SEC, ACC, and so on. The top teams in the Division I FBS (Football Bowl Subdivision), which constitute the largest schools that offer the most money for athletic scholarships, advance via invitation to postseason bowl games or a four-team playoff for the national championship. Beginning with the 2014–2015 season, the top four teams play in two semifinal games, with the winners facing each other in the College Football Championship Game. This playoff system replaced the controversial BCS system, which had been in place from 1998 through the 2013–2014 season. Read more about college football in Chapter 16.

- **NFL teams** play 16 regular-season games, preceded by a minimum of 4 preseason games that are played in August. The 32 NFL teams are divided into two conferences, the NFC (National Football Conference) and the AFC (American Football Conference), and the four division leaders and two wild card teams from each conference advance to the playoffs with hopes of reaching the Super Bowl, which is played in early February. Chapter 17 gives you all the details about the NFL.

Football is pretty much a weekend sport, although a few games are played on Monday and Thursday, particularly in the NFL. In general, however, the football season, which begins in earnest right around Labor Day, follows this orderly pattern:

- High school games are usually played on Friday nights.

- College games are played on Saturdays, mostly during the day, although a few are held on Thursday and Friday nights.

- The NFL plays on Sundays for the most part. For television purposes, games are played in the early and late afternoon (Eastern time).

How Television Helped Increase Football's Popularity

Today, most football fans are introduced to the game through television, which brings the game right into everyone's home. The action in a football game translates well to television. The field and all the action that takes place upon it fit just as nicely on a big screen as they do on a smaller model. Because television networks use up to 20 cameras for most games, viewers rarely miss out on plays. And with replay machines, the networks can show critical plays from several different angles, including a viewer-friendly angle for fans watching at home or at the neighborhood tavern.

Television shows like *FOX NFL Sunday* also help to make the game more personal by promoting the personalities under the helmets. Fans, for example, can watch and listen to a Drew Brees interview and feel like they know the New Orleans quarterback as a person.

In addition, with round-the-clock NFL coverage on sports cable networks like ESPN, FOX Sports, and the NFL Network, fans can tune in pretty much 24 hours a day to get the latest news and updates about their favorite players and teams. This kind of coverage keeps football at the forefront of fan awareness all season long.

Why Millions Cheer Each Year for College Football

As much as I prefer the NFL, I have to acknowledge that for many fans, college football is the game to watch. The level of play isn't as high in college, but the collegiate game has more history and pageantry. Marching bands, mascots, pep rallies, and cheerleaders add a fun dimension to college football. Some teams, such as Notre Dame and Michigan, are steeped in folklore and tradition. Notre Dame, for example, has the Four Horsemen, the Seven Mules, and the Gipper.

College football fans can be every bit as passionate as NFL fans, especially when they root for a team that represents the college or university they attend or once attended or when they don't have a professional team to cheer on. Los Angeles, for example, doesn't have an NFL football team — the Rams left for St. Louis in 1995, and the Raiders returned to Oakland that same year — but its football fans make do based on the strength of two local college football teams, the USC Trojans and the UCLA Bruins. USC and UCLA consistently field excellent teams.

What Makes the Super Bowl Number One

Almost every year, the highest-rated show on network television is the Super Bowl, with whatever the number-two show is running a distant second. Of the ten most-watched shows in the history of television, four of them are Super Bowl games. Clearly, the Super Bowl has become an event that all of America, both casual and hard-core fans alike, focuses on. Even if it's the only game they watch all season, people tune into the Super Bowl and attend Super Bowl parties in massive numbers (would you believe these parties are more popular than New Year's Eve parties?).

The Super Bowl has also become an international event. More than 200 countries and territories, including Slovenia and the People's Republic of China, televised 2014's Super Bowl XLVIII. In the United States, an estimated 112.2 million fans watched the game, making it the most watched show in the history of American television. People all over the world saw the Seattle Seahawks defeat the Denver Broncos on that Super Bowl Sunday.

The main reason the Super Bowl is so popular is that pro football is the only major professional team sport with a single-elimination playoff system. The other major sports declare their champions after a team wins four games in a best-of-seven series. The Super Bowl is do-or-die; that's what makes the game so special.

And it isn't just the game itself that attracts viewers. Companies pay advertising firms lots of money to create commercials. In fact, watching the Super Bowl to see the commercials has become a part of what makes Super Bowl Sunday so special. All the commercials are judged and summarized because hundreds of millions of potential customers are watching, making the commercial stakes almost as high as those on the field.

The road to the Super Bowl

I played in my only Super Bowl after my third season in the NFL, and I thought I'd make it back at least two or three more times during my career. Unfortunately, that never happened.

The media attention back in 1984 wasn't nearly as expansive as it is today. In fact, tracing the growth of the media from 1984 to today is like comparing the size of Rhode Island to the size of Montana. I remember taking a cab to Tampa Stadium to play in the Super Bowl. The traffic was so bad that I ended up walking the last three-quarters of a mile to the stadium. Today, the NFL provides police escorts for the players. The fanfare surrounding a team's arrival is as if the president is coming to town.

Chapter 2

Meet Me on the Gridiron

· ·

In This Chapter

▶ Comparing domes and outdoor stadiums

▶ Taking a look at the field and the ball

▶ Getting a rundown of the many players

▶ Gearing up for football with uniforms, helmets, pads, and shoes

· ·

I've spent a lot of time on football fields. Although the dimensions are the same, from high school to the NFL, every field seems different. That's because all across America, the atmosphere inside each stadium, or the architectural character of the stadium itself, tends to be unique to that region. But every field shares some common characteristics.

In this chapter, I explain the basics of a football field and why teams don't always play on my favorite surface — good old green grass. I also talk about the number of players on the field, what they wear, and that odd-shaped ball they play with.

The Big Picture: Stadiums

As you probably know, a *stadium* is the whole structure or area in which football and other games are played: the field, the stands, and so on. Stadiums come in all shapes and sizes. The important thing is that they allow room for the 100-yard-long football field, which is, of course, obligatory. (See the next section for more on the football field.)

NFL and college stadiums come in two main varieties: domed stadiums and outdoor stadiums. Domed stadiums are designed so that the players and the fans don't have to deal with the weather; they always have a roof over their heads, and the teams always play on artificial turf. When you're talking about big-time football, both types of stadiums generally seat between 50,000 and 107,000 screaming fans.

The best stadium in pro football

There's no better setting in pro football than Lambeau Field in Green Bay, Wisconsin. With its circular seating and lack of an upper deck, Lambeau is a fan-friendly stadium. Every seat offers a good view of the action.

For a potentially cold arena, Lambeau is also a player-friendly stadium. To improve their field in freezing conditions, the Packers installed SportGrass in 1997. This new surface consists of natural grass planted on a recyclable, synthetic surface below field level. This setup creates a stable base that can't be destroyed by the physical wear and tear on the field when coupled with soggy, wet conditions. The old field, by the way, was packed into "Frozen Tundra" boxes and sold to fans to help pay for the new field.

New stadiums, many financed through public support and tax dollars, have become one of the NFL's top priorities. Between 1992 and 2010, a total of 22 new stadiums were built. These stadiums offer luxury boxes, state-of-the-art video systems, and other amenities for fans. Reliant Stadium, home of the Houston Texans, boasts natural grass and a retractable roof, the first of its kind in the NFL. Ford Field, the home of the Detroit Lions, includes a six-story atrium. In 2010, proving once and for all that Texans like all things big, the Dallas Cowboys inaugurated Cowboys Stadium, the largest domed stadium in the world. The stadium includes an 11,520-square-foot video display screen, the — you guessed it — largest high-definition screen in the world.

Getting Down to Business: The Field

There's nothing like a football field. If I could wish something for everyone, it would be for them to stand on the sideline at an NFL game and hear, sense, and feel the impact of the collisions and see the speed of the game up close. The selected areas around the sidelines for photographers and television cameramen are my favorite places to watch the game. The following sections tell you what you see on a football field, whether you're on the field or in the stands.

Field dimensions

The dimensions of a football field haven't changed much through the years. The field has been 100 yards long and 53⅓ yards wide since 1881. In 1912, the two end zones were established at 10 yards deep and have remained so ever since. Consequently, all football games are played on a rectangular field that's 360 feet long and 160 feet wide.

The marks on the field

All over the field, you see a bunch of white lines. Every line has a special meaning, as shown in Figure 2-1:

- ✔ **End lines:** The lines at each end of the field are called the *end lines.*
- ✔ **Sidelines:** The lines along each side of the field are called the *sidelines.*
- ✔ **Goal lines:** The *goal lines* are 10 yards inside and parallel to each end line.
- ✔ **Field of play:** The area bounded by the goal lines and sidelines is known as the *field of play.*
- ✔ **50-yard line:** The field is divided in half by the *50-yard line,* which is located in the middle of the field.
- ✔ **End zones:** The two areas bounded by the goal lines, end lines, and sidelines are known as the *end zones.*

To make all these white lines, teams use paint or marking chalk. They're even painting grass fields these days. The end lines and sidelines are 4 inches wide and rimmed by a solid white border that's a minimum of 6 feet wide. All boundary lines, goal lines, and marked yard lines are continuous lines until they intersect with one another.

The field also contains yard lines, hash marks, and lines marking the player benches, which I describe in detail in the following sections.

Yard lines

Yard lines, at intervals of 5 yards, run parallel to the goal lines and are marked across the field from sideline to sideline. These lines stop 8 inches short of the 6-foot solid border in the NFL.

Yard lines give players and fans an idea of how far a team must advance the ball in order to record a *first down.* As Chapter 3 explains in detail, an offensive team must gain 10 yards in order to post a first down. Consequently, the field is numbered every 10 yards, starting from the goal lines. All these lines and numbers are white.

Figure 2-1:
The playing
field.

Hash marks

Hash marks mark each yard line 70 feet, 9 inches from the sidelines in the NFL. On high school and college football fields, the hash marks are only 60 feet from the sidelines. Two sets of hash marks (each hash is 1 yard in length) run parallel to each other down the length of the field and are approximately 18½ feet apart. When the ball carrier is either tackled or pushed out of bounds, the officials return the ball in bounds to the closest hash mark. Punted balls that go out of bounds are also marked on the nearest hash mark.

When you've gone too far

A player is *out of bounds* whenever he steps from the field of play and touches (or flies over) the white sidelines or end lines. To remain in bounds for a catch, an NFL player must have both feet (including the toes of his shoes) touching the ground inside the end lines and sidelines and must be in possession of the football; in college and high school football, a player needs to have only one foot inside the end lines and sidelines to be considered in bounds.

The hash marks are used for ball placement prior to most offensive plays so more of the game can be played in the middle of the field, which makes the game more wide open. If the ball was placed 20 feet from where it went out of bounds rather than on the closest hash mark, offenses would be restricted to one open side of the field for many of their run and pass plays. In other words, they would have to run or pass to the right or the left, and wouldn't have the option to do either. But, when teams run the football and the ball carrier is tackled between the hash marks, the ball is declared dead at that spot and generally is placed where the ball carrier was tackled and stopped.

An important thing to remember is that an incomplete pass is returned to the spot of the preceding play, not where it actually goes out of bounds or where the quarterback was standing when he threw it.

Player benches

Six feet outside the border of the field, or 6 feet from the sidelines, is an additional broken white line that defines an area in which only coaches and substitute players may stand. Six feet farther behind this broken white line is where the *bench area* begins (refer to Figure 2-1). The team congregates in the bench area during a game, watching teammates play or resting on the benches. Within this area, team doctors and trainers also examine injured players.

The playing surface

Two types of surfaces are used in football — natural grass and artificial turf. Each has its pros and cons.

- ✔ **Natural grass:** Many natural grass surfaces exist, depending on the region's temperature and the stadium's drainage system. Generally, though, natural grass is similar to your backyard lawn or any baseball outfield: It's green, soft, and beautiful, but it needs to be mowed, watered, and replaced. Many companies have invested a lot of time and effort into perfecting a combination of natural grasses that can withstand the heavy and destructive wear that football presents (after all, cleats can rip up turf).

✔ **Artificial turf:** Some artificial surfaces are made from synthetic nylon fibers that resemble very short blades of grass; other artificial surfaces have tightly woven fibers that give the feel of a cushioned carpet. Artificial surfaces are cheaper to maintain than natural grass. Plus, many football stadiums are multipurpose facilities that are used for outdoor concerts, political and religious rallies, and other sports, such as baseball and soccer. When such events are held, some areas of the grass can become trampled and destroyed by the thousands of fans sitting or walking on it, so having an artificial surface is advantageous.

Then again, in many stadiums, the artificial surface is also harder than natural grass because it's often laid over cement, blacktop, or dirt. And on extremely hot days, artificial surfaces retain the heat, making a day that's 95 degrees Fahrenheit feel like a 100-degree day.

Most players prefer natural grass to artificial turf. Playing on an artificial surface is much like playing on green-colored wall-to-wall carpeting.

Grass beats artificial surfaces

I never liked playing on artificial surfaces. The problem with these surfaces, in my opinion, is that your shoes get stuck, which makes you more susceptible to injury. The game is faster on this surface, but when players make quick cuts or attempt to move too quickly, they seem to twist their knees and feet because their shoes stick to the surface.

I never could find the right shoe for artificial surfaces. I even tried basketball sneakers. I think I tried on maybe a thousand different styles of nub-tipped shoes. I tried everything on turf, and I retired never being satisfied with any of the shoes.

Players also suffer what I call *turf burns* when they dive to make a tackle or when a ball carrier

skids across the surface. I've had the skin on my elbows and knees rip right off me. Some teams use what doctors give burn victims — it's called *second skin*. A thin, jellylike material, second skin can be cut to size and placed on the turf burn. The problem with any turf burn is that it can last for two to three weeks, and even if you don't play on turf again, the scab gets ripped off every day in practice.

To prevent these types of injuries, a lot of players wear elastic sleeves over their elbows, forearms, and knees. I tried playing with them, but they kept slipping down after I started sweating. I didn't like having to pull them up or back on for every play — it was an unnecessary, useless activity.

Goalposts and other on-the-field equipment

The *goalpost* serves as the guideline for the kicker, whose goal is to sail the ball high between the goalpost's two vertical bars, an act that's sometimes called *splitting the uprights*. The goalpost rises from the back of the end zone. When a ball carrier reaches the end zone, he has scored a touchdown worth six points. The *goal line* is 8 inches wide (twice as wide as the typical yard line) in the NFL, and 4 inches wide at the high school and college levels. The goalposts were originally located on the goal line, but they were moved inside the goal line, and finally, in 1974, they were moved permanently from the goal line to the end zone's end line (refer to Figure 2-1).

NFL goalposts are a single standard type, known as the *sling-shot* design; on some high school and youth fields, however, you may still find goalposts in the shape of an H. A sling-shot goalpost has one post in the ground and a curved extension that sweeps the crossbar into place, as shown in Figure 2-2. This post is fully padded to protect players when they collide with it in the back of the end zone. The *crossbar* is 10 feet above the ground and 18 feet, 6 inches long in the NFL and college. In high school football, the crossbar is 23 feet, 4 inches long. The *uprights,* the two poles extending up from both ends of the crossbar, rise about 35 feet (30 feet in college and 20 feet in high school) and are 3 to 4 inches in diameter.

Figure 2-2:
The NFL
goalpost.

The goalposts generally are painted yellow or white. A 4-x-42-inch ribbon is attached to the top of each goalpost to aid the officials in determining the exact top of the upright when judging whether a kick has passed through the uprights. The ribbons also give kickers an idea of the wind conditions.

Goalposts aren't the only things you see sitting on the field; you also see the chains and down marker along one sideline, marking the spot of the ball and other important information. For more information about the chains and the people who work them, see Chapter 3.

Looking at That Funny-Shaped Ball

The ball is an important component of a football game — you couldn't very well play *football* without the *ball* part. But you can't use just any old ball; strict rules govern the ball's size, weight, and even brand.

In the NFL, the ball must be a Wilson brand, bearing the signature of the commissioner of the league, Roger Goodell. The ball can be inflated to between 12½ and 13½ pounds of air pressure. It's made of an inflated rubber bladder enclosed in a pebble-grained, leather case of natural tan color without grooves or ridges of any kind. The ball is the form of a *prolate spheroid* (basically an oblong shape with pointed ends). You may have heard a football referred to as a *pigskin*. But, don't worry, footballs just *resemble* a toughened pig's skin, and in the game's early days, they were swollen like a chubby little piggy.

To make it easier to grip and throw, the ball has eight raised white laces in its center. A quarterback can wrap his pinkie, fourth finger, and middle finger between these laces for a perfect grip. The size and weight of the ball must conform to these specifications:

- **Long axis:** 11 to 11½ inches
- **Long circumference:** 28 to 28½ inches
- **Short circumference:** 20¾ to 21¼ inches
- **Weight:** 14 to 15 ounces

College and high school balls are the same size as NFL balls, although you may find a white stripe encircling the tip area at both ends of the college and high school ball. The white stripe supposedly helps receivers see the ball better, which may be helpful for night games.

In the NFL, the home club supplies 36 footballs in an open-air stadium or 24 footballs in a domed stadium, and the league supplies another 12 K-balls used only for kicking. (*K-balls* are sealed in a special box to be opened by the officiating crew and held in their custody until two hours before kickoff so they can't be "doctored" by kickers and punters.) Outdoor stadiums require more balls in case of inclement weather, such as rain, sleet, or snow. The referee is the sole judge as to whether all balls comply with league specifications. The referee tests each football with a pressure gauge approximately two hours prior to kickoff.

Meeting the Cast of Characters

Each football team has 11 players per side: 11 on offense and 11 on defense. Teams are allowed to play with fewer than 11 players (why would they want to do that?), but they're penalized for having more than 11 players on the field during play, which is also known as *live action*. In high school, three or more talented players may play both offense and defense. And a few rare athletes may play both offense and defense in major college football and the NFL.

The *nonstarting players* (that is, those who aren't among the 22 or so players who are listed in the starting lineup) are considered reserves, and many of them are specialists. For example, defenses may play multiple schemes employing a *nickel back* (a fifth defensive back) or two *pass rushers* (linebackers or defensive ends who are used strictly on passing downs to rush the quarterback). Also, an extra player is often used as the *long snapper* who snaps (hikes) the ball for punts, field goal attempts, and extra point attempts. Some of the reserves make the team because they're excellent special teams players who are great on punt and kick coverages because they're fearless tacklers in the open field. (See Chapter 12 for the scoop on special teams.)

The roster sizes in high school and college football tend to be unlimited, especially for home games. The NFL, however, limits active, uniformed players to 45 per team on game day. A typical NFL game-day roster includes three quarterbacks, a punter, a placekicker, a kick return specialist, eight offensive linemen, four running backs, five receivers, two tight ends, seven defensive linemen, seven linebackers, and six defensive backs.

In the NFL, an additional player can be in uniform, but he must be a quarterback and enter the game only after the other quarterbacks have been removed from the game because of injury. When this extra quarterback, or 46th player, enters the game, the other quarterbacks are deemed ineligible and can't return to that game even if they're healthy.

What Football Uniforms Are All About

Youth football (described in Chapter 15) has weight and size limitations, but as boys advance in football from high school to college to the pros, the uniform is the one common denominator. If you can play (and play well), a uniform will always be waiting for you in some team's locker room.

It isn't the uniform that separates one player from the others; it's his talent and heart. But the uniform and its protective pads are a necessary part of the game, something any player would be foolhardy to take the field without. Think of this: Only 60 years ago, many men wore helmets without face masks, meaning they had some pretty rugged noses and required more dental work during football season.

Why the need for all this protection? Well, the NFL is made up of players ranging in weight from 150 to 360 pounds and in height from 5'5" to 6'9". Some of these assorted sizes are able to bench press 550 pounds and run the 40-yard dash in as fast as 4.2 seconds. Because of the varied weights, sizes, strengths, and speeds of NFL players, the best protection possible is necessary. Smaller players want to be able to play without worrying about being crushed by all those large bodies. (Chapter 17 looks at health risks and the challenge of keeping football players healthy.)

Figure 2-3 shows a typical football uniform, and the following sections talk about the various components of the uniform and the pads that go underneath it.

The jersey

The *jersey* is the uniform's shirt. The jersey is basically each player's identity and marks his allegiance to a specific team. The jersey must be large enough to cover the shoulder pads.

Every NFL team jersey comes with a different numeral to distinguish one player from another. The numerals, which appear on the front and back of the jersey, are 8 inches high and 4 inches wide. Most high school and college teams have the same specifications, and some also place the number on the jersey's sleeve.

In the NFL, specific positions wear certain numerals. For example:

- Quarterbacks and kickers wear from 1 to 19.
- Running backs and defensive backs wear from 20 to 49.

✔ Linebackers wear from 50 to 59 or 90 to 99.

✔ Offensive linemen wear from 50 to 79.

✔ Defensive linemen wear from 60 to 79 or 90 to 99.

✔ Receivers wear from 10 to 19 or 80 to 89.

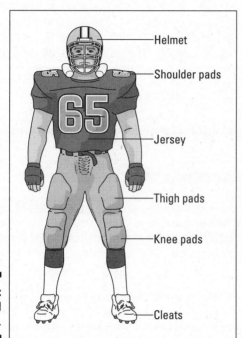

Helmet

Shoulder pads

Jersey

Thigh pads

Knee pads

Cleats

Figure 2-3:
The football
uniform.

On the back of each NFL jersey is the player's surname in letters that are 2½ inches high. His name appears across the upper back just above the numerals.

Team jersey colors and designs further separate one team from another. And most team colors have been with particular teams since their inception. In Green Bay, for example, the jerseys are green with gold trim. In Oakland, the Raiders always wear black. At Nebraska, the color is bright red; at Texas, it's orange. The different colors add to the spectacle of the game. In the NFL and college, the visiting team usually wears a white jersey. The colors for visiting teams vary on the high school level.

Throwback jerseys

A *throwback jersey* is a uniform from a team's past. In 1994, to mark the 75th anniversary of the NFL, the league started permitting teams to wear throwback jerseys. Throwback jerseys add a little more color and pageantry to the pro game. They give teams a chance to reconnect with their past. And let's face it, throwback jerseys are a great merchandising tool. Fans who like to wear their favorite team's jersey sometimes shell out a few more dollars to purchase the throwback jersey, too.

NFL teams can decide when they want to wear throwbacks, and some teams actually wear their throwback uniforms in every game. Not that these teams like reliving the past — they wear throwback jerseys because they've always had the same jersey. The Indianapolis Colts, New Orleans Saints, and Cleveland Browns have never redesigned their jerseys. They've worn the same uniforms, more or less, from the beginning.

Helmets and face masks

The helmet and face mask are designed to protect a player's face and head from serious injury. Many players also wear a mouth guard to protect their teeth and prevent themselves from biting their tongues. A few players even wear another protective cap on the outside of the helmet for added protection.

Helmets are equipped with chin straps to keep them snugly in place. To prevent serious concussions, many helmets have air-filled pockets inside them. A player tests his helmet by sticking his head inside it and then shaking it for comfort, also making sure that it's snug. If it's too tight, he simply releases air from the air pockets.

Player safety is an increasingly important issue in the NFL with concussion and other head injuries becoming a major concern. Helmet manufacturers have been updating their designs in an attempt to increase player safety and comfort. Helmet technology is continually advancing, and it's very likely that helmet designs will continue to evolve over the next few years.

When you're watching a game, you may notice players wearing helmets of slightly different shapes and designs. Players are allowed to choose the helmet design that works best for them as long as the helmet design is certified by the National Operating Committee on Standards for Athletic Equipment.

All helmets are equipped with face masks. The rounded metal material that composes all face masks can't be more than ⅝-inch in diameter. Most linemen wear a face mask called a *cage,* which has a bar extending down from the middle and top of the helmet to below the nose area. There, this bar joins two or three bars that extend from both sides that completely prevent an opponent's hands from reaching inside the face area and under the chin. However, few quarterbacks and receivers have a face mask with a bar coming between their eyes, because they want to ensure they can see clearly; many also leave the chin exposed. Twenty years ago, some quarterbacks wore a helmet with a single bar across the face. Today, you may see a punter or kicker with a helmet that has a single bar, but players who encounter more contact during games want more protection.

Some helmets also have a sunshade across the eyes to prevent sun glare from interfering with the player's vision. This sunshade also keeps opponents from seeing the player's eyes, which may give the player an advantage because opponents can't see where the player is looking.

Pads

Pads are necessary to absorb the many physical blows a player takes during a game and protect every part of his body. Next to the helmet, the shoulder pads are probably the number-one protective gear players wear. These pads protect a player's shoulders, plus his sternum region, from injury. Some of these pads also cover the top of the arm and the rotator cuff. Other pads include thigh pads, elbow pads, hip pads, tail pads, and knee pads, although not all players wear them. Some quarterbacks even wear flak jackets to protect their rib cages, which are vulnerable when they lift their arms to throw the ball.

Shoes and cleats

Football cleats come in ½-inch, ⅝-inch, ¾-inch, and 1-inch lengths. Wearing the right cleat is definitely important for traction. If a player doesn't have the proper traction indoors or outside on a muddy surface, he simply can't do his job and perform at the highest level. The shorter cleat, which makes a player less prone to injury, is worn on dry, firm fields because it provides the ideal traction for these fast fields. On a slippery grass field, a player — especially a big lineman across the line of scrimmage — needs to dig deep to gain traction. In that situation, the player switches to a ¾- or 1-inch cleat, depending on how he's maneuvering (stopping and going) during warm-ups. Receivers and running backs often wear shoes with fewer cleats than the larger, more physical players do.

For artificial surfaces, most players wear a shoe that has a sole of dozens of rubber-nubbed, ½-inch cleats. Some linemen prefer a basketball-type shoe, especially on indoor turf where there's no chance of rain and the surface isn't as slick. Because artificial surfaces tend to be sticky, players want to be able to glide over the surface. They don't want to stop on a dime and change directions. Many players believe that instant stop and restart can be hazardous to their knees and ankles.

Most teams are equipped with all sizes and types of shoes in case the weather changes during the course of a game. You often see players changing their shoes on the sidelines. On mushy days, you see them cleaning the cleats on their shoes to maintain the necessary traction. In the NFL, players test the playing surface an hour prior to the game and then go into the locker room and, if necessary, have an equipment manager change their cleats with a power drill, like a pit crew changing tires at a stockcar race.

NFL uniform codes

In a high school game, you may see a player wearing a torn jersey or exposing his midriff area, or you may see five different styles or brands of shoes on 11 different players. None of this occurs in the NFL, where violations of strictly enforced uniform codes can lead to players being fined. Here are some of the NFL rules:

- The NFL shield or logo must be visible on pants, jerseys, and helmets.

- Tear-away jerseys, which would make it more difficult for defensive players to grab and tackle their opponents on the other side of the ball, are prohibited.

- All jerseys must remain tucked into the uniform pants.

- Sleeves can't be torn or cut.

- Stockings must cover the entire leg area from the shoe to the bottom of the pants and meet the pants below the knee. Uniform stockings may not be altered, and they must be white from the top of the shoe to about mid-calf.

- Size and locations of shoe logos must be approved by NFL Properties. Players aren't allowed to wear shoes from companies not approved by the league.

- All tape used on shoes, socks, or pants must be either transparent or a color that matches the team uniform.

- Towels can be only 8 inches long and 6 inches wide and must be tucked into the front waist of the pants. (Quarterbacks and wide receivers often wear towels tucked into their waists to wipe their hands clean of mud and moisture between plays.)

Chapter 3

Them's the Rules
(And Regulations)

In This Chapter

▶ Keeping time in a game, starting with the kickoff

▶ Understanding the down system

▶ Scoring via touchdowns, field goals, and other methods

▶ Defining the officials' roles and interpreting their signals

▶ Calling penalties, from offside to personal fouls

Football is a pretty complicated game. Twenty-two players are on the field at all times, plus a host of officials, not to mention all those people running around on the sidelines. But after you figure out who's supposed to be where, and what they're supposed to do there, following a football game is pretty easy.

This chapter walks you through all the phases of a game, from the coin toss to the opening kickoff to halftime to the time when the fat lady sings. It also explains how the clock works, how you score points, what the officials do, what every penalty means, and much more.

The Ins and Outs of the Game Clock

To keep things in small, easily digestible chunks, every football game is divided into *quarters*. In college and pro football, each quarter lasts 15 minutes; high school teams play 12-minute quarters. After the second quarter comes halftime, which lasts 12 minutes in the NFL, 15 minutes in college, and 15 to 20 minutes in high school. Halftime gives players time to rest and bands and cheerleaders time to perform (it also gives fans time to go get a hot dog). Coaches, players, or alumni are sometimes honored at halftime.

The game clock, which is operated by a timekeeper in the press box, doesn't run continuously throughout those 15- or 12-minute quarters. (If it did, when would they show the television commercials?) The clock stops for the following reasons:

- ✔ Either team calls a timeout. Teams are allowed three timeouts per half.

- ✔ A quarter ends. The stoppage in time enables teams to change which goal they will defend (they change sides at the end of the first and third quarters).

- ✔ The quarterback throws an incomplete pass.

- ✔ The ball carrier goes out of bounds.

- ✔ A player from either team is injured during a play.

- ✔ An official signals a penalty by throwing a flag. (I tell you all about penalties in the later "Penalties and Other Violations" section.)

- ✔ The officials need to measure whether the offense has gained a first down, or they need to take time to *spot* (or place) the ball correctly on the field.

- ✔ Either team scores a touchdown, field goal, or safety. (I explain what these achievements are and how much they're worth in the later "Scoring Points" section.)

- ✔ The ball changes possession via a kickoff, a punt, a turnover, or a team failing to advance the ball 10 yards in four downs.

- ✔ The offense gains a first down (college and high school only).

- ✔ Two minutes remain in the half or in overtime (NFL only).

- ✔ A coach has challenged a referee's call, and the referees are reviewing the call (college and NFL only).

- ✔ A wet ball needs to be replaced with a dry one.

Unlike college and professional basketball, where a shot clock determines how long the offense can keep possession of the ball, in football the offense can keep the ball as long as it keeps making first downs (which I explain a little later in this chapter). However, the offense has 40 seconds from the end of a given play, or a 25-second interval after official stoppages, to get in proper position after an extremely long gain. If the offense doesn't snap the ball in that allotted time, it's penalized 5 yards and must repeat the down.

With the exception of the last two minutes of the first half and the last five minutes of the second half of an NFL game, the officials restart the game clock after a kickoff return, after a player goes out of bounds on a play, or after a declined penalty.

Overtime and sudden death

If a game is tied at the end of regulation play, the game goes into overtime. To decide who gets the ball in overtime, team captains meet at the center of the field for a coin toss. The team that wins the toss gets the ball and the first crack at scoring.

✔ In the NFL, this method of handling tie games is sometimes called *sudden death* because, in regular season play, the game is over immediately after the first team scores. The sudden-death method of deciding a tie game has been criticized as unfair to the team that loses the coin toss. After all, if your team loses the toss, it may not get a chance to get the ball or score. Critics of the overtime system claim that both teams should get the ball and a chance to score in overtime. To calm the critics, the NFL instituted a new overtime policy in 2010. Now if the team that wins the coin toss scores

only a field goal during its first possession, the opposing teams gets a crack at scoring too, and if this team scores a touchdown, it wins the game. If the game is still tied after both teams have had a chance to score, the game goes into sudden death, and the first team to score wins.

✔ Under college rules, each team gets the ball for alternate possessions starting at the 25-yard line. If the team that wins the coin toss scores, its opponent still gets a chance to score and tie the game again. If a college football game goes past two overtimes, teams must try for two-point conversions after touchdowns (instead of kicking for an extra point — a PAT) until one prevails. (See the later section "Extra points and two-point conversions" for additional information on PAT kicks versus going for two.)

The Coin Toss and Kickoff

Every football contest starts with a *coin toss.* Selected members of each team (called *captains*) come to the center of the field, where the referee holds a coin. In the NFL, the coin toss is restricted to three captains from each team. In college football, four players may participate. However, only one player from the visiting team calls heads or tails, and that player must do so before the official tosses the coin into the air (hence the name *coin toss*). If that player calls the toss correctly, his team gets to choose one of three privileges:

✔ **Which team receives the kickoff:** Generally, teams want to start the game on offense and have the opportunity to score as early as possible, so the team who wins the toss usually opts to receive. They're known as the *receiving team.* The referee, swinging his leg in a kicking motion, then points to the other team's captains as the *kicking team.*

✔ **Which goal his team will defend:** Instead of receiving the kickoff, the captain may elect to kick off and choose a goal to defend. Captains sometimes take this option if they believe that weather will be a factor in the outcome of the game. For example, in choosing which goal to defend, the player believes that his team will have the wind at its back for the second quarter and the crucial final quarter of the game.

✔ **When to decide:** The team that wins the coin flip can *defer,* giving it the right to choose between kicking and receiving the second-half kickoff.

The team that earns the right to receive the ball gets the ball via a *kickoff.* To perform this kickoff, the kicking team's *placekicker* places the ball in a holder (called a *tee,* which is 1 inch tall in the NFL and 2 inches tall in high school and college) on his team's 35-yard line (NFL and college), or 40-yard line (high school). The kicker then runs toward the ball and kicks it toward the other team. Figure 3-1 shows how teams typically line up for a kickoff in the NFL.

Figure 3-1:
Players line up in this formation for a kickoff in the NFL.

At the far end of the field from the kicker, one or more *returners* from the other team await the kickoff. The returner's goal is to catch the ball and score a touchdown or run the ball as far back toward the opponent's goal line as he can. After the return is complete, the first set of *downs* begins.

Downs Plus Yardage Equals Excitement

Watching a game in which the offense keeps running plays but never goes anywhere would be really boring. To prevent that, the fathers of football created the *down system*. The offense has four downs (essentially four plays) to go 10 yards. If the offensive team advances the ball at least 10 yards in four tries or fewer, it receives another set of four downs. If the offense fails to advance 10 yards after three tries, it can either punt the ball on the fourth down (a *punt* is a kick to the opponent without the use of a tee) or, if it needs less than a yard to get a first down, try to get the first down by running or passing.

You may hear television commentators use the phrase "three and out." What they mean is that a team failed to advance the ball 10 yards and has to punt the ball. You don't want your team to go three and out very often. But you do want to earn lots of *first downs,* which you get after your team advances the ball 10 yards or more in the allotted four downs. Getting lots of first downs usually translates to more scoring opportunities.

Football has its own lingo to explain the offense's progress toward a first down. A first down situation is also known as a "first and 10," because the offense has 10 yards to go to gain a first down. If your offense ran a play on first down in which you advanced the ball 3 yards, your status would be "second and 7"; you're ready to play the second down, and you now have 7 yards to go to gain a first down. Unless something really bad happens, the numbers stay under 10, so the math is pretty simple.

As a viewer, you aren't expected to remember what down it is and how many yards the offense needs to advance to gain a first down. Football makes it easy by providing people and signs to help you keep track. On the sideline opposite the press box is a group of three people, known as the *chain gang* or *chain crew,* who hold three 8-foot-high poles. Here's an explanation of that crew:

✔ Two people called *rodmen* hold metal rods with Xs at the top connected by a thin metal chain that stretches exactly 10 yards when the two rods are thoroughly extended. One rod marks where the possession begins, and the other extends to where the offensive team must go in order to make another first down.

✔ The third person, known as the *boxman,* holds a marker that signifies where the ball is and what down it is. Atop this rod is the number 1, 2, 3, or 4, designating whether it is the first, second, third, or fourth down.

✔ In all NFL stadiums, a person also marks where the *drive* began (that is, where the offensive team assumed possession of the ball). Many high school and college fields don't have these markers.

Whenever the officials need to make a critical measurement for a first down, the chain crew comes to the hash marks nearest where the ball is positioned, and the officials use the rods to measure whether the offense has obtained a first down. The home team supplies the chain crew and also the *ball boys,* who are responsible for keeping the balls clean and free of excessive moisture.

Thanks to the miracle of technology, determining where a team has to advance the ball to get a first down is easier than ever — but only if you're watching television. On the television screen during a game, you see an electronic line across the field that marks where a team must go to get a first down.

Scoring Points

Teams can score points in several ways — and scoring more points than the other team is the object of the game. The following sections explain each method of scoring.

Touchdowns

A *touchdown* is worth six points — the ultimate goal. A team scores a touchdown, plus the loudest cheers from fans, when an offensive player carrying the ball, or a defensive player who has obtained the ball from the other team after recovering a fumble or intercepting a pass, advances from anywhere on the field and breaks the plane of his opponent's goal line with the ball. (*Breaking the plane* means that a ball carrier can soar over the goal line in midair and have his efforts count for a touchdown — even if he's hit in midair and lands back on the 1-yard line — as long as the ball crosses the plane.) Figure 3-2 shows New Orleans Saints' running back Pierre Thomas scoring a touchdown in the Super Bowl.

A team is also awarded a touchdown when any player who's inbounds catches or recovers a loose ball behind his opponent's goal line. This sort of touchdown can occur on a kickoff, a punt, or a *fumble* (when a player drops the ball).

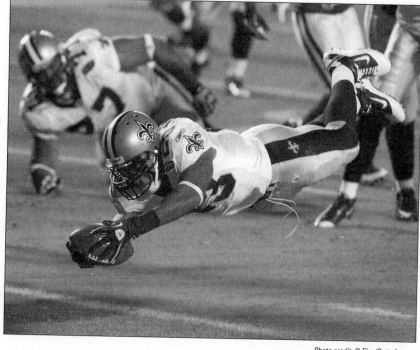

Figure 3-2:
Pierre
Thomas of
the New
Orleans
Saints
scores a
touchdown
against the
Indianapolis
Colts in
Super Bowl
XLIV.

Photo credit: © Elsa/Getty Images

Extra points and two-point conversions

A try for an *extra point,* also known as a *point after touchdown (PAT),* is attempted during the scrimmage down that's awarded after a touchdown. The extra point is successful when the kicker kicks the ball between the uprights of the goalpost and above the crossbar, provided that the ball was snapped 2 yards away from the opponent's goal line (or 3 yards away in high school and college). Teams almost always make their extra point attempts — especially beyond the high school level — because the kick is a fairly easy one. (See Chapter 2 for more information about the goalposts.)

When a team is feeling particularly confident — or desperate — it might attempt a *two-point conversion* after scoring a touchdown. (Chapter 8 talks about situations in which a coach might decide to have his team "go for two.") Two-point conversions, which were added to the NFL for the 1994 season, have always been a part of high school and college football. The offense gets the ball on the 2-yard line (the 3-yard line in high school and college) and must advance the ball across the goal line, or break the plane, as if scoring a touchdown. In the NFL, the try (called a *conversion attempt*) is over when the officials rule the ball dead or if a change of possession occurs (meaning the defense intercepts a pass or recovers a fumble). In college, the defensive team can return a fumble or interception to its opponent's end zone and score two points.

Field goals

A *field goal,* often the consolation prize for an offense that tries to score a touchdown but stalls within its opponent's 30-yard line, is worth three points. A team scores a field goal when a kicker boots the ball entirely through the uprights of the goalpost without the ball touching either the ground or any of the offensive players. The kicked ball must travel between the uprights and above the crossbar of the goalpost.

You get the distance of a field goal by adding 10 yards (the distance from the goal line to the end line where the goalposts are placed) to the yard line from which the ball is kicked. Or simply add 17 to the number of yards that the offense would have to advance to cross the goal line (the extra 7 yards represents the typical distance of a snap for a field goal attempt). For example, if the offense is on its opponent's 23-yard line, they're attempting a 40-yard field goal.

An extra point experiment

In the preseason games of the 2014 season, the NFL moved the spot where extra points are kicked from the 2-yard line to the 15-yard line, making the kick 33 yards. (Two-point conversion attempts remained at the 2-yard line.) The reason for this experiment was to see if the game would be impacted at all if extra points were made more difficult. As the game currently stands, 99.6 percent of extra point attempts are good. Well, in the 2014 preseason, the success rate dropped slightly to 94.3 percent. So increasing the distance of the extra point attempt didn't really make a difference.

The league will likely continue to experiment with rule changes involving extra points and two-point conversions. Many fans of the game think that extra points are too easy and that two-point conversions should be attempted more often.

Safeties

A *safety* occurs when a player on the offensive team is tackled in his own end zone or goes out of bounds in his own end zone. A safety scores two points for the defensive team. After a safety, the team that was scored on must punt the ball to the other team from its own 20-yard line. For the offensive team, a safety is bad thing. The other team gets not only two points but also the ball in good field position. Normally, teams kick off from the 35-yard line. Having to punt from the 20-yard line allows the other team to advance the ball further up the field after the punt.

Frankly, a safety is embarrassing to the offense, and offensive players will do just about anything to prevent a safety. Besides being tackled in the end zone, here are other instances when a safety is awarded:

✔ A quarterback knows he's about to be tackled in his end zone, and to prevent the other team from scoring a safety, he chucks the ball out of bounds. If a referee thinks the quarterback threw the pass solely to prevent a safety, the referee awards the safety to the defensive team.

✔ The offensive team commits a penalty (say, holding a defensive player who's preparing to tackle the ball carrier in the end zone) that would otherwise require it to have the ball marked in its own end zone.

✔ A blocked punt goes out of the kicking team's end zone.

✔ The receiver of a punt muffs the ball and then, when trying to retrieve the ball, forces or illegally kicks it into the end zone and it goes out of the end zone.

✔ A muffed ball is kicked or forced into the end zone and then recovered there by a member of the receiving team.

The Role of the Officials

Officials play many important roles in a football game. In fact, they basically have control of every game. For example:

✔ They're responsible for any decision involving the application of a rule, its interpretation, or its enforcement.

✔ They keep players from really hurting each other and making other illegal actions.

✔ They enforce and record all fouls and monitor the clock and all timeouts that are charged.

All officials carry a whistle and a weighted, bright yellow flag, which they throw to signal that a penalty has been called on a particular play. In the event that an official throws his yellow flag during a play and then sees yet another penalty, he throws his hat.

Officials are part-time workers for NFL, college, and high school football. They're paid for working the game and are given travel expenses. In the NFL and in college football, the work can be financially rewarding. For instance, depending on seniority and experience, these officials may earn between $25,000 and $80,000 a season. High school officials, on the other hand, aren't paid nearly as well; they generally do it for the love of the game.

If you want, you can just call them "the officials," or — if you're in a particularly belligerent mood — you can call them "the idiots who aren't even qualified to officiate a peewee football game." Either way, true diehards know that each of the seven officials (five or six at some levels) has a different title and task. The sections that follow explain who they are and what they do.

Referee

The *referee* has general oversight and control of the game. He's the final authority for the score, the number of a down in case of a disagreement, and all rule interpretations when a debate arises among the other officials. He's the only official who wears a white hat; all the other officials wear black hats.

The referee announces all penalties and confers with the offending team's captain, explaining the penalty. Before the snap of the ball, he positions himself in the offensive backfield, 10 to 12 yards behind the line of scrimmage, and favors the right side if the quarterback is right-handed or the left side if the quarterback is left-handed. The referee also monitors any illegal hits on the quarterback, such as *roughing the passer* (you can read more about this penalty in Chapter 5). He follows the quarterback throughout the game and watches for the legality of blocks made near him.

At the end of any down, the referee can request the head linesman (see the later related section for details on this official's role) and his assistants to bring the yardage chains onto the field to determine whether the ball has reached the necessary line for a new first down. The referee also notifies the head coach when any player is ejected for unnecessary roughness or unsportsmanlike conduct.

Umpire

The *umpire* is responsible for the legality of the players' equipment and for watching all play along the *line of scrimmage,* the division line between the offensive and defensive players. He makes sure that the offensive team has no more than 11 players on the field prior to the snap of the ball. At the start of a play in college football, he positions himself 4 to 5 yards off the line of scrimmage on the defensive side of the ball. In the NFL, he's positioned in the offensive backfield until the final five minutes of each half, when he takes his traditional position on the defensive side.

Because he's responsible for monitoring the legality of all contact between the offensive and defensive linemen, this official calls most of the holding penalties. He also assists the referee on decisions involving possession of the ball in close proximity to the line of scrimmage. He records all timeouts, the winner of the coin toss, and all scores, and he makes sure the offensive linemen don't move downfield illegally on pass plays. Finally, when it's raining, the umpire dries the wet ball prior to the snap.

Head linesman

The *head linesman* sets up on the side of the field designated by the referee. He straddles the line of scrimmage and watches for encroachment, offside, illegal men downfield, and all the other line-of-scrimmage violations (which you can read more about in the later "Penalties and Other Violations" section). He's also responsible for ruling on all out-of-bounds plays to his side of the field.

The chain crew (described earlier in this chapter) is the responsibility of the head linesman. He grabs the chain when measuring for a first down. He's usually the official who runs in after a play is whistled dead and places his foot to show where forward progress was made by the ball carrier at the end of the play. He assists the line judge (who stands opposite the head linesman) with illegal motion calls and any illegal shifts or movement by running backs and receivers to his side. Also, during kicks or passes, he checks for illegal use of hands, and he must know who the eligible receivers are prior to every play.

Line judge

The *line judge* lines up on the opposite side of the field from the head linesman and serves as an overall helper while being responsible for illegal motion and illegal shifts. He has a number of chores. He assists the head linesman with offside and encroachment calls. He helps the umpire with holding calls and watching for illegal use of hands on the end of the line, especially during kicks and pass plays. The line judge assists the referee with calls regarding false starts and forward laterals behind the line of scrimmage. He makes sure that the quarterback hasn't crossed the line of scrimmage prior to throwing a forward pass. And if all that isn't enough, he also supervises substitutions made by the team seated on his side of the field. On punts, he remains on the line of scrimmage to ensure none of the ends move downfield prior to the ball being kicked.

One of the line judge's most important jobs is supervising the timing of the game. If the game clock becomes inoperative, he assumes the official timing on the field. He advises the referee when time has expired at the end of each quarter. In the NFL, the line judge signals the referee when two minutes remain in a half, stopping the clock for the *two-minute warning*. This stopping of the clock was devised to essentially give the team in possession of the ball another timeout. During halftime, the line judge notifies the home team's head coach when five minutes remain before the start of the second half.

Back judge

The *back judge* has similar duties to the field judge (see the following section) and sets up 20 yards deep on the defensive side, usually to the tight end's side of the field. He makes sure that the defensive team has no more than 11 players on the field and is responsible for all eligible receivers to his side.

After the receivers have cleared the line of scrimmage, the back judge concentrates on action in the area between the umpire and the field judge: It's vital that he's aware of any passes that are trapped by receivers. He makes decisions involving catching, recovery, or illegal touching of loose balls beyond the line of scrimmage. He rules on the legality of catches or pass interference, whether a receiver is interfered with, and whether a receiver has possession of the ball before going out of bounds.

The back judge calls clipping when it occurs on punt returns. (The upcoming "Recognizing 15-yard penalties" explains clipping and similar penalties.) During field goal and extra point attempts, the back judge and field judge stand under the goalpost and rule whether the kicks are good.

Field judge

The *field judge* lines up 20 yards downfield on the same side as the line judge. In the NFL, he's responsible for the 40/25-second clock. (When a play ends, the team with the ball has 40 seconds in which to begin another play before it's penalized for delay of game. If stoppage occurs due to a change of possession, a timeout, an injury, a measurement, or any unusual delay that interferes with the normal flow of play, a 25-second interval exists between plays.)

The field judge also counts the number of defensive players. He's responsible for forward passes that cross the defensive goal line and any fumbled ball in his area. He also watches for pass interference, monitoring the tight end's pass patterns, calling interference, and making decisions involving catching, recovery, out-of-bounds spots, or illegal touching of a fumbled ball after it crosses the line of scrimmage. He also watches for illegal use of hands by the offensive players, especially the ends and wide receivers, on defensive players to his side of the field.

Side judge

With teams passing the ball more often, the *side judge* was added in 1978 as the seventh official for NFL games. Some high school games are played without a side judge, but, like the NFL, college teams have adopted the use of the seventh judge. The side judge is essentially another back judge who positions himself 20 yards down field from the line of scrimmage and opposite the field judge. He's another set of eyes monitoring the legalities downfield, especially during long pass attempts. On field goal and extra point attempts, he lines up next to the umpire under the goalpost and decides whether the kicks are good.

Familiarizing Yourself with Referee Signals

Because it's awfully hard to yell loud enough for a stadium full of people to hear you, and because someone has to communicate with the timekeepers way up in the press box, the referee uses signals to inform everyone of penalties, play stoppages, touchdowns, and everything else that transpires on the field. Table 3-1 shows you what these signals look like and explains what they mean.

Table 3-1 Signaling Scoring Plays, Penalties, and Other Stoppages

Signal	*What It Means*
	Clock doesn't stop. The referee moves an arm clockwise in a full circle in front of himself to inform the offensive team that it has no timeouts, or that the ball is in play and that the time-keeper should keep the clock moving.
	Delay of game. The referee signals a delay of game by fold-ing his arms in front of his chest. This signal also means that a team called a timeout when it had already used all its allocated timeouts.
	Encroachment. The referee places his hands on his hips to signal that an offside, encroachment, or neutral zone infraction occurred.
	Face mask. The referee gestures with his hand in front of his face and makes a downward pulling motion to signal that a player illegally grabbed the face mask of another player.
	False start/illegal formation. The referee rotates both forearms over and over in front of his body to signify a false start, an ille-gal formation, or that the kickoff or the kick following a safety is ruled out of bounds.
	First down. The referee points with his right arm at shoulder height toward the defensive team's goal to indicate that the offensive team has gained enough yardage for a first down.
	Fourth down. The referee raises one arm above his head with his hand in a closed fist to show that the offense is facing fourth down.
	Holding. The referee signals a holding penalty by clenching his fist, grabbing the wrist of that hand with his other hand and pulling his arm down in front of his chest.

Signal	What It Means
	Illegal contact. The referee extends his arm and an open hand forward to signal that illegal contact was made.
	Illegal crackback block. The referee strikes with an open right hand around the middle of his right thigh, preceded by a personal foul signal, to signal an illegal crackback block.
	Illegal cut block. From the side, the referee uses both hands to strike the front of his thighs to signal that a player made an illegal cut block. When he uses one hand to strike the front of his thigh, preceded by a personal foul signal, he means that an illegal block below the waist occurred. When he uses both hands to strike the sides of his thighs, preceded by a personal foul signal, he means that an illegal chop block occurred. When he uses one hand to strike the back of his calf, preceded by a personal foul signal, he means that an illegal clipping penalty occurred.
	Illegal forward pass. The referee puts one hand waist-high behind his back to signal an illegal forward pass. The referee then makes the loss of down signal.
	Illegal motion. The referee flattens out his hand and moves his arm to the side to show that the offensive team made an illegal motion at the snap or prior to the snap of the ball.
	Illegal push. The referee uses his hands in a pushing movement with his arms below his waist to show that someone on the offensive team pushed or illegally helped a ball carrier.
	Illegal shift. The referee uses both arms and hands in a horizontal arc in front of his body to signal that the offense used an illegal shift prior to the snap of the ball.
	Illegal substitution. The referee places both hands on top of his head to signal that a team made an illegal substitution or had too many men on the field on the preceding play.

(continued)

Table 3-1 *(continued)*

Signal	What It Means
	Illegal use of hands. The referee grabs one wrist and extends the open hand of that arm forward in front of his chest to signal illegal use of the hands, arms, or body.
	Illegally touched ball. The referee uses the fingertips of both hands and touches his shoulders to signal that the ball was illegally touched, kicked, or batted.
	Illegally touched pass. The referee is sideways and uses a diagonal motion of one hand across another to signal an illegal touch of a forward pass or a kicked ball from scrimmage.
	Incomplete pass. The referee shifts his arms in a horizontal fashion in front of his body to signal that the pass is incomplete, a penalty is declined, a play is over, or a field goal or extra point attempt is no good.
	Ineligible player downfield. The referee places his right hand on top of his head or cap to show that an ineligible receiver on a pass play was downfield early or that an ineligible member of the kicking team was downfield too early.
	Intentional grounding. The referee waves both his arms in a diagonal plane across his body to signal intentional grounding of a forward pass. This signal is followed by the loss of down signal.
	Interference. The referee, with open hands vertical to the ground, extends his arms forward from his shoulders to signify pass interference or interference of a fair catch of a punted ball.
	Invalid fair catch. The referee waves one hand above his head to signal an invalid fair catch of a kicked ball.

Signal	What It Means
	Juggled pass. The referee gestures with his open hands in an up-and-down fashion in front of his body to show that the pass was juggled inbounds and caught out of bounds. This signal follows the incomplete pass signal.
	Loss of down. The referee places both hands behind his head to signal a loss of down.
	Player ejected. The referee clenches his fist with the thumb extended, a gesture also used in hitchhiking, to signal that a player has been ejected from the game.
	Personal foul. The referee raises his arms above his head and strikes one wrist with the edge of his other hand to signify a personal foul. If the personal foul signal is followed by the referee swinging one of his legs in a kicking motion, it means roughing the kicker. If the signal is followed by the referee simulating a throwing motion, it means roughing the passer. If the signal is followed by the referee pretending to grab an imaginary face mask, it's a major face mask penalty, which is worth 15 yards.
	Reset 25-second clock. The referee makes an open palm with his right hand and pumps that arm vertically into the air to instruct the timekeeper to reset the 25-second play clock.
	Reset 40-second clock. With the palms of both hands open, the referee pumps both arms vertically into the air to instruct the timekeeper to reset the 40-second play clock.
	Safety. The referee puts his palms together above his head to show that the defensive team scored a safety.

(continued)

Table 3-1 *(continued)*

Signal	*What It Means*
	Stop the clock. The referee raises one arm above his head with an open palm to signify that excessive crowd noise in the stadium has made it necessary for the timekeeper to stop the clock. This signal also means that the ball is dead (the play is over) and that the neutral zone has been established along the line of scrimmage.
	Timeout. The referee signals a timeout by waving his arms and hands above his head. The same signal, followed by the referee placing one hand on top his head, means that it's an official timeout, or a referee-called timeout.
	Touchback. The referee signals a touchback by waving his arms and hands above his head and then swinging one arm out from his side.
	Touchdown. The referee extends his arms straight above his head to signify that a touchdown was scored. He also uses this signal to tell the offensive team that it successfully converted a field goal, extra point, or two-point conversion.
	Tripping. The referee repeats the action of placing the right foot behind the heel of his left foot to signal a tripping penalty.
	Uncatchable pass. The referee holds the palm of his right hand parallel to the ground and moves it back and forth above his head to signal that a forward pass was uncatchable and that no penalty should be called.
	Unsportsmanlike conduct. The referee extends both arms to his sides with his palms down to signal an unsportsmanlike conduct penalty.

Penalties and Other Violations

A *penalty* is an infraction of the rules. Without rules, a football game would devolve into total chaos because the game is so physically demanding and the collisions are so intense. A dirty deed or a simple mistake (like a player moving across the line of scrimmage prior to the ball being snapped) is a penalty. Football has more than 100 kinds of penalties or rule violations. Don't worry, though. The next sections get you acquainted with several of them.

The specific penalties and their ramifications can get pretty complicated. You may want to read through Parts II and III to get a handle on the offense and defense first if you're a beginner and really want to understand this stuff. If you have trouble with a particular term, turn to the Appendix. By the way, I describe how these penalties are called and enforced in the NFL. Some of these penalties are slightly different in the college ranks.

Looking at 5-yard penalties

The following common penalties give the offended team an additional 5 yards. Some of these penalties, when noted, are accompanied by an automatic first down.

- ✔ **Defensive holding or illegal use of the hands:** When a defensive player tackles or holds an offensive player other than the ball carrier. Otherwise, the defensive player may use his hands, arms, or body only to protect himself from an opponent trying to block him in an attempt to reach a ball carrier. This penalty also includes an automatic first down.

- ✔ **Delay of game:** When the offense fails to snap the ball within the required 40 or 25 seconds, depending on the clock. The referee can call a delay of game penalty against the defense if it repeatedly charges into the neutral zone prior to the snap; when called on the defense, a delay of game penalty gives the offense an automatic first down. The ref can also call this penalty when a team fails to play when ordered (because, for example, the players are unsure of the play called in the huddle), a runner repeatedly attempts to advance the ball after his forward progress is stopped, or a team takes too much time assembling after a timeout.

- ✔ **Delay of kickoff:** Failure of the kicking team to kick the ball after being ordered to do so by the referee.

- ✔ **Encroachment:** When a player enters the neutral zone and makes contact with an opponent before the ball is snapped.

- **Excessive crowd noise:** When the quarterback informs the referee that the offense can't hear his signals because of crowd noise. If the referee deems it reasonable to conclude that the quarterback is right, he signals a referee's timeout and asks the defensive captain to use his best influence to quiet the crowd. If the noise persists, the referee uses his wireless microphone to inform the crowd that continued noise will result in either the loss of an existing timeout or, if the defensive team has no timeouts remaining, a 5-yard penalty.

- **Excessive timeouts:** When a team calls for a timeout after it has already used its three timeouts allotted for the half.

- **Failure to pause for one second after the shift or huddle:** When any offensive player doesn't pause for at least one second after going into a set position. The offensive team also is penalized when it's operating from a no-huddle offense and immediately snaps the ball without waiting a full second after assuming an offensive set.

- **Failure to report change of eligibility:** When a player fails to inform an official that he has entered the game and will be aligned at a position he normally doesn't play, like an offensive tackle lined up as a tight end. In the NFL, all players' jersey numbers relate to the offensive positions they play; consequently, the officials and opposing team know when it's illegal for a player wearing number 60 through 79 (offensive linemen generally wear these numbers) to catch a pass.

- **False start:** When an interior lineman of the offensive team takes or simulates a three-point stance and then moves prior to the snap of the ball. The official must blow his whistle immediately. A false start is also whistled when any offensive player makes a quick, abrupt movement prior to the snap of the ball.

- **Forward pass is first touched by an eligible receiver who has gone out of bounds and returned:** When an offensive player leaves the field of play (even if he's shoved out), returns inbounds, and is therefore an ineligible receiver.

- **Forward pass is thrown from behind the line of scrimmage after the ball crosses the line of scrimmage:** When a player catches a pass, runs past the line of scrimmage, and then retreats behind the line of scrimmage and attempts another pass. However, a player is permitted to throw the ball to another player, provided that the ball isn't thrown forward. A ball thrown this way is called a *lateral.*

- **Forward pass touches or is caught by an ineligible receiver on or behind the line of scrimmage:** When an offensive lineman catches a pass that isn't first tipped by a defensive player.

- **Grasping the face mask of the ball carrier or quarterback:** When the face mask is grabbed unintentionally and the player immediately lets go of his hold, not twisting the ball carrier's neck at all.

✔ **Illegal formation:** When the offense doesn't have seven players on the line of scrimmage. Also, running backs and receivers who aren't on the line of scrimmage must line up at least 1 yard off the line of scrimmage and no closer, or the formation is considered illegal.

✔ **Illegal motion:** When an offensive player, such as a quarterback, running back, or receiver, moves forward toward the line of scrimmage moments prior to the snap of the ball. Illegal motion is also called when a running back is on the line of scrimmage and then goes in motion prior to the snap. It's a penalty because the running back wasn't aligned in a backfield position.

✔ **Illegal return:** When a player returns to the field after he has been ejected. He must leave the bench area and go to the locker room within a reasonable time.

✔ **Illegal substitution:** When a player enters the field during a play. Players must enter only when the ball is dead. If a substituted player remains on the field at the snap of the ball, his team is slapped with an unsportsmanlike conduct penalty (see the later section "Recognizing 15-yard penalties" for more on this penalty). If the substituted player runs to the opposing team's bench area in order to clear the field prior to the snap of the ball, his team incurs a delay of game penalty.

✔ **Ineligible member(s) of kicking team going beyond the line of scrimmage before the ball is kicked:** When a player other than the two players aligned at least 1 yard outside the end men go downfield when the ball is snapped to the kicker. All the other players must remain at the line of scrimmage until the ball is kicked.

✔ **Ineligible player downfield during a pass down:** When any offensive linemen are more than 2 yards beyond the line of scrimmage when a pass is thrown downfield.

✔ **Invalid fair catch signal:** When the receiver simply extends his arm straight up. To be a valid fair catch signal, the receiver must fully extend his arm and wave it from side to side.

✔ **Kickoff goes out of bounds between the goal lines and isn't touched:** When the kicking team fails to keep its kick inbounds, the ball belongs to the receivers 30 yards from the spot of the kick or at the out-of-bounds spot unless the ball went out-of-bounds the first time an onside kick was attempted. In this case, the kicking team is penalized five yards and the ball must be kicked again.

✔ **More than 11 players on the field at the snap:** When a team has more than 11 players on the field at any time when the ball is live. The offense receives an automatic first down if the penalty is committed by the defensive team.

- **More than one man in motion at the snap of the ball:** When two offensive players are in motion simultaneously. Having two men in motion at the same time is illegal on all levels of football in the United States. Two players can go in motion prior to the snap of the ball, but before the second player moves, the first player must be set for a full second.

- **Neutral zone infraction:** When a defensive player moves beyond the neutral zone prior to the snap and continues unabated toward the quarterback or kicker even though no contact is made by a blocker. If a defensive player enters the neutral zone prior to the snap and causes an offensive player to react immediately and prior to the snap, the defensive player has committed a neutral zone infraction.

- **Offside:** When any part of a player's body is beyond the line of scrimmage or free kick line when the ball is put into play.

- **Player out of bounds at the snap:** When one of the 11 players expected to be on the field runs onto the field of play after the ball is snapped.

- **Running into the kicker or punter:** When a defensive player makes contact with a kicker or punter. Note that a defender isn't penalized for running into the kicker if the contact is incidental and occurs after he has touched the ball in flight. Nor is it a penalty if the kicker's own motion causes the contact, or if the defender is blocked into the kicker, or if the kicker muffs the ball, retrieves it, and then kicks it.

- **Shift:** When an offensive player moves from one position on the field to another. After a team huddles, the offensive players must come to a stop and remain stationary for at least one second before going in motion. If an offensive player who didn't huddle is in motion behind the line of scrimmage at the snap of the ball, it's an illegal shift.

Surveying 10-yard penalties

These penalties cost the offending team 10 yards:

- **Deliberately batting or punching a loose ball:** When a player bats or punches a loose ball toward an opponent's goal line, or in any direction if the loose ball is in either end zone. An offensive player can't bat forward a ball in a player's possession or a backward pass in flight. (The nearby sidebar titled "The Holy Roller" explains the genesis of this rule.)

- **Deliberately kicking a loose ball:** When a player kicks a loose ball in the field of play or tries to kick a ball from a player's possession. The ball isn't dead when an illegal kick is recovered, however.

✔ **Helping the runner:** When a member of the offensive team pushes or pulls a runner forward when the defense has already stopped his momentum.

✔ **Holding, illegal use of the hands, arms, or body by the offense:** When an offensive player uses his hands, arms, or other parts of his body to hold a defensive player from tackling the ball carrier. The penalty is most common when linemen are attempting to protect the quarterback from being *sacked* (tackled behind the line of scrimmage). The defense is also guilty of holding when it tackles or prevents an offensive player, other than the ball carrier, from moving downfield after the ball is snapped. On a punt, field goal attempt, or extra point try, the defense can't grab or pull an offensive blocker in order to clear a path for a teammate to block the kick or punt attempt.

✔ **Offensive pass interference:** When a forward pass is thrown and an offensive player physically restricts or impedes a defender in a manner that's visually evident and materially affects the opponent's opportunity to gain position to catch the ball. This penalty usually occurs when a pass is badly underthrown and the intended receiver must come back to the ball and interfere rather than allow the defender to intercept the pass.

✔ **Tripping a member of either team:** When a player, usually close to the line of scrimmage, sees someone running past him and sticks out his leg or foot, tripping the player.

The Holy Roller

The rule that forbids offensive players from batting the ball forward came about after a controversial play that took place in a 1978 game between the Oakland Raiders and San Diego Chargers. Trailing the Chargers 20–14 with 10 seconds left in the game and desperately needing a touchdown to win, Raider quarterback Ken "The Snake" Stabler deliberately fumbled the ball forward at the Charger 14 yard line. The ball bounced to the 8-yard line, where Raider Pete Banaszak swatted the ball across the goal line. There, Raiders' Hall of Fame tight end Dave Casper fell on the ball for a touchdown.

The controversial play became known as the "Holy Roller." Said Oakland guard Gene Upshaw about the episode, "The play is in our playbook. It's called 'Win at Any Cost.'" Whatever you want to call the play, the NFL made it illegal to advance the ball by kicking or swatting it the following season.

Recognizing 15-yard penalties

These are the penalties that make coaches yell at their players because they cost the team 15 yards — the stiffest penalties (other than ejection or pass interference) in football:

- ✓ **A tackler using his helmet to butt, spear, or ram an opponent:** When a player uses the top and forehead of the helmet, plus the face mask, to unnecessarily butt, spear, or ram an opponent. The officials monitor particular situations, such as when a

  - Passer is in the act of throwing or has just released a pass

  - Receiver is catching or attempting to catch a pass

  - Runner is already in the grasp of a tackler

  - Kick returner or punt returner is attempting to field a kick in the air

  - Player is on the ground at the end of a play

- ✓ **A punter, placekicker, or holder simulates being roughed by a defensive player:** When these players pretend to be hurt or injured or act like a defensive player caused them actual harm when the contact is considered incidental.

- ✓ **Chop block:** When an offensive player blocks a defensive player at the thigh or lower while another offensive player occupies that same defensive player by attempting to block him or even simulating a blocking attempt.

- ✓ **Clipping below the waist:** When a player throws his body across the back of the leg(s) of an opponent or charges, falls, or rolls into the back of an opponent below the waist after approaching him from behind, provided that the opponent isn't a ball carrier or positioned close to the line of scrimmage. However, within 3 yards on either side of the line of scrimmage and within an area extended laterally to the original position of the offensive tackle, offensive linemen can block defensive linemen from behind.

- ✓ **Delay of game at the start of either half:** When the captains for either team fail to show up (or fail to show up in uniform) in the center of the field for the coin toss three minutes prior to the start of the game. A team whose captains fail to show loses the coin toss option and is penalized from the spot of the kickoff. The other team automatically gets the coin-toss choice.

- ✓ **Face mask:** When a tackler twists, turns, or pulls an opponent by the face mask. Because this move is particularly dangerous, the penalty is 15-yards and an automatic first down. If the referee considers his action flagrant, the player may be ejected from the game.

✔ **Fair catch interference:** When a player from the kicking team prevents the punt or kick returner from making a path to the ball or touching the ball prior to the ball hitting the ground. This penalty isn't called when a kick fails to cross the line of scrimmage or a player making a fair catch makes no effort to actually catch the ball.

✔ **Illegal crackback block by the offense:** When an offensive player who lines up more than 2 yards laterally outside an offensive tackle, or a player who's in a backfield position at the snap and then moves to a position more than 2 yards laterally outside the tackle, clips an opponent anywhere. Moreover, the offensive player may not contact an opponent below the waist if the blocker is moving toward the position from which the ball was snapped and the contact occurs within a 5-yard area on either side of the line of scrimmage.

✔ **Illegal low block:** When a player on the receiving team during a kick-off, safety kick, punt, field goal attempt, or extra point try blocks an opponent below the waist.

✔ **Piling on:** When a ball carrier is helpless or prostrate, defenders jump onto his body with excessive force with the possible intention of causing injury. Piling on also results in an automatic first down.

✔ **Roughing the kicker:** When a defensive player makes any contact with the kicker, provided the defensive player hasn't touched the kicked ball before contact. Sometimes this penalty, which also results in an automatic first down, is committed by more than one defensive player as they attempt to block a kick or punt.

✔ **Roughing the passer:** When, after the quarterback has released the ball, a defensive player makes direct contact with the quarterback subsequent to the pass rusher's first step after the quarterback releases the ball. The NFL wants to protect its star players, so this penalty is watched closely. Pass rushers are called for this penalty if they fail to avoid contact with the passer and continue to *drive through* or forcibly make contact with the passer. The defensive player is called for roughing if he commits intimidating acts such as picking up the passer and stuffing him into the ground, wrestling with him, or driving him down after he has released the ball. Also, the defender must not use his helmet or face mask to hit the passer. Finally, the defender must not strike the quarterback in the head or neck area or dive at his knees. Roughing the passer results in an automatic first down.

✔ **Taking a running start to attempt to block a kick:** When a defender takes a running start from beyond the line of scrimmage in an attempt to block a field goal or extra point and lands on players at the line of scrimmage. This penalty prevents defensive players from hurting unprotected players who are attempting to block for their kicker.

✔ **Unnecessary roughness:** This penalty has different variations:

- Striking an opponent above the knee with the foot, or striking any part of the leg below the knee with a whipping motion

- Tackling the ball carrier when he's clearly out of bounds

- A member of the receiving team going out of bounds and contacting a player on the kicking team

- Diving or throwing one's body on the ball carrier when he's defenseless on the ground and is making no attempt to get up

- Throwing the ball carrier to the ground after the play is ruled dead (when an official has blown the whistle)

- Hitting a defenseless receiver in one of the following ways: leaving one's feet and launching into the receiver or using any part of the helmet to initiate forceful contact

✔ **Unsportsmanlike conduct:** When a player commits any act contrary to the generally understood principles of sportsmanship, including the use of abusive, threatening, or insulting language or gestures to opponents, officials, or representatives of the league; the use of baiting or taunting acts or words that engender ill will between teams; and unnecessary contact with any game official.

Identifying specific pass-play penalties

These penalties occur only when the offensive team has attempted a forward pass. Here are three of the most common penalties you see on pass plays:

✔ **Illegal contact:** When a defensive player makes significant contact with a receiver who's 5 yards beyond the line of scrimmage. Illegal contact is a 5-yard penalty and an automatic first down. This penalty has become much more prevalent in the NFL as the league no longer wants to see receivers impeded as they go out into their pass patterns.

✔ **Intentional grounding:** When a passer, facing an imminent loss of yardage due to pressure from the defense, throws a forward pass without a realistic chance of completing it. If he throws such a pass in his own end zone, a safety (two points) is awarded to the defense. It is *not* intentional grounding when a passer, while out of the *pocket* (the protected area within the area of two offensive tackles), throws a pass that lands at or beyond the line of scrimmage with an offensive player having a realistic chance of catching the ball. When out of the pocket, the passer is allowed to throw the ball out of bounds. The penalty is loss of down and 10 yards from the previous line of scrimmage if the passer is in the field of play, or loss of down at the spot of the foul if it occurs more than 10 yards behind the line.

> ✔ **Pass interference:** When a defensive player physically restricts or impedes a receiver in a visually evident manner and materially affects the receiver's opportunity to gain position or retain his position to catch the ball. This penalty is an automatic first down, and the ball is placed at the spot of the foul. If interference occurs in the end zone, the offense gets a first down on the 1-yard line. However, when both players are competing for position to make a play on the ball, the defensive player has a right to attempt to intercept the ball.

Disputing a Call: The Instant Replay Challenge System

Under the *instant replay challenge system,* a coach who disagrees with a call can ask the referees to review it with instant replay. (The NFL resurrected this system in 1999 after trying and abandoning it in the late 1980s and early 1990s, and the NCAA has been using it since 2004.) Coaches can challenge up to two calls per game. However, if they challenge a call and the referees decide after reviewing it that the call stands, the team that issued the challenge loses a timeout. In the rare instance of a coach making two successful challenges within a game, he is allowed a third challenge.

To challenge a call, the coach must make the challenge before the ball is snapped and the next play begins. To signal a challenge, the coach throws a red flag onto the field of play. Usually, coaches wait for the replay to be reviewed in the coaches' booth upstairs, or they view the play on the stadium's big screen before issuing a challenge.

In the NFL, in the final two minutes of each half, neither coach may challenge a call. A replay official monitors all plays and signals down to the field to the referee if any play or call needs to be reviewed. In addition, in the NFL, all scoring plays and turnovers (fumbles and interceptions) are automatically reviewed by the replay official.

Supporters of instant replay challenges say that challenges make the game fairer. The speed of the modern game puts a real strain on a referee's ability to make accurate calls. Instant replay challenges offer teams an opportunity to reverse the occasional bad call. Detractors say that instant replay challenges slow down the game and aren't "instant" at all. As well as the usual interruptions for timeouts, clock stoppages, and penalties, instant replay challenges take away the very thing that fans love most about football — its speed and excitement.

Part II
Go, Offense!

In this part . . .

- ✔ Find out what it takes to be a quarterback, physically and mentally
- ✔ Discover how teams throw and run the ball and compare passing patterns
- ✔ Examine offensive strategies and get to know the people who play the ground game

Chapter 4

The Quarterback, Football's MVP

. . . .

In This Chapter

▶ Understanding what a quarterback does

▶ Recognizing the qualities that make a good quarterback

▶ Deciphering quarterback language and fundamentals

▶ Figuring out a quarterback's rating

. . . .

Being a former defensive player, I hate to admit that the quarterback is the most important player on a football team. My only consolation is that although quarterbacks command the highest salaries in the NFL, my fellow defensive linemen are number two on the list. That's because their job is to make the quarterback's life miserable. Quarterbacks get all the press during the week, and defensive guys knock the stuffing out of them on weekends.

I like my quarterback to be the John Wayne of the football team. He should be a courageous leader, one who puts winning and his teammates ahead of his personal glory. Joe Montana, who won four Super Bowls with the San Francisco 49ers, and John Elway, who won two Super Bowls with the Denver Broncos, quickly come to mind. Both of them played with toughness, although they also had plenty of talent, skill, and flair to somehow escape the worst situations and throw the touchdown pass that won the game.

In this chapter, I reveal the fundamental skills necessary for a quarterback. I also discuss stance, vision, and arm strength and solve the puzzle of that mysterious quarterback rating system.

Taking a Look at the Quarterback's Job

With the exception of kicking plays (described in Chapter 12), quarterbacks touch the ball on every offensive play. A quarterback's job is to direct his team toward the end zone and score as many points as possible. The typical team scores on one-third of its offensive possessions, resulting in either a touchdown or a field goal. So you can see that the quarterback is under enormous pressure to generate points every time the offense takes the field.

The quarterback (QB) is the player directly behind the center receiving the ball, as shown in Figure 4-1, where the center is the X. He's the player who announces the plays in the huddle, but he doesn't call them on his own. Coaches on all levels of football (peewee, high school, college, and the NFL) decide what plays the offense will use.

Figure 4-1:

The QB lines up directly behind the center at the beginning of each play. In the NFL, a quarterback receives plays from a coach on the sidelines via an audio device placed in his helmet. In high school and college football, an assistant coach generally signals in the plays from the sidelines after conferring with the head coach or offensive coordinator. In critical situations, a player may bring in the play when being substituted for an offensive player already on the field.

When Terry Bradshaw, my partner at FOX, played in the NFL in the 1970s, many coaches allowed their veteran quarterbacks to call their own plays after practicing and studying all week. But eventually the coaches wrested control of the play calling away from the quarterbacks, believing that the responsibility was too much of a mental burden for them. When the game became more specialized (with multiple substitutions on both offense and defense) in the 1980s, coaches decided that they wanted the pressure of making the play calls. They didn't think that a quarterback needed the additional responsibility of facing the media after a game and explaining why he called certain plays in a losing game. Head coaches wanted to be the ones to answer those tough questions.

Although NFL coaches don't allow quarterbacks to call their own offensive plays (except in no-huddle situations when little time remains on the clock), a player must be prepared to change the play at the line of scrimmage if it doesn't appear that the play will succeed. Changing the play at the line of scrimmage in this way is called *audibilizing* (see the later "Calling Plays and Audibilizing" section for more on this topic).

After the quarterback is in possession of the ball, he turns and, depending on which play was called, hands the ball to a running back, runs with the ball himself, or moves further back and sets up to attempt a pass. Depending on the design of the offense, the quarterback takes a three-step, five-step, or seven-step drop before throwing the ball.

The area in which the quarterback operates, most likely with a running back (RB) and the offensive line protecting him from the defense, is called the *pocket*. It's as wide as the positioning of the quarterback's offensive tackles (refer to Figure 4-1). The quarterback is instructed to stay within this so-called protective area; if he ventures out of the pocket, he's likely to suffer a bone-crushing tackle. And the last thing a coach wants is for his quarterback, the leader of his team, to get injured.

The quarterback's main job is to throw the football and encourage his team-mates to play well. In college, especially if the team runs a spread formation, the quarterback may run the ball as often as he passes, but in the NFL, the quarterback doesn't run the ball very often unless he's being chased out of the pocket or instructed to run a quarterback sneak. Teams run this play when the offense needs a yard or less for a first down. In a *quarterback sneak,* the quar-terback takes a direct snap from the center and either leaps behind his center or guard or dives between his guard and center, hoping to gain a first down.

In passing situations when the team has many yards to go for a first down or touchdown, quarterbacks sometimes take a *shotgun snap.* In this instance, the quarterback stands 6 to 8 yards behind the center and receives the ball through the air from the center much like a punter does. Starting from the shotgun position, the quarterback doesn't have to drop back. He can survey the defense and target his receivers better. However, defending against a quarterback who lines up in the shotgun position is easier for the defensive players, because they know the play is very likely to be a pass instead of a run.

While the quarterback is setting up a play, he must also be aware of what the defense is attempting to do. Later in this chapter, I explain how quarterbacks "read" a defense.

Determining What a Quarterback Needs to Succeed

When scouts or coaches examine a quarterback's potential to play in the NFL, they run down a checklist of physical, mental, and personality traits that affect a quarterback's success on the field. These qualities are required for success at all levels of football. However, in this chapter, I discuss them in terms that relate to a professional athlete.

Note: Some scouts and coaches break down a quarterback's talent and abilities further, but for this book's purposes, the following are the main criteria necessary to excel. If a quarterback has five of these eight traits, he undoubtedly ranks among the top 15 players at his position.

Arm strength

Unlike baseball, football doesn't use a radar gun to gauge the speed of the ball after the quarterback releases it. But velocity is important when throwing a football because it allows a quarterback to complete a pass before a single defensive player can *recover* (react to the pass) and possibly deflect or intercept the ball. The more arm strength a quarterback has, the better his ability to throw the ball at a high speed.

Many good quarterbacks, with practice, could throw a baseball between 75 and 90 miles per hour, comparable to a Major League Baseball pitcher. Because of its shape, a football is harder to throw than a baseball, but NFL quarterbacks like the Denver Broncos' Peyton Manning and the New York Jets' Michael Vick throw the fastest passes at over 45 miles per hour.

Accuracy

Defensive coverage has never been tighter than in today's NFL. When a receiver goes out into a route, most of the time he's open for only a tiny window of space and time. The best quarterbacks can put the ball in the ideal spot for the receiver to not only catch the ball but to catch it in stride to gain more yards down field. Elite quarterbacks make the perfect throw play after play. Plenty of quarterbacks have strong arms, but the ones who succeed at the highest levels make their living with accurate throws.

Competitiveness

A player's competitiveness is made up of many subjective and intangible qualities. A quarterback should have the desire to be the team's offensive leader and, ideally, overall leader. No one should work harder in practice than he does.

The quarterback's performance affects the entire offensive team. If he doesn't throw accurately, the receivers will never catch a pass. If he doesn't move quickly, the offensive linemen won't be able to protect him. He also should have the courage to take a hard hit from a defensive player. During games, quarterbacks must cope with constant harassment from the defense. They must stand in the pocket and hold onto the ball until the last split second, knowing that they're going to be tackled the instant they release the ball.

To be a competitive player, a quarterback must have an inner desire to win. The quarterback's competitive fire often inspires his teammates to play harder. Competitiveness is a quality that every coach (and teammate) wants in his quarterback.

Intelligence

The quarterback doesn't have to have the highest IQ on the team, but intelligence does come in handy. Many NFL teams have a 3-inch-thick playbook that includes at least 50 running plays and as many as 200 passing plays. The quarterback has to know them all. He has to know not only what he's supposed to do in every one of those plays but also what the other *skilled players* (running backs, receivers, and tight ends) are required to do. Why? Because he may have to explain a specific play in the huddle or during a timeout. On some teams, the quarterback is also responsible for informing the offensive linemen of their blocking schemes.

Many quarterbacks are what coaches call *football smart:* They know the intricacies of the game, the formations, and the defenses. They play on instinct and play well. Former San Francisco quarterback Steve Young is both football smart and book smart. Young was a lot like former great quarterbacks Otto Graham of the Cleveland Browns and Roger Staubach of the Dallas Cowboys. Being book smart and football smart can be an unbeatable combination on game days.

Mobility

A quarterback's mobility is as important as his intelligence and his arm. He must move quickly to avoid being tackled by defensive players. Therefore, he must move backward (called *retreating*) from the center as quickly as possible in order to set himself up to throw the ball. When a quarterback has excellent mobility, you hear him described as having *quick feet*. This term means that he moves quickly and effortlessly behind the line of scrimmage with the football. A quarterback doesn't have to be speedy to do this. He simply must be able to maneuver quickly and gracefully. In one simple step away from the line of scrimmage, a good quarterback covers 4½ feet to almost 2 yards. While taking these huge steps, the quarterback's upper body shouldn't dip or lean to one side or the other. He must be balanced.

Mobility is also critical when a quarterback doesn't have adequate pass protection and has to move out of the pocket and pass while under pressure and on the run. Coaches call this type of mobility *escapability.* Both Michael Vick and Mark Sanchez, shown in Figure 4-2, are great at escaping defensive pressure. Maybe the best of the old-timers was Fran Tarkenton, who played with the New York Giants and the Minnesota Vikings. Roger Staubach of the Cowboys was nicknamed "Roger the Dodger" because he was tough to trap.

Release

If a quarterback doesn't have exceptional arm strength, he'd better have a quick *release.* After the quarterback raises the ball in his hand, usually near his head or slightly above and behind it, he *releases,* or rapidly brings his arm forward and lets the ball loose. Former Miami Dolphins quarterback Dan Marino probably had the game's quickest release. His arm and hand remained a blur when filmed and replayed in slow motion.

Figure 4-2:
Quarterback Mark Sanchez of the New York Jets throws on the run in a game versus Cleveland.

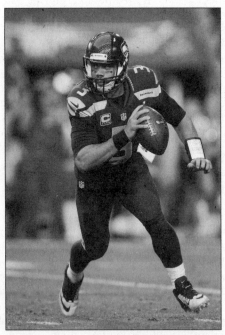

Photo credit: © Joe Robbins/Getty Images

Quarterbacks with great releases generally are born with the ability. Average quarterbacks can improve and refine their releases, but their releases will never be great. A quarterback either has this coordinated motion between his arm, elbow, and wrist, or he doesn't. Throwing a football isn't a natural arm movement like slinging your arm to roll a bowling ball.

Size

Players of all different heights and weights have played the quarterback position, but NFL quarterbacks are preferably over 6'1" and 210 pounds. A quarterback who's 6'5" and 225 pounds is considered ideal. A quarterback wants to be tall enough to see over his linemen — whose average height in the NFL is 6'5" to 6'7" — and look down the field, beyond the line of scrimmage, to find his receivers and see where the defensive backs are positioned.

Weight is imperative to injury prevention because of the physical wear and tear that the quarterback position requires. A quarterback can expect a lot of physical contact, especially when attempting to pass. Defenders relentlessly pursue the quarterback to hit him, tackling him for a *sack* (a loss of yards behind the line of scrimmage) before he can throw a pass or making contact after he releases a pass. These hits are sometimes legal and sometimes illegal. If the defensive player takes more than one step when hitting the quarterback after he releases the ball, the hit is considered late and therefore illegal. Regardless, defensive linemen and linebackers are taught to inflict as much punishment as possible on the quarterback. They want to either knock him out of the game or cause him enough pain that he'll be less willing to hold on to the ball while waiting for his receivers to get open. When a quarterback releases a pass prematurely, it's called *bailing out of the play*.

Vision

A quarterback doesn't necessarily need keen peripheral vision, but it doesn't hurt. A quarterback must quickly scan the field when he comes to the line of scrimmage prior to the snap of the ball. He must survey the defense, checking its alignments and in particular the depth of the defensive backs — how far they are off the receivers, off the line of scrimmage, and so on. After the ball is snapped, the quarterback must continue to scan the field as he moves backward. Granted, he may focus on a particular area because the play is designed in a certain direction, but vision is critical if he wants to discover whether a receiver other than his first choice is open on a particular play. Most pass plays have a variety of options, known as *passing progressions.* One pass play may have as many as five players running pass routes, so the quarterback needs to be able to check whether any of them is open so that he has an option if he's unable to throw to his intended (first choice) receiver.

A quarterback needs to have a sense of where to look and how to scan and quickly react. Often, a quarterback has to make a decision in a split second or else the play may fail. Vision doesn't necessarily mean that the quarterback has to jerk his head from side to side. Instead, his *passing reads* (how a quarterback deciphers what the defense is attempting to accomplish against the offense on a particular play) often follow an orderly progression as he looks across the field of play. A quarterback must have an understanding of what the defensive secondary's tendencies are — how they like to defend a particular play or a certain style of receiver. Sometimes, after sneaking a quick glance at his intended target, the quarterback looks in another direction in order to fool the defense. (Many defensive players tend to follow a quarterback's eyes, believing that they'll tell where he intends to throw the pass.)

Quarterbacking Fundamentals

Playing quarterback requires a lot of technical skills. Although a coach can make a player better in many areas of the game, I don't believe that any coach can teach a player how to throw the football. Otherwise, every quarterback would be a great passer. And if such a coach existed, every father would be taking his son to that coach, considering the millions of dollars NFL quarterbacks earn every season.

You can teach a quarterback how to deal with pressure, how to make good decisions, and how to make good connections with his receivers and predict where they'll be. But quarterbacks either have the innate talent to throw the football — that natural arm motion and quick release — or they don't. Think of how many good college quarterbacks fail to survive in the NFL. Plus, NFL scouts, coaches, general managers, and so on will tell you that the league has only 10 to 15 really good quarterbacks. If throwing could be taught, all quarterbacks would be great.

Quarterbacks *can* improve and refine their skills in the following areas with a lot of practice and hard work.

Settling into the stance

To play the most important position in football, a quarterback must begin with his stance under center. The quarterback takes his stance behind the center to receive the ball; the center snaps it back to him, as shown in Figure 4-3. The quarterback's stance under center starts with both feet about shoulder width apart. He bends his knees, flexes down, and bends forward at the waist until he's directly behind the center's rear end. The quarterback then places his hands, with the thumbs touching each other and the fingers spread as far apart as possible, under the center's rear end. Because some centers don't bring the ball all the way to the quarterback's hands, the quarterback will lower his hands below the center's rear end in order to receive the ball cleanly. The quarterback needs to avoid pulling out early, a common mistake when the quarterback and the center haven't played together very much.

Dropping back

After he masters the stance, a quarterback learns how to *drop back* and set up to pass. Dropping back is what a quarterback does after he receives the ball from the center. Before he passes the ball, he must move away from the line of scrimmage (and the opposing defense) and put himself in a position to be able to throw the football.

Figure 4-3:
A quarter-
back usually
lines up
behind the
center, who
snaps the
ball to him
to start the
play.

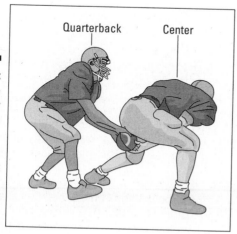

You see quarterbacks backing up from center, or *backpedaling,* when the offensive formation is aligned to the left of a right-handed quarterback. Backpedaling is essential in those alignments so that the quarterback can see whether the linebacker on that side is *blitzing* (rushing across the line of scrimmage in an attempt to tackle the quarterback). The quarterback must be alert to a possible blitz; consequently, he can't afford to half-turn his back to that side.

The depth to which a quarterback drops in the pocket generally is determined by how far from the line of scrimmage the receiver is running. If the receiver is running 5 to 6 yards down the field and then turning to catch the ball, for example, the quarterback takes a drop of no more than three steps. The quarterback generally moves further away from the line of scrimmage as the *pass routes* (the paths receivers take when going out for a pass) of his receivers get longer. For instance, if the receiver is running 10 to 12 yards down the field, the quarterback takes five steps to put himself about 7 yards back from the line of scrimmage.

On a *post route* (a deep pass in which the receiver angles in to the goalpost) or a *streak route* (a deep pass straight downfield), the quarterback takes a seven-step drop. Taking a longer drop when a shorter one is required enables the defense to recover and may lead to an interception or an incompletion.

All these drop-backs are critical to the timing of the receiver's run, move, and turn and the quarterback's delivery and release. In practice, the quarterback works on the depth of his steps according to the pass route.

Handing off

One of the most important things for a quarterback to master is the running game and how it affects his steps from center (head to Chapter 6 for the scoop on the running game). Some running plays call for the quarterback to open his right hip (if he's right-handed) and step straight back. This technique is called the *six o'clock step*. The best way to imagine these steps is to picture a clock. The center is at twelve o'clock, and directly behind the quarterback is six o'clock. Three o'clock is to the quarterback's right, and nine o'clock is to his left.

For example, a right-handed quarterback hands off the ball to a runner heading on a run around the left side of his offensive line (it's called a *sweep*) at the five o'clock mark. When handing the ball to a runner heading on a sweep across the backfield to the right, the quarterback should hand off at the seven o'clock mark.

Getting a grip

Because different quarterbacks have different-sized hands, one passing grip doesn't suit everyone. Some coaches say that a quarterback should hold the ball with his middle finger going across the ball's white laces or trademark. Other coaches believe both the middle and ring finger should grip the laces.

Many great quarterbacks have huge hands, allowing them to place their index finger on the tip of the ball while wrapping their middle, ring, and small fingers around the middle of the ball. However, the ball slips from many quarterbacks' hands when they attempt to grip the ball this way. So, basically, every quarterback needs to find the grip that works for him.

Reading a Defense

When a quarterback prepares for a game, he wants to be able to look at a specific defensive alignment and instantly know which offense will or won't succeed against it.

Many quarterbacks are taught to read the *free safety,* or the safety positioned deepest in the *secondary,* the part of the field behind the linebackers that the safeties and cornerbacks are responsible for. (See Chapter 10 for more on the secondary and Chapter 11 for the full scoop on defensive schemes and strategies.) If the free safety lines up 5 to 7 yards deeper than the other defensive backs, the safeties are probably playing a zone defense. A quarterback also knows that the defense is playing zone if the cornerbacks are aligned 10 yards off the line of scrimmage. If the cornerbacks are on the line of scrimmage, eyeballing the receivers, they're most likely playing man-to-man. Knowing whether the defense is playing zone or man-to-man is important to the quarterback because he wants to know whether he's attacking a zone defense or man-to-man alignment with his pass play.

Although a defense may employ 20 to 30 different pass coverages in the secondary, four basic coverages exist. Because most defenses begin with four players in the secondary, the coverages are called *cover one, cover two, cover three,* and *cover four.* The following list gives a description of each:

 ✔ **Cover one:** In this coverage, shown in Figure 4-4, one deep safety is about 12 to 14 yards deep in the middle of the field, the two cornerbacks (CB) are in *press coverage* (on the line of scrimmage opposite the two receivers), and the strong safety (SS) is about 5 yards deep over the tight end. Cover one is usually man-to-man coverage. A running play works best against this type of coverage.

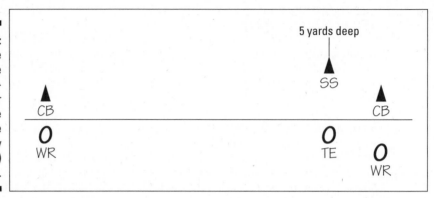

Figure 4-4:
Cover one
puts one
safety or sec-
ondary player
close to the
line while the
free safety
(not pictured)
plays deep.

✔ **Cover two:** This time, both safeties are deep, 12 to 14 yards off the line of scrimmage, as shown in Figure 4-5. The two cornerbacks remain in press coverage, while the two safeties prepare to help the corners on passing plays and come forward on running plays. A deep comeback pass, a crossing route, or a swing pass works well against this type of coverage.

Figure 4-5:
Cover two
puts both
safeties
deep.

✔ **Cover three:** This coverage, shown in Figure 4-6, has three defensive backs deep. The free safety remains 12 to 14 yards off the line of scrimmage, and the two cornerbacks move 10 to 12 yards off the line of scrimmage. Cover three is obvious zone coverage. The strong safety is 5 yards off the line of scrimmage, over the tight end. This cover is a stout defense versus the run, but it's soft against a good passing team. In this cover, a quarterback can throw *underneath passes* (short passes to beat the linebackers who are positioned underneath the defensive back's coverage). Staying with faster receivers in this area is difficult for some linebackers to do.

Figure 4-6: In cover three, three defensive backs line up deep.

✔ **Cover four:** In cover four, what you see is what you get, as shown in Figure 4-7. All four defensive backs are off the line of scrimmage, aligned 10 to 12 yards deep. Some teams call this coverage "Four Across" because the defensive backs are aligned all across the field. The cover four is a good pass defense because the secondary players are told to never allow a receiver to get behind them. If offensive teams can block the *front seven* (a combination of defensive linemen and linebackers that amounts to seven players), a running play works against this coverage.

Figure 4-7: Cover four aligns all four secondary players off the line of scrimmage.

Calling Plays and Audibilizing

The quarterback relays to his teammates in the huddle what play the coach has called. The *play* is a mental blueprint or diagram for every player on the field. And everything the quarterback says refers specifically to the assignments of his receivers, running backs, offensive linemen, and center.

For example, the quarterback may say "686 Pump F-Stop on two." The first three numbers (686) are the passing routes that the receivers — known as X, Y, and Z — should take. Every team numbers its pass routes and patterns (look for them in Chapter 5), giving receivers an immediate signal of what routes to run. On this play, the X receiver runs a 6 route, the Y receiver an 8 route, and the Z receiver another 6 route. "F-Stop" in this case refers to the fullback's pass route. And "two" refers to the *count* on which the quarterback wants the ball snapped to him. In other words, the center will snap the ball on the second sound.

Most teams snap the ball on the first, second, or third count unless they're purposely attempting to draw the opposition offside by using an extra-long count. For example, if the quarterback has been asking for the ball on the count of two throughout the game, he may ask for the ball on the count of three, hoping that someone on the defense will move prematurely.

After the quarterback reaches the line of scrimmage and puts his hands under the center, he says "Set" (at which point the linemen drop into their stances) and then something like "Green 80, Green 80, Hut-Hut." The center snaps the ball on the second "Hut." "Green 80" means absolutely nothing in this case. However, sometimes the quarterback's remarks at the line of scrimmage prior to the snap count inform his offensive teammates of how the play will be changed. The offensive linemen also know that the play is a pass because of the numbering system mentioned at the beginning of the called play.

Teams give their plays all sorts of odd monikers, such as Quick Ace, Scat, Zoom, and Buzz. These names refer to specific actions within the play; they're meant for the ears of the running backs and receivers. Each name (and every team has its own terms) means something, depending on the play called.

Quarterbacks are allowed to *audibilize,* or change the play at the line of scrimmage. A changed play is called an *audible.* Quarterbacks usually audibilize when they discover that the defense has guessed correctly and is properly aligned to stop the play. When he barks his signals, the quarterback simply has to say "Green 85," and the play is altered to the 85 pass play. Usually, the quarterback informs his offensive teammates in the huddle what his audible change may be.

A quarterback may also use an offensive strategy known as *check with me,* in which he instructs his teammates to listen carefully at the line of scrimmage because he may call another play, or his call at the line of scrimmage will be the play. To help his teammates easily understand, the play may simply change colors — from Green to Red, for example.

Acing Quarterback Math

Quarterbacks are judged statistically on all levels of football by their passing accuracy (which is called *completion percentage*), the number of touchdowns they throw, the number of interceptions they throw, and the number of yards they gain by passing. This last statistic — passing yards — can be deceiving. For example, if a quarterback throws the ball 8 yards beyond the line of scrimmage and the receiver runs for another 42 yards after catching the ball, the quarterback is awarded 50 yards for the completion. (You may hear television commentators use the term *yards after the catch* to describe the yards that the receiver gains after catching the ball.) Quarterbacks also receive positive passing yards when they complete a pass behind the line of scrimmage — for example, a screen pass to a running back who goes on to run 15 yards. Those 15 yards are considered passing yards.

For a better understanding of what the quarterback's numbers mean, take a look at Denver Broncos quarterback Peyton Manning's statistics for the 2013 season. He played in all 16 regular-season games.

Att	Comp	Pct Comp	Yds	Yds/Att	TD	Int	Rating
659	450	68.3	5,477	8.3	55	10	115.1

Examining Manning's statistics, you see that he attempted 659 passes (Att) and completed 450 of those passes (Comp) for a completion percentage of 68.3 (Pct Comp). In attempting those 659 passes, his receivers gained 5,477 yards (Yds), which equals an average gain per attempt of 8.3 yards (Yds/Att). Manning's teammates scored 55 touchdowns (TD) via his passing while the defense intercepted (Int) 10 of his passing attempts.

When you see a newspaper article about a football game, the story may state that the quarterback was 22 of 36, passing for 310 yards. Translation: He completed 22 of 36 pass attempts and gained 310 yards on those 22 completions. Not a bad game.

Last but not least you have the NFL quarterback rating formula, also called the passer rating formula. It makes for an unusual math problem. Grab your calculator and follow these steps to figure it out:

1. **Divide completed passes by pass attempts, subtract 0.3, and then divide by 0.2.**

2. **Divide passing yards by pass attempts, subtract 3, and then divide by 4.**

3. **Divide touchdown passes by pass attempts and then divide by 0.05.**

4. **Divide interceptions by pass attempts, subtract that number from 0.095, and divide the remainder by 0.04.**

The sum of each step can't be greater than 2.375 or less than zero. Add the sums of the four steps, multiply that number by 100, and divide by 6. The final number is the quarterback rating, which in Manning's case is 115.1.

A rating of 100 or above is considered very good; an average rating is in the 80 to 100 range, and anything below 80 is considered a poor quarterback rating.

Chapter 5

The Passing Game

In This Chapter

▶ Catching up with the receivers

▶ Getting a handle on common passing-game terms

▶ Finding out about different pass patterns

Although the strategies of offenses change and sometimes favor running over passing, throwing the football is a major part of football's excitement. Some of the most memorable plays in football are those long passes (or throws) that win games in the final seconds or pull a team ahead in the score and turn the game around. Who can resist joining in the collective cheer that erupts when the ball is hurtling through the air and looks as if it's about to drop into a receiver's hands? And when the defense catches the ball (known in football jargon as an *interception*), the play can be just as exciting and influential to the outcome of the game.

An offense scores points by moving the ball into the opponent's end zone. This chapter focuses on one half of the offensive attack: the passing game. The other half, the running game, is covered in Chapter 6. In the 1980 NFL season, pass plays exceeded running plays for the first time since 1969, and that trend has continued ever since.

Getting to Know the Passing Game

To many fans, the passing game is the most exciting aspect of football. Seeing the quarterback throwing a long pass and a fleet-footed receiver jumping up to grab it is exciting. Earl "Curly" Lambeau, the founder and player/coach of the Green Bay Packers, made his offenses throw the football in the mid-1930s. But teams eventually moved away from throwing the ball. In the 1960s and 1970s, the running game and zone defenses (where players defended deep and covered every area of the field) choked the life out of the passing game.

Two significant rule changes in 1978 spurred the growth of the passing game in the NFL. First, defenders were permitted to make contact with receivers only within 5 yards of the line of scrimmage. Previously, defenders were allowed to hit, push, or shove ("chuck") a receiver anywhere on the field. (In 2014, NFL officials were instructed to pay close attention to illegal contact by defenders against receivers, further opening up the passing game.) Also, offensive linemen were allowed to use open hands and fully extend their arms to block a pass-rusher. The liberalization of this offensive blocking technique led to better protection for the quarterback and ultimately more time for him to throw the football.

Prior to these rules, offenses had begun to rely on running backs as their main pass receivers. Then Bill Walsh became the head coach of the San Francisco 49ers in 1979, and he melded every aspect of these new rules and the running-back-as-receiver concept into his *West Coast offense*. For the first time, teams were running out of passing formations, and the pass was setting up running plays instead of vice versa.

To make a pass successful, quarterbacks and receivers (wide receivers, tight ends, and running backs) must work on their timing daily. To do so, the receivers must run exact *pass patterns* with the quarterback throwing the football to predetermined spots on the field. Although passing the football may look like a simple act of the quarterback throwing and a receiver catching the ball (often in full stride), this aspect of the game is very complex. For it to be successful, the offensive linemen must provide the quarterback with adequate protection so that he has time to throw the football (more than two seconds), while the receivers make every attempt to catch the ball, even if it's poorly thrown. Sometimes, a receiver must deviate from his planned route and run to any open space to give the quarterback a target. .

Recognizing the Role of Receivers

A quarterback wouldn't be much good without receivers to catch the ball. *Wide receivers* and *tight ends* are the principal players who catch passes, although *running backs* also are used extensively in every passing offense. (See Chapter 6 for more on running backs.) During the 2014 season, 23 players in the NFL had over 1,000 receiving yards, and of those 23, only 2 were tight ends. The rest were wide receivers.

Receivers come in all sizes and shapes. They are tall, short, lean, fast, and quick. To excel as a receiver, a player must have nimble hands (hands that are very good at catching the ball) and the ability to concentrate under defensive duress; he must also be courageous under fire and strong enough to withstand physical punishment. Although receiving is a glamorous job, every team expects its receivers to block defensive backs on running plays as well (head to Chapter 7 to find out more). Every team wants its receivers to be able to knock a defensive cornerback on his back or at least prevent him from making a tackle on a running back.

Tight ends aren't as fast as wide receivers because they play the role of heavy-duty blockers on many plays. Teams don't expect tight ends, who may outweigh a wide receiver by 60 pounds, to have the bulk and strength of offensive linemen, but the good ones — like Vernon Davis of the San Francisco 49ers and Rob Gronkowski of the New England Patriots — are above-average blockers as well as excellent receivers.

Basic offenses have five possible receivers: the two running backs, the tight end, and the two wide receivers. The wide receivers are commonly referred to as X and Z receivers. The X receiver, or *split end,* normally aligns to the weak side of the formation, and the Z receiver, or *flanker,* aligns to the strong side of the formation. The tight end is known as the Y receiver. (In simplest terms, the strong side of the formation is the side with the most distance to the sideline.)

The split end received his name because he was the end (the offenses of the 1930s used two ends) who aligned 10 yards away from the base offensive formation. Hence, he *split* from his teammates. The other end, the tight end, aligned next to an offensive tackle. The *flanker* position was originally a running back, and as offenses developed, he flanked to either side of the formation, but never on the line of scrimmage like the split end and tight end.

In many offenses, on passing downs, the tight end is replaced by another receiver. In Figure 5-1, the Y receiver is the one who replaces the tight end.

Figure 5-1:
The Y receiver can replace the tight end on passing downs.

The following sections offer insight into the nitty-gritty details of the receiver's role in the passing game. Read on to find out everything from the stance that receivers use to the ways they overcome man-to-man coverage.

Achieving the proper stance

Before receivers work on catching the ball, they need to learn the proper stance to create acceleration off the line of scrimmage while also using their upper bodies to defend themselves from contact with defensive backs. Receivers must understand, even at the beginning level, that they must get open before they can catch the ball and that the proper stance enables them to explode from the line of scrimmage. A quarterback won't throw the ball to a receiver who isn't open, and when it comes to being able to complete a pass to an open receiver, every step counts.

In the *stand-up stance,* the receiver's feet remain shoulder width apart and are positioned like they're in the starting blocks — with his left foot near the line of scrimmage and his right foot back 18 inches. With his shoulders square to the ground, he should lean forward just enough so that he can explode off the line when the ball is snapped. The receiver's lean shouldn't be exaggerated, though, or he may tip over.

A good receiver uses the same stance on every play because he doesn't want to tip off the defense to whether the play is a run or a pass. Bad receivers line up lackadaisically on running plays.

Teaching kids the receiver's stance

The best way for a youngster to learn the stand-up stance is to take him to a track meet and show him the sprinters. If you can't go to a track meet, watch one on television or your computer. Watch how a great 100-meter sprinter starts with her feet in the starting blocks and then explodes at the sound of the gun. This starting position is the same in football, with the snap of the ball representing the starter's pistol. Teaching receivers their stance by using sprinter's starting blocks is a good idea.

First, put the receiver in a *four-point stance,* both hands and feet on the ground, and have him get a feel for the burst out of the blocks (or what football calls the *burst off the line of scrimmage*). His feet should be shoulder width apart. Next, have the receiver try a *three-point stance,* with only one hand on the ground. The receiver should try this stance 100 times before advancing to the stand-up stance that's common on all levels of football, from youth to the pros.

Lining up correctly

One wide receiver, usually the split end, lines up on the line of scrimmage. The other receiver, the flanker, must line up 1 yard behind the line of scrimmage. A combination of seven offensive players must always be on the line of scrimmage prior to the ball being snapped. A smart receiver checks with the nearest official to make sure he's lined up correctly.

The tight end and the split end never line up on the same side. If a receiver is aligned 15 to 18 yards away from the quarterback, he can't hear the quarterback barking signals. Therefore, he must look down the line and move as soon as he sees the ball snapped. Once off the line of scrimmage, a receiver should run toward either shoulder of a defensive back, forcing the defender to turn his shoulders perpendicular to the line of scrimmage to cover him. The receiver hopes to turn the defender in the direction that's opposite of the one in which he intends to go.

Catching the ball

Good receivers catch a football with their hands while their arms are extended away from their bodies. They never catch a football by cradling it in their shoulders or chest, because the ball frequently bounces off.

The best technique a receiver has for using his hands is to place one thumb behind the other while turning his hands so that the fingers of both hands face each other. He spreads his hands as wide as possible while keeping his thumbs together. Then he brings his hands face-high, like he's looking through a tunnel (see Figure 5-2). He wants the ball to come through that tunnel. He wants to see the point of the ball coming down the tunnel, and then he wants to trap it with his palms, thumbs, and fingers. This technique is called *getting your eyes in line with the flight of the ball.* If a ball is thrown below a receiver's waist, he should turn his thumbs out and his little fingers should overlap. A receiver with good fundamentals also keeps his elbows close to his body when catching a football, which adds power to his arms.

Beating man-to-man coverage

Man-to-man coverage is a style, like in basketball, in which one man guards (or defends) another. The defender stays with a single receiver no matter where he runs. His responsibility is to make sure the receiver doesn't catch a pass. (Head to Chapter 10 for more on man-to-man coverage.)

Figure 5-2:
The right
way to
catch a
football.

Defensive players use the in-your-face technique of putting their bodies on the line of scrimmage and trying to knock the receivers off stride and out of their routes (see the later section "Looking at Passing Patterns" for more info on routes). The defensive back's objective is to "hurt" the receiver first and then try to push him out of bounds (it's illegal for a receiver to return to the field and catch a pass) while trying to get the receiver's mind off running a perfect route and making a catch. The entire defensive attitude is to take the receiver out of the game, mentally and physically.

A receiver must approach this in-your-face technique as if he's in an alley fight against someone who wants to take him down. When the center snaps the ball, the receiver must bring his arms and hands up to his face just like a fighter would. The receiver wants to prevent the defensive player from putting his hands into his chest by counter-punching his attempts. The working of the receiver's hands is similar to the "wax on, wax off" style taught in the movie *The Karate Kid*.

After the receiver fights off the defensive back's hands, he must dip his shoulder and take off running. This technique is called *dip and rip* because the receiver dips his shoulder and rips through the defender's attempt to hold or shove him with a strong punch, like a boxer throwing a great uppercut to his opponent's chin. This move was a favorite of Hall-of-Famer Jerry Rice, who's possibly the greatest receiver of all time.

Another method of defeating man-to-man coverage is to use the *swim technique*. With the swim, the receiver's arms and hands are still in the same position as the dip and rip, and the receiver must again get his hands up in a boxing position. But at the snap of the ball, instead of lowering his shoulder and ripping through, the receiver tries to slap the defensive back's hands one way while heading in the opposite direction. When the defensive back reacts, the receiver uses his free arm and takes a freestyle stroke (raises an arm up and forward and then brings it back to the side) over the defensive back while trying to pull the arm back underneath and behind him. This entire action takes a split second. With the swim technique, it's critical that the receiver doesn't allow the defensive back to catch his arm and grab hold under his armpit to prevent him from running downfield.

Note: Bigger, stronger receivers use the dip and rip method, whereas smaller, faster receivers usually use the swim technique.

Defining Important Passing Terms

This section lists the words and descriptions frequently mentioned when discussing the passing game. As a player, my favorite word was *sack:* a defender's dream and a quarterback's nightmare (you can find a definition in the following list). I had 84 sacks in my career, every one a great thrill. I deflected quite a few pass attempts, too. Read on and you'll get my meaning:

- ✔ **Deflection:** A *deflection* happens when a defensive player uses his hands or arms to knock down (or deflect) a pass before it reaches the receiver. This act usually occurs near the line of scrimmage when defensive linemen jump, arms raised, into a quarterback's visual passing lane, hoping to deflect the pass. Deflections can lead to an interception or incompletion.

- ✔ **Holding:** *Holding* is the most common penalty called against the offense when it's attempting to pass. The offense receives a 10-yard penalty (and repeat of down) when any offensive player holds a defensive player by grabbing his jersey or locking his arm onto the defensive player's arm while that player is trying to sack the quarterback. This penalty is also known as illegal use of the hands, arms, or any part of the body.

- ✔ **Illegal forward pass:** A quarterback can't cross the line of scrimmage and throw the ball. This penalty often occurs when the quarterback runs forward, attempting to evade defensive players, and forgets where the line of scrimmage is. The offense is penalized 5 yards from the spot of the foul and loses a down.

- ✔ **Intentional grounding:** This penalty occurs when a quarterback standing in the pocket deliberately throws the ball out of bounds or into the ground. It can be interpreted in the following three ways, with the first two drastically penalizing the offense:

  - • **No. 1:** The quarterback is attempting to pass from his own end zone and, prior to being tackled, intentionally grounds the ball, throwing it out of bounds or into the ground. The defense is awarded a safety, worth two points, and the offense loses possession of the ball and has to kick the ball from its own 20-yard line. (NFL teams usually kick off from the 30-yard line.)

- **No. 2:** The quarterback is trapped behind his own line of scrimmage and intentionally grounds the ball for fear of being tackled for a loss. This penalty is a loss of down, and the ball is placed at the spot of the foul, which in this case is where the quarterback was standing when he grounded the ball. Otherwise, the intentional grounding penalty calls for loss of down and 10 yards.

- **No. 3:** The quarterback steps back from the center and immediately throws the ball into the ground, intentionally grounding it. This is referred to as *spiking the ball.* This play is common when an offense wants to stop the clock without calling a timeout because it either wants to preserve its timeouts or is out of timeouts. For this type of intentional grounding, the penalty is simply a loss of a down.

✔ **Interception:** An *interception* is the act of any defensive player catching a pass. Along with a fumble, an interception is the worst thing that can happen to a quarterback and his team. It's called a *turnover* because the defensive team gains possession of the ball and is allowed to run with the ball in an attempt to score. (Deion Sanders was probably the greatest threat on an interception because of his open-field running ability.)

✔ **Roughing the passer:** This penalty was devised to protect the quarterback from injury. After the ball leaves the quarterback's hand, any defensive player must attempt to avoid contact with him. Because a defensive player's momentum may cause him to inadvertently run into the quarterback, he's allowed to take one step after he realizes that the ball has been released. But if he hits the quarterback on his second step, knowing that the ball is gone, the *referee* (the official standing near the quarterback) can call *roughing.* It's a 15-yard penalty against the defense and an automatic first down. This penalty is difficult to call unless the defensive player clearly hits the quarterback well after the quarterback releases the ball. After all, it's pretty tough for defensive ends, who are usually over 6 feet and weigh 250 pounds, to come to an abrupt stop from a full sprint.

Roughing the passer penalties can also be called on defenders who

- Strike the quarterback in the head or neck area, regardless of whether the hit was intentional

- Flagrantly hit the quarterback in the knee area or lower when the defender has an unrestricted path to the quarterback

Keep in mind that these penalties apply only when the quarterback is acting as a passer. If the quarterback tucks the ball and runs, defenders can hit him just like any other ball carrier. However, quarterbacks have the option of giving themselves up while running, which basically means that they slide feet first to avoid being hit. If a defender hits a sliding quarterback, he's assessed a 15-yard unnecessary roughness penalty.

- ✔ **Sack:** A *sack* happens when the quarterback is tackled behind the line of scrimmage by any defensive player. The sack is the most prominent defensive statistic, one the NFL has officially kept since 1982. (All other kinds of tackles are considered unofficial statistics because individual teams are responsible for recording them.) Colleges have been recording sacks for the same length of time.

- ✔ **Trapping:** Receivers are asked to make a lot of difficult catches, but this one is never allowed. *Trapping* is when a receiver uses the ground to help him catch a pass that's thrown on a low trajectory. For an official to not rule a reception a trap, the receiver must make sure either his hands or his arms are between the ball and the ground when he makes a legal catch. Often, this play occurs so quickly, only instant replay can show that the receiver wasn't in possession of the ball — instead it shows that he trapped it.

Looking at Passing Patterns

When watching at home or in the stands, you can look for basic pass patterns used in all levels of football. These pass patterns (also known as *pass routes*) may be a single part of a larger play. In fact, on a single play, two or three receivers may be running an equal number of different pass patterns.

By knowing passing patterns, you can discover what part of the field or which defensive player(s) the offense wants to attack, or how an offense wants to compete with a specific defense. (Sometimes, a pass pattern is run to defeat a defensive scheme designed to stop a team's running game by moving defenders away from the actual point of attack.) The following list includes the most common patterns receivers run during games:

- ✔ **Comeback:** Teams use this pass pattern effectively when the receiver is extremely fast and the defensive player gives him a 5-yard cushion, which means that the defensive player stays that far away from him, fearing his speed. On the comeback, the receiver runs hard downfield, between 12 and 20 yards, and then turns sharply to face the football. The comeback route generally is run along the sideline. To work effectively, the quarterback usually throws the ball before the receiver turns. He throws to a spot where he expects the receiver to stop and turn. This kind of pass is called a *timing pass* because the quarterback throws it before the receiver turns and looks toward the quarterback or before he makes his move backward.

✔ **Crossing:** The crossing pattern is an effective pass against man-to-man coverage because it's designed for the receiver to beat his defender by running across the field. The receiver can line up on the right side of the line of scrimmage, run straight for 10 yards, and then cut quickly to his left. When the receiver cuts, he attempts to lose the man covering him with either a head or shoulder *fake* (a sudden jerk with his upper body to one side or the other) or a quick stutter-step. This route is designed for two receivers, usually one on either side of the formation. It allows one receiver to interfere with his teammate's defender as the two receivers cross near the middle of the field. The play is designed for the quarterback to pass to the receiver on the run as the receiver crosses in front of his field of vision.

✔ **Curl:** For this 8- to 12-yard pass beyond the line of scrimmage, the receiver stops and then turns immediately, making a slight curl before facing the quarterback's throw. The receiver usually takes a step or two toward the quarterback and the ball before the pass reaches him. The curl tends to be a high-percentage completion because the receiver wants to shield the defender with his back, and the intention is simply to gain a few yards. Big tight ends tend to like the curl.

✔ **Hook:** This common pass play, which is also known as a buttonhook, is designed mostly for a tight end, who releases downfield and then makes a small turn, coming back to face the quarterback and receive the ball. A hook is similar to a curl, except the turn is made more abruptly and the pass is shorter, at 5 to 8 yards. It's a timing pass, so the quarterback usually releases the ball before the tight end starts his turn.

✔ **Post:** This is a long pass, maybe as long as 40 to 50 yards, in which the receiver runs straight downfield, and then cuts on a 45-degree angle toward the "post," or goalposts. (Most teams use the hash marks as a guiding system for both the quarterback and the receiver.) A coach calls this play when one safety is deep and the offense believes it can isolate a fast receiver against him. The receiver runs straight downfield, possibly hesitating a split second as if he might cut the route inside or outside, and then cuts toward the post. The hesitation may cause the safety, or whoever is positioned in the deep center of the field, to break stride or slow down. The receiver needs only an extra step on the defender for this play to be successful. The quarterback puts enough loft on the ball to enable the receiver to catch the pass in stride.

✔ **Slant:** This pass is designed for an inside receiver (a flanker) who's aligned 5 yards out from the offensive line, possibly from a tight end or the offensive tackle. The receiver runs straight for 3 to 8 yards and then slants his route, angling toward the middle of the field. A slant is effective against both zone and man-to-man coverage because it's designed to find an open space in either defensive scheme (see Chapter 10 for details on both of these types of coverage).

✔ **Square-out:** The receiver on this pattern runs 10 yards down the field and then cuts sharply toward the sideline, parallel to the line of scrimmage. The square-out is also a timing play because the quarterback must deliver the pass before the receiver reaches the sideline and steps out of bounds, sometimes before he even cuts. The quarterback must really fire this pass, which is why commentators sometimes refer to it as a *bullet throw.* The route works against both man-to-man and zone coverage. The receiver must roll his shoulder toward the inside before cutting toward the sideline. The quarterback throws the pass, leading the receiver toward the sideline.

✔ **Streak (or Fly):** This is a 20- to 40-yard pass, generally to a receiver on the quarterback's throwing side (which is right if he's right-handed or left if he's left-handed). The receiver, who's aligned wide and near the sidelines, runs as fast as he can down the sideline, hoping to lose the defensive man in the process. This pass must be thrown accurately because both players tend to be running as fast as they can, and often the cornerback is as fast as the receiver. This play is designed to loosen up the defense, making it believe the quarterback and the receiver have the ability to throw deep whenever they want to. Moving a defense back or away from the line of scrimmage allows the offense an opportunity to complete shorter passes and execute run plays. To complete this pass, the quarterback makes sure a safety isn't playing deep to that side of the field. Otherwise, with the ball in the air for a long time, a free safety can angle over and intercept the pass. If the quarterback sees the safety near his streaking receiver, he must throw to another receiver elsewhere on the field.

✔ **Swing:** This is a simple throw to a running back who runs out of the backfield toward the sideline. The quarterback generally throws the pass when the running back turns and heads upfield. The swing is usually a *touch pass,* meaning the quarterback doesn't necessarily throw it as hard as he does a deep square-out (described earlier in this list). He wants to be able to float it over a linebacker and make it easy for the running back to catch. The area in which the back is running is known as *the flat* because it's 15 yards outside the hash marks and close to where the numbers on the field are placed. The receiver's momentum most likely will take him out of bounds after he catches the ball unless he's able to avoid the first few tacklers he faces.

Figure 5-3 shows the many pass patterns and how they funnel off what's called a *route tree.* The tree is numbered: 4 is a square-out; 5 is a slant; 6 is a curl or a hook; 7 is a post; 8 is a streak or fly; and 9 is a corner route. When calling a pass play, these numbers, which can vary by team, refer to the specific pass pattern (or route) called by the quarterback.

Figure 5-3:
A route
tree with
the pass
patterns
numbered.

Getting into the Shotgun Formation

In football terminology, *formation* describes how the players on offense line up before the ball is snapped. As football has evolved, so have the formations. The *shotgun* passing formation was devised by San Francisco 49ers head coach Red Hickey in 1960. Hickey feared the Baltimore Colts' great pass rush, so he had his quarterback, John Brodie, line up 7 yards behind the line of scrimmage (see Figure 5-4). Hickey figured that Brodie would have more time to see his receivers and could release the ball before the defensive rush reached him. The strategy worked, and the 49ers upset the mighty Colts.

Offenses use the shotgun when they have poor pass blocking or when they're facing excellent pass rushers. Teams also use the shotgun when they want to pass on every down, usually when they're behind. However, many offenses use the shotgun simply because the quarterback and the coach like to use it. Other teams use the shotgun only when they're in obvious passing situations — such as on third down when they need 4 or more yards for a first down, or anytime they need more than 10 yards for a first down.

Figure 5-4:
The shotgun
formation
puts the
quarterback
7 yards
behind
the line of
scrimmage.

Passing and catching greats

A football team needs all kinds of warriors to make the passing game work. Here are a few snapshots of the performers who are worth remembering. Many of them mixed style with grace, talent, and toughness.

✔ The San Diego Chargers had a receiver named "Bambi." Lance Alworth hated his nickname, which was given to him by a teammate who thought he had the speed and grace of a deer. Alworth had short hair and brown eyes and ran like the wind — right into the Pro Football Hall of Fame. Alworth was the second player to reach 10,000 receiving yards.

✔ Joe Willie Namath was one of the first players to wear white football shoes. "Broadway Joe" was a flashy bachelor quarterback for the New York Jets in the 1960s and early 1970s who once wore a fur coat on the sidelines. In the 1967 season, he threw for 4,007 yards in just 14 games. And Namath followed through on his guarantee

to beat the heavily favored Baltimore Colts in Super Bowl III.

✔ Earl "Curly" Lambeau was the first quarterback/coach of the Green Bay Packers. In the 1930s, Coach Lambeau (the Green Bay stadium is named after him) opted for a wide-open passing game when most NFL teams were still slugging each other with the running game. Lambeau made stars of players like receiver Don Hutson (whom I describe in Chapter 20).

✔ Johnny Unitas is in the Hall of Fame, but he wasn't always a Baltimore Colts' star. He played minor league football in 1955 for $3 a game. The Pittsburgh Steelers drafted him but then didn't believe that he was good enough to make their team and released him from their roster. Unitas, famous for his black high-top football shoes, ended up being the first quarterback to pass for 40,000 yards.

Despite its versatility, the shotgun formation has a couple downsides:

- ✔ The center must be able to make an accurate, chest-high, 7-yard snap to the quarterback.

- ✔ You can't fool the defensive players; they know you're probably throwing the ball, and the pass rushers won't hesitate to sprint for your quarterback in hopes of a sack.

Teams need a quick-thinking quarterback who can set his feet quickly in order to use the shotgun formation effectively.

Chapter 6

Hitting the Ground Running

. . . .

In This Chapter

▶ Looking at the roles of the fullback and running back

▶ Understanding why all sizes and shapes can excel at the running game

▶ Getting acquainted with the running game's nuances

▶ Taking a look at three running back–focused offensive formations

▶ Reviewing basic running plays

. . . .

Running back may be the most physically demanding position in football. A great running back, whose productivity dictates his team's success, is asked to take a tremendous beating on a weekly basis. Every game he faces 11 angry men who have a license to physically punish him. Rarely does one defensive player bring down a great running back. He gets hit from every angle — high and low. Often, one player grabs hold of the running back while a number of defenders take clean shots at him.

One of the toughest football players I played with was running back Marcus Allen. Despite the continual beating he took, Allen would pick himself off the ground and, without showing any emotion, walk back to the huddle and prepare for the next play. I don't know how many times I saw Marcus look like he'd just gotten his head taken off and then come right back for more on the very next play. He was especially determined at the goal line, scoring a then-NFL-record 123 rushing touchdowns even though everyone in the stadium knew he would be running with the ball.

This chapter goes into detail about what makes a great running back — or a good one, for that matter. Obviously, a running back needs to be able to do more than just run with the football. A running back must also know his assignments, know the opposing defenses, and be aware of all the players on the field. So, in this chapter, I explain the many different running plays and the varied styles and types of people who fit the mold of a running back.

An Overview of the Ground Game

In football, the *ground game* refers to running the football (as opposed to passing it). Running the ball is the basic premise of football, and it's the easiest way to move the ball. A team runs three times and gains 10 yards, and that's good enough for a first down and another set of four downs. What could be easier? In youth football, every team runs. After all, what 11-year-old can pass like former Miami Dolphins quarterback Dan Marino? Plus, learning the fundamentals of running the ball is much easier than learning how to run pass routes.

Most championship football teams are excellent at running the football. The Denver Broncos won the Super Bowl in 1998 because they had a better running game than the Green Bay Packers. The Broncos could run, and the Packers couldn't stop them and their talented running back, Terrell Davis. In fact, Denver's offensive line was really fired up for that game — they wanted to block and open holes — because they felt that the Packers, the media, and some NFL insiders weren't giving them enough respect.

The New York Giants won their second Super Bowl after the 1990 season, beating a superior Buffalo Bills team, because they could run the ball and keep the clock moving. They also kept the ball away from Buffalo's high-powered offense. This ploy is called *ball control,* which is a common football term. Running the ball is the best way to maintain possession and keep the clock moving when a team is ahead because the clock doesn't stop if a player is tackled in bounds. However, if the quarterback throws an incompletion, the clock stops. Stopping the clock is advantageous to the defense; it gives them a breather and the hope that they may get the ball back. So when a team is running the football successfully, usually it's physically whipping the other team. And that's the object of the game!

The NFL has become somewhat of a pass-happy league, but the running game is still vitally important. In 2013, 13 running backs rushed for more than 1,000 yards, with LeSean McCoy of the Philadelphia Eagles leading the way with 1,607 yards. He averaged 5.1 yards per carry.

Football's predecessor: Rugby

Men have been running with a ball for almost two centuries. Before football, people were fascinated by a sport called *rugby,* which was developed by an Englishman in 1823. Players in this sport are tackled by more than one opponent, and the runner isn't protected by a helmet or shoulder pads. Football is based on rugby — but the men who designed football were smart enough to add protective gear to the mix.

Meeting the Men Who Play the Ground Game

Understanding what's going on during running plays is much easier when you know who's responsible for the running game. The next time you see an offense set up, look for the two players who line up in the *offensive backfield* (the area of the field behind the quarterback and the line of scrimmage). These players are the *running backs.* The smaller one is the main ball carrier, and the larger one is the guy charged with protecting the ball carrier. Read on to find out what each type of running back does, who tends to play in these positions, and how each player lines up behind the quarterback.

The halfback, a team's principal ball carrier

On most teams, the principal ball carrier is called the *halfback* (also called the *tailback* or the *running back*). When teams — be they high school, college, or NFL teams — find a good running back, they give him the ball. And they give it to him as often as he's willing and able to carry it. (Check out Figure 6-1 to see former Alabama tailback Mark Ingram in action.)

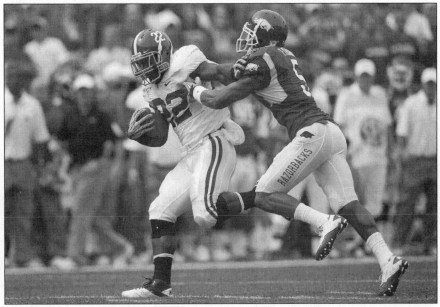

Figure 6-1: Tailback Mark Ingram (22) of the Alabama Crimson Tide fights off an Arkansas Razorbacks' tackler in 2010.

Photo credit: © Joe Robbins/Getty Images

Most runners would probably tell you that they wouldn't mind carrying the ball even more often than they actually do. Toting the football is a status symbol, after all. The NFL record for rushing attempts in a single season belongs to Larry Johnson, then of the Kansas City Chiefs, who carried the ball 416 times in the 2006 season. That's an astonishing 26 carries per game!

The fullback, protector of the halfback

When a team employs two running backs in the offensive backfield, the bigger of the two is usually called the *fullback*. He's there to block and clear the way for the *halfback,* who's the main ball carrier. You may think that the fullback's job is a thankless one, but most fullbacks get a lot of satisfaction from making a great block (generally on a linebacker) and winning the physical battle against players who tend to be bigger than they are.

In the old days, some of the best runners were fullbacks. Marion Motley of the 1949 Cleveland Browns weighed almost 240 pounds and carried defenders down the field. Cookie Gilchrist was a 252-pound fullback with the Buffalo Bills in the mid-1960s; he was one devastating blocker and could run, too. So could 237-pound Larry Csonka, a former Miami Dolphin, who, along with 230-pound John Riggins of the Washington Redskins, was the dominant fullback of the 1970s.

It's interesting to note that because of the way offenses have evolved, especially in college football, the traditional fullback position appears to be going the way of the dinosaur. Some NFL teams have no true fullback on their roster. The spread offense, with its emphasis on passing, doesn't require a fullback. Big, strong, fast players who in previous years might have played fullback are now playing on the other side of the ball, in the linebacker position.

Recognizing that Running Backs Come in All Sizes and Shapes

You may hear football coaches say that a particular player is the prototype performer at a particular position, but no such prototype exists at running back. Running backs come in all sizes and shapes. Little guys like former Detroit Lion Barry Sanders, former Chicago Bear Walter Payton, and former Buffalo Bill Thurman Thomas, who were quick and slippery players, excelled at the highest level. Big brutes like Jim Brown of the Cleveland Browns, Earl Campbell of the Houston Oilers (now the Tennessee Titans), John Riggins of the Washington Redskins, and Jim Taylor of the Green Bay Packers also had successful NFL careers.

Running back Emmitt Smith, who scored a then-record 25 touchdowns in 1995 and who holds the NFL record for yards gained, was an example of the tough, physical inside runner who weighed only 210 pounds. Pittsburgh Steelers tailback Jerome "The Bus" Bettis was 40 pounds heavier than Smith, but I still considered him a halfback rather than a fullback because he was the main runner on his team. And I can't forget former Dallas Cowboy Tony Dorsett, the great Marcus Allen, and former San Francisco 49ers Roger Craig and Tom Rathman — all good backs, but never listed as little guys *or* big brutes.

Next, let me clear up the myth that you have to be extremely fast to be an excellent running back. Marcus Allen had only average speed; in fact, some scouts thought he was too slow. But in his outstanding career, he scored 145 touchdowns and gained 12,243 yards rushing. Allen was elected to the Football Hall of Fame on his first try in 2003. He was football's finest *north/south runner* — which means he didn't mess around dancing "east" or "west" behind the line of scrimmage. When trapped by defensive players, the quickest and best way to gain yards is to go straight ahead; that's the primary trait of a north/south runner.

Little guys slip by opponents in the open field. They're difficult to grab hold of and tackle — it's almost like their shoulder pads are covered with butter. Barry Sanders fell into that group. So did Dorsett and Lionel "Little Train" James, who played for San Diego in the 1980s. On the other hand, big brutes like Jim Brown simply run over everyone. Brown never concerned himself with making tacklers miss him. At some point, every coach looks for a big back who can run over everyone in his way.

Regardless of their size or skill level, the common denominator among all these men is that they were physically tough, determined, and talented football players. Any type of runner can be a good running back, as long as he's playing in the right system and gets help from his teammates.

Exploring Running Back Fundamentals

Running backs need more skills than players at other positions. That's because on any given play, a running back may run the ball, catch a pass, or block an opposing player. Occasionally running backs are even called upon to throw a pass or kick the ball. To help you appreciate what running backs do, the sections that follow look at what goes into playing this very important position.

The basic skills

On most football teams, the running back is the best athlete on the team. The demands on him, both physical and mental, are great. Every running back must be able to do the following well:

✔ **Line up in the right stance:** The most common stance for a running back is the *two-point stance.* A tailback in the I formation (I tell you all about this in the later "Lining Up: The Formations" section) often uses the two-point stance with his hands on his thighs, his feet shoulder width apart, and his weight on the balls of his feet. His head is up, his legs are slightly bent at the knees, and his feet are parallel to one another, with his toes pointed toward the line of scrimmage. (For more information on running back stances, see the later "The stances" section.)

✔ **Receive a handoff:** A runner must receive the football from the quarterback without fumbling. To do this properly, his arms must form a pocket outside his stomach. If the back is right-handed, he bends his left arm at the elbow in a 90-degree angle, keeps his forearm parallel to the ground, and turns up the palm of his left hand. His right arm is up to receive the ball so that when the quarterback places the ball in his stomach area, his right forearm and hand close around it. Figure 6-2 shows how a running back takes a handoff and holds the ball while running. After he has possession of the ball, the back grips the ball at the tip and tucks the other end into his elbow with one side of the ball resting against his body (so his arm is in somewhat of a V-shape).

Figure 6-2:
One of a running back's main concerns is protecting the ball by receiving the quarterback's handoff properly.

✔ **Run at top speed:** Ideally, a running back is running at near top speed when he grabs a handoff. His head is upright and his shoulders are square to the line of scrimmage. He's also leaning forward slightly to keep his body low, and his legs are driving forward. When making cuts, the back plants and accelerates off the foot that's opposite of the direction he's running (for example, if he wants to go left, he plants on his right foot). When running behind a blocker, he's behind the blocker's outside hip. When the block is made, the back cuts quickly behind the blocker's inside hip when turning upfield. For *cut-back running,* the back fakes a step away from the defender (trying not to shift too much weight) and then turns quickly to the inside of the defender (of course, the defender must move for the cut-back to be successful).

✔ **See the field:** When you watch video highlights of a great running back like Barry Sanders of the Detroit Lions, you'd swear he had eyes in the back of his head. How else can you explain his cuts and moves and his escapes from defensive trouble? Like a basketball guard running a fast break, a back needs to have peripheral vision. He needs to be able to see what's coming at him from the corners of the field. Backs with exceptional speed (4.4 seconds in the 40-yard dash) can gain many more yards by seeing where the defensive pursuit is coming from and running away from it. However, backs without great speed can be successful by sensing danger while trying to maintain a straight line to the end zone (these backs are called *north/south runners*). But backs with great speed can outrun many defenders by heading to the corner of the end zone if a defender is 10 yards away to their left or right.

✔ **Block for another back:** A team's principal running back is rarely a good blocker. The best blockers among the backs are the fullbacks, who are asked to block players 30 to 100 pounds heavier than they are. A running back needs to stay low and explode into the defender's upper body while using his hands (in closed fists) and forearms to make contact. A lot of backs try to block a linebacker or defensive back low (at his legs), but this technique is rarely successful. Many defensive players are capable of jumping up and then shoving the back down to the ground as they move past him. Coaches want their backs to get a piece of the defender and knock him off his line to the quarterback or ball carrier.

The job description

A running back has a responsibility, or assignment, on every play. I think running backs have the toughest job on the football field because they have to not only know every play like a quarterback but also make physical contact on virtually every down.

No matter how fast an athlete is, how big a brute he is, or how slippery or quick he is, he won't be able to play as a running back if he doesn't have a brain and can't think on his feet. I think the main reason many outstanding college runners never make it in professional football is that the pro game simply overloads their brains.

Here's a rundown of a running back's job description:

- ✔ **He's an every-minute player.** While he's on the field, he never has a minute to let up, and he never has a chance to take a play off. He can't afford to line up and merely go through the motions. When he doesn't have the ball, he must follow through with his fakes and pretend that he has the ball.

- ✔ **On every play, he must know what down it is and how many yards the team needs for a first down.** He must know when to lower his shoulder and go for a first down and when to keep a drive alive by making a move and gaining a little extra yardage, helping his team move into scoring range.

- ✔ **He must know the time on the clock in order to know when to go out of bounds and when to turn upfield and gain extra yardage.** Stopping the clock is critical when a team is behind in the score.

- ✔ **He must know the defense's various alignments and then adjust his thinking to those alignments on pass plays and running plays.** On a pass play, he must know the protection scheme because he may be asked to throw a block to give the quarterback time to pass.

- ✔ **He must know every play and all its variations.** For example, on one running play, he may have to block a linebacker. But on the same play called against a different defensive front, he may be asked to block a defensive end.

  On running plays, a running back must know the opposition's defensive schemes so he can predict which defender will be the first guy coming to make the tackle. Although this information may not be important to the runner carrying the ball, it's valuable for the other back who's asked to block on the play.

- ✔ **He must know every pass route called because he may be the first receiving option on a play.** He must know the defense's coverage in order to adjust his route accordingly. For example, if the linebacker goes out, he may have to go in, and vice versa. He must know how deep he has to get on every pass route so that he's timed up with the quarterback's drop. Because the quarterback may throw the ball before the runner turns to catch the ball, he must run the exact distance; if he doesn't, the timing of the play will be messed up.

- ✔ **He must know every hole number in the playbook.** A typical NFL playbook may contain between 50 and 100 running plays. The *holes* (the spaces opened up by blockers), which are numbered, are the only things that tell the running back where he's supposed to run with the ball. The play will either specify the hole number or be designed for a specific hole.

College running backs versus pro running backs

In college, coaches give a great high school running back a scholarship, and they have him for four years. Now, it doesn't look good for your program if you beg a player to come to your school and then end up cutting him or taking away his scholarship because he doesn't live up to your expectations. This is what I mean when I say that he's yours for four years.

The difference for pro running backs is that the NFL is a big business. Running backs can be signed to big contracts, but teams can always cut them and lose nothing but a few days or weeks of coaching time and a few dollars. Today, such dismissals are viewed simply as bad money deals or bad investments. Therefore, when a head coach finds a runner who can run for more than 1,000 yards a season, score whenever he needs to, and carry the team when the quarterback is having an off day, he knows he has a winner.

The stances

A running back can use two stances: One is the *up stance,* in which he has his hands resting on his thighs, a few inches above his knees, as shown in Figure 6-3. This stance is also called the *two-point stance.* The second is the *down stance,* in which he puts his right hand on the ground like a lineman, as shown in Figure 6-4. It's also called the *three-point stance* because one hand and both feet are on the ground.

Figure 6-3: A running back's up stance (or two-point stance).

Figure 6-4:
A running
back's down
stance (or
three-point
stance).

Runners can use the two-point stance when they're in the *split-back forma-tion,* with one back aligned to the left of the quarterback and one to the right. However, most coaches prefer their runners to use the three-point stance in this alignment because they believe it provides the runner with a faster start than the two-point stance — much like a sprinter bursting from his blocks. Some runners remain in the two-point stance in split backs, which can tip off the defense that they're going to pass-protect for the quarterback or run out for a pass. The running backs can then resort to a three-point stance with the intention of confusing the defense.

In the *I formation,* so named because the center, quarterback, fullback, and halfback line up behind one another to form a letter *I,* the deep back is always in a two-point stance. The fullback in the I formation is in front of the tailback. He can be in either a two-point or a three-point stance because he's blocking on 95 percent of the plays. The two-point stance is better on passing downs because it enables the running back to see the defensive alignment better — meaning he can see whether a linebacker may be blitzing, especially if he must block this defender. The three-point stance is better for blocking because the running back can exert his force upward and into the defender's chest and upper body.

The number one priority

The most important aspect of a running back's game is protecting the football. On the first day of practice, the first thing the coach tells his running backs is this: If you don't protect the football, you won't play. By *protecting the football,* I mean not fumbling the ball and leaving it on the ground where the opposition can recover it and gain possession. How well you protect the football is more a matter of how well you concentrate, not how big you are.

To help them protect the ball (and themselves), running backs have to know *pursuit* and *angles*. I'm talking football language here, not physics. What I mean is that the runner must understand where the defensive players are coming from (the pursuit) and from what direction (the angle) they plan on tackling him. If a runner understands these basic principles, he can figure out the direction the defensive players are coming from and prepare for contact and protecting the football.

Before contact, the running back braces the ball against his body while protecting the outside of the ball with his hand and forearm. Some backs prepare for the collision by wrapping their other arm around the football as well. Also, the back dips his shoulders and head and rolls his shoulders inward away from where he expects the first contact to come from. When facing smaller defenders, the running back may use a *stiff arm* (extending his free hand) to jostle the defender in his face mask or shoulder area. A back uses a stiff arm to push a tackler away from him or to reduce the tackler's ability to go after his legs.

HALL OF FAME

Dorsett goes the distance

A player can return a kick, punt, or interception for 100 yards or more to score a touchdown, but the longest possible run is 99 yards. Former Dallas Cowboys running back Tony Dorsett, a Heisman Trophy award winner from the University of Pittsburgh, covered exactly that distance in 1983.

The amazing part about the play is that Ron Springs, the Cowboys' other running back, was supposed to get the ball; the play was designed for him. But Springs misunderstood quarterback Danny White's call and left the huddle, returning to the sidelines. With Springs gone, Dallas had only ten players on the field. And because quarterbacks don't do much blocking, only 8 Cowboys were available to block 11 Minnesota Vikings (I say only 8 because one of the remaining 9 was Dorsett, who was carrying the ball).

Dallas, coached by the highly specialized and inventive Tom Landry, always did a lot of substituting. But White didn't know that Springs had left the huddle. As White turned away from the line of scrimmage, looking for Springs, he instead came face to face with Dorsett. White did what any panicked quarterback would do: He handed the ball to Dorsett. But the play didn't end up being a flop. Dorsett faked left, stopped, and then headed around the right end. He broke through the first line of defenders and was off to the races.

Dorsett's run still stands as the longest run from the line of scrimmage in NFL history. It may be equaled someday, but it will never be surpassed.

Lining Up: The Formations

An offensive *formation* is how the offense aligns all 11 of its players prior to using a particular play. A team can run or pass out of many formations, but for this chapter, I selected three backfield formations that focus specifically on running backs. One is the *pro-set,* which is also known as the *split-back* or *split T formation.* Another is the *I formation* — where both runners are aligned together behind one another and behind the quarterback and center. The third formation is the I formation's hybrid, the *offset I formation.* Most teams give these offset formations names like Jack, Queen, Far, Near, and so on.

Here's a breakdown of what the three formations look like:

✔ **Split-back formation:** In the split-back formation, the runners are aligned behind the two guards about 5 yards behind the line of scrimmage, as shown in Figure 6-5. Teams use this formation because it's difficult for the defense to gauge whether the offense is running or passing. With split backs, the backfield is balanced and not aligned toward one side or the other, making it more difficult for the defense to anticipate what the play will be. This formation may be a better passing formation because the backs can swing out of the backfield to either side as receivers.

Figure 6-5: In the split-back formation, the two RBs line up behind the two guards.

✔ **I formation:** In the I formation, the tailback (TB) — the runner who will carry the ball — can place himself as deep as 7 yards from the line of scrimmage, as shown in Figure 6-6. By stepping this far back, the runner believes he'll be in full stride when he nears the line of scrimmage. Consequently, the I formation is ideally suited to a team with a great running back. Also, the depth allows him to have complete vision of his blockers and the defensive players' first reaction to the run. This formation is called the I because the quarterback (QB), fullback (FB), and tailback form an *I,* with the fullback between the quarterback and tailback.

Figure 6-6:
In the I
formation,
the TB lines
up 7 yards
behind
the line of
scrimmage
with a FB in
front of him.

✔ **Offset I formation:** In the offset I formation, the running back (RB) remains deep, 5 to 7 yards from the quarterback. When the running back is this deep, the majority of the time the team plans to run the ball. The fullback (FB), or blocking back, can be as close as 3 yards to the line of scrimmage, as shown in Figure 6-7. The other back wants to be close to his target: the defender he must block. A good fullback needs only 2 yards before making blocking contact. Also, he's deep enough in case the play requires him to go in motion to either side and swing to the outside for a possible reception. The fullback can be set to the strong side or the weak side of the formation.

Figure 6-7:
The FB is
set to the
strong side
in this ver-
sion of the
offset I for-
mation; the
RB remains
deep.

Single wing

The *single wing* was an offensive formation that was popular in the early years of the NFL. Pop Warner developed the formation around 1908. It used four players in the backfield: the quarterback, tailback, wingback, and fullback. In the single wing, the tailback, not the quarterback, was the primary passer and runner. The quarterback was a blocking back like today's fullback.

In this formation, the quarterback was positioned close to the line of scrimmage and in a gap (the spacing) between two offensive linemen. The wingback was aligned behind and outside the strong-side end. The fullback was a few steps from the tailback and also aligned to the strong side. Back then, the offensive line generally was unbalanced — two linemen were to one side of the center and four were to the other side. The strong side was the side where the four offensive linemen were lined up. The ball was snapped to the tailback, not the quarterback, who was about 4 yards behind the center.

Most of the time, offenses ran the ball from the single wing; it was a power football formation. However, with the tailback doing a lot of spinning and faking, the single wing added deception. The tailback often would lateral the ball to another back. Teams would run reverses, counters, and trap plays from the formation while also passing the ball.

Walking through the Basic Running Plays

If you're watching closely, you may notice your local high school football team using some of the same running plays that the NFL pros do. That's because the following basic running plays are used in all levels of football:

- ✔ **Blast or dive:** Every team has the blast or dive run in its playbook; it's the simplest of carries. Usually led by a blocking fullback, the running back takes a quick handoff from the quarterback and hits a hole between an offensive guard and a tackle. On some teams, this run ends up between a guard and the center. The offense calls this run when it needs a yard or two for a first down. The runner lowers his head and hopes to *move the pile* (or push through defenders) before the middle linebacker tackles him.

- ✔ **Counter:** This play is an intentional misdirection run on the part of the offense. The quarterback fakes a lateral toss to one back who's heading right, running parallel to the line of scrimmage. He's the decoy. The quarterback then turns and hands off to the remaining runner in the backfield, generally a fullback, who runs toward the middle of the line, hoping to find an opening between either guard and the center.

✔ **Draw:** This is a disguised run, which means it initially looks like a pass play. The offensive linemen draw back like they're going to pass-protect for the quarterback (QB). The quarterback then drops back and, instead of setting up to pass, he turns and hands the ball to the runner, as shown in Figure 6-8. After the running back (RB) receives the ball, he wants to reach his maximum speed quickly to take advantage of the anticipated huge holes at the line of scrimmage. The goal of every draw play is to get the defensive linemen charging at the quarterback, only to be pushed aside by the offensive linemen at the last second. To fool the defense with this run, a team must have an above average passing game.

Figure 6-8:
How the RB moves in the draw play.

✔ **Off-tackle:** The off-tackle is the oldest run around — it's a byproduct of the old single wing offense from more than 100 years ago (see the nearby "Single wing" sidebar for more information on this offense). It's a strong-side run, meaning the halfback (HB) heads toward the end of the line where the tight end, the extra blocker, lines up. The runner wants to take advantage of the hole supplied by the tackle, tight end, and his running mate, the fullback (FB). He can take the ball either around the tight end, as shown in Figure 6-9, or outside the tackle. He hopes that the fullback will block the outside linebacker.

Figure 6-9:
The FB clears a path for the HB in the off-tackle run.

✔ **Pitch:** This run is usually from a two-back formation. The quarterback (QB) takes the snap and fakes a handoff to the first back (HB), who's heading directly toward the line of scrimmage; he then tosses (or pitches) the ball laterally to the other runner (FB), who has begun to move to the outside, as shown in Figure 6-10. The runner can either take the pitch outside or cut back toward the inside. Pitch plays can be designed to go in either direction.

Figure 6-10: Faking a handoff to the HB and tossing the ball to the FB in the pitch run.

✔ **Reverse:** For this play, the halfback (HB) receives the handoff from the quarterback (QB) and then runs laterally behind the line of scrimmage. (The play can be designed for the back to run in either direction.) The ball carrier meets up with a wide receiver (WR) or flanker running toward him and then hands the ball to that receiver or flanker, as shown in Figure 6-11. The offensive line blocks as if the ball were intended for the halfback so that the defensive players follow him. After the receiver is in motion and has the ball, he runs in the opposite direction, or against the flow of his own blockers. This play really works if the receiver is a fast and tricky runner. It helps if the interior defensive players and linebacker fall for the halfback's initial fake. Also, the weak-side defender, the last line of defense, must leave his position and chase the halfback. Otherwise, this weak-side defender is in perfect position to tackle the receiver.

Figure 6-11: For a reverse, the QB hands off to the HB, who then hands the ball to the WR.

✔ **Slant:** This run is exactly like it sounds. Instead of running straight toward the line of scrimmage, the runner (HB) slants his angle outside after he receives the ball, as shown in Figure 6-12. A slant is used to take advantage of defenses that over pursue, allowing offensive linemen to be more effective by pushing the defenders to one side.

Figure 6-12:
The HB runs to his right after aligning on the left side in a slant play.

✔ **Sweep:** This run is pretty common in every team's playbook. As shown in Figure 6-13, it begins with two or more offensive linemen (which in the figure are labeled as LG and RG) *pulling,* or leaving their stances and running toward the outside of the line of scrimmage. The ball carrier (HB) takes a handoff from the quarterback (QB) and runs parallel to the line of scrimmage, waiting for his blockers to lead the way around the end. The run is designed to attack the defensive end, outside linebacker, and cornerback on a specific side. Most right-handed teams (that is, teams that have a right-handed quarterback) run the sweep toward the left defensive end. The sweep can begin with the other back faking receipt of a handoff and running in the opposite direction of where the sweep run is headed. Many teams simply have the other back, a fullback (FB), help lead the blocking for the ball carrier.

Figure 6-13:
The sweep calls for the HB to follow the two pulling guards and FB around to the weak side.

✔ **Stretch:** The stretch play, or outside zone run, has become more popular in recent years. The quarterback (QB) takes the snap from under center and sprints into the backfield to meet the ball carrier (HB) as he runs toward the edge of the formation, outside the tight end. As shown in Figure 6-14, the strong side guard and tackle pull to lead the runner as the tight end blocks down to seal off any defenders coming from the inside.

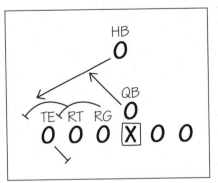

Figure 6-14: The stretch play allows the running back to quickly reach the edge of the formation.

✔ **Trap:** Teams don't use this run very often because it requires quick and agile offensive linemen, and most teams use big blockers these days. As shown in Figure 6-15, the trap is a sucker run that, like the draw, is intended to take advantage of the defensive players' willingness to attack the offense. The trap works well against an aggressive defensive line and linebackers. On the trap, a guard (LG in the figure) vacates his normal area, allowing the defensive player to cross the line of scrimmage and have a clear lane into the backfield. The guard from the opposite side then moves across the line and blocks the defender. This action by the guard is called *pulling*, hence the term *pulling guard*. The trap play has to be well-timed, and after the ball carrier receives the ball, he must quickly dart through the hole behind the trap block.

Figure 6-15: As the FB takes a handoff for the trap play, the LG pulls to his right.

✔ **Veer:** College teams run this play more often than pro teams do because it generally requires a quarterback who's quick-footed and an excellent ball-handler — in other words, a quarterback who can run if he has to. As shown in Figure 6-16, the veer is a quick-hitting run in which the ball can be handed to either running back, whose routes are determined by the slant or charge of the defensive linemen. The term *veer* comes from the back veering away from the defense. In Figure 6-16, the quarterback (QB) hands off to the halfback (HB), who veers to the right behind his blockers.

Figure 6-16:
In the veer run, the QB hands off to the HB, who veers to the hole on the right.

Chapter 7

The Offensive Line at Work in the Trenches

. . . .

In This Chapter

▶ Surveying the center's (and everyone else's) duties

▶ Examining lineman body types

▶ Getting to know the keys to good line play

▶ Understanding blocking, holding, and other things that linemen do

. . . .

*F*ootball isn't a relationship-driven business. If any positions could be used to illustrate that point, they would be the offensive and defensive line. The offensive and defensive lines are the sharks and the dolphins, the mongooses and the cobras, of football. In other words, they're natural enemies. Being a defensive lineman, I never encouraged friendships with offensive linemen, but I always respected them. My job was to beat and overpower them in order to help my team win.

When I was with the Raiders in the 1980s, two opposing offensive linemen stuck out: Anthony Muñoz, a tackle with the Cincinnati Bengals, and Dwight Stephenson, the Miami Dolphins' center. Unlike many offensive linemen, both of these men were very athletic in addition to being rugged and physical. That's the ideal combination for this position. I've seen Muñoz play basketball, and for a 280-pounder, he moved as if he were 100 pounds lighter. Great feet. When the ball was snapped, I wanted to be quicker than the man blocking me. My plan was to beat him off the ball and get by him before he could react.

The job of offensive linemen? To protect the most hunted commodity in the game — the quarterback — and to block for the ball carrier. The line also opens up *holes* in the defense for the running backs (by *blocking,* or impeding the movement of, defenders). Ball carriers try to go through these holes, which are also called *running lanes.* The ability to run effectively in a football game is the end result of the offensive line winning the war at the line of scrimmage. It's man against man, and whoever wants it more usually wins.

The offensive line is also essential to the passing game. Its job is to shield the quarterback, allowing him two or three seconds of freedom in which to throw the ball. The more time the line gives the quarterback to scan the field and find an open receiver, the better chance the quarterback has of a completion or a touchdown pass. Without the offensive line (or *O line*), the offense would never get anywhere.

This group, more than any other, needs to work together like the fingers on a hand. The linemen want their offensive teammates to gain yards — the more the merrier. You'll notice that when a team has a great running back who's gaining a lot of yards, the offensive line is usually mentioned as doing its job.

In this chapter, I explain the positions that make up the offensive line, give some insight into the personalities of offensive linemen, and cover some of the techniques that offensive linemen use to block for the quarterback and running backs.

Looking Down the Line

The offensive line is made up of five players, with the man in the middle called the *center.* Every offensive line position is based on the center. To the right of him is the *right guard,* and outside the right guard is the *right tackle.* To the left of the center is the *left guard,* and outside the left guard is the *left tackle.* Figure 7-1 helps you see the positioning of the offensive line's personnel.

If the quarterback is right-handed, the left tackle is also referred to as the *blind-side tackle.* Why? Well, a right-handed quarterback generally drops back to pass and turns his head to the right while doing so. He can't see behind him, so his left side is his blind side.

Figure 7-1:
The personnel on the offensive line.

Line of scrimmage

O O X O O

Left tackle · Left guard · Center · Right guard · Right tackle

© John Wiley and Sons, Inc.

The following sections give some generalities about the players at the three main offensive line positions — center, guard, and tackle.

Centers

Like a center in basketball, a football center is in the middle of the action. He's the player who *snaps* (or delivers) the ball to the quarterback. As the snapper, he must know the *signal count* — when the quarterback wants the ball to be snapped, indicated by a series of commands, such as "Down. Set. Hut hut hut!"

This center-quarterback exchange initiates every offensive play. Before the play begins, the center stands over the ball and then bends down, usually placing both hands around the front tip of the football. He snaps (or *hikes*) the ball between his legs to the quarterback. (Refer to Chapter 4 for an illustration of the snap.)

The most special offensive lineman: The blind-side tackle

Most coaches put their best athlete at left tackle if their quarterback is right-handed (and more than 90 percent are). Ideally this player has quick feet and a good sense of balance.

The blind-side tackle doesn't have to be the biggest, baddest player on the team; he can weigh 300 pounds and be quite adequate. But *reach* (arm length) is important, and knowing how to use your arms and hands to block or *jam* (place your hands on the top of your opponent's jersey number) is critical. Getting his hands on the defensive player's numbers, so to speak, guarantees that the lineman is keeping a distance between himself and the defensive player. Gaining this advantage is imperative.

By maintaining proper distance, the offensive lineman isn't as susceptible to the defensive lineman's techniques and moves. If he keeps that distance, he has more time to get his feet into position to block the defender on each move. Also, distance gives the lineman time to adjust laterally and get in front of his man. If the defender is body to body or hip to hip with the offensive lineman, the lineman is beaten because the defensive player can grab him. The closer the defensive player gets to you, the harder it is to recover and get the correct positional leverage on him.

In his 2006 book *The Blind Side: Evolution of a Game* (W.W. Norton & Company), author Michael Lewis described why the blind-side tackle became such an important position and how blind-side tackle Michael Oher rose from poverty with the help of friends and family to become a promising football player. *The Blind Side* was made into a movie in 2009 starring Sandra Bullock as the wealthy society lady who adopted Oher. I highly recommend the book and the movie, and not just to football fans. Oher's story is heartwarming and gives a good glimpse into the inner workings of football.

The exchange of the football is supposed to be a simple action, but occasionally it gets bungled, resulting in a *fumble*. A fumble can be caused by the center not snapping the ball directly into the quarterback's hands (perhaps because he's worried about being hit) or by the quarterback withdrawing his hands before the ball arrives. Because hands are essential to good blocking, centers sometimes worry more about getting their hands into position to block than cleanly snapping the ball to the quarterback. Coaches refer to those poor snaps as *short-arming the ball*. In other words, the center doesn't bring the ball all the way back to the quarterback's hands.

In addition to delivering the ball cleanly to the quarterback, a center must know the blocking responsibilities of every other offensive lineman. The offense never knows beforehand how the defense will set up. And unlike the offense, the defense may move before the ball is snapped, which allows a defense to set up in a vast array of formations. The center is essentially a coach on the field, redirecting his offensive line teammates as necessary based on how the defense aligns itself. On nearly every play, the center points to the defenders and, using terminology that the defense can't decipher, gives his fellow linemen their blocking assignments.

Centers tend to be quick, smart, and even-keeled. The other linemen look to the center for leadership and stability. In addition to being mentally tough, a center needs to be physically tough so he can absorb hits from defensive players while he's concentrating on cleanly delivering the football to the quarterback.

Guards

Guards, who line up on either side of the center, should be some of the best blockers. In a *block,* an offensive lineman makes contact with a defensive player and uses his hands, arms, and shoulders to move him out of the way. A guard is doing his job if he clears the way, creating a hole for a running back to run through. A guard also must be able to fight off his man — stopping the defender's forward momentum — and prevent him from rushing the quarterback on a pass play.

The neutral zone

The *neutral zone* is the area between the offensive and defensive lines. It's the length of the ball in width. Only the center is allowed in the neutral zone until he snaps the ball. If a lineman from either team lines up in this zone prior to the snap of the ball, his team incurs a 5-yard penalty.

Tackles

Tackles tend to be the biggest linemen, and in the NFL they're generally the most athletic. (Figure 7-2 shows one of the NFL's best tackles, Ryan Clady of the Denver Broncos.) Tackles should be the stars of the offensive line because their job on the ends of the line is to repel some of the game's best defensive linemen and pass-rushers. They need to have great agility and the strength necessary to seal off the outside when a running play occurs. (*Sealing off the outside* means preventing the defensive players from reaching the corner of the line and tackling the ball carrier.)

Sometimes a tackle must shove a defensive player outside when the play is designed to go toward the middle of the field. He has a lot of responsibility on the *edge* (the outside shoulder of the defensive end or linebacker aligned over him) because, if the tackle succeeds in containing the defensive players, the ball carrier has an open field in which to run. Sometimes the tackle must block his man toward the inside, thus allowing the ball carrier to run wide and outside the edge. In some plays, a tackle blocks down on the defensive tackle while the guard pulls to block the defender aligned over the tackle, moving that defender away from the running lane.

Figure 7-2: Ryan Clady of the Denver Broncos is one of the premier offensive tackles in the NFL.

Photo credit: © Paul Jasienski/Getty Images

Not all running plays are designed to go inside the tackles. *Off-tackle* runs are usually run to the strong side of the formation, where the tight end, who serves as another blocker, lines up. On off-tackle runs, the tackle must contain his man and push him inside toward the center of the line as the ball carrier runs wide, or outside the tackle. If the tackle can't move his man, he must prevent this defensive end or linebacker from reaching the edge of the line of scrimmage, shielding the ball carrier from the defensive pursuit.

The Lineman Physique: Fat Guys Doing the Job

Fans often look at offensive linemen and say that they're out of shape because they have big, round bodies. But that's the kind of physique most offensive line coaches look for. They don't want sculpted bodies; they want bulky players like Bill Bain, who played for the Los Angeles Rams in the 1980s, and Cleveland Browns tackle Joe Thomas. These players have great body mass and great natural strength. If you've been carrying 300+ pounds around most of your life, you tend to develop good leg strength and a powerful torso. If you're a big man, though, you must have quick feet and good athletic ability to play on the offensive line — that way you can move the weight and move people out of the way. That's what Thomas has.

The perception used to be that you should stick the biggest, least athletic men on the offensive line, but today's offensive linemen have gone a long way toward shattering that notion. Players like Joe Thomas, Joe Staley, and Ryan Clady range in size from 310 to 325 pounds, and they're fast, agile, and mean.

Today, offensive linemen fall in two categories:

✔ **The big, burly (heavyset) lineman:** During the Cowboys' Super Bowl run from 1992 to 1995, when Emmitt Smith was the best runner in pro football, the Dallas line consisted of this type of lineman. These players imposed their will on their opponents and pounded them repeatedly — considered a *power offense*. Their style was to beat their opponents into submission. They limited their running plays to maybe five or six; they had those plays and stuck with them.

The power offense is common when a coach believes that his offensive line is bigger and stronger than the opposition's defensive line. The Cleveland Browns had such an offensive line for Jim Brown. The problem defensive players face against such a powerfully built line isn't the first running play, or the second running play, but the ninth play and beyond. As a defensive player, you get tired of 300-pound guys hammering at your head.

✔ **The smaller, quicker lineman:** This type of lineman is light and agile, with the ability to run and block on every play (they call that *pulling*). This lineman takes more of a surgical approach, slicing and picking the defense apart. The best example of this type of line play is the classic *West Coast offense.* This scheme involves a lot of *angle blocking,* which means an offensive lineman rarely blocks the defensive player directly in front of him; he does everything in angles.

The San Francisco 49ers used this finesse offense exclusively while winning four championships in the 1980s. The Denver Broncos won Super Bowl XXXII and XXXIII in 1998 and 1999 with what's considered by today's standards to be a small offensive line, with an average size of 290 pounds. The Broncos used a variation of the West Coast offense, which their head coach, Mike Shanahan, incorporated into his offense after serving as the 49ers' offensive coordinator for three seasons.

I see the difference between these two offensive line styles as the difference between heavyweight boxers George Foreman and Muhammad Ali, with the West Coast style being Ali and the power offense style being Foreman. Every one of Foreman's body punches is magnified by ten — all brute force — whereas Ali works you over like a surgeon, slicing and picking you apart.

What style a team chooses often depends on its quarterback, the size and ability of its offensive linemen, and the coach's offensive preference. If your quarterback has the ability to escape the rush, the West Coast finesse works fine. If you have an immobile quarterback, you may want Foreman-like blockers who are difficult to get past.

Understanding the Keys to Successful Offensive Line Play

Because the offensive line's job is so important, linemen need to develop certain characteristics, both individually and as a unit. The sections that follow outline some of those critical traits.

The proper stance

Offensive linemen often use a *two-point,* or *up, stance,* especially if the team plans to pass. The best two-point stance for a lineman is to be balanced, meaning that the right foot isn't way back. When the foot is back too far, the lineman has a tendency to turn a little more. A lineman must not turn his body to the outside or to the interior. If he gets caught leaning to the outside, he could give the defensive player the corner (the outside edge). When a lineman gives the defensive player the corner, the defender simply dips his shoulders and then runs forward to that corner. Figure 7-3 shows the proper two-point stance for an offensive lineman.

On normal downs in which the offense may opt to run or pass the football, many teams put their linemen in a three-point stance, which means right hand on the ground and right foot back, as shown in Figure 7-4. A player must get comfortable in this stance and also maintain his balance so that he doesn't telegraph what he intends to do. The hand on the ground shouldn't be too far forward as to cause a dip in the shoulders; those should be square. From that stance, you can pull to the right, pull to the left, set up and hold your ground, or drive straight ahead.

Figure 7-3:
An offensive lineman's two-point stance ensures that he remains balanced.

© John Wiley and Sons, Inc.

Figure 7-4:
On normal downs, offensive linemen assume a three-point stance.

© John Wiley and Sons, Inc.

But in a definite passing situation, such as third-and-long, being in a two-point stance is perfectly fine. Moving and maintaining positional leverage is easier and quicker from a two-point stance (see the "Leverage" section later in this chapter for more information). You can also run a draw or trap play from that position.

By the same token, if it's first-and-10, an offensive tackle may be able to remain in the up position. Say the play is a run designed away from the tackle. From a two-point, up position, he can pull to the inside and help block for the ball carrier. *Note:* Linemen want to change stances occasionally to prevent defensive players from zeroing in on exactly what the offense is doing; this changing is known as *giving the defensive player different looks.*

A solid base

An excellent offensive lineman is able to maintain proper balance. The key to proper balance is having a solid base. A lineman's feet should be set a little wider than the width of his shoulders; that way, the torso is set like a perfect upside-down *T.* If the lineman can maintain this stance, in most cases he won't be knocked off his feet.

If offensive linemen can maintain a good base, they can utilize their feet and whatever quickness they have. The same principle applies in boxing and basketball. A boxer always maintains that good base while keeping any lean to a minimum. He doesn't want to overextend his body to one side, thus becoming more susceptible to being knocked off his feet. A basketball player on defense wants to be able to move right and left while maintaining a good center of gravity.

Leverage

Maintaining positional leverage is important for an offensive lineman. He needs to anticipate where the defensive player is going and then get himself between that player and the quarterback, whom he's trying to protect. The point between the blocker and the quarterback, where the offensive lineman wants to meet the defender he plans to block, is called the *intersection point.* The offensive lineman needs to reach that point as quickly as possible. The slower the lineman assumes that position, the easier it is for his opponent to get him turned. That's really what the defensive player is trying to do — turn the offensive lineman. After the offensive lineman is turned, the defensive player can shorten his distance to the corner. And after he accomplishes that, the defender can make an inside move because he has the offensive lineman pointed in the wrong direction.

Toughness

An important ingredient in offensive line play is toughness. Generally, toughness is an attitude a player develops over time. He must have a lot of self-pride and tell himself that no one will beat him. Being tough is a big part of every sport, and it's a sign of a true competitor.

So much of toughness is mental. Many times, a football game is like a 15-round prizefight. At some point, one of those boxers slows down. I don't want to say that he quits, but working hard simply becomes less important to him. That phenomenon happens on a football field, too, and that's where mental toughness comes in. Toughness is essential when run-blocking because it's basically about being tougher than your opponent and wearing him down. Linemen win the fight when they rob their opponents of mental toughness.

HALL OF FAME

Standing together: The offensive line

Offensive linemen tend to hang in a group: They practice together and go out together.

For example, in 1997, the Denver Broncos had a typical group. Denver's offensive line instituted a kangaroo court — no defense attorneys allowed — in which they fined each other for being quoted in newspapers or talking on radio shows. The plan was for them to be anonymous; they were against publicity. In fact, they fined each other if they received a game ball, usually awarded by the captain or coach for a well-played game. And they fined Pro-Bowler Gary Zimmerman for being a prima donna because he missed training camp during a contract negotiation.

Prior to the Super Bowl, when the NFL ordered the Bronco linemen to talk — 2,000 reporters were asking questions every day — they bit their tongues when they heard how the more-talented Green Bay Packers defensive line was too powerful for them. On game day, they opened huge holes for running back Terrell Davis, who scored three touchdowns and rushed for 157 yards in Denver's 31-24 victory.

When their teammates declared that the offensive line deserved the Super Bowl MVP award for blocking for Davis and protecting quarterback John Elway, the linemen thought that was definitely a bad idea. They would have had to fine themselves $1,000 or more for accepting such an honor.

Repetition

Another key to an effective and cohesive offensive line lies in its practice repetition. On any level, many of the best running teams are those that run three or four basic plays. They keep repeating them, doing them over and over until they're so proficient that no opponent can stop them. In NFL training camps, offensive lines constantly work together, everyone going through the hard times, the long, hot muggy days — everyone working when he's tired. At some point, you have to rely on the guy next to you. Working together over and over in the heat of the day can develop real cohesiveness.

Uncovering a Lineman's Worst Offense: Penalties

When the ref blows the whistle because an offensive lineman committed a transgression, he blows the whistle because the lineman did one of the following:

- **Clipping:** When an offensive lineman blocks an opponent from behind, hitting him in the back of the legs or in the back. The infraction costs the offense 15 yards. However, clipping above the knee is legal within 3 yards of the line of scrimmage.

- **Chop blocking:** This dirty play (which draws a 15-yard penalty) is when a lineman dives at an opponent's knees anywhere outside a designated area 3 yards beyond the line of scrimmage. The same block is considered legal when it occurs within 3 yards of the line of scrimmage. Go figure. The worst chop block is when linemen double-team a defender; one restrains the player around the shoulders while another hits him below the waist.

- **Encroachment:** Encroachment happens when a player enters the neutral zone before the ball is snapped and makes contact with the opposition. This is a 5-yard penalty. The offense repeats the down.

- **False start:** A false start is when an offensive lineman who's in a stance or set position moves prior to the snap of the ball. This is a 5-yard penalty with a replay of the down.

- **Helping the runner:** After the ball carrier crosses the line of scrimmage, an offensive lineman can't push or pull him forward, helping him gain extra yardage. Helping the runner is a 10-yard penalty with a replay of the down.

✔ **Holding:** When an offensive lineman grabs and holds onto a defensive player, it's called *holding,* and it's one of the worst things an offensive lineman can get caught doing. An offensive lineman is whistled for holding when he grabs an arm or a jersey, or even tackles a player who has managed to get around him. Linemen are allowed to use their hands, but they can't use them to clamp onto an opposing player and limit his movement. If a lineman is caught holding a defensive player in the NFL, the penalty is 10 yards from the line of scrimmage.

Now, some people will tell you that offensive linemen hold on every play, but mainly those accusations are coming from defensive guys like me. Generally, if the offensive lineman's hands are inside the opponent's shoulder and his chest area (where the jersey number is), he can grab and hold all he wants as long as he keeps the defender in front of him. But if a defender goes to the ground really fast for no apparent reason, it's obvious that he's being held, even if the offensive lineman's hands are inside.

✔ **Ineligible receiver downfield:** A quarterback would never throw the ball to his blockers, but the blockers can be penalized for running downfield if they aren't trying to block defensive players. Linemen who are no longer blocking or have lost their man can't run past the line of scrimmage when the quarterback is attempting to pass. Ineligible receiver downfield is a 5-yard penalty with a repeat of the down.

✔ **Offside:** This happens when an offensive player lines up over the designated line of scrimmage, trying to gain an edge on blocking or simply forgetting where he should be. Generally, the lineman either places his hand over the line of scrimmage or tilts his upper body over the line of scrimmage. Offside is a 5-yard penalty with a repeat of the down.

Getting Acquainted with Blocking Terms

You hear a lot of terms thrown around when it comes to blocking. Knowing one type of block from another really isn't that important unless you're trying to impress a diehard fan or you happen to play on the offensive line. If you're interested, here's the lowdown on some of the most common blocking terms:

✔ **Cut-off block:** Generally used on running plays, which are designed to allow a defensive player to come free, or untouched, across the line of scrimmage. After that happens, an offensive lineman deliberately gets in the way of this on-rushing defender. This block is sometimes called an *angle block* because the offensive lineman hits the defensive player from the side, or from an angle.

✔ **Chop block:** The legal variety is used within 3 yards of the line of scrimmage to slow the opposition's pass rush. A lineman blocks down low with his shoulders and arms, attempting to take the defender's legs from underneath him and stop his momentum. If this play occurs 3 yards or more beyond the line of scrimmage, the blocker is penalized 15 yards. Defensive players wish this type of block would be outlawed permanently on all parts of the playing field.

✔ **Drive block:** This one-on-one block is used most often when a defensive lineman lines up directly over an offensive lineman. The blocker usually explodes out of a three-point stance and drives his hips forward, delivering the block from a wide base while keeping his head up and his shoulders square.

✔ **Double-team:** Two linemen ganging up on one defensive player is known as double-teaming. It's more common on pass plays when the center and a guard work together to stop the penetration of a talented inside pass-rusher. However, the double-team also works well on running plays, especially at the point of attack or at the place where the play is designed to go. The double-team blockers attack one defender, clearing out the one player who might stop the play from working.

✔ **Man-on-man blocking:** This is the straight-ahead style of blocking, with a defender playing directly over you and you driving straight into him. Most defenses use four linemen, so man-on-man blocking is common on pass plays, with each offensive lineman choosing the opponent opposite him, and the center helping out to either side.

✔ **Reach block:** A reach block is when an offensive lineman reaches for the next defender, meaning he doesn't block the opponent directly in front of him but moves for an opponent to either side. The reach block is common on run plays when the play calls for a guard to reach out and block an inside linebacker.

✔ **Slide block:** This is when the entire offensive line slides down the line of scrimmage — a coordinated effort by the line to go either right or left. It's a good technique when the quarterback prefers to roll or sprint right, running outside the tackle while attempting to throw the football. In that case, the line may slide to the right to give the quarterback extra protection to that side. With a talented cutback runner, this scheme may give the illusion of a run to the right, as the line slides that way while the ball carrier takes an initial step to the right and then cuts back to his left, hoping to gain an edge.

✔ **Trap block:** In a trap block, the offensive line deliberately allows a defensive player to cross the line of scrimmage untouched and then blocks him with a guard or tackle from the opposite side or where he's not expecting it. The intent is to create a running lane in the area that the defender vacated. The trap block is really a mind game. The offense wants the defender to believe it has forgotten about him or simply missed blocking him. After the defender surges upfield, across the line of scrimmage by a yard or two, an offensive lineman blocks him from the side.

Depending on the play's design, this block can come from a guard or a tackle. Teams run this play to either side, and it's important for the center to protect the back side of this lane, negating any pursuit by the defense. The trap block is also called an *influence block* because you want to draw the defender upfield and then go out and trap him. Good passing teams tend to be good trapping teams because defenders usually charge hard upfield, hoping to reach the quarterback.

✔ **Zone block:** In this block, each lineman protects a specific area or zone. Even if the defensive player leaves this area, the blocker must stay in his zone because the play or ball may be coming in that direction and the quarterback wants that area uncluttered. Blocking in a zone is generally designed to key on a specific defensive player who's disrupting the offensive game plan.

Chapter 8

Examining Offensive Plays and Strategies

In This Chapter

▶ Running specialized pass offenses and exploring new offensive formations

▶ Defeating different defensive fronts

▶ Discovering how to gain yards

▶ Deciding when to gamble on offense

▶ Choosing a goal-line offense

*W*hen I played defense, I knew that the offensive coaches were trying to get into my head and into the minds of my defensive buddies. When calling a specific play, the offensive coaches wanted to not only beat us but also make us look foolish. This chapter unmasks some of the tricky tactics those offensive geniuses come up with when they're burning the midnight oil studying defensive tendencies.

When football teams decide which play or formation to use, they base the decision on the personnel matchups they want. Coaches study the opposition and examine hours of film hoping to find the weak links in the opposing defense. No defensive team has 11 great players. So, the offense's design is to move away from the opposition's strengths and attack the weaknesses.

Here's another thing you should know about offensive strategy: No perfect play exists for every occasion. In strategy sessions prior to a game, a play may look like it will result in a long gain, but in reality it may not succeed for various reasons. It may fail because someone on the offensive team doesn't execute or because a defensive player simply anticipates correctly and makes a great play. Things happen!

In this chapter, I explain the basic offensive approaches to the game and walk you through some particular plays and overall schemes. Then I discuss which offensive plays or formations work well against particular defenses and in specific situations. When does a quarterback sneak work? When is play-action passing ideal? What goal-line run plays really work? What does a team do on third-and-long? This chapter has answers for all these questions and a whole lot more.

Offense Begins with Players

The first thing you should know about offense is that *players* win games — schemes, formations, and trick plays don't. If a player doesn't execute, none of the decisions that the coaches made will work. And I'm not talking merely from the point of view of an ex-player; coaches, owners, and scouts all know that this is true.

The opposite scenario applies, too: A play designed to gain the offense only a couple of yards can turn into a score unexpectedly if a defensive player misses a tackle or turns the wrong way or if an offensive player makes a spectacular move. Having been a defensive player, I know that we sometimes had players placed in the right situations to defend a play perfectly, but the play still succeeded because of an offensive player's outstanding effort.

Helping offenses by enforcing an important rule

What has aided offensive production in the last dozen or so NFL seasons is the enforcement of the *5-yard bump rule,* which forbids defensive backs from pushing or shoving receivers 5 or more yards beyond the line of scrimmage in hopes of pushing them off their pass routes. The 5-yard bump rule was originally instituted in 1978, but through the years, officials started allowing defensive backs to again use their hands and arms in this manner. This liberal interpretation of the rule hurt the passing game because it prevented offenses from executing their carefully designed plays.

But because the rule is being enforced properly in the NFL today, offenses seem to be taking charge. Referees are calling many more illegal contact and defensive holding penalties, resulting in defenders not playing as aggressively as they once did. Offenses are doing a much better job of spreading out the defenses, knowing that they can throw to their outside receivers. Forcing defenses to defend a larger area of the field has not only improved the passing game, but also created more opportunities for running backs. With defenders spread out across the line of scrimmage, a runner now has a chance at a longer run if he breaks through the first line of defense.

And look at the size of today's offensive players — who can stop them? So many runners and receivers weigh 200 pounds or more, and they all can run 40 yards in 4.5 seconds or faster. (The 40-yard dash is a common test that teams use to measure players' talents.) Peyton Manning, quarterback of the Denver Broncos, weighs 230 pounds and is 6 feet 5 inches tall. Quarterback Ben Roethlisberger of the Pittsburgh Steelers is 6 feet 5 inches tall and weighs 241 pounds.

And it isn't just the quarterbacks, runners, and receivers who are growing in size. Some teams have 325-pound offensive linemen who can run 40 yards in 5 seconds flat, and some are as agile as men half their size. They're as big as the defensive linemen, therefore giving the skilled players on offense an opportunity to succeed. Every great ball carrier will tell you that he can't gain his 1,000 yards a season without a very good offensive line.

Zeroing in on Specialized Pass Offenses

Few passes travel more than 10 or 12 yards. I'm sure you've heard about *the bomb* — a reference to a long pass — but those 35- to 40-yard or longer pass plays are pretty rare, thanks to the modern pass offenses that are run in the NFL and college football. As a fan, you should be aware of two types of pass offenses, which I describe in the sections that follow.

West Coast offense

Currently, Aaron Rodgers and a handful of other NFL quarterbacks operate a short, ball-control passing game called the *West Coast offense*. It got this name because it was developed by coach Bill Walsh, who directed the San Francisco 49ers to three Super Bowls. The West Coast offense's popularity spread throughout the NFL as Walsh disciples such as Mike Holmgren, Mike Shanahan, and Jon Gruden began using it. Many college teams use variations of this offense, depending on the talent of their receivers.

The West Coast offense uses all the offense's personnel in the passing game, as opposed to an I-formation team that's structured to run the ball and rarely throws to the running backs. (I tell you all about the I formation in Chapter 6.) Rather than running long routes downfield, the wide receivers run quick slants or square-out patterns toward the sidelines, hoping to receive the ball quickly and gain extra yards after the catch. The receivers run a lot of *crossing routes,* meaning they run from left to right or right to left in front of the quarterback, maybe 10 yards away. Crossing routes are effective because they disrupt many defensive secondary coverages.

If a running back is good at catching the ball, he becomes a prime receiver in the West Coast offense. This offense also uses a tight end on deeper routes than most other offenses. Because the offense has so many potential pass catchers (two receivers and two running backs or three receivers and one running back) on a typical pass play, the tight end can often find open areas after he crosses the line of scrimmage. The defensive players in the secondary tend to focus their attention on the wide receivers. The West Coast offense incorporates the tight end into most pass plays, so that player must be an above-average receiver.

The premise of the West Coast offense is to maintain possession of the ball. Although it has quick-strike scoring possibilities, it's designed to keep offensive drives alive by passing rather than running the ball. One of the basic theories of this offense is as follows: If the defense is suspecting a run, pass the ball to the running back instead.

Shotgun offense

For obvious passing downs, some teams use the *shotgun offense*. In the shotgun, the quarterback (QB) lines up 5 to 7 yards behind the center and receives a long snap, as shown in Figure 8-1. The pass plays used in this offense are identical to those used when the quarterback is under center; offenses use the shotgun simply to allow the quarterback more time to visualize the defense, particularly the secondary's alignment. On an obvious passing down, nothing can be gained by keeping the quarterback under center. Why have him spend time dropping back to pass when he can receive a long snap and be ready to throw?

The QB is positioned 5 to 7 yards behind the center in the shotgun offense. To run this offense, you want a quarterback who's quick with his decisions and also able to run with the football if the defense's actions make it possible for him to gain yardage by carrying the ball himself.

Figure 8-1: The QB is positioned 5 to 7 yards behind the center in the shotgun offense.

The best shotgun quarterback I ever saw was John Elway of the Denver Broncos. Jim Kelly of the Buffalo Bills truly excelled in the shotgun, too. Elway and Kelly seemed more comfortable and confident in this formation than other quarterbacks.

From a defensive lineman's viewpoint, the shotgun is okay because you don't have to concentrate on defending the run; you know that the offense is going to pass. In other formations, a defender has to be prepared for both possibilities: run or pass. He has to think before reacting. When facing the shotgun, a defensive lineman has only one mission: to get to the quarterback as fast as he can.

Red gun (or run-and-shoot) offense

The *red gun offense,* or *run-and-shoot offense,* uses four receivers, one running back, and no tight end. The Houston Oilers and the Atlanta Falcons used this offense in the early 1990s, but both teams have since abandoned it for a more conventional approach because it places too much emphasis on passing. (The Houston Oilers have since moved out of Texas, and now they're called the Tennessee Titans with a home in Nashville.)

The red gun is a great offense for fans to watch because it uses so many pass plays. Also, only five offensive linemen are blocking on every play, which creates more opportunities for the defense to place more pass-rushers to one side (called *overloading*); the offensive linemen can't possibly block every one of these pass-rushers. These types of gambles may lead to a sack or a big play — feast or famine. When a red gun offense gives the ball to a running back, he has a chance to make a big play because the defense is concentrating on pressuring the four wide receivers. Depending on how deep the receivers run their patterns, the running back may have a lot of open area on the field in which to run.

No NFL team has won with the red gun, but the University of Florida won two national championships with it. Defenses need to practice and prepare for running offenses, too, and with a limited amount of practice time on a typical weekday, the red gun offense never gives the defense that opportunity. Instead, the defensive players become accustomed to defending the pass. Defenses have to be good at stopping the run, too, in order to win. Also, the red gun doesn't employ a tight end — another thing the defense needs to know how to defend.

I always had problems with the red gun offense as a player because it was an unconventional system. It was difficult to key on the lone running back and anticipate what the play was going to be. This running back usually was in the same alignment, so, to me, some passes looked like run plays, and run plays ended up being pass plays. Offenses often ran *draw plays* (running plays) from an unusual perspective. For example, the team would run a draw as the quarterback was faking like he was going to run around the end (called a *bootleg*), but actually he had already given the ball to the running back; the quarterback was simply pretending to have the ball while running wide. I know this offense frustrated our defensive coaches. They never seemed sure of which defense worked best against it, especially for us defensive linemen.

Looking at Some Newfangled Offenses

One of the great pleasures of following the game of football is seeing it evolve over time. Coaches are always trying innovative new schemes on offense and defense to catch their opponents off guard. Consequently, the game keeps changing. If you watch a football game from years past (you can watch these games on DVD, on ESPN Classic, and at www.nflnetwork.com/nflnetwork), the first thing you notice is how different the game is now, especially on offense. The previous century saw offenses use and abandon these formations: the flying wedge, the single wing, the wing T, the Notre Dame Box, and the wishbone. Recent years have seen three new offensive formations: the wildcat, the spread, and the pistol. I describe them in the next sections.

The wildcat

The *wildcat* formation is unique in football because, when an offense runs the wildcat, the quarterback isn't on the field. His place is taken by a running back or sometimes a wide receiver, who takes the snap shotgun-style from 5 to 7 yards behind the center. The running back or receiver then runs the ball (or sometimes hands it to another running back).

The wildcat offers a couple advantages to the offense. Without a quarterback on the field, the offense has an extra blocker to help the runner advance the ball. And because the halfback takes the snap from center, the offense wastes no time handing off the ball. The runner can make his move as soon as the ball is snapped. Moreover, by starting from 5 to 7 yards behind the offensive line, the runner has a good field of vision. He can better see where the defenders are and where his offensive line has busted a hole in the defense for him to run through.

In the 2008 season, the Miami Dolphins ran the wildcat with talented running backs Ricky Williams and Ronnie Brown, and they won 11 games. But for the most part the wildcat is used sparingly in the NFL and in college. If a team runs the wildcat, it frequently does so only when it needs 2 to 3 yards to get a first down. The wildcat is a one-dimensional offensive formation. Most of the advantages of running the wildcat are cancelled out by the fact that the defense can focus on the run — it doesn't have to defend against a player who is good at passing the ball — when it sees its opponent lining up in the wildcat.

The spread

The *spread* gets its name because, in this formation, the offense spreads out across the width of the field, causing the defensive players to spread out accordingly. The quarterback takes the snap shotgun-style, after which he can run the ball, pass it, or hand it off, often to a runner who's going in motion across the backfield. The idea behind the spread is to open up the field and create more offensive opportunities — more seams for runners to attack and more space in which receivers can get open.

The spread is used far more often in college football than in the pro game for a very important reason: In the spread, the quarterback runs as well as passes the ball, and in the NFL, where players are faster and bigger, and where the quarterback is a very valuable commodity, teams don't want to risk an injury to the quarterback by allowing him to run the ball.

Still, with all its option and misdirection plays, the spread formation makes for very exciting football, and many college teams have found success with the spread. The 2011 Bowl Championship Series (BCS) championship game (see Chapter 16 for information about the BCS) featured two teams that ran the spread offense — the Oregon Ducks and the Auburn Tigers.

The pistol

The pistol, like the wildcat and the spread formation, is run from a shotgun snap. The quarterback lines up 4 yards behind center, and a running back lines up 3 yards behind the quarterback. The pistol combines the advantages of the shotgun formation and the I formation. Lining up 4 yards behind center gives the quarterback a better view of the defense and allows him the opportunity to throw quick passes without having to drop back before passing the ball. The running back, meanwhile, also gets a good look at the defense, because he's even farther behind the line of scrimmage than the quarterback. Like the spread, the pistol requires a quarterback who can run as well as pass. Running quarterbacks, however, take a lot more hits than pocket quarterbacks, and injuries are often a factor over the course of a season. Colin Kaepernick of the San Francisco 49ers and Robert Griffin III of the Washington Redskins both have had success running plays from the pistol formation.

Beating a Defense

One of the primary factors that helps a coach decide what offense to run and what plays to call is how the defense sets up. Various defenses call for different strategies to beat them. The following sections describe some defenses and the offensive plays or formations that may work against those defensive schemes. For more information about any of these defenses, flip to Chapter 11.

Battling a 3-4 front

When facing a *3-4 front* (three down linemen and four linebackers), the offense's best strategy is to run *weak side,* or away from the tight end (which is always the strong side of any offensive formation). One possible running play is called the *weak-side lead.* With this play, the defensive end (DE) usually attempts to control and push the offensive tackle (LT) inside toward the center of the line, leaving the linebacker behind him (OLB) to defend a lot of open area. The offense is in the I formation, and the fullback (FB) runs to the weak side and blocks the linebacker, shoving him inside. The left offensive tackle allows the defensive end to push him a little, letting the defender believe that he's controlling the play. However, the offensive lineman then grabs the defender, containing him, and moves him out of the way to the right. The ball carrier should have a clear running lane after he hits the line of scrimmage. Figure 8-2 diagrams this play.

Figure 8-2: Running the ball to the weak side is a good offensive strategy against a 3-4 defense.

Running against a 4-3 front

An offense can attack a *4-3 front* (four down linemen, three linebackers) in many different ways, but one common strategy is to attack what coaches call the *bubble side* (the defensive side where the two linebackers are positioned). Remember, the 4-3 defense employs both over and under slants that the four-man defensive line uses. *Overs* and *unders* are basically the alignments of defensive linemen to one particular side of the offensive center (see Chapter 11 for further details). When the defensive front lines up in an under look, the offense attacks the bubble.

The offensive play shown in Figure 8-3 is called a *delay draw* to the strong side (the tight end side) of the offensive formation. When the defense is positioned like this, three defensive linemen line up over the center, left guard, and left tackle. These offensive linemen are also called the weak-side guard and tackle. This defensive alignment leaves only one lineman and two smaller linebackers (DE, ILB, and OLB) to defend the strong side of the offense's I formation (turn to Chapter 6 for the scoop on this formation).

Figure 8-3: The delay draw takes advantage of the fact that only one lineman and two linebackers are on the strong side.

On the delay draw, the right guard (RG) blocks down on the defensive nose tackle (N), and the fullback (FB) runs into the hole and blocks the front-side linebacker (ILB). The right tackle (RT) blocks the defensive end (DE), keeping him out of the middle, and the tight end (TE) blocks and contains the outside linebacker (OLB). This approach is known as *running at the defense's weakest point*. When the ball carrier reaches the line of scrimmage, he should find open space between the offense's right guard and right tackle.

Defeating the four-across defense

In the *four-across defense,* the defense plays all four secondary players deep, about 12 yards off the line of scrimmage. To beat this defense, the offense wants to have two wide receivers (WR) run comeback routes, have the tight end (TE) run a 16-yard in route, and have the two backs (RB) swing out to the right and left. The running back to the quarterback's left side should run more of a looping pass pattern. The quarterback (QB) throws the ball to the wide receiver on the left, as shown in Figure 8-4.

Figure 8-4: This play is good for beating the four-across defense.

The quarterback throws to his left because the ball is placed on the left hash mark, which is the short side of the field. Throwing a 15-yard comeback pass to his left is much easier than throwing a 15-yard comeback to the right, or the wide side of the field. The pass to the wide side would have to travel much farther, almost 42 yards, as opposed to just 15 yards. From the left hash mark to the numbers on the right side of the field, the distance is more than 19 yards. And the comeback to the right is always thrown beyond those numbers (10, 20, 30, 40), going down the length of the field.

If the defense senses that the quarterback is going to throw to the wide receiver on the left side and then decides to drop a linebacker into underneath coverage, hoping to intercept, the quarterback can't throw that pass. By *underneath,* I mean that the linebacker is dropping back to defend the pass, but safeties are still positioned beyond him. Hence, the linebacker is underneath the safeties. Instead, the quarterback throws to the running back on the same side. The quarterback simply *keys* (watches) the linebacker. If the linebacker drops into coverage, the quarterback throws to the running back because he won't be covered. If the linebacker takes the running back, the quarterback throws to the receiver.

Beating press coverage

Press coverage is when the defensive team has its two cornerbacks on the line of scrimmage, covering the outside receivers man-to-man. One tactic against this defense is to throw to the tight end (TE), who runs to the middle of the field, as shown in Figure 8-5. Another option is to throw to the running back (RB), who's swinging out to the left. The wide receivers (WR), who are being pressed, run in the opposite direction, away from the area in which either the tight end or the running back is headed, as shown in Figure 8-6.

Passing against a zone coverage

When I say "passing against a zone coverage," I'm talking about a defensive secondary that's playing zone — meaning the cornerbacks are playing off the line of scrimmage. They aren't in press coverage. The best pass against a zone coverage is the curl, and the best time to use it is on first-and-10. A receiver (WR) runs 10 to 12 yards and simply *curls,* or hooks back, toward the quarterback (QB), as shown in Figure 8-7. He usually curls to his left and attempts to run his route deep enough to gain a first down. The coverage should be *soft* enough (meaning the defensive back, CB, is playing 5 to 7 yards off the receiver) on these routes that the receiver's size shouldn't matter. However, against a man-to-man scheme, a smaller receiver may be ineffective when running patterns against a taller, stronger defensive back.

Figure 8-5:
One option for beating press coverage is to throw to the tight end in midfield.

Figure 8-6:
Throwing to the running back, who swings out to the left, is another way to beat press coverage.

Figure 8-7: The receiver runs 10 to 12 yards out and then curls back toward the quarterback when facing zone coverage.

Selecting an offense versus a zone blitz

Pittsburgh Steelers defensive coordinator Dick LeBeau invented the *zone blitz* in the late 1980s, giving his team the nickname "Blitzburgh" (see Chapter 11 for details on the zone blitz). Sustaining a running offense is difficult against teams that run a zone blitz. Some offenses have had success running against zone blitz defenses, but I don't think you can beat them consistently by running the ball.

When facing a defense that blitzes a lot off the corner (linebackers or safeties coming from either wide side of the line of scrimmage against your offensive tackles), the offense should align with two tight ends in order to help pass-protect. To beat a zone blitz with a passing attack, the offense must find its opponent's weakest defender in the passing game (be that cornerback, safety, or linebacker).

The quarterback must throw to the side opposite where the defense is *overloaded* (has more players). For example, if the defense positions four players to the quarterback's left, as shown in Figure 8-8, the quarterback should throw to his right. But the offense must still block the side from which the defense is attacking.

Throwing the post versus blitzing teams

Most defenses protect against quarterbacks attempting to throw the *post route,* which is when a receiver fakes to the outside and then runs straight down the field toward the goalpost. The quarterback lines up the throw by focusing on the hash marks. When he releases the ball, he tries to *lead the receiver,* or throw the ball slightly in front of him, so that the pass drops to the receiver over his shoulder. That way, if a defensive player is chasing the receiver, the defender shouldn't be able to intercept the pass.

The deep post doesn't really work well against zone blitz defenses. Why? Because these teams rarely leave the post open. They defend it pretty well.

However, other teams that blitz from a basic 4-3 defense may use a safety to blitz the quarterback. When a team uses a safety to blitz, usually the defense is vulnerable in the center of the field, where both safeties should be. Still, very few teams leave the deep post wide open because it can give the offense a quick six points.

Wearing out a defense with the no-huddle offense

In need of a score late in a game, every team runs a *no-huddle offense* in an attempt to move down the field quickly. (See "Doing the two-minute drill" later in this chapter for more info on late-game tactics.) In essence, by quickly running plays without pausing to huddle, the offense prevents the defense from substituting players and changing its scheme. The quick pace of play can tire out a defense, leaving it vulnerable to a score.

A handful of teams with elite quarterbacks — the New England Patriots with Tom Brady, the Denver Broncos with Peyton Manning, the New Orleans Saints with Drew Brees, and the Green Bay Packers with Aaron Rodgers — run their two-minute, or no-huddle, offense, throughout the game.

Gaining Better Field Position

Of course, scoring is always an offense's ultimate goal, but to score, you have to move down the field toward your opponent's end zone. In the next sections, I describe the various strategies for gaining yards and, consequently, a better field position.

Throwing a field position pass

When offenses face third down and more than 6 yards, which is known as *third-and-long,* the safest play is for the quarterback to throw to a running back who's underneath the coverage of the defensive secondary. Why? Because in such situations, the defensive secondary, which is aligned well off the line of scrimmage, is always instructed to allow the receiver to catch the ball and then come up and tackle him, preventing a first down.

Early in the game, when your offense is down by ten or fewer points, you want to run a safe play on third-and-long, knowing that you'll probably end up punting the ball. In other words, your offense is raising its white flag and giving up. That's why this pass to the running back is called a *field position pass.* Maybe the back will get lucky, break a bunch of tackles, and gain a first down, but basically you're playing for field position. The odds of beating a good defensive team under third-and-long conditions are pretty slim.

Opting for possession passes

Most of the time, a *possession pass* is a short throw, between 8 and 10 yards, to either a running back or a tight end. The intent isn't necessarily to gain a first down but to maintain possession of the ball while gaining yardage. Often, teams call possession passes several times in a short period to help the quarterback complete some easy passes and build his confidence.

If the quarterback wants to throw a possession pass to a wide receiver and the defensive secondary is playing off the line of scrimmage, his best option is to throw a 5-yard hitch. A *5-yard hitch* is when the receiver runs up the field 5 yards, stops, and then turns back so that he's facing the quarterback. When the receiver turns, the ball should almost be in his hands. Coaches call these throws when the quarterback has thrown some incompletions, giving him a chance to calm down and complete a few easy passes.

Moving downfield with play-action passes

In a *play-action pass,* the quarterback fakes a handoff to a running back and then drops back 4 more yards and throws the football. The fake to the running back usually causes the linebackers and defensive backs to hesitate and stop coming forward after they realize that it isn't a running play. They stop because they know they must retreat and defend their pass responsibility areas.

If neither team has scored and the offense is on its own 20-yard line, that's a perfect time to throw the football. Some conservative offensive teams run play-action only in short-yardage situations (for example, second down and 3 yards to go). But play-action works whenever the defense places its strong safety near the line of scrimmage, wanting to stuff the run. Because the defensive pass coverage is likely to be soft, the offense has a good opportunity to throw the ball. And the defense shouldn't be blitzing, which in turn gives the quarterback plenty of time to throw.

Surveying Offenses for Sticky Situations

One of the biggest challenges of being a coach — or a quarterback, for that matter — is to lead your team out of the sticky situations that arise. This section explains some of the strategies that offenses use to gain the necessary yardage for a first down, move downfield with little time left on the clock, and more.

Deciding whether to gamble on fourth-and-1

The game is tied, and on fourth-and-1 you have a decision to make: Should your team kick a field goal or go for the first down and maintain possession, hoping to end your offensive possession with a touchdown?

For most coaches, the decision depends on the time of the game and the team they're playing. If a team is on the road against a solid opponent, one that has beaten the team consistently in the past, most coaches elect to kick a field goal. In the NFL, some teams are especially difficult to beat at home. For example, the New England Patriots won 21 consecutive home games (including playoff games) in the 2002 through 2005 seasons. The thought process is that any lead, even a small one, is better than risking none at all against such a team when you're on the road. So, at Gillette Stadium, where the Patriots play, you kick the field goal and take your three points.

A coach's strategy may change drastically when his team is playing the same opponent in its own stadium. If I'm playing in my stadium and I'm leading 17–7 in the fourth quarter, I may go for it on fourth-and-1 — especially if we're inside the other team's 20-yard line. I may let my team take a shot, especially if the offense hasn't been very effective. If my team doesn't make the first down, the other team has to go more than 80 yards to score, and it has to score twice to beat me. You'd rather be in the other team's territory when you gamble. Never gamble in your own territory — it could cost your team three points or a touchdown.

The toughest area in which to make a decision is between your opponent's 35- and 40-yard lines — a distance that may be too far for your field goal kicker but too close to punt. If your punter kicks the ball into the end zone, for example, your opponent begins possession on the 20-yard line, giving you a mere 15-yard gain in field position. When you're making the decision whether to kick or punt in this 35- to 40-yard line area, you may as well toss a coin.

Making a first down on a fourth-down gamble

It's fourth down and 1 yard to go for a first down, and your offense just crossed midfield. You want to gamble, believing that your offense can gain enough yards for a first down. The best play to call in this situation is a run off the tackle and the tight end on the left side of the formation, as shown in Figure 8-9.

Your offense has three tight ends in the game: the standard short-yardage personnel. These players always practice running a few specific plays during the week. Your offense knows that the defense plans to plug up the middle; they don't want an interior running play to beat them. They'll defend that area. To fool the defense and maximize the offense's chance to succeed, the offensive alignment puts two tight ends to the right, hoping the defense will react to the formation and slant its personnel to that side because it believes that the play is centered there. With the defense slanted to prevent a run to the right, the offense runs to the left.

Figure 8-9:
Run to
the left in
a short-
yardage
situation
when the
defense
believes
that the play
is centered
to the right.

Running a quarterback sneak

The *quarterback sneak* is one of the oldest plays in the book. But it isn't that simple to execute, and it doesn't always succeed. The play is designed for the quarterback to run behind one of his guards, using the guard as his principal blocker. Teams run the quarterback sneak when they need less than a full yard, sometimes only a few inches, for a first down.

To be successful with the sneak, the quarterback delays for a moment and determines the angle the defensive linemen are coming from. Then he dives headfirst, pushing his shoulders into the crack behind whichever guard (the right or left side) is called in the huddle.

The quarterback wants to run at the weakest defensive tackle. For example, you don't want to run at the Seattle Seahawks' Kevin Williams; you want to run at the other tackle. If the Baltimore Ravens' Haloti Ngata is aligned over your right guard, you want to sneak over your left guard. You make the sneak work by having your center and guard double-team the defensive tackle (or whoever's playing in this gap opposite the two offensive linemen). These two blockers must move the defensive tackle or the defender in that gap.

Doing the two-minute drill

Your team has two minutes left in the game to drive 70 yards for a score. You must score a touchdown (and successfully kick the extra point) to tie the game. As an offensive coach, you're hoping the defense decides to play a *prevent defense,* which means they use seven players in pass coverage while rushing only four linemen or linebackers at the quarterback. When a defense plays a prevent defense, you may want to run the ball because the running back has plenty of room to run after he crosses the line of scrimmage.

The best pass play to use in this situation is the *triple stretch,* which is also known as the *vertical stretch.* In this play, one receiver runs a deep pattern through the secondary, another receiver runs a route in the middle, and another simply runs underneath, as shown in Figure 8-10. The underneath route may be only 5 yards across the line of scrimmage and *underneath* the linebackers' position in pass coverage.

The intermediate receiver runs a route behind the linebackers and in front of the secondary coverage players. Teams don't necessarily want to throw deep, knowing that the defense is focused on preventing a huge gain, but that receiver must *stretch the defense,* or force the defense to retreat farther from the line of scrimmage. You use the deep receiver as a decoy.

Figure 8-10: The triple (or vertical) stretch pass play is great for a two-minute offense.

The quarterback's intention is to find the intermediate receiver (WR who comes in from the left). If the intermediate receiver can run behind the linebackers and catch the ball, he'll probably have a 15-yard gain, but he'll have to make sure that he runs out of bounds to stop the clock and conserve time. If the short receiver catches the ball, the linebackers are probably playing deep to prevent the intermediate receiver from catching the ball. In this situation, you dump it to the running back. He catches it and has a chance to run, but he must make sure he gets out of bounds, too. If the defense blitzes, you may be able to complete the deep route for a long touchdown pass. The quarterback normally reads progression from deep to intermediate and underneath, knowing that the defense is set up for the middle route.

Scoring Offenses

After you get the ball downfield and get out of all those sticky situations, your offense is ready to score. In the following sections, you can find plays for various scoring situations.

Making the best run play on the goal line

Actually I can't tell you the *best* run play on the goal line because there's no best play. But I can tell you that teams that have the most success running on the goal line have a great back like Hall of Famers Jim Brown or Marcus Allen in their backfield. Teams are always searching for a great running back, someone who can fight through three defenders, for example, and still reach the end zone.

The best running back in the NFL isn't necessarily the one that coaches choose when their teams are near the goal line. The "dodger and dancer" type of runner who can break out in the open field isn't as valuable near the goal line as the "pound it in there" guy. Down on the 1-yard line, you need a powerful runner — a tough, physical player — who can bowl over people. Because he's going to be hit, he needs to be able to bounce off one or two tacklers. Well, okay. The best play at the goal line is always something straight ahead.

Scoring inside the opponent's 10-yard line

One pass in today's NFL offenses is perfectly suited to the part of the field inside the 10-yard line: the *quick out*. As shown in Figure 8-11, the outside receiver (WR on the left) runs straight for 5 to 7 yards and then breaks quickly to the outside. Offenses use this pass play a lot because many defenses play the old college zone defense of putting their four defensive backs deep and back, which is called the *four-across alignment* (see the earlier "Defeating the four-across defense" section for more).

If you have a big, physical receiver, the quick out is the ideal pass. The receiver and the quarterback have to be in unison and time it right. If the quarterback completes the pass, the receiver has a chance to break a tackle and run in for a touchdown. The opportunity to score is there because in the four-across alignment, the defensive back doesn't have help on that side; he must make the tackle by himself. If he doesn't, the receiver can score an easy six points. Of course, the quick out is also a dangerous pass to throw. If the cornerback reads the play quickly and the quarterback fails to throw hard and accurately, the ball is likely to be intercepted by the defensive player and returned for a touchdown.

Figure 8-11:
The quick out to the WR on the left is the perfect pass to throw from inside an opponent's 10-yard line.

Going for two-point conversions

After scoring a touchdown, a team has two options: kick the ball through the uprights for one point or try for a *two-point conversion.* The team earns two points if it successfully reaches the end zone on either a pass or a run after a touchdown.

For a two-point conversion in the NFL, the ball is placed on the 2-yard line, the same spot as for a kick. (College and high school teams must score from the 3-yard line.) You'd think that the two points would be automatic, but over the years, two-point conversions have been successful just 47 percent of the time, whereas kickers convert extra-point attempts at a rate of around 99 percent.

Coaches have a universal chart that tells them when to kick and when to attempt a two-point conversion (the chart was supposedly devised by UCLA coach Tommy Prothro in 1970 with the help of his offensive coordinator, Dick Vermeil). Coaches like the chart because they dislike being second-guessed by players and the media for making the wrong choice — a decision that may result in a defeat. Here's what the chart says:

- ✔ If you're behind by 2, 5, 9, 12, or 16 points, attempt a two-point conversion.

- ✔ If you're ahead by 1, 4, 5, 12, 15, or 19 points, attempt a two-point conversion.

- ✔ If you're behind by 1, 4, or 11 points, you have to make the dreaded judgment call — it can go either way.

Teams elect to go for two points when they need to close the point differential with their opponent. For example, if a team is behind by five, kicking the extra point would close the gap to four. That means the team could kick a field goal (worth three points) and still lose the game. But a two-point conversion would reduce the deficit to three, and a field goal would tie the game. When behind by nine points, a two-point conversion reduces the deficit to seven, meaning that a touchdown and an extra point could tie the game.

The two-point conversion, with the right multiples of field goals and touchdowns, can close a deficit or widen it, depending on the situation. It's a gamble. But when a team is trailing, it may be the quickest way to rally and possibly force overtime. Most coaches prefer to tie in regulation and take their chances with an overtime period. However, some coaches, especially if their teams have grabbed the momentum or seem unstoppable on offense, may elect to try two points at the end of the game and go for the win rather than the tie. The previous play is more common in high school and college football than in the NFL, where coaches tend to be conservative because of playoff implications — and because a loss might mean unemployment.

Most teams use zone pass plays in two-point conversion situations because defenses aren't playing man-to-man coverages as much anymore. So the following play was designed to succeed against a zone defense. Remember that the offense simply has to gain 2 yards (or 3 in high school and college) to reach the end zone, which doesn't sound complicated.

To attempt a two-point conversion, the offense lines up three receivers to one side. One receiver runs the flat; another receiver runs up about 6 or 7 yards and runs a curl; and the third receiver runs to the back of the end zone, turns, and waits. Figure 8-12 shows three receivers (TE and WR) to one side — the right side. This group of receivers can be a tight end and two wide receivers — it doesn't matter as long as the receivers are bunched together in a close group. One receiver runs straight ahead and about 2 yards deep into the end zone. Another receiver is the inside guy. He runs straight up the field. He heads first to the back of the end zone and turns to run a deep square-out. The other receiver just releases into the flat area, outside the numbers on the field. If the quarterback looks into the secondary and believes that he's facing a zone defense, he wants the receiver running the 6-yard curl to come open.

If the defense is playing a man-to-man coverage, the quarterback wants the receiver in the flat to come open immediately. If the defense reads the play perfectly, the quarterback is in trouble because he must find a secondary target while under a heavy pass-rush. Still, this pass is almost impossible to defend because the offense is prepared for every defensive concept.

If the coverage is man-to-man, the offense opens with a *double pick,* which is illegal if the officials see it clearly. By a *pick,* I mean that an offensive receiver intentionally blocks the path of a defensive player who's trying to stay with the receiver he's responsible for covering. Both the tight end and one receiver on the right side attempt to pick the defensive player covering the receiver (refer to Figure 8-12) running toward the flat area. If the receiver who's benefiting from the illegal pick doesn't come open, the first receiver attempting a pick runs 2 yards into the end zone and curls, facing the quarterback. After trying to pick a defender and if he believes he's wide open, the tight end settles, stops to the right of the formation, and waves his arm so the quarterback can see him.

Figure 8-12:
A common
two-point
conversion
against
a zone
coverage,
with three
receivers
(TE and WR)
to one side.

Disguising a Successful Play

During the course of a game, a team often finds that one pass play works particularly well against a certain defense and matchup. To keep using the play in that game and to continue to confuse the defense, the offense often runs the pass play out of different formations while maintaining similar pass routes.

As an example, here's what an offense originally does: It lines up with three receivers (WR), a tight end (TE), and a running back (RB), as shown in Figure 8-13. One receiver is to the left, and the running back is also behind the line to the left, behind the left tackle. The tight end is aligned to the right, and two other receivers are outside of him. The receiver on the left runs down the field 18 yards and runs a square-in (for more on this passing route, see Chapter 5). The tight end runs a crossing route, about 7 or 8 yards from the line of scrimmage. The running back swings out of the backfield to the left.

The receiver located in the slot to the right simply runs right down the middle of the field. He's the deep decoy receiver who's going to pull all the defensive players out of the middle. The quarterback wants to hit the receiver who lined up on the left side. If he isn't open, he tries the middle with the tight end; lastly, he dumps the ball to the running back.

To modify this successful play, the same receiver on the left runs the same 18-yard square-in, as shown in Figure 8-14. The running back on the left releases to that side, but this time he runs across the line of scrimmage 7 or 8 yards and curls back toward the quarterback. The back is now assuming the role of the tight end in the original formation. This time, the tight end runs down the middle of the field. The receiver in the slot now runs right between the two hashes and hooks. So it's pretty much the same play. The offense's target remains the receiver to the left. And all those other receivers are simply decoys.

Figure 8-13:
An example of a successful offensive play.

Figure 8-14:
An offense can modify a successful play by varying passing routes.

Part III
The Big D

In this part . . .

✔ Take a look at the defensive line and understand sacks and tackles

✔ Look at how the secondary — the last line of defense — operates

✔ Brush up on defensive tactics and how to handle difficult situations on the field

Chapter 9

These Guys Are Huge: The Defensive Line

In This Chapter

▶ Looking at the different types of defensive linemen, from noses to ends

▶ Getting the lowdown on linebackers

▶ Understanding how the defense lines up

▶ Finding out about sacks, tackles, and more

The game of football has changed a lot since I entered the NFL in 1981. Today's defensive linemen are bigger, and maybe faster, than those who played 30 years ago. Of course, they've had to keep pace with their main opposition, the offensive linemen. When I played in the NFL, you could count the number of 300-pound offensive linemen on one hand. Now, you need more than two hands to count a single team's 300-pounders!

Defensive linemen have to battle these huge offensive linemen. Then they have to deal with running backs and quarterbacks, whose main function in life is to make the defensive line look silly. Few linemen can run and move, stop and go, like running back LeSean McCoy of the Buffalo Bills and quarterback Russell Wilson of the Seattle Seahawks. These guys are two of the best offensive players in the NFL, and they're also superb all-around athletes. Linemen, who generally weigh 100 pounds more than McCoy or Wilson, have a difficult time catching and tackling players like them. The few who can are the great linemen. However, many linemen have the ability to put themselves in position to stop a great offensive player. The key is: Can they make the tackle?

In this chapter, I address the responsibilities of every defensive lineman and talk about all the linebacker positions, explaining how those two segments of the defense interact.

Those Big Guys Called Linemen

Defensive linemen are big players who position themselves on the line of scrimmage, across from the offensive linemen, prior to the snap of the ball. Their job is to stop the run, or in the case of a pass play, sack the quarterback, as shown in Figure 9-1.

The play of the defensive linemen (as a group) can decide the outcome of many games. If they can stop the run without much help from the linebackers and defensive backs, they allow those seven defensive players to concentrate on pass defense (and their coverage responsibilities). Ditto if they can sustain a constant pass-rush on the quarterback without help from a blitzing defensive back or linebacker.

For the defense to do its job effectively, linemen and linebackers (the players who back up the defensive linemen) must work together. This collaboration is called *scheming* — devising plans and strategies to unmask and foil the offense and its plays. To succeed as a group, a defense needs linemen who are selfless — willing to go into the trenches and play the run while taking on two offensive linemen. These players must do so without worrying about not getting enough pass-rush and sack opportunities.

The following sections take an in-depth look at the defensive line, which is also known as the *D line*.

Figure 9-1:
Nose tackle
Vince
Wilfork
sacks the
quarter-
back —
again.

Photo credit: © Bernie Nunez/Getty Images

Looking closely at the D line

Defensive linemen usually start in a *three-point stance* (one hand and two feet on the ground). In rare situations, they align themselves in a *four-point stance* (both hands and both feet on the ground) to stop short-yardage runs. The latter stance is better because the lineman wants to gain leverage and get both of his shoulders under the offensive lineman and drive him up and backward. He needs to do anything he can to stop the offensive lineman's forward charge.

Defensive linemen are typically a rare combination of size, speed, and athleticism, and, in terms of weight, they're the largest players on the defense. A defensive lineman's primary job is to stop the run at the line of scrimmage and to *rush* (chase down) the quarterback when a pass play develops.

Defensive linemen seldom receive enough credit for a job well done. In fact, at times, a defensive lineman can play a great game but go unnoticed by the fans and the media, who focus more on offensive players, like quarterbacks and wide receivers, and defensive playmakers, such as defensive backs and linebackers. Defensive linemen *are* noticed in some situations, though, like when they

- ✔ Record a *sack* (tackle a quarterback for a loss while he's attempting to pass)

- ✔ Make a tackle for a loss or for no gain

Often, defensive linemen *contain* an opponent (neutralize him, forcing a stalemate) or deal with a *double-team block* (two offensive linemen against one defensive lineman) in order to free up one of their teammates to make a tackle or sack. The defensive lineman position can be a thankless one because few players succeed against double-team blocks. The only place where one guy beats two on a regular basis is in the movies.

Identifying types of defensive linemen

The term *defensive lineman* doesn't refer to a specific position, as you might think. A player who plays any of the following positions is considered a defensive lineman:

- ✔ **Nose tackle:** The defensive lineman who lines up directly across from the center, "nose to nose," as shown in Figure 9-2. Like in baseball, you build the strength of your team up the middle, and without a good nose tackle, your defense can't function. This player needs to be prepared for a long day because his job is all grunt work, with little or no chance of making sacks or tackles for minus yardage.

Figure 9-2:
The nose
tackle (N)
lines up
opposite the
center.

© John Wiley and Sons, Inc.

The nose tackle knows he'll be double-blocked much of the game. He's responsible for gaps on each side of the center (known as the *A gaps*). Prior to the snap, the nose tackle looks at the ball. When the center snaps the ball, the nose tackle attacks the center with his hands. Because the nose tackle is watching the ball, the center can sucker him into moving early by suddenly flinching his arms and simulating a snap.

✔ **Defensive tackles:** The two players who line up inside the defensive ends and usually opposite the offensive guards. The defensive tackles' responsibilities vary according to the defensive call or scheme; they can be responsible for the *A gaps* (the space between the center and guards) or the *B gaps* (the space between the guards and tackles), as shown in Figure 9-3.

Figure 9-3:
The defen-
sive tackles
(DT) line up
inside the
defensive
ends (DE).

© John Wiley and Sons, Inc.

Defensive tackles do a great deal of *stunting*, or executing specific maneuvers that disrupt offensive blocking schemes. They also adjust their alignments to the inside or outside shoulders of the offensive guards based on where they anticipate the play is headed. Often, they shift to a particular position across from the offensive linemen when the game unfolds and they discover a particular weakness to an offensive lineman's left or right side.

✔ **Defensive ends:** The two defensive linemen who line up opposite the offensive tackles or on those players' outside shoulders. Where the defensive ends line up varies according to the defensive call or scheme. For example, in a *4-3 defense,* the defensive ends align wide because they have two defensive tackles to the inside of them (refer to Figure 9-3). In a *3-4 defense,* the defensive ends align tighter, or closer to the center of the line, because they have only a nose tackle between them, as shown in Figure 9-4. To find out more about 3-4 or 4-3 defenses, turn to Chapter 11.

Figure 9-4:
The defen-
sive ends
(DE) in a 3-4
defense.

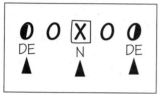

© John Wiley and Sons, Inc.

The defensive ends are responsible for chasing the quarterback out of the pocket and trying to sack him. These players are usually smaller than nose tackles and defensive tackles in weight (that is, if you consider 270 pounds small), and they're generally the fastest of the defensive linemen. The left defensive end is usually a little stronger against the run, a better tackler, and maybe not as quick to rush the quarterback. He's generally tougher for an offensive lineman to move off the line of scrimmage. The right defensive end (who's usually on the blind side of the quarterback) is the better pass-rusher. On a few teams, these ends flip sides when facing a left-handed quarterback, making the left defensive end the better pass-rusher.

Understanding what makes a good defensive lineman

Great defensive linemen, like J. J. Watt of the Houston Texans, are very rare players. Their combination of size, speed, strength, and durability isn't found in many players. A good defensive lineman has the majority of these qualities:

- **Size:** A defensive lineman needs to be 260 pounds or bigger.

- **Durability:** Defensive linemen must be able to withstand the punishment of being hit or blocked on every play. Because they play 16 or more games a season, with about 70 plays per game, defensive linemen are hit or blocked about 1,000 times a season.

- **Quickness:** Speed is relative, but quickness is vital. A lineman's first two steps after the ball is snapped should be like those of a sprinter breaking from the starting blocks. Quickness enables a defensive lineman to react and get in the proper position before being blocked. I call this "quickness in a phone booth." A defensive lineman may not be fast over 40 yards, but in that phone booth (5 yards in any direction), he's a cat!

✔ **Arm and hand strength:** Linemen win most of their battles when they ward off and shed blockers. Brute strength helps, but the true skill comes from a player's hands and arms. Keeping separation between yourself and those big offensive linemen is the key not only to survival but also to success. Using your hands and arms to maintain separation cuts down on neck injuries and enables you to throw an offensive lineman out of your way to make a tackle.

✔ **Vision:** Defensive linemen need to be able to see above and around the offensive linemen. They also need to use their heads as tools to ward off offensive linemen attempting to block them. A defensive lineman initially uses his head to absorb the impact and stop the momentum of his opponent. Then, using his hands, he forces separation. But before the ball is snapped and before impact, the opponents' backfield formation usually tells him what direction the upcoming play is going in. Anticipating the direction of the play may lessen the impact that his head takes after the ball is snapped.

✔ **Instincts:** Defensive linemen need to know the situation, down, and distance to a first down or a score. And they must be able to know and read the stances of all the offensive linemen they may be playing against. In an effort to move those big bodies where they need to go a little more quickly, offensive linemen often cheat in their stances more than any position in all of football. By doing so, they telegraph their intentions. Defensive linemen must assess these signs prior to the snap in order to give themselves an edge.

For example, if an offensive lineman is leaning forward in his stance, the play is probably going to be a run. The offensive lineman's weight is forward so that he can quickly shove his weight advantage into his opponent and clear the way for the ball carrier. If the offensive lineman is leaning backward in his stance (weight on his heels, buttocks lower to the ground, head up a bit more), the play is usually going to be a pass; or he may be preparing to *pull* (run to either side rather than straight forward).

Delving into D-line lingo

Every football team has its own vocabulary for referring to different positions. For example, some teams give male names to all the defenders who line up to the offense's *tight end side* — they call these defenders Sam, Bart, Otto, and so on. The defenders who align on the *open end side* (away from the tight end) are occasionally — but not always — given female names like Liz, Terri, and Wanda.

Here are some of the most common terms that teams use to refer to defensive linemen and their alignments:

✔ **Under tackle:** A defensive tackle who lines up outside the offensive guard to the split end side, as shown in Figure 9-5. The entire defensive line aligns under (or inside) the tight end to the split end side. Some of the NFL's best players are positioned as the under tackle. They possess strength and exceptional quickness off the ball, but they aren't powerful players.

✔ **Open end:** A defensive end who lines up to the split end or open end side of the formation — away from the tight end side, as shown in Figure 9-6. (If the offensive formation has two tight ends, there's no open side and therefore no open end.) Coaches generally put their best pass-rusher at the open end position for two reasons: He has the athletic ability to match up with the offensive tackle, and if he's positioned wide enough, a running back may be forced to attempt to block him, which would be a mismatch. Philadelphia Eagles end Trent Cole, who had 8 sacks in 2013, typifies the all-around open end.

Figure 9-5:
The under tackle (UT) lines up outside an offensive guard.

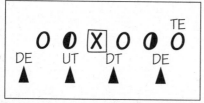

© John Wiley and Sons, Inc.

Figure 9-6:
The open end (OE) goes head-to-head with an offensive tackle or a running back.

© John Wiley and Sons, Inc.

✔ **Elephant end:** The elephant end lines up on the tight end side of the offense, as shown in Figure 9-7, and then attempts to disrupt the tight end's *release* (his desire to escape the line of scrimmage and run down the field) on each play. This position was made famous by the San Francisco 49ers and was suited to the specific skills of Charles Haley, the only player to have earned five Super Bowl rings. Haley was ideal for the position because he was a great pass-rusher as well as strong, like an elephant, which enabled him to hold his position against the run. This position gives the defense an advantage because the tight end generally has trouble blocking this talented defensive end.

✔ **Pass-rushing end:** A player on the defense who has superior skills at combating offensive linemen and pressuring the quarterback. These ends can line up on either side of the defensive line. A pass-rushing end, like the Buffalo Bills' Mario Williams, has the job of getting the best possible pass-rush, although he reacts to the run if a pass play doesn't develop. If the quarterback is in a *shotgun formation* (see Chapter 5), the pass-rushing end must focus on where he expects the quarterback to be when he attempts to throw his pass.

Figure 9-7:
The elephant
end (EE)
is the tight
end's great-
est foe.

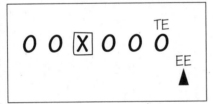

© John Wiley and Sons, Inc.

Unlocking the keys to a defensive lineman

A *key* is what a defensive player looks at prior to the snap of the ball. For example, if it's first-and-5, odds are that the offense will attempt to run the ball. The defensive lineman must *key* (watch) the offensive lineman and be prepared to react to his movements.

Here's a quick rundown of a defensive lineman's thought process prior to any play:

✔ **Alignment:** The defensive lineman has to make sure he's aligned correctly.

✔ **Stance:** The stance he's using should be to his advantage.

- ✔ **Assignment:** Does he know exactly what to do?

- ✔ **Key:** The lineman considers what/whom he should be looking at.

- ✔ **Get off:** He has to be quick off the football.

- ✔ **Attack:** The lineman thinks about attacking and controlling the offensive lineman with his hands, and then escaping by using his arms and shoulder to push by him.

- ✔ **Execute:** The lineman wants to execute his stunt to a specific area or gap and then react to where the ball is.

- ✔ **Pursue:** He always follows the football.

- ✔ **Tackle:** Finally, he can make the tackle.

And you thought tackling was the only chore of a defensive lineman! Now you know that they have many responsibilities (some of them thankless tasks), and they really have to be thinking to put themselves in a position to make a tackle.

Linebackers: The Leaders of the Defense

By the design of the defense, linebackers are the leaders of that 11-man squad. They're the defensive quarterbacks and coaches on the field, beginning every play by giving the defensive call. They set the standard for every defense by being able to get to the ball before anyone else. They're usually emotional leaders who excel in leading by example. If they play hard, their winning attitude carries over to the rest of the defense.

Although a linebacker's main intention is to tackle the offensive player with the ball, the term *linebacker* has become one of the most complicated terms in football. Linebackers have become football hybrids due to their wide variety of responsibilities and enormous talent.

Football is in an age of specialization, and linebackers are used a great deal because they're superior athletes who can learn a variety of skills and techniques. Some of them are suited to combat specific pass or run plays that the coaches believe the opposing offense plans to use. For that reason, coaches make defensive adjustments mainly by putting their linebackers in unusual alignments, making it difficult for the opposing quarterback and offensive players to keep track of the linebackers. Sometimes in a game, three linebackers leave the field and are replaced by two defensive backs and one linebacker who excels in pass defense. The roles are constantly changing as defenses attempt to cope with the varied abilities of a team's offense.

Because linebackers play so many different roles, they come in all sizes, from 215 pounds to 270 pounds. Some are extremely fast and capable of sticking with a running back. Others are very stout and strong and are known for clogging the middle of a team's offensive plans. Still others are tall and quick and extremely good pass-rushers. Regardless of skill or size differences, all linebackers have a few key characteristics in common: They have good instincts, are smart on their feet, can react immediately when the offense snaps the ball, and dominate each individual opponent they face.

The following sections offer insight into just what it is linebackers do, how they get those jobs done, and what kinds of linebackers you may see.

Figuring out what linebackers do

The job description of all linebackers is pretty lengthy: They must defend the run and also pressure the quarterback. (Vacating their assigned areas to go after the quarterback is called *blitzing.*) They must execute stunts and defend against the pass in a zone or in what are paradoxically known as *short-deep areas* on their side of the line of scrimmage. Also, the middle linebacker generally makes the defensive calls (he informs his teammates of what coverages and alignments they should be in) when the offense breaks its huddle.

Linebackers also are often responsible on pass defense to watch and stay with the tight end and backs. In other pass defense coverages, a linebacker may be responsible for staying with a speedy wide receiver in what's known as *man-to-man coverage* (more on this in Chapter 10).

To fully understand linebacker play, you need to be aware that every linebacker wants to coordinate his responsibilities with those of the defensive line. A linebacker is responsible for at least one of the *gaps* — the lettered open spaces or areas between the offensive linemen — in addition to being asked to ultimately make the tackle.

Every team wants its linebackers to be the leading tacklers on the team. It doesn't want its players in the *secondary,* the last line of the defense (see Chapter 10), to end up as the top tacklers, because that means the other team's running backs have consistently broken through the line.

 To keep your sanity when watching a game, just try to remember which players are the linebackers and that the bulk of their job is to do what Patrick Willis of the San Francisco 49ers (shown in Figure 9-8) does: make tackles from sideline to sideline and constantly pursue the ball carrier.

Figure 9-8:
Linebackers
like all-pro
Patrick
Willis of
the San
Francisco
49ers guard
against the
run and the
pass.

Photo credit: © Michael Zagaris/Getty Images

Dealing with the senses

Linebackers must take full advantage of what they can see, feel, and do. Every drill they do in practice, which carries over to the game, is based on these things:

- ✔ **Eyes:** Linebackers must train their eyes to see as much as possible. They must always focus on their target prior to the snap of the ball and then mentally visualize what may occur after the snap.

- ✔ **Feet:** Everything linebackers do involves their ability to move their feet. Making initial reads of what the offense is going to do, attempting to block offensive linemen and defeat them, and tackling the ball carrier are all directly related to proper foot movement.

- ✔ **Hands:** A linebacker's hands are his most valuable weapons. They also protect him by enabling him to ward off blockers and control the offensive linemen. A linebacker uses his hands to make tackles, recover fumbles, and knock down and intercept passes.

Naming all the linebackers

The following definitions can help you dissect the complex world of the line-backer:

- ✔ **True linebacker:** Linebackers who line up in the conventional linebacker position — behind the defensive linemen — are true linebackers. They align themselves according to the defensive call. Their *depth* (or distance) from the line of scrimmage varies, but it's usually 4 yards.

- ✔ **Sam linebacker:** A linebacker who lines up directly across from the tight end (the strong side of the formation) and keys the tight end's movements, as shown in Figure 9-9. His responsibility is to disrupt the tight end's release off the line of scrimmage when he's attempting to run out for a pass. The linebacker must then react accordingly. Depending on the defensive call, he either rushes the passer or moves away from the line of scrimmage and settles (called a *pass drop*) into a specified area to defend potential passes thrown his way. The ideal Sam linebacker is tall, preferably 6 feet 4 inches or taller, which enables him to see over the tight end. (Tight ends also tend to be tall.)

Figure 9-9:
The Sam linebacker disrupts the tight end during the play.

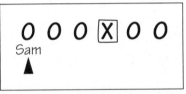

© John Wiley and Sons, Inc.

When he played with the New York Giants in the 1980s, Carl Banks was a perfect fit for the Sam linebacker position. He had long arms and viselike hands, giving him the ability to control the tight end or *shed* him (push him away) if he needed to run to a specific side. The Sam linebacker needs to immobilize the tight end as well as have the athletic ability to pursue any ball carrier.

- ✔ **Willy linebacker:** The macho term for a *weak-side linebacker* (see Figure 9-10), the Willy linebacker has the most varied assignments of any line-backer: He rushes the passer or drops into coverage, depending on the defensive call. He tends to be smaller, nimbler, and faster than most other linebackers.

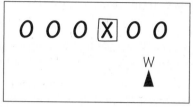

Figure 9-10:
The Willy linebacker (W) covers the weak side.

© John Wiley and Sons, Inc.

✔ **Mike linebacker:** This is the glory position of the linebacker corps. Every defensive player — from boys playing pickup games on the sandlot to men playing in the NFL — wants to play this position. The Mike linebacker is also known as the *middle linebacker* in 4-3 defenses (which I explain in Chapter 11). He lines up in the middle, generally directly opposite the offense's center and off him 3 to 4 yards, as shown in Figure 9-11. His job is to make tackles and control the defense with his calls and directions. He keys the running backs and the quarterback because he's in the middle of the defense and wants to go where the ball goes.

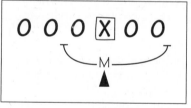

Figure 9-11:
The Mike linebacker (M) lines up across and back from the center.

© John Wiley and Sons, Inc.

Defensive Alignments

To better understand the inner workings of defensive football, you need to know how a defense lines up. Most defenses line up according to where the tight end on offense lines up. A defensive player, generally a linebacker, yells "left" or "right," and the remaining players react and align themselves. Alignments are critical to a defense's success. If the defense isn't in the proper alignment, the players put themselves at a great disadvantage prior to the snap of the ball.

Here are some helpful explanations of terms used to describe defensive players and their alignments:

✔ **On or over a player:** The defensive player is directly across from the offensive player and no more than a yard apart — virtually helmet to helmet.

✔ **Inside a player:** The defensive player lines up with his right shoulder across from the offensive player's right shoulder. The defensive player's right shoulder can be directly across from the offensive player's helmet.

✔ **Wide of a player:** The defensive player is facing forward, and his entire upper body is outside the nearest shoulder of an offensive player. When the center snaps the ball, the defensive player wants a clear path forward so he can use his quickness to beat the offensive blocker off the line of scrimmage.

✔ **Over defense:** In this defensive alignment, four members of the defensive team shift position in order to put themselves directly opposite each player aligned on the strong side (tight end side) of the offensive formation.

✔ **Under defense:** This is exactly the opposite of the over shift. This time, three defensive players line up directly across from the center, guard, and tackle on the weak side (non–tight end side) of the offensive formation, leaving only a defensive end opposite the offensive tackle on the strong side of the formation.

The *open end side,* or weak side, is opposite the tight end, where the split end lines up on offense. Most defenses design their schemes either to the tight end or to the open end side of the field. When linebackers and defensive linemen line up, they do so as a group. For example, they align *over* to the tight end or maybe *under* to the open end.

Sacks, Tackles, and Other Defensive Gems

Defensive players work all game hoping to collect a tangible reward: a sack. Former Los Angeles Rams defensive end Deacon Jones coined the term *sack* in the 1960s when referring to tackling the quarterback for a loss behind the line of scrimmage. (The name comes from hunting: When hunters go into the field planning to shoot a quail or pheasant, they place their trophies in a gunnysack.) Unfortunately for Jones, who had as many as 30 sacks in some of his 14 seasons, the NFL didn't begin to officially record this defensive statistic until the 1982 season. Consequently, Jones doesn't appear on the all-time sack leader list, which is headed by Bruce Smith with 200.

When two defensive players tackle the quarterback behind the line of scrimmage, they must share the sack. Each player is credited with half a sack; that's how valuable the statistic has become. In fact, many NFL players have performance clauses in their contracts regarding the number of sacks they collect, and they receive bonuses for achieving a certain number of sacks.

Unfortunately, in the quest to rack up sacks, defensive players can get penalized for roughing the passer if they're not careful. The NFL has placed special emphasis on protecting quarterbacks from late hits and unnecessary roughness. Defensive players can no longer strike the quarterback in the head or neck area, even with an incidental, glancing blow. Nor can they tackle quarterbacks at the knee or lower. They must also avoid driving the quarterback into the ground when tackling. The bottom line is you can't hit 'em high, you can't hit 'em low, and you can't hit 'em hard. That makes a pass rusher's job pretty tough.

Alan Page, Hall of Famer and defensive end of the Minnesota Vikings, was so quick that opposing quarterbacks often rushed their throws in anticipation of being tackled. Some quarterbacks would rather risk throwing an incompletion — or an interception — than be sacked. Page's coach, Bud Grant, called this action a *hurry*. The term remains popular in football, and pressuring the quarterback remains the number-one motive of defensive linemen on pass plays.

The term *tackling* has been around for more than 100 years. A player is credited with a *tackle* when he single-handedly brings down an offensive player who has possession of the ball. Tackles, like sacks, can be shared. A shared tackle is called an *assist*. Many teams award an assist whenever a defensive player effectively joins in on a tackle. For example, some offensive players have the strength to drag the first player who tries to tackle them. When that occurs, the second defensive player who joins the play, helping to bring down the ball carrier, is credited with an assist.

You may have heard the term *stringing out a play*. Defenders are coached to force the ball carrier toward the sideline after they cut off the ball carrier's upfield momentum. Consequently, the sideline may be the best "tackler" in the game.

A lineman who preferred keyboards to QBs

Mike Reid was raised in Altoona, Pennsylvania — about the craziest high school football town in the country. Reid became an all-state defensive lineman and a punishing fullback. Before football, his mother made him take piano lessons. So when Penn State offered him a football scholarship, he accepted and majored in classical music.

Reid was a demon on the football field. In 1969, he won the Outland Trophy, emblematic of the best lineman in college football. The next April, he was the first-round draft choice of the Cincinnati Bengals. He enjoyed football, but music remained his passion. He taped his fingers before every game, hoping to prevent them from being broken so that he could play the piano on Monday afternoons. After playing five pro seasons and twice being named to all-pro teams, Reid quit the Bengals in 1975 to join a little-known rock band. Five years later, he moved to Nashville, Tennessee, and began writing country western songs.

Reid has since written such hits as "There You Are" for Willie Nelson and "I Can't Make You Love Me" for Bonnie Raitt. He has won three Grammys and even wrote an opera about football, titled *Different Fields*.

Chapter 10

The Secondary: Last Line of Defense

In This Chapter

▶ Meeting the secondary's members: Cornerbacks, safeties, and nickel and dime backs

▶ Getting to know the tricks of the secondary trade

▶ Recognizing the difference between zone and man-to-man coverages

▶ Understanding the eight men in a box and Nickel 40 coverage variations

The *secondary* is the name given to the group of players who make up the defensive backfield. The basic *defensive backfield* consists of four position players: a right cornerback, a left cornerback, a strong safety, and a free safety. The secondary is the final line of defense, right after the defensive line and the linebackers (head to Chapter 9 for details on these defenders). The players who make up the secondary are known collectively as *defensive backs*, or *DBs*. Basically, their job is to tackle runners who get past the defensive line and the linebackers and to defend — and hopefully break up — pass plays.

Depending on the defensive scheme the coaching staff employs, the secondary can consist of anywhere from three to seven defensive backs on the field at the same time. (In rare instances, I've even seen eight defensive backs on the field at once.) However, most conventional defensive alignments use four defensive backs: two cornerbacks and two safeties. If all of this sounds confusing, never fear — this chapter is here to help you understand how and why a secondary acts in a particular way.

Be aware that a majority of big offensive plays (gains of 25 yards or more) and touchdowns come from the offense's ability to execute the passing game. Therefore, on the defensive side of the ball, a great deal of attention on television is devoted to the secondary. Often, a defensive back is in proper position or has good coverage technique, but the offensive receiver still catches the pass. Other times, the secondary player is out of position, failing to execute his assignment, or is physically beaten by a better athlete. If you know the difference and what to look for, you'll be regarded as an expert.

Presenting the Performers

All the players who make up the secondary are called defensive backs, but that category is further divided into the following positions: cornerbacks, safeties, and nickel and dime backs. In a nutshell, these players are responsible for preventing the opponent's receivers from catching the ball. If they fail, they must then make the tackle, preventing a possible touchdown. The different players work in slightly different ways, as you find out in the following sections.

Cornerbacks

The *cornerback* is typically the fastest of the defensive backs. For example, Deion Sanders, who played on Super Bowl championship teams in the 1990s with the San Francisco 49ers and the Dallas Cowboys, had Olympic-caliber speed and the explosive burst necessary for this position. The *burst* is when a secondary player *breaks* (or reacts) to the ball and the receiver, hoping to disrupt the play.

The ideal NFL cornerback can run the 40-yard dash in 4.4 seconds, weighs between 180 and 190 pounds, and is at least 6 feet tall. However, the average NFL cornerback is about 5 feet 10 inches tall. Although speed and agility remain the necessary commodities, height is becoming a factor in order to defend the ever-increasing height of today's wide receivers. How many times have you seen a great little cornerback like Antoine Winfield, who's 5 feet 9 inches, put himself in perfect position simply to be out-jumped for the ball by a much taller receiver with longer arms?

The ultimate thrill for a cornerback is the direct challenge he faces on virtually every play, but this is especially true on passing downs. A defensive lineman can win 70 percent of his battle against an offensive lineman and leave the field feeling relieved. However, the same odds don't necessarily apply to a cornerback. He can't afford to lose many challenges because he's exposed one-on-one with a receiver. If his man catches the ball, everyone in the stadium or watching on television can see. And if he's beaten three out of ten times for gains over 25 yards, he may be in the unemployment line or find himself demoted come Monday. Cornerback is a job that accepts no excuses for poor performance. The next sections describe the cornerback's role in two specific types of coverage.

Cornerbacks in man-to-man coverage

Most defensive schemes employ two cornerbacks (CB) in man-to-man coverage (which I explain further in the later "Man-to-man coverage" section) against the offense's wide receivers (WR), as shown in Figure 10-1. The cornerbacks align on the far left and right sides of the line of scrimmage, at least 10 to 12 yards from their nearest teammate (usually a linebacker or defensive end) and opposite the offense's wide receivers. The distance varies depending on where the offensive receivers align themselves. Cornerbacks must align in front of them.

Figure 10-1: The two CBs generally line up on the far left and right sides of the line of scrimmage.

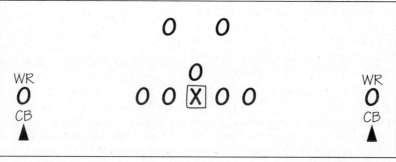

© John Wiley and Sons, Inc.

Most teams attempt to place their best cornerbacks against the opposition's best receivers. Coaches generally know who these players are and design their defenses accordingly. Often, they simply need to flop cornerbacks from one side to the other. Some offensive formations place a team's two best receivers on the same side of the field, requiring the defense to place both of its cornerbacks accordingly, as in Figure 10-2.

Figure 10-2: Placing two top WRs on the same side of the field forces the defense to place both CBs on that side.

© John Wiley and Sons, Inc.

HOWIE SAYS

An outstanding cornerback pair

To win in the NFL today, a team needs to have a good pair of cornerbacks. When I played for the Raiders, we had an excellent pair: Mike Haynes, who was inducted into the Pro Football Hall of Fame in 1997, and Lester Hayes, who may still be inducted. When you have two great players like Haynes and Hayes — guys who can cover the best receivers one-on-one without surrendering any long gains — your front seven defensive players (some combination of linemen and linebackers) are all the more effective.

Cornerbacks are a special breed of athlete. They must be both physically gifted and mentally strong. Haynes was an effortless player, with a fluid stride and graceful movements. And *graceful* isn't a term that's generally associated with football players. Sometimes an opposing coach — the type who likes to take a hit on 17 when playing blackjack — would decide to test him and throw the ball his way, but rarely with

any success. More often than not, when you throw toward a great cornerback, your play doesn't succeed. And in the worst-case scenario, the corner intercepts the ball and returns it for a touchdown. Haynes never talked much on or off the field, but he was deadly as a player.

Hayes was just the opposite. He enjoyed talking to newspaper and television reporters and seemed to have an opinion on most subjects. He loved talking on the field, too. He also believed in putting tacky goo on his hands and uniform. We called it "stickum." Stickum was so sticky that it was like having a Velcro glove or playing with a Velcro ball. Hayes covered himself with the stuff. When a pass would come his way, it generally would stick to his body, and then he would grab hold of it. In 1980, Hayes had 13 interceptions, the second-best total in NFL history. Soon after, the NFL outlawed stickum, claiming that it gave players an unfair advantage.

Cornerbacks in zone coverage

Cornerbacks are also used in zone coverage (which I fill you in on in the later "Zone coverage" section). If a team's cornerbacks are smaller and slower than its opponent's receivers, that team usually plays more zone coverages, fearing that fast receivers will expose its secondary's athletic weaknesses. However, if you have two talented cornerbacks, like the Cincinnati Bengals had in the 2010 season with Leon Hall and Johnathan Joseph, your team can play more man-to-man coverage.

Safeties

Most defenses employ two safeties — a strong safety and a free safety. Safeties often are called the defense's quarterbacks, or the quarterbacks of the secondary. They must see and recognize the offense's formations and instruct their teammates to make whatever coverage adjustments are necessary. These instructions are different from what the middle linebacker (whom I describe in Chapter 9) tells his teammates.

For example, the middle linebacker focuses more on his fellow linebackers and the alignment of the defensive linemen. Also, he's generally too far away from the defensive backs to yell to them. The safeties must coordinate their pass coverages after finding out what assistance the linebackers may offer in specific situations. They often have to use hand signals to convey their instructions in a noisy stadium.

Strong safety

Of the two types of safeties, the *strong safety* is generally bigger, stronger, and slower.

Coaches often refer to (and judge) their safeties as small linebackers. These players should be above-average tacklers and should have the ability to backpedal and quickly retreat in order to cover a specified area to defend the pass (which is called *dropping into pass coverage*). The strong safety normally aligns to the tight end side of the offensive formation (also known as the *strong side,* hence the name *strong safety*), and 99 percent of the time, his pass coverage responsibility is either the tight end or a running back who leaves the backfield.

Good strong safeties like Polamalu are superior against the run offense. Many strong safeties are merely adequate in pass coverage and below average when playing man-to-man pass defense. When you hear a television analyst inform viewers that the strong safety "did a great job of run support," he means that the strong safety read his key (the tight end) and quickly determined that the play was a run rather than a pass. (Chapter 8 has more information on keys.)

The sole reason strong safeties are more involved with the run defense is because they line up closer to the line of scrimmage. Coaches believe that strong safeties can defend the run while also having the necessary speed and size to defend the tight end when he runs out on a pass pattern.

Free safety

The *free safety* (FS) is generally more athletic and less physical than the strong safety. He usually positions himself 12 to 15 yards deep and off the line of scrimmage, as shown in Figure 10-3. He serves the defense like a center fielder does a baseball team: He should have the speed to prevent the inside-the-park home run, which in football terms is the long touchdown pass. He also must have the speed and quickness to get a jump on any long pass that's thrown in the gaps on the field. Ed Reed of the Baltimore Ravens is a quality free safety.

I would be remiss if I didn't talk about Ronnie Lott, a Hall of Fame safety. What made Lott so special was that he could play either safety position. And he was so fast that he began his career as a cornerback. Never has a more intuitive player played in the secondary than Lott, who always seemed to know where the pass was headed.

Figure 10-3: The FS lines up deep and off the line of scrimmage, hoping to prevent the long pass.

Being the final line of the defense against the long pass, the free safety must be capable of making instant and astute judgments. Some people say that an excellent free safety can read the quarterback's eyes, meaning he knows where the quarterback is looking to throw the football. The free safety is the only defensive back who's coached to watch the quarterback as his key. The quarterback directs him to where the ball is going.

A free safety must also be able to cover a wide receiver in man-to-man coverage, because many offenses today employ three wide receivers more than half the time. (The first two are covered by the cornerbacks.)

Nickel and dime backs

Some experts try to equate learning the nickel and dime defensive schemes with learning to speak Japanese. Not so! All it's about is making change. When defensive coaches believe that the offense plans to throw the football, they replace bigger and slower linebackers with defensive backs. By substituting defensive backs for linebackers, defensive coaches ensure that faster players — who are more capable of running with receivers and making an interception — are on the field.

The fifth defensive back to enter the game is called the *nickel back,* and the sixth defensive back to enter is termed the *dime back.* The *nickel* term is easy to explain — five players equal five cents. The dime back position received its name because, in essence, two nickel backs are on the field at once. And, as you well know, two nickels equal a dime. However, each team has its own vernacular for the nickel and dime back positions. For example, the Raiders used to refer to their nickel back as the *pirate*. Regardless of the name, these players are generally the second-string cornerbacks. In other words, no team has a designated nickel back or dime back job.

The one downside of using a defensive scheme that includes nickel and dime backs is that you weaken your defense against the running game. For instance, many modern offenses opt to run the ball in what appear to be obvious passing situations because they believe that their powerful running backs have a size and strength advantage over the smaller defensive backs after the ball carrier breaks the line of scrimmage. Although defensive backs should be good tacklers, the prerequisite for the position is being able to defend pass receivers and tackle players who are more your size.

Substituting nickel and dime backs is part of a constant chess game played by opposing coaching staffs. Defensive coaches believe they've prepared for the occasional run and that these extra defensive backs give the defense more blitzing and coverage flexibility.

Figure 10-4 shows a common nickel/dime alignment that has a good success rate against the pass, especially when offenses are stuck in third-and-20 situations. This alignment enables teams to use many different defensive looks, which help to confuse the quarterback. But this scheme is poor against the run, so the defense has to remain alert to the possibility that the offense will fake a pass and run the ball instead.

Figure 10-4: A common nickel/dime alignment that works well against the pass.

© John Wiley and Sons, Inc.

Studying Secondary Tricks and Techniques

Being a defensive back is pretty scary. Often, the entire weight of the game is on your shoulders. One misstep in pass coverage or one missed tackle can lead to a touchdown. Also, a defensive back may be the only player between the ball carrier and the end zone. So this means that the defensive back has to be a good, smart tackler rather than an aggressive one.

When defensive backs line up, they rarely know whether the play will be a pass or a run. In a split second after the ball is snapped, they must determine the offense's intentions and, if it's a pass play, turn and run with one of the fastest players (the wide receiver) on the field. In the following sections, I introduce you to some of the tricks of their trade.

Doing a bump and run

The meaning of the term *bump and run* has been altered through the years. Thirty years ago, a cornerback could bump a receiver and then bump him again. Many cornerbacks held on for dear life, fearful the receiver would escape and catch a touchdown pass. Mel Blount, a Hall of Fame cornerback with the champion Pittsburgh Steelers of the 1970s, may have had the strongest hands of any defensive back. When he grabbed a receiver, even with one hand, the man could go nowhere; Blount would ride him out of the play. By *ride* I mean Blount (or any strong defensive back) could push the receiver away from his intended pass route. Most defensive backs tend to ride their receivers, if they can, toward the sidelines.

Blount perfected his hands-on technique so well that in 1978, the NFL's Competition Committee (coaches, owners, and general managers who are appointed to study and make rule changes) rewrote the chuck rule, or what's known as the *bump* in bump and run. Consequently, defensive backs are still allowed to hit receivers within 5 yards of the line of scrimmage, but beyond that, hitting a receiver is a penalty. The penalty for this illegal use of the hands gives the offense an automatic first down and 5 free yards (turn to Chapter 3 for the full scoop on penalties).

Today, you may see defensive backs with their hands on receivers beyond 5 yards. Sometimes the officials catch them, and sometimes they don't. The intent remains the same: Defensive backs want to get in the faces of the receivers and chuck them or jam them (using both hands) as they come off the line of scrimmage. The idea is to disrupt the timing of the pass play by hitting the receiver in the chest with both hands, thereby forcing the receiver to take a bad step. Often, the defensive back pushes the receiver in order to redirect him. A defensive back generally knows which way a receiver wants to go. By bumping him to one side, the defensive back may force the receiver to alter his pass route.

Staying with a receiver

After bumping or attempting to jam a receiver, a defensive back must be able to turn and run with the receiver. Sometimes, the defensive back (especially a cornerback) ends up chasing the receiver. When he needs to turn, the defensive back should make half-turns, rotating his upper body to the same side as the receiver. When the receiver turns to face the ball in the air, the defensive player should turn his body to the side of the receiver to which his arms are extended.

A defensive back must practice his footwork so he can take long strides when backpedaling away from the line of scrimmage while covering a receiver. When he turns, he should be able to take a long crossover step with his feet while keeping his upper body erect. This technique is difficult because the defensive back often has to move backward as quickly as the receiver runs forward. When he turns to meet the receiver and the pass, the defensive back should be running as fast as he can to maintain close contact with the receiver.

Stemming around

The term *stemming around* sounds foolish, and, in all honesty, defensive backs may look foolish while they're stemming around. Well, at least they're not standing around. Anyway, *stemming* describes the action of the defensive backs when they move around after appearing to be settled in their alignments prior to the offense's snap of the ball. By stemming, they attempt to fool the quarterback and force him into making a bad decision about where to throw the football. This tactic is becoming quite popular in defensive football (all players can do it, but it's most noticeable in defensive backs and linebackers) because it creates an uncertainty in the quarterback's mind, thus disrupting his decision making.

The most successful stemming ploy by the secondary is to give the quarterback the impression that they're playing man-to-man coverage when they're really playing zone coverage. This ploy usually results in a *poor read* (an inaccurate interpretation of the defense) by the quarterback. A poor read can lead to a deflected pass, an incomplete pass, or an interception — the secondary's ultimate goal.

Making a Mark: A Good Day in the Life of a Defensive Back

Quarterbacks and receivers tend to pick on defensive backs. Former Miami Dolphins quarterback Dan Marino passed them silly, and receivers like Andre Johnson and Larry Fitzgerald simply push them aside with their size and strength. The only way a defensive back can retaliate is to make a play.

This list shows some of the positive plays a defensive back can use to make his mark. The first three plays are reflected on the statistical sheet after the game; the rest just go into the receiver's or quarterback's memory bank. Of course, all tackles are recorded, but the ones I list here have a unique style of their own.

- ✔ **Interception:** The ultimate prize is an *interception,* which is when a defensive back picks off a pass intended for a receiver. An even bigger thrill is returning the catch for a defensive touchdown, which is called a *pick-six* (*pick* because the pass was picked off, and *six* because returning the catch for a touchdown scores six points).

- ✔ **Pass defensed:** *Pass defensed* is a statistic that a defensive back achieves every time he deflects a pass or knocks the ball out of a receiver's hands. You can also say that the defensive back *broke up a pass.* A pass defensed means an incompletion for the quarterback.

- ✔ **Forced fumble:** A *forced fumble* is when a defensive back forces the ball away from a receiver after he gains possession of the ball. Defensive backs have been known to use both hands to pull the ball away from the receiver's grasp. This play is also known as *stripping the ball.* Any defensive player can force a fumble, and forced fumbles can happen on running plays, too.

- ✔ **Knockout tackle:** The *knockout tackle* is the ultimate tackle because it puts a wide receiver down for the count. Every safety in the league wants a knockout tackle; it's a sign of intimidation. Defensive backs believe in protecting their (coverage) space and protecting it well. Cornerbacks want these hits, too, but many of them are satisfied with bringing an offensive player down any way they can.

- ✔ **Groundhog hit:** A *groundhog hit* is a perfectly timed tackle on a receiver who's leaping for the ball. Instead of aiming for the body, the defensive back goes for the feet, flipping the receiver headfirst into the ground.

The Problem of Pass Interference and Illegal Contact

When a receiver is running in a pass pattern and is more than five yards away from the line of scrimmage, a defensive player can't push, shove, hold, or otherwise impede the progress of the receiver. If he does any of those things before the quarterback throws the ball, he's called for either *defensive holding* or *illegal contact*. Both penalties result in five yards and an automatic first down for the offense.

When a pass is in the air, if a defensive player pushes, shoves, holds, or otherwise physically prevents an offensive receiver from moving his body or his arms in an attempt to catch the pass, he's called for *pass interference*. Except for being ejected from a game, pass interference is the worst penalty in professional football for any member of the defensive team. Why? Because the number of yards that the defense is penalized is determined by where the penalty (or foul) is committed. So when the officials call pass interference against a defensive player on a pass attempt that travels 50 yards beyond the line of scrimmage, the penalty is 50 yards. The offensive team is given the ball and a first down at that spot on the field. If a defensive player is *flagged* (penalized) in the end zone, the offensive team is given the ball on the 1-yard line with a first down. (The offense is never awarded a touchdown on a pass interference penalty.)

This penalty is a judgment call, and you often see players from both sides arguing for or against a pass interference penalty. Officials don't usually call pass interference when a defensive player, who also has a right to try to catch any ball, drives his body toward a pass, gets his hand or fingers on the ball, and then instantaneously makes physical contact with the receiver. The critical point is that the defensive player touched the ball a split second *before* colliding with the receiver. On these plays, the defensive back appears to be coming over the receiver's shoulder to knock down the pass. Often, you can't tell whether the official made the right call on these types of plays until you see them in a slow-motion replay on television. These plays (called *bang-bang plays*) occur very quickly on the field.

In recent years, the NFL has asked officials to pay special attention to defensive coverage of receivers. The result has been a tremendous increase in the number of holding, illegal contact, and pass interference penalties on the defense. Defensive players feel like they can't even breathe heavily on receivers without getting flagged. Any sort of incidental bumping or pushing now warrants a flag.

Defensive backs (safeties and cornerbacks) now can't afford to cover receivers tightly, so they have to give the receivers a bit of a cushion. This softer style has allowed offenses throughout the league to rack up huge passing numbers. Receivers are catching more passes and offenses are gaining more yards. If you like this style of football, the game is more exciting. But if you prefer low-scoring defensive struggles, you're not a happy fan.

Examining the Two Types of Coverage (And Their Variations)

Football teams employ two types of pass coverage: man-to-man coverage and zone coverage. Both coverages have many variations and combinations, but the core of every coverage begins with either the man-to-man concept or a zone concept. I get you familiar with the core coverages first, and then I show you some of the variations.

Man-to-man coverage

Simply stated, *man-to-man coverage* is when any defensive back, or maybe even a linebacker, is assigned to cover a specific offensive player, such as a running back, tight end, or wide receiver. The defender must *cover* (stay with) this player all over the field until the play ends. His responsibility is to make sure the receiver doesn't catch a pass. The most important rule of man-to-man coverage (which is also known as *man coverage*) is that the defensive back must keep his eyes on the player that he's guarding or is responsible for watching. He's allowed to take occasional peeks toward the quarterback, but he should never take his eyes off his man.

Here are the three main types of man-to-man coverage:

✔ **Man free:** In this coverage, all defensive backs play man-to-man coverage except the free safety, who lines up or drops into an area and becomes a safety valve to prevent a long touchdown completion. This style of coverage is used when the defense *blitzes,* or rushes four or five players at the quarterback. So, man free is man-to-man coverage with one roaming free safety. Linebackers also cover running backs or even tight ends man-to-man.

✔ **Straight man:** The free safety doesn't serve as a safety valve in this alignment — or, as coaches say, no safety help is available. Each defender must know that he (alone) is responsible for the receiver he's covering. The phrase "the player was stuck on an island" refers to a cornerback being isolated with an offensive receiver and having no chance of being rescued by another defensive back. This style of man-to-man coverage is generally used when the defense is blitzing or rushing a linebacker toward the backfield, hoping to sack the quarterback. Defenses use it depending on the strength and ability of their own personnel and the receiving talent of the offense they're facing. So, straight man is pure man-to-man coverage with no roaming free safety.

✔ **Combo man:** This category contains any number of combinations of man-to-man coverage. For example, when a team wants to double-team a great wide receiver (with two defensive backs), it runs a combo man defense. A great receiver is someone like Jerry Rice, who owns virtually every pass-receiving record in the history of pro football. The object of such a defense is to force the quarterback to throw the football to a less-talented receiver than someone like Rice (namely, anybody but him!).

In Figure 10-5, the cornerback (CB) is responsible for the star receiver's outside move, while the safety (S) is prepared in case the star receiver decides to run his route inside, or toward the middle of the field. A team's pass defense may be vulnerable on the side of the field opposite where it's double-teaming a receiver. Also, the pass defense may be vulnerable to a short pass on the same side of the field and underneath the double-team.

What's fun about man-to-man coverages, especially for players, are the endless personnel matchup possibilities that they provide. Also, against an excellent throwing quarterback like the Denver Broncos' Peyton Manning or the New Orleans Saints' Drew Brees, these combinations create something of a chess match between the quarterback and the defensive secondary.

Figure 10-5: Combo man coverage can prevent a talented receiver from making a big play.

Zone coverage

In *zone coverage,* the defensive backs and linebackers drop into areas on the field and protect those *zones* against any receivers who enter them. The biggest difference between zone coverage and man-to-man coverage is that in the latter coverage, a defender is concerned only about the player he's covering. In virtually all zone coverages, two defensive backs play deep (12 to 15 yards off the line of scrimmage) and align near the hash marks.

In a zone coverage, each defensive back is aware of the receivers in his area, but his major concentration is on the quarterback and reacting to the quarterback's arm motion and the ball in flight. Coaches employ zone coverage against teams that love to run the football because it allows them to better position themselves to defend the run. Other teams use zone coverage when the talent level of their secondary personnel is average and inferior to that of the offensive personnel they're facing.

For defensive backs, zone coverage is about sensing what the offense is attempting to accomplish against the defense. Also, in zone coverage, each defensive player reacts when the ball is in the air, whereas in man-to-man coverage, he simply plays the receiver.

The simplest way to recognize a zone defense is to observe how many defenders line up deep in the secondary. If two or more defensive players are aligned deep (12 to 15 yards off the line of scrimmage), the defense is in a zone.

Eight men in the box

I'm sure you've heard television commentators mention the term *eight men in the box.* They aren't talking about a sandbox, and they aren't discussing a new pass coverage. Instead, they're talking about a setup that enables a team to defend the run more effectively when it has a strong secondary.

The *box* is the imaginary area near the line of scrimmage where the defensive linemen and linebackers line up prior to the offense putting the ball into play. Usually, a team puts seven defenders, known as the *front seven,* in that box. But a team can put an eighth man — the strong safety (SS) — in the box, as shown in Figure 10-6, if it has two outstanding cornerbacks (CB) who can cover wide receivers (WR) man to man.

Figure 10-6: The defense puts an eighth man, the SS, in the box to improve its odds against six run blockers.

So how does a talented pair of cornerbacks drastically improve a team's defense against the run? By allowing the defense to play an extra (eighth) man in the box, where the defense has to deal with the runner. By placing eight defenders against six blockers — five offensive linemen and a tight end — the odds are pretty good that the running back will have trouble finding open territory. And when a team has talented cornerbacks who can defend the pass effectively, the defensive linemen and linebackers perform with the utmost confidence. They know that they can attack without worrying about their pass coverage responsibilities.

The Nickel 40 defense

By definition, the *Nickel 40 defense* is strictly a pass defense that can employ either a linebacker or another defensive back as the sixth player in pass coverage. It's a substituted defense (one that generally isn't used on every down) by skill and ability level. A defensive team wants to put its four best pass-rushers on the line of scrimmage, with one linebacker and six defensive backs.

The sixth, or dime back (DB), position can end up being a defensive back as well as a linebacker at times. In this alignment, the linebacker aligns in the middle about 5 yards away from the line of scrimmage (see Figure 10-7). He should be one of the team's fastest linebackers as well as a good tackler. Most teams use four defensive backs near the line of scrimmage with two safeties playing well off the ball, toward the middle of the field near the hash marks.

Figure 10-7: In the Nickel 40, the defense puts a sixth player (DB) in pass coverage.

The pressure of being a cornerback

A matchup between a great cornerback and a great receiver is as eagerly awaited as an Old West gunslinger's final duel. On January 7, 1990, the Los Angeles Rams and New York Giants were in overtime of a playoff game. With the ball on their own 30-yard line, the Giants had their defensive backs on the line of scrimmage (called *pressing*), hoping to prevent the Rams from moving into ideal field goal range.

Rams receiver Willie "Flipper" Anderson was lined up on the right side, and Giants cornerback Mark Collins had him one-on-one. If Anderson were to run past Collins, no safety would be available to help. Rams quarterback Jim Everett recognized the coverage and elected to try for the home-run play (a *bomb pass*) rather than a running play.

When the ball was snapped, Collins missed his bump or jam on Anderson. The game was now on the line. Everett floated a *rainbow* (a high-arching pass) down the right sideline toward Anderson, who had a 1-yard advantage on Collins. Near the goal line, Collins jumped, praying that he could deflect the pass. His fingertips missed the spiraling ball by 6 inches. Anderson caught the ball, the officials raised the touchdown signal, and the Rams won the playoff game. Anderson actually ran through the end zone, through the Giants Stadium tunnel, and into the locker room, the ball firmly in his grasp.

Afterward, Collins stood in his locker room aware of his failure, but his confidence wasn't shattered. "That's the life of a cornerback," Collins said. "You make ten good plays and one bad one, and all anyone wants to talk about is the bad. If you're going to play cornerback in this league, you've got to accept that this is your life."

The object of the Nickel 40 is to pressure the quarterback, hoping to either sack or harass him. Teams use their four best pass-rushers on the field in this alignment, and these four players will most likely be opposed by only five offensive linemen. Defenses use a Nickel 40 defense only when the offense uses three or more receivers in its alignment.

From this defensive look, the pass-rushers may stem or *stunt* (move about on the line of scrimmage), trying to apply pressure by using their best linemen against the offense's weakest blockers. Defenses also have been known to blitz the quarterback with one of the defensive backs or a linebacker in order to overwhelm the offensive blocking scheme. The defensive pass coverage in the secondary can be a mixture of man-to-man and zone alignments.

The Nickel 40 is a good defense against an offense that's fond of *play-action passes* (when the quarterback fakes a handoff to a running back, keeps the ball, and then attempts a pass; see Chapter 8 for more on these) or against an offense that likes to substitute a lot of receivers into the game. I'm talking about offenses that use formations that employ four wide receivers rather than the customary two wide receivers. The Nickel 40 defense, with faster personnel, can compensate and deal with an offense that prefers to always have a player in motion prior to the snap of the ball. It's also adept against other unusual formations.

Chapter 11

Delving into Defensive Tactics and Strategies

In This Chapter

▶ Discovering how coaches pick which defenses to use

▶ Familiarizing yourself with the 4-3 defense, the 3-4 defense, and other defenses

▶ Finding out what to do in the sticky situations

Coaches will tell you that defenses win championships, and I'm not being prejudiced when I say that I agree with that statement. When I was in the right defense, in the proper alignment, that was when I had the best chance to succeed. When you're in the right defense, it comes down to you beating the man in front of you. As an athlete, that's all you can ask for.

The defense's battle plans are exactly what this chapter is about. Every team enters a game with a basic strategy. This chapter explains the common strategies — the defense's alignment and look — and how the defense can be "offensive" by dictating the style of play in a game. In this chapter, I cover all the basic defenses and help you figure out which defensive package works best against which offense.

Choosing a Base Defense

NFL coaches love to copy one another, primarily when a coach is successful with a particular offense or defense. For example, a lot of winning teams in the 1970s began to use the 3-4 defense (which uses three down linemen and four linebackers) as their base, or primary, defense. The 3-4 was the defense of choice in the 1980s; only Dallas, Chicago, and Washington preferred a 4-3 scheme (four down linemen and three linebackers). By the time the 1990s came to a close, the 4-3 defense was back in vogue, thanks mostly to the success that Jimmy Johnson had with the Dallas Cowboys in the 1990s. In the

2014 season, a slight majority of NFL teams used some form of the 4-3 as their base defense.

Basically, what you need to understand is that the goals of any type of defense are to

- ✔ Stop the opposition and get the ball back for the offense.
- ✔ Seize possession of the ball via a turnover. A *turnover* occurs when the defense recovers a fumble or secures an interception.

To compete with sophisticated offenses, defenses have had to keep pace. In fact, some rules have changed simply to negate suffocating defenses. These rule changes have caused defensive coaches to return to the chalkboards and film rooms to devise more dastardly plans — and nowadays, they even use computers to uncover offensive tendencies.

Most defenses are named by their *fronts,* or the number of defensive linemen and linebackers who align in front of the defensive backs. The most common front is the *front seven:* four defensive linemen and three linebackers, or three defensive linemen and four linebackers. It's assumed in football parlance that a front seven also includes four defensive backs: 7 + 4 = 11 players on the field.

How I prepared to take on an opponent's offense

When I played for the Raiders in the 1980s, I brought computer printouts to the locker room to glance over on game days. Those computer sheets showed every formation the opposition planned to use against us (or so we thought).

When I went on the road, I carried my own VCR and brought tapes that Johnny Otten, the Raiders' film guy, put together for me. I had him put every run play the team used on one tape, called a *run cut-up,* and every pass play on another, called a *pass cut-up.* These cut-ups showed every play that the opposition ran from a two-back formation, from the I-formation, and from the one-back formation (I fill you in on these formations in Chapter 6).

We watched hours of film during the week, but on Saturday nights I watched a couple more hours on my own and broke down every formation. By studying and reviewing all the formations, I was prepared. For example, when the opposition's offense came to the line of scrimmage in a split-back formation, my mind immediately computed to "full left, 18 Bob Tray 0," a run play.

I know that jargon means nothing to you, but it tipped off my mind. I knew which play was coming, which is more than half the battle as a player. The other half is stopping the play.

I want you to fully understand the history, the reason, and the success/failure rates for each defensive scheme. Knowing why a team uses a specific strategy is important. Choosing a defense is like a game of checkers: A coach wants his team to stay a few offensive moves ahead of its opponent, anticipating the opponent's next move or play. The defense wants to prevent the offense from jumping over its defenders and reaching the end zone (or as they say in checkers, "King me!"). And, like checkers, you may sacrifice a piece in one area of the board (or field) to prevent the opponent from reaching your end of the board. The ultimate goal with any defense is to prevent a touchdown, so sometimes surrendering a field goal is a moral victory.

Examining the Different Defenses

The next time you watch a football game, try this little experiment: Right before the offense snaps the ball, glance at the defense and note where the defensive players are on the field. Then very quickly ask yourself, "What defensive scheme is that?" If you do this for a whole game, you'll start to understand — and appreciate — the different defensive strategies. You'll see why the defense lines up differently, for example, when it's making a goal-line stand or when it's defending against a long pass. You'll begin to see precisely what the defense is trying to do to stop the offense from gaining yards and scoring.

To help you recognize different defensive strategies, the following sections describe a handful of common lineups that defenses use to keep the offense in check.

4-3 front

The majority of NFL teams use the *4-3 defense,* which consists of two defensive tackles (DT), two defensive ends (DE), two outside linebackers (LB), a middle linebacker (MLB), two cornerbacks (CB), and two safeties (S), as shown in Figure 11-1. The 4-3 was devised in 1950 by New York Giants coach Steve Owen, who needed a fourth defensive back to stop the Cleveland Browns from completing long passes. Owen, whose cornerback was future Dallas Cowboys head coach Tom Landry, called the 4-3 his *umbrella defense* because the secondary opened in a dome shape as the linebackers retreated into pass coverage. In the first game in which the Giants used it, the defense clicked, and the Giants beat Cleveland 6–0, shutting out the Paul Brown-coached team for the first time in its history.

Figure 11-1: The 4-3 defense consists of four linemen (DE and DT), three linebackers (LB and MLB), and four defensive backs (CB and S).

Although it was initially devised to stop the pass, the 4-3 defense should be able to stop both the pass and the run. The 4-3 was first widely used in the late 1950s, when Sam Huff became the Giants' middle linebacker and the Detroit Lions, who also liked the scheme, made Joe Schmidt their middle linebacker. Both of these Hall of Fame players were instinctive and played run defense well because they were strong and exceptional at lateral pursuit of the ball carriers. But they also played the pass well. They could move away from the line of scrimmage (in other words, *drop into coverage*) and effectively defend a team's short-passing game.

On paper, this defense is well-balanced. As with all defenses, having talented personnel is important. The 4-3 defense needs ends who are strong pass-rushers and physically tough against the run. The ideal middle linebacker is someone like former Chicago Bear Dick Butkus (see Chapter 19), who could single-handedly make defensive stops and possessed the all-around savvy to put his teammates in favorable positions. The defensive tackles should be strong against the run and agile enough to sustain pass-rush pressure on the quarterback.

In the 4-3, the stronger and more physical of the two outside linebackers lines up over the tight end, leaving the other, quicker outside linebacker to be more of a pass-rusher. With the exception of all-star teams, it's almost impossible for a team to have superior players at every position. However, teams tend to use a 4-3 when they have four pretty good defensive linemen and a good middle linebacker. If three of those five players have all-star potential, this scheme should be successful.

Later in this chapter, I tell you about variations of the 4-3, including the Dallas 4-3, the over/under, and the Chicago Bears' 46 defense of the mid-1980s. Some teams also use four-man lines but use more defensive backs rather than linebackers behind their four-man fronts.

3-4 front

Bud Wilkinson created the *3-4 defense* at the University of Oklahoma in the late 1940s, but the 1972 Miami Dolphins, who went undefeated that year, were the first NFL team to begin using it in earnest. And the Dolphins did so out of necessity; they had only two healthy defensive linemen. Chuck Fairbanks, another Oklahoma coach, used the 3-4 as an every-down defense with the New England Patriots in 1974; also in 1974, Houston Oilers coach O. A. "Bum" Phillips did the same.

Unlike the 4-3 defense, the 3-4 defense uses only three defensive linemen, with the one in the middle called the *nose tackle* (N), as shown in Figure 11-2. The prototype nose tackle was the Oilers' 265-pound Curley Culp, who combined strength with exceptional quickness; he was an NCAA wrestling champion. The 3-4 also employs four linebackers (LB), with the other two defensive linemen (DE) usually consisting of one superior pass-rusher and a rugged run-defender. In some 3-4 defenses, all three down linemen are *two-gappers,* meaning they plug the gap between two offensive linemen and aim to neutralize those two blockers, allowing the linebackers to go unblocked and make the majority of the tackles.

Figure 11-2: The 3-4 defense lines up with three linemen (DE and N) and four linebackers (LB).

NFL teams in the 1970s adopted the 3-4 because they lacked quality defensive linemen and had more players who were suited to play outside linebacker. This is also true today in high school and college, where teams may lack quality defensive linemen but have no shortage of athletes who are capable of playing linebacker. The outside linebacker position fits an NFL player who's at least 6 feet 3 inches, 240 pounds (the bigger and taller, the better). This player should have the ability to play the run and rush the passer like a defensive end.

The 3-4 can be a flexible defense. In some instances, the defense may decide to drop seven or eight players into pass coverage. Conversely, the interchangeable personnel of a 3-4 could end up sending three to five players to rush the quarterback. In the 1970s, Miami actually called its 3-4 defense "the 53" after linebacker Bob Matheson's jersey number. Matheson moved around, but he was primarily a pass-rushing linebacker.

The 3-4 defense is ideally suited to defending multiple offensive formations, meaning a defensive coordinator can match his personnel with that of the offense. Also, the physically dominant nose tackle can prove to be a nightmare for the offensive center. The nose tackle can neutralize the center's pass-blocking attempts by constantly shoving his strong head and shoulders to the ground or moving the center sideways, thus negating his effectiveness as a blocker.

The 3-4 defense also spawned the term *two-gap style*. With this technique, the defensive linemen and inside linebackers actually block the offensive linemen to either side, opening a lane for the untouched outside linebacker to make the play. The 3-4 defense focuses on the outside linebackers; in fact, they're the stars of this defense.

The greatest defensive player I ever saw, Lawrence Taylor of the New York Giants, was essentially an outside linebacker in a 3-4 scheme. Although Taylor was great at sacking the quarterback in this scheme, the 3-4 defense generally is better at stopping the run than rushing the passer. And Taylor was exceptional at both aspects of the game — he could rush but also stand his ground and contain the run. Plus, he had the speed to pursue a running back moving away from him and still make the tackle.

The NFL in recent years has seen an increase in the number of teams using the 3-4 defense. The New England Patriots and Pittsburgh Steelers, who between them won five Super Bowls in the first decade of the 2000s, used the 3-4. But for the most part, NFL teams have shied away from the 3-4 defense because, to be successful, they need tall, 250-pound outside linebackers who also have speed. That kind of player is hard to come by.

3-4 eagle

Fritz Shurmur started using the *3-4 eagle defense* with the Los Angeles Rams in the late 1980s. Shurmur's defense used another linebacker in the role of the nose tackle, as shown in Figure 11-3. Instead of having a 300-pound player over the center, Shurmur inserted a 240-pound linebacker, a player who was susceptible to the run because most offensive centers outweighed him by 60 pounds. To succeed against the run, this linebacker needed to use his quickness and guile to shoot offensive line gaps. However, this linebacker was a solid tackler and was also good at dropping into pass coverage. The remaining personnel were identical to a typical 3-4 scheme, so it was sometimes referred to as a 2-5 eagle because of the five linebackers.

Figure 11-3: The 3-4 eagle defense uses a linebacker (LB) in place of the nose tackle.

© John Wiley and Sons, Inc.

Shurmur devised this defense to confront (and ideally confuse) San Francisco 49ers quarterback Joe Montana, who had an exceptional ability to read a defense correctly and complete a pass to the open man. Having a lighter and faster linebacker drop into passing lanes was a totally foreign concept to any quarterback, who was used to that player remaining along the line of scrimmage rather than roaming in the defensive backfield like a defensive back.

The 3-4 eagle evolved from Buddy Ryan's 46 defense (described in detail later in this chapter), which is all about applying pass-rush pressure at the end of the offensive line. The eagle places a premium on above-average linebackers who can sack the quarterback by rushing around the last blocker at the end of the offensive line. Most pass-rushers in this scheme prefer to line up away from the outside shoulder of the man responsible for blocking them. Outside linebacker Kevin Greene, who collected 46 quarterback sacks in three seasons (1988–1990), was the star (and benefactor) on Shurmur's Rams teams. Greene used his speed and exceptional strength for a 248-pounder to later lead the NFL in sacks twice (in 1994 and 1996). His 160 career sacks are the most ever by a linebacker.

The eagle is more successful with above-average cornerbacks who can play man-to-man defense, or man coverage. Man coverage complements the deep zone drops of two of the five linebackers. To me, it makes more sense to drop a 240-pound linebacker into pass coverage than to use a 310-pound nose tackle, which is what some zone blitz defenses do. That's one of the big differences between these two defenses. This defense can be very effective against a team running the West Coast offense (see Chapter 8), especially one that has a versatile running back who can damage a defense with his receiving as well as his running ability. Linebackers are better suited to catching and tackling this kind of ball carrier, while also being capable of defending the tight end, who's always an important performer in the West Coast offense.

Despite the lack of a big body over the center, the eagle 3-4 defense isn't susceptible to the run because it employs two very physical inside linebackers and can bring a strong safety close to the line of scrimmage to serve as another tackler (or linebacker). This maneuver allows the eagle to put eight defensive players in the *box,* which is the area near the line of scrimmage where the defense is most effective at stopping the run. Some teams, however (particularly those with a good, versatile running back), have tremendous success running the football against this defense. Why? Because the offense is able to neutralize the light linebacker playing nose tackle and run the ball from formations from which it had always thrown the football. Such tactics confuse the defensive personnel, who are unable to predict what the offense intends to do.

Dallas 4-3

I want to make a distinction here: When Jimmy Johnson coached the Dallas Cowboys in Super Bowl XXVII and XXVIII, Dallas's defense had an abundance of talented players among the front seven but didn't have particularly speedy or skillful cornerbacks. The *Dallas 4-3 defense* used four down linemen and three linebackers but gambled more than Johnson would have allowed and occasionally used more of a nickel scheme, inserting another defensive back in place of a linebacker, as shown in Figure 11-4. This defense is predicated more on a team's personnel than on a particular alignment.

Figure 11-4: The Dallas 4-3 defense uses four linemen (DE and DT) but may use an extra defensive back in place of one of the three linebackers (OLB, MLB, and LB).

But what Dallas was able to accomplish, and what has been copied, was the scheme *cover four* or *four across* in the secondary. Because Dallas's front seven was so talented and could apply extreme pressure on the quarterback, the secondary was able to play deeper and prevent the deep pass. Of course, this scheme puts extra pressure on the two cornerbacks, who are expected to be able to take the opposition's two best receivers man-to-man and shut them down without any help.

In the Dallas 4-3 defense, the safeties also can creep up toward the line of scrimmage to provide support against running plays. Basically, this defense allows the safeties to cheat and overplay one aspect of the offense when they anticipate the play correctly. With the rest of the defense attempting to funnel almost every running play toward these physical safeties, the back goes down if the safeties make good reads. In modern football, in which teams may have physically gifted tight ends, the Dallas 4-3 defense puts the safety in a better position to defend the *seam pass,* the throw right down the hash marks to the tight end or to a receiver running straight upfield.

Flex

Coach Tom Landry invented the *flex defense* for the Dallas Cowboys teams of the 1970s and 1980s. It's a 4-3 alignment, too, but it *flexes* (moves back) two defensive linemen (DT and DE) off the line of scrimmage by 2 or 3 yards, as shown in Figure 11-5. These two offset linemen read the blocking combinations of the offense and attempt to make the tackle (or the sack) while their teammates try to break down the offense's blocking patterns.

Figure 11-5: The flex defense puts two defensive linemen (DT and DE) 2 or 3 yards off the line of scrimmage.

The flex defense works only if you have talented defensive tackles. These flexed defensive linemen must have exceptional speed and the ability to react. By being a couple of yards off the line of scrimmage, they should be able to see how an offensive play is developing. But to be able to stop a play from their positions, they also must have the speed to recover the 2 yards while moving forward. Being off the line of scrimmage makes it more difficult for offensive linemen to block them. The blockers have to run a couple of yards to strike them, but meanwhile the defensive linemen are also moving, quite possibly in a different direction.

Bob Lilly (whom I tell you more about in Chapter 19) was one of the greatest defensive tackles of all time; Randy White (nicknamed *The Manster* because he was half man and half monster) was very close to him in ability. The keys to both players' success were their exceptional quickness and strength. White was a converted linebacker playing defensive tackle; you don't find many players capable of making that change. Shifting White's defensive position was a bold move by Landry more than 30 years ago, but this defensive scheme wouldn't work well today. The basic premise of the flex — to have defensive linemen reading — hinders the pass-rush. A player can't be reading and waiting for something to come his way. Instead, he has to react and attack if he wants to tackle the quarterback. The flex seemed like a great defense against the run until Eric Dickerson of the Los Angeles Rams ran for 248 yards against it in a playoff game at the end of the 1985 season.

Zone blitz

Zone blitz sounds like a contradiction in terms: Teams that like to play zone pass coverage generally don't blitz. Zones are safe; blitzes are all-out gambles. Dick LeBeau, a player and coach for 45 years in the NFL, is usually credited with inventing this defense in the late 1980s to take advantage of his huge safety, David Fulcher.

The Pittsburgh Steelers and the Carolina Panthers were the proponents of the exotic zone blitz in the mid-1990s (Figure 11-6 shows a zone blitz). From a base 3-4 alignment, they would overload one side of the offense by placing as many as three of the four linebackers to that side. They might stick a cornerback there, too, or put a safety there in place of a linebacker. The object was to confuse the quarterback and the offensive linemen, forcing them to wonder: How many people (four, five, or six) are really coming at the quarterback?

Figure 11-6:
The defense lined up in a zone blitz.

© John Wiley and Sons, Inc.

The down linemen in this scheme usually engage the center and guards. Their intent is to occupy these players and give them the impression that they may be rushing the quarterback. Often, the defensive linemen merely hold their ground while waiting for the run, or they stop, peel back off the line of scrimmage (by 5 yards or so), and then attempt to cover that area (this move is referred to as *short zone coverage*) against a possible pass play. The object of a zone blitz is to create one or two free lanes to the quarterback for the linebackers or defensive backs who do the blitzing.

The zone blitz is an ideal defense against an inexperienced or gun-shy quarterback. The defense wants to get the quarterback thinking. Before any quarterback drops back to pass, he scans the secondary to try to figure out what kind of defense it's playing. This is called *reading the secondary*. When a quarterback looks at a zone secondary, he doesn't usually equate it with blitzing. But in this defense, the quarterback checks out the defensive front, too. He wants to have an idea where the blitz or the most pass-rush pressure will come from. A good quarterback believes that he can move away from the pressure from the suspected overloaded side and gain enough time to complete his pass.

The combinations and varieties of zone blitzes are endless. However, offenses have discovered that a short pass play to the *flat* (outside the hash marks) may be effective against this defense. Most zone blitzing teams give offenses considerable open areas to one side or the other underneath their final line of pass defense. Often, blitzing teams send a player who normally would be in pass coverage toward the quarterback. When a defense blitzes like that, it always keeps two people deep because it doesn't want to surrender a long touchdown.

46

The team most often associated with the *46 defense* is the Chicago Bears of the 1980s. The 46 didn't receive its name from its alignment, but rather because Bears free safety Doug Plank wore jersey number 46 and often lined up as a linebacker. Buddy Ryan, the Bears' defensive coordinator, altered Chicago's original personnel in the 46 defense — five defensive linemen, one linebacker, and five defensive backs — to four defensive linemen, four linebackers, and three defensive backs, as shown in Figure 11-7. The fourth so-called linebacker, the "46," is generally considered a cross between a linebacker and a strong safety.

Figure 11-7: The Bears' 46 defense used four down linemen (DE, DT), four linebackers (OLB, MLB, 46), and three defensive backs (CB, FS).

© John Wiley and Sons, Inc.

In the 46, three defensive linemen line up across from the offense's center and two guards, making it impossible for those offensive players to double-team the defender opposite the center. In Chicago, this defensive player was Dan Hampton. When Ryan became head coach of the Philadelphia Eagles, the player over the center was Reggie White. Hall-of-Famers Hampton and White were the strongest linemen on their teams; they were also excellent pass-rushers. Their exceptional ability made it possible for them to collapse the offense's pocket, thus ruining the quarterback's protection. They were good enough to beat two blockers in their prime, paving the way for teammates to have a clean shot at the quarterback as White and Hampton occupied his protectors.

The Bears had sensational success with the 46 defense. In 1984, they recorded 72 quarterback sacks, and the following year, they allowed only ten points in three playoff games en route to their Super Bowl XX championship. In one six-game stretch, the defense scored 27 points and allowed 27 points. When the Bears won the Super Bowl, the defensive players carried Buddy Ryan off on their shoulders, while the offensive players took care of head coach Mike Ditka.

In the 46, no defender lines up over the two offensive tackles. Instead, defenders are placed off both of the offensive tackles' outside shoulders. From there, their intentions are straightforward: rush and sack the quarterback.

The biggest downsides to the 46 defense are the pass-coverage limitations. Your cornerbacks are stuck in man-to-man coverage 90 percent of the time, with only one safety to help. You can drop an inside linebacker or two into zone coverage; however, when you line up with basically only three defensive backs on the field, often a linebacker gets stuck one-on-one with the tight end. If the tight end can run, this matchup may be a mismatch for the defense. Also, the 46 defense can struggle against a three-wide-receiver offense because of the man-coverage situations. But, the philosophy of this defense is to attack the quarterback before he can pick apart the secondary.

The 46 is a good defense against offenses with two-back sets. Why? Because such an offense doesn't spread the 46; instead, it condenses it. And that's perfect, because the 46 is an aggressive defense designed to attack. The two-back offense affords the 46 defense the opportunity to send its pass rushers off the corner. When they come off the corner, the edge of the offensive line, no one is there to impede their path into the backfield, where they can cause the most damage.

The 46 defense can have a soft spot if the offense believes it can run wide against it, particularly in the direction of one of the offensive tackles. If the offense can block the two outside defenders, pushing them outside, the runner can cut inside the offensive tackle and run through that lane. And when the cornerbacks drop deep, the back may be able to gain a lot of yards. In college football, offenses beat the 46 defense by having the quarterback run an *option play.* In the option, the quarterback starts running around the end. He can either turn upfield or lateral the ball to a running back. (Note that pro coaches don't usually allow their quarterbacks to run an option play.)

Over/under 4-3

The over/under 4-3 is basically a scheme with four down linemen and three linebackers — what I call a Sam linebacker on the tight end and then two inside linebackers. The object of this defense is to shift more defensive linemen to the offense's suspected point of attack, which is called the *over,* or to shift the linemen to the weak side of the offensive formation, which is called the *under.* The down linemen are the stars of this show.

In the *under 4-3,* shown in Figure 11-8, one defensive lineman is on an offensive tackle, another is on the guard and center, and another is on the *open side* offensive tackle (the side opposite the tight end). In the *over 4-3,* three of the four defensive linemen shift toward the strong side of the offensive formation (the tight end side), as shown in Figure 11-9. A defender is always directly opposite the tight end in both of these defenses.

The over-and-under scheme gives the defense flexibility in the way it uses its players in the secondary. Tony Dungy, former coach of the Tampa Bay Buccaneers and Indianapolis Colts, used to bring his strong safety close to the line of scrimmage, and suddenly he had an eight-man front. For a change-up look, defenses can drop safeties to their traditional spots 12 yards off the line of scrimmage and roll the two cornerbacks up to or within 3 yards of the line of scrimmage, making the defense look like a nine-man front.

Figure 11-8:
The under 4-3 aligns on the weak side of the defense.

© John Wiley and Sons, Inc.

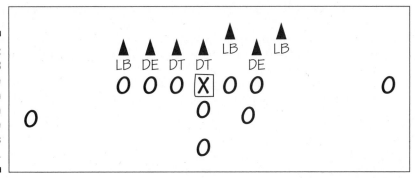

Figure 11-9:
The over 4-3 shifts the down linemen toward the offense's strong side.

© John Wiley and Sons, Inc.

For this defense to succeed, a team needs talented people up front — players capable of dominating the line of scrimmage. This scheme works only if the down linemen are special players like Dungy had with Warren Sapp in Tampa Bay. This defense can survive with average linebackers, decent safeties, and good cornerbacks, but it must have hard-charging linemen who are physically capable of beating offensive linemen.

The over/under 4-3 was a perfect defense for Dungy. Unlike Dungy, some teams and their coaches are very impatient; they want to attack and be aggressive, maybe pushing the panic button and blitzing the opposition before the time is right. But a coach like Dungy was able to sit back. He wasn't emotional. He folded his arms and let the offense keep the ball for seven or eight plays, believing that sooner or later the offense would panic and make a mistake. This defense can force an offense into making mistakes, too. Believe me when I say that some NFL offenses have trouble running eight plays without screwing something up.

Cover two (and Tampa two)

The cover two defense was devised to stop the *West Coast offense,* which relies on short passing routes and running backs coming out of the backfield to catch passes (for more about the West Coast offense, see Chapter 8). When running backs as well as tight ends and receivers all catch passes, how can the defense cover so many receivers?

The answer is the *cover two,* a 4-3 zone defense. Rather than cover receivers man to man, the defensive side of the field is divided into zones, with each zone the responsibility of a safety, cornerback, or linebacker. The deep part of the field (the area starting about 15 yards from the line of scrimmage) is divided into two large zones, each of which is the responsibility of a safety. (The cover two gets its name from these two large zones.) The safeties guard against receivers running downfield to catch long passes. Meanwhile, the area between the line of scrimmage and the deep part of the field is divided into five small zones, each of which is the responsibility of a cornerback or linebacker. The idea is to stop the short pass, or if a receiver succeeds in catching a short pass, to keep him from gaining more than a few yards. If a receiver breaks a tackle and gets downfield, one of the two safeties for which the defense is named is supposed to stop the receiver from breaking off a long gain. The cover two defense requires talented linemen who can pressure the quarterback into throwing the ball before receivers can break into the open areas between zones.

The cover two, designed to stop short passes, is susceptible to a strong running attack. What's more, the area in the middle of the field beyond 10 or 15 yards from the line of scrimmage is vulnerable because it falls between the two major zones. A speedy receiver who slips into this area and catches a pass can torch a team playing the cover two defense.

To protect the middle of the field, the Tampa two, a variation on the cover two, was invented. In the *Tampa two,* the middle linebacker drops back into the defensive secondary to protect against the pass, as shown in Figure 11-10. The Tampa two gets its name from the Tampa Bay Buccaneers, who used this defense starting in the mid-1990s under defensive coordinator Monte Kiffin. Running the Tampa two defense requires a stellar middle linebacker, somebody like Derrick Brooks, who played for the Buccaneers. Brooks had the speed to drop back and cover receivers as well as the strength and stamina to guard against runs up the middle. Most middle linebackers aren't blessed with that combination of speed and strength.

Figure 11-10:
In the Tampa two, a variation of the cover two, the middle linebacker (LB) drops back into pass coverage.

Tackling Tricky Situations

Defenses are under constant pressure in every game: one mistake (a missed tackle in the open field or a blown assignment, for example) and the opponent has points on the board. The sections that follow tackle a couple of the tricky situations that defenses face and give advice for handling them.

Stopping a superstar

When playing against a superstar, whether he's a running back or a quarterback, the defense must decide what facet of the offense it wants to focus on. In other words, the defense says, "I'm stopping Maurice Jones-Drew (who actually just retired, so just an example) and forcing the quarterback to throw the ball to beat me." Defenses can't do both — stop the run and the pass — against great offensive teams.

A team with a great safety, such as Troy Polamalu, can move its safety closer to the line of scrimmage without sacrificing its ability to cover receivers. The safety becomes another linebacker, the eighth man in the box. In other words, you have four defensive linemen and three linebackers, and you bring an extra run defender out of the secondary. If your safety reacts poorly, the defense can be susceptible to being beaten consistently by the pass. The consolation, though, is that the running back isn't going to run for 150 yards.

Defenders must at least attempt to tackle a great back like Jones-Drew. They should never stand around and wait for a good shot; they should fly at him. If they miss, they miss, but they're definitely not going to bring him down if they don't at least give it a shot.

Stopping the two-point conversion

The two-point play can make or break a game — and ultimately a season. (Check out Chapter 8 for more details on the two-point conversion.) On a two-point conversion attempt, teams try to spread the defense and then run some kind of *pick pass pattern*. Here's how that pattern starts: The offense aligns two receivers on one side of the formation. The outside receiver runs toward the middle of the field, while the inside receiver runs, stops, and then heads in the direction of the outside receiver. When the two receivers cross, that's called a *pick play* because the inside receiver tries to rub the man guarding him against the defender who's covering his teammate. The desired result is an open receiver in the *flat,* the area beyond the defensive linemen but in front of the secondary.

In an effort to prevent the pick play, defenses trying to prevent two-point conversions are playing more and more zone coverage in the secondary. After all, they just can't stop all the combinations of different pass routes, especially when offenses use a three-wide-receiver set. And the pick play is particularly successful against man-to-man coverage. So in trying to prevent a two-point play, the defense anticipates that most teams won't run. Most offenses line up in a one-back formation with three receivers to one side.

The key to defending against a two-point conversion attempt is not to blitz. Instead, the defense should use a four-man line and play a zone defense behind it. You can play as many as six or seven defensive backs across because the defense doesn't have to worry about the depth of the field. (After all, the end zone is only 10 yards deep.)

Stuffing short yardage

The first thing you have to realize in *short-yardage situations* (third down and 1 yard or fourth down and 1 yard or less) is that you can't stop everything. So you have to prepare your defensive front people — the defensive line and the linebackers — to stop one or two particular plays. Usually, you have eight defenders on the line, a combination of linemen and linebackers, and defensive players over both tight ends. The key play that you have to be able to stop is the offense's isolation play.

An *isolation play* is what happens on a blast play, when a fullback runs inside to block a defensive player standing by himself before the quarterback hands off the ball to the running back behind him. The running play is called the *blast play,* but it works because the fullback isolates a specific defensive player. On this type of play, the defensive linemen must establish positive gap control.

Here's what I mean: In addition to lining up across from an offensive lineman and defeating his block, each defensive lineman must get his body into a gap, either by *stunting* (when the defensive linemen jump to one side or the other, confusing the offensive linemen) or by lining up on the shoulder of an offensive lineman and securing the gap. Next, someone on defense must get some penetration across the line of scrimmage in order to have any chance of disrupting the play. (**Remember:** Offensive linemen have trouble blocking quicker players who are charging straight ahead into a gap.)

Part IV
Meet the Rest of the Team

In this part . . .

✔ Examine the ins and outs of special teams play

✔ Understand what coaches and other team members do on a
football team

Chapter 12

Special Teams, Masters of the Kicking Game

In This Chapter

▶ Taking a look at special teams and who's on them

▶ Beginning each game with a kickoff and kickoff return

▶ Making (and blocking) field goal and extra point attempts

▶ Recognizing the importance of punting

As you probably know, every football game begins with a kickoff. More than 97 percent of the time, a team kicks an extra point after scoring a touchdown. And every time a team scores, the team must kick off again. These are just a few examples of what's known as the *kicking game.* The proper name for the group of players who take care of these tasks is *special teams.*

Overall, this group of players is remarkable. A lot of effort, skill, and courage are involved in manning these positions. But you can play ten years in the NFL, be a tremendous special teams performer, and play in virtual anonymity. Kickers and some return men garner attention, but for the other players — the guys who cover kicks and punts and block for kickers — the job is often pretty thankless in the eyes of the public and the media (and even within the team). Special teams players generally are noticed only for doing a poor job — when a punt or field goal attempt is blocked or when the opposition returns a kickoff for a touchdown. After you read this chapter, however, you should have a much greater appreciation for these fine athletes and the important tasks they do.

Finding Out Who's Who on Special Teams

The players who put their foot to the ball are the *placekickers, punters,* and *field goal kickers.* They're all also known as *specialists.* On some teams, the punter handles kickoff duties, and the placekicker is responsible for field goal and extra point attempts. Other teams have players for all three positions. But there's a lot more to the kicking game than these two or three players.

When a punter attempts a punt, for example, 21 other players are on the field. The ten remaining men on the punting team have two tough responsibilities: to protect the punter's kick from being blocked and then to run down the field and cover the punt. They face ten players who are trying to slow them down, as well as the player who's catching the punt (the *punt returner*). The returner is generally one of the fastest runners on a team and a specialist in his own right. The punting team wants to prevent the return man from gaining a single yard, whereas the punt returner obviously wants to go the distance and score a touchdown. At the very least, he wants to place his team's offense in good field position, shortening the distance that the offense must travel to score.

Specialists have their own coach, known as a *special teams coach,* who serves in a capacity similar to that of an offensive or defensive coordinator in that he coaches a large group of players and not merely a specific position (flip to Chapter 13 for full insight into the coaching lineup). Some teams also have a kicking coach who coaches basically two players, the punter and the kicker.

Special teams are *so* specialized that a single group of players can't cover every situation. Four special teams units exist:

✔ The group of players that handles punts, kickoffs, and punt returns

✔ The unit that handles field goal and extra point attempts

✔ The group that takes care of kickoff returns

✔ The unit that attempts to block field-goal and extra-point attempts

Generally, great special teams players are unusual. Travis Jervey, who played for the Atlanta Falcons, Green Bay Packers, and San Francisco 49ers, and was selected for the Pro Bowl, had a pet lion. Special teams players are often the wild and crazy guys on a team, too. When coverage men stop a returner in his tracks, for example, they're usually as excited as offensive players scoring touchdowns.

My own special teams experiences

I was a special teams player during my first two years in the NFL. Being a small-college player from Villanova, playing on special teams gave me the opportunity to work my way up through the ranks on the Raiders. The NFL is kind of like the Army in that you have to prove you belong.

I was on most of the special teams units. I covered punts and kickoffs, plus I was part of the unit that tried to block field goal and extra point attempts. Matt Millen and I were the two bulldozers on the kick-blocking team. We used to get down in a *four-point stance* (both hands and feet on the ground) and line up on either side of the center, who snaps the ball. Ted Hendricks, who was over 6 feet 7 inches tall

and had the longest arms I'd ever seen, would stand right behind us. Millen and I would basically function as a snowplow and clear a path for Hendricks. Ted was in charge; he'd tell us where to line up and what to do, and I remember him blocking a number of kicks.

When I became an All-Pro player in my third year in the NFL, my defensive line coach wouldn't allow me to play on special teams anymore because he didn't want me getting hurt. That's pretty much the philosophy in the NFL today. For example, quarterbacks used to be the holders for field goals and extra points, but it's pretty rare to see any of them holding these days. They don't want to hurt those pretty fingers!

Understanding What's So Special about Special Teams

A key thing to know about special teams is that these 11-man units are typically on the field for about 20 percent of the plays in a football game. But coaches often say that special teams play amounts to one-third of a football game — by that, they mean its total impact on the game.

Take scoring, for example — how games were won and lost in the 2014 NFL regular season:

- ✔ **Offenses** scored 1,187 touchdowns and 28 two-point conversions for a total of 7,178 points. Remember, teams earn six points for a touchdown and two points for a two-point conversion.

- ✔ **Special teams** accounted for 829 field goals made and 1,222 extra points for a total of 3,709 points just from kicking. Plus teams scored 13 touchdowns on punt returns and 6 touchdowns on kickoff returns for an additional 114 points.

- ✔ **Defenses** scored 73 touchdowns on interception returns and fumble recoveries, which totals 438 points.

Field position terminology

The main line of demarcation on a football field is the 50-yard line. The area on both sides of the 50 is known as *midfield territory.* A lot of football terms are defense-oriented. Consequently, when a commentator says, "The Chicago Bears are starting from their own 18," it means that the ball is on the 18-yard line and that the opposition, should it recover the ball, is only 18 yards away from scoring a touchdown. The Bears may be on offense, but they should be mindful of the precarious offensive position they're in. They want to move the ball away from their goal line, and probably in a conservative fashion (say, by running the ball rather than throwing risky passes that could be intercepted).

So while the offense does most of the scoring, as you would expect, special teams contribute a pretty big chunk of the total points. Another important function of the special teams unit is to maintain good field position and to keep the opposition in bad field position. The main objective of the kickoff, for example, is to pin the opponent as far away from its end zone, and thus a score, as possible. Kickoff coverage teams strive, though, to put the opponent 80 yards or more away from scoring.

Placekicking

Placekicking, which is one half of the special teams' duties, involves kickoffs, field goal attempts, and extra point attempts (an extra point is also known as a *point after touchdown,* or PAT). Unlike punting, which I describe later in this chapter, a kicker boots the ball from a particular spot on the field. You can read about the three types of kicks and the rules and objectives behind them in the next sections.

Kicking off

For fans, the opening kickoff is an exhilarating start to any game. They see the two-sided thrill of one team attempting to block the other, helping its returner run through, over, and past 11 fast-charging players of the kicking team. (Well, make that ten players. The kicker usually stands around the 50-yard line after kicking the ball, hoping he doesn't have to make a tackle.) And the kicking team wants to make a statement by stopping the returner inside his own 20-yard line. This is the object on every level of football, from peewee to college to the NFL.

The following sections help you understand what happens during a kickoff, from the decision made at the coin toss to the rules regulating kickoffs in the NFL.

Deciding whether to kick or to receive

At the coin toss, when captains from both teams meet the referee in the center of the field, the captain who correctly calls the flip of the referee's coin decides whether his team is to receive or to defend a particular goal. For example, if the captain says he wants to defend a certain end zone, the opponent automatically receives the ball. If the winning captain wants the ball, the opponent chooses which end of the field his team will kick from (and the goal it will defend). Except in bizarre weather conditions — when it's snowing, raining, or extremely windy — most teams elect to receive the kickoff because they want the ball for their offense.

On some occasions, a team may allow its opponent to receive after winning the coin toss, meaning it *defers* its right to kick off because the head coach probably believes that his defensive unit is stronger than the opposition's offense and wants to pin the offense deep in its own territory, force a turn-over, or make it punt after three downs. Adverse weather conditions are also a factor because they may jeopardize the players' ability to field the kick cleanly, and some kickers have difficulty achieving adequate distances against a strong wind. In these conditions, a team may opt to receive the ball at the end of the field where the weather has less of an effect.

Setting up for the kickoff

For kickoffs, NFL and college kickers are allowed to use a 1-inch tee to support the ball. High school kickers may use a 2-inch tee. The kicker can angle the ball in any way that he prefers while using the tee, but most kickers prefer to have the ball sit in the tee at a 75-degree angle rather than have it perpendicular to the ground. During some games, strong winds prevent the ball from remaining in the tee. In those instances, a teammate holds the ball steady for the kicker by placing his index finger on top of the ball and applying the necessary downward pressure to keep it steady.

The kickoff team generally lines up five players on either side of the kicker. These ten players line up in a straight line about 8 yards from where the ball is placed on the kicking tee. If the kicker is a soccer-style kicker (I describe this type of kicker in the later related sidebar), he lines up 7 yards back and off to one side (to the left if he's a right-footed kicker, or vice versa). As the kicker strides forward to kick the ball, the ten players move forward in unison, hoping to be in full stride when the kicker makes contact with the ball.

In both the NFL and college football, teams kick off from the 35-yard line. But that wasn't always the rule. In the NFL from 1994 to 2010, the kick off was moved back five yards to the 30-yard line. In college, kickoffs came from the 30 from 2007 to 2011.

So why was the kickoff moved up to the 35? The rules committees in both the NFL and college want to improve player safety. When the kickoff comes from the 35 yard line, most kickers place the ball deep in the opposite end zone. These deep kicks mean that the receiving team is less likely to attempt a return and instead accept a touchback. A *touchback* occurs when a receiving player possesses the ball in the end zone and takes a knee (known as downing the ball) or when the kicked ball is allowed to bounce past the end line. Touchbacks automatically give the offense the ball on its own 20-yard line.

When a kickoff isn't deep in the end zone, the receiving team is more likely to attempt a return. If the ball carrier has great blocking and can avoid a few tackles, he might return the ball past the 20-yard line, and that makes for exciting football. Unfortunately, kickoffs feature 22 players running full speed at each other, resulting in dangerous collisions. To reduce injuries, the NFL and the NCAA (National Collegiate Athletic Association) now require kick off from the 35-yard line.

The move to the 35-yard line has definitely increased the number of touchbacks in the NFL. From 1994 to 2010, the touchback percentage from all kickoffs was around 11 percent. From 2011 to 2013, touchbacks increased to 45 percent.

Kicking the ball

When the referee blows his whistle, the kicker approaches the ball. His objective is to hit the ball squarely in the lower quarter in order to get the proper loft and distance. As soon as the kicker's foot makes contact with the ball, his ten teammates are allowed to cross the line of scrimmage and run downfield to *cover* the kick — basically, to tackle the player who catches the ball and attempts to return it back toward the kicking team. The ideal kickoff travels about 70 yards and hangs in the air for over 4.5 seconds. Maximizing *hang time* (the length of time the football is in the air) is important because it enables players on the kicking team to run down the field and cover the kick, thus tackling the return man closer to his own end zone.

Again, the kicking team's objective in a kickoff is to place the ball as close to its opponent's end zone as possible. After all, it's better for your opponent to have to travel 99 yards to score a touchdown than it is for them to have to move the ball only, say, 60 yards. Plus, if you can keep the ball close to your opponent's end zone, your defense has a better chance of scoring a touchdown if it recovers a fumble or intercepts an errant pass. And by pinning the opposition deep in its own territory and possibly forcing a punt, a team can expect to put its offense in better field position when it receives a punt.

To keep the kick returner from making many return yards, kickers may attempt to kick the ball to a specific side of the field (known as *directional kicking*) to force the return man to field the kick. The basis of this strategy is the belief that your kick coverage team is stronger than your opponent's kick return unit and that the return man isn't very effective. In this situation, the returner is often restricted, and the defense can pin him against the sidelines and force him out of bounds.

Many teams now opt to force the receivers into a touchback by either kicking the ball to deep into the end zone or out of the end zone completely. This tactic minimizes the risk of a long return. The offense then takes the ball at the 20-yard line.

The kickoff formation shown in Figure 12-1 typifies directional kicking. Instead of simply kicking the ball straight down the middle of the field, the kicker angles the ball to the left side. This style is ideal against a team that lines up with only one kick returner. The directional kick forces the returner to move laterally and take his eyes off the ball. The kicking team's purpose is to focus its coverage to one side of the field, where it hopes to have more tacklers than the return team has blockers.

Following the rules of the kickoff

Like virtually everything else in football, kickoffs are strictly governed by a set of rules:

- ✔ The receiving team must line up a minimum of 10 yards from where the ball is kicked.

- ✔ Members of the kicking team can recover the ball after the kick travels 10 yards or the ball touches an opponent. If the kicked ball goes out of bounds before traveling 10 yards, the kicking team is penalized 5 yards and must kick again. If a member of the kicking team touches the ball before it travels 10 yards, the kicking team must kick again and is again penalized 5 yards.

- ✔ A member of the kicking team can recover the ball in the end zone and be awarded a touchdown.

- ✔ Members of the kicking team must give the receiving team's returner the opportunity for a *fair catch*. If he signals for a fair catch, the players can't touch him and can't come within 3 feet of him until he touches the ball.

- ✔ The receiving team gets the ball on its own 40-yard line (25 yards from the spot where the ball was kicked) if the kickoff goes out of bounds before reaching the end zone. If it bounces out before the 40-yard line, the receiving team receives the ball where it went out of bounds.

Figure 12-1:
Kicking the ball to a specific side of the field forces the returner to field it and allows the kicking team to focus its coverage on that side of the field.

© John Wiley and Sons, Inc.

The wackiest kickoff ever

Alumni and fans of the Stanford/University of California at Berkeley rivalry know it simply as "The Play." It's also the only known touchdown scored while running through the opposition's band — as in *marching band*.

Stanford and UC Berkeley have faced each other in more than 110 games, and The Play occurred in the 85th meeting, on November 20, 1982. Stanford was ahead 20–19 with four

seconds remaining, and most of the 75,662 fans were heading for the exits in Cal's Memorial Stadium when Stanford's Mark Harmon kicked off from his own 25-yard line because his team had been assessed a 15-yard penalty for excessive celebration following its go-ahead field goal. Given the field position and in an attempt to prevent a run-back, Harmon made a *percentage kick* — a low-bouncing squibber. Such kicks are usually difficult to field and, because the ball isn't kicked a great distance, allow the coverage team a shorter distance in which to tackle the opposition. At the time of the kick, the Stanford band, a legendary group known for its zany attire and performances, poured onto the south end of the field (Cal's end zone), believing the game was over.

What happened next goes into football history under the "pretty unbelievable" category. Cal's Kevin Moen caught the bouncing ball on his own 46-yard line and ran forward 10 yards, where he was surrounded by Stanford tacklers. But before he was downed, Moen lateralled to Richard Rodgers. (A *lateral* is a legal play in which the ball is passed or tossed backward; it's illegal to pass forward on any type of running play.) Rodgers kept the ball

briefly before tossing it back to running back Dwight Garner, who carried the ball to the Stanford 48-yard line. Garner was being tackled when he flipped the ball back to Rodgers, who started running forward again and, before he was tackled, lateralled to Mariet Ford, who sidestepped two tacklers and rushed to the Stanford 25-yard line.

As Ford was being tackled and falling to the ground, he tossed the ball up in the air, and backward, to Moen, the player who had originally fielded Harmon's kickoff. By this time, Moen and the players who remained were running through the Stanford band. Moen sidestepped some band members and then smashed through the Stanford trombone player to score the winning touchdown.

Final score: Cal 25, Stanford 20.

Returning the kickoff

The ultimate purpose of a kickoff return is to score or advance the ball as close to midfield (or beyond it) as possible. A team's ability to start out on offense in better-than-average field position greatly increases its chances for success.

Kickoff returners don't usually figure greatly in a team's success, but during the 1996 season, Desmond Howard was a major reason that the Green Bay Packers were Super Bowl champions. Howard returned only one kickoff for a touchdown that season, but his long returns always supplied tremendous positive momentum swings for his team. When he didn't go all the way, Howard was adept at giving his team excellent field position. Anytime he advanced the ball to his own 30-yard line or beyond, he put his offensive teammates in better field position and, obviously, closer to the opponent's end zone and a score.

Great kickoff returners possess the innate ability to sense where the tackling pursuit is coming from, and they can move quickly away from it. A great returner follows his initial blocks and, after that, relies on his open-field running ability or simply runs as fast as he can through the first opening. Both Gayle Sayers of the Chicago Bears and Terry Metcalf of the former

St. Louis Cardinals were excellent at changing directions, stopping and going, and giving tacklers a small target by twisting their bodies sideways.

Teams want their kick returners to be able to run a 4.3-second 40-yard dash, but they also want them to have enough body control to be able to use that speed properly. Being the fastest man doesn't always work because there's rarely a free lane in which to run. Usually, somebody is in position to tackle the kickoff returner. Great returners cause a few of these potential tacklers to miss them in the open field.

The sections that follow offer insight into what happens when the ball lands in the returner's hands, both from the offensive and defensive perspective, and present the kickoff return rules to know.

Understanding the kickoff return rules

The following rules govern the kickoff return:

- ✔ No member of the receiving team can cross the 45-yard line until the ball is kicked.
- ✔ Blockers can't block opponents below the waist or in the back.
- ✔ If the momentum of the kick takes the receiver into the end zone, he doesn't have to run the ball out. Instead, he can down the ball in the end zone for a *touchback,* in which case his team takes it at the 20-yard line.
- ✔ If the receiver catches the ball in the field of play and retreats into the end zone, he must bring the ball out of the end zone. If he's tackled in the end zone, the kicking team records a safety and scores two points.

Before 2009, good return teams set up a *blocking wedge* with three or more huge players aligned together to clear a path for the ball carrier behind them. But in 2009, in the interest of player safety, the NFL prohibited teams from using more than two players to form a wedge on kickoff returns. Why the rule change? When you create a wall of three huge blockers in front of the ball carrier, the kicking team naturally wants to break through that wall to make the tackle. So defenders on the kicking team would get a 50-yard head of steam and crash into the wedge. Players who did this were known as *wedge busters,* and they were celebrated for their toughness and courage. Unfortunately, wedge busters were constantly risking injury to themselves and the blockers they collided into. The NFL decided that using wedges and busting wedges were just too dangerous.

Covering the kickoff return

Coverage men (the guys whose job it is to tackle the kick returner) must be aggressive, fast, and reckless in their pursuit. They must avoid the blocks of the return team. Special teams coaches believe that a solid tackle on the opening kickoff can set the tone for a game, especially if the return man is stopped inside his own 20-yard line. But the job of the kickoff coverage man isn't an easy one. Players get knocked down once, twice, and sometimes three times during their pursuit of the kickoff returner. Not for nothing is the coverage team sometimes called the "suicide squad."

Kicking field goals and PATs

Most special teams scoring involves the placekicker or field goal kicker. During the 2009 NFL season, the 32 pro teams attempted 930 field goals and converted 756 of them, which is an 81 percent success rate. For the last 35 years, field goal kicking has played a pivotal, often decisive, role in the outcomes of NFL games. Kickers can become instant heroes by converting a last-second field goal to win a game.After an NFL offense has driven to within 30 yards of scoring a touchdown, the coaches know the team is definitely within easy field goal range. In the 2009 NFL season, field goal kickers converted 265 of 274 attempts inside 30 yards for an impressive 97 percent conversion rate. Between 30 and 39 yards, NFL kickers made 85 percent of their attempts. However, teams saw a significant drop-off beyond 39 yards. Kickers made only 216 of 363 attempts from 40 yards or longer for a completion rate of 60 percent. Despite the decline in accuracy, you can see that coaches were still willing to at least attempt to score three points, knowing that a missed field goal gives the defensive team the ball at the spot of the kick.

Reliable kickers can often claim a job for a decade or more because their ability to convert in the clutch is so essential. For example, Morton Andersen played 25 seasons in the NFL with six teams. He holds the record for most career field goals with 565.

Hidden yardage

Jimmy Johnson, who coached the Dallas Cowboys and the Miami Dolphins, called positive return yards *hidden yardage*. For example, Johnson equated a 50-yard advantage in punt/kick return yards to five first downs. In some games, it may be extremely difficult for an offense to produce a lot of first downs, so return yardage is key.

Johnson reported that his teams won games while making only 12 first downs because they played great both defensively and on special teams. He believed that the team with the best field position throughout the game, attained by excellent punt and kick coverage, generally wins. Also, he believed that if you have a great punt and kick returner, opponents may elect to kick the ball out of bounds, thus giving your offense fine field position.

The following sections explain the roles of the folks involved in field goal and extra point attempts, what makes a kick count, and the rules regarding both types of kicks.

Who does what

On field goal and extra point (PAT, which stands for *point after touchdown*) attempts, the kicker has a holder and a snapper. He also has a wall of nine blockers in front of him, including the snapper, who's sometimes the offensive center. On many teams, the player who snaps the ball for punts also snaps for these kicks. The snap takes approximately 1.3 seconds to reach the holder, who kneels on his right knee about 7 yards behind the line of scrimmage. He catches the ball with his right hand and places the ball directly on the playing surface. (Placekicking tees are allowed in high school football but not in college and the NFL.) The holder then uses his left index finger to hold the ball in place.

The kicker's leg action, the striking motion, takes about 1.5 milliseconds, and the ball is usually airborne about 2 seconds after being snapped.

It's good!

For an extra point or a field goal try to be ruled good, the kicked ball must clear the crossbar (by going over it) and pass between (or directly above one of) the uprights of the goalpost (see Chapter 2 for the specs of the goalpost). Two officials, one on each side of the goalpost, stand by to visually judge whether points have been scored on the kick.

Most college and NFL teams expect to convert every extra point, considering that the ball is snapped from the 2- or 3-yard line. A field goal is a different matter, though, due to the distance involved.

The rules

A few rules pertain strictly to the kicking game. Most of them decide what happens when a kick is blocked or touched by the defensive team. Because three points are so valuable, special teams place a great emphasis on making a strong effort to block these kicks. The team kicking the ball works just as diligently to protect its kicker, making sure he has a chance to score.

The byproduct of these attempts often leads to the defensive team *running into* or *roughing the kicker*. This infraction occurs when a player hits the kicker's body or leg while he's in the act of kicking. A penalty is also enforced when a player knocks down the kicker immediately after he makes the kick. The rules are fairly strict because the kicker can't defend himself while he's concentrating on striking the ball. (Check out Chapter 3 for more on these and other penalties.)

Some of the other rules regarding field goals and extra points:

✔ Either team can advance a blocked field goal recovered behind the line of scrimmage.

✔ A blocked field goal that crosses the line of scrimmage may be advanced only by the defense. If the ball is muffed or fumbled, however, it's a free ball and either team can recover it.

✔ On a blocked PAT in an NFL game, the ball is immediately dead. Neither team is allowed to advance it. In college football, the defense can pick up the ball and return it to the kicking team's end zone for a two-point score (if they're lucky).

✔ The guards may lock legs with the snapper only. The right guard places his left foot inside the snapper's right foot after both players assume a stance so that their legs cross, or lock. The left guard places his right foot on the opposite side of the center. By locking legs, the guards help stabilize the snapper from an all-out rush on his head and shoulders while he leans down over the ball. All other players on the line of scrimmage must have their feet outside the feet of the players next to them.

✔ The holder or kicker may not be roughed or run into during or after a kick. The penalty for running into the kicker is 5 yards; the penalty for roughing the kicker is 15 yards and an automatic first down.

However, roughing the holder or kicker is legal if the kick is blocked, the ball touches the ground during the snap, or the holder fumbles the ball before it's kicked.

✔ On a missed field goal, the ball returns to the line of scrimmage if it rolls dead in the field of play, is touched by the receiving team, goes into the end zone, or hits the goalpost. The defensive team assumes possession at that time.

Blocking field goals and PATs

Blocking either a PAT or a field goal attempt can change the momentum of a game and eventually decide its outcome. To block kicks, players must be dedicated, athletic, and willing to physically sacrifice themselves for the good of the team, as the players in Figure 12-2 are doing. To have a successful block, each man must do his job.

Drop-kicking: The lost art

Before the ball was made thinner and distinctly more oblong to assist passers, the plumped version was easily drop-kicked. Yes, players would simply drop the ball and kick it after it touched the ground. The action was perfectly timed.

The current rules still allow drop-kicking, but the ball's tapered design stops most players from trying it. The last successful drop kick in the NFL occurred on January 1, 2006, when Doug Flutie of the New England Patriots drop-kicked an extra point in the final game of his career. Prior to Flutie's drop-kick, no one in

the NFL had succeeded in making a drop-kick since the 1941 championship game, when the Chicago Bears' Ray "Scooter" McLean successfully drop-kicked a PAT.

In a 2010 Thanksgiving Day game, Dallas Cowboys' punter Mat McBriar fumbled the snap from the center, and after the ball bounced a couple times on the grass, kicked the ball in what might be described as a drop kick. The referees, however, ruled that McBriar's kick wasn't a drop kick at all, but a fumble followed by an illegal kick. Nice try, Mat!

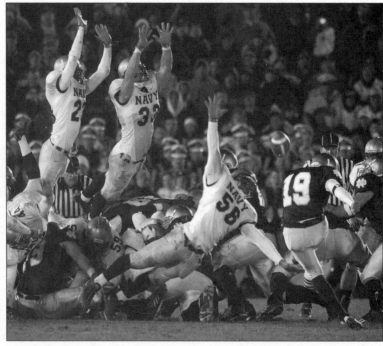

Figure 12-2:
Navy defenders try to block a field goal attempt by Notre Dame's D.J. Fitzpatrick in 2003.

Photo credit: © U.S. Navy/Getty Images

Blocked kicks may appear easy, but, as shown in Figure 12-3, a play such as the *middle field goal block* requires talented defensive linemen who can win the battle up front. These defensive linemen position themselves near the center snapping the ball because the quickest way to any field goal or extra point attempt is up the middle. With the ball 7 yards off the line of scrimmage, teams place their best pass-rushers in the middle, believing that one of them can penetrate the blocking line a couple of yards and then raise his arms, hoping to tip the booted ball with his hands. If the kicker doesn't get the proper trajectory, the kick can be blocked.

Figure 12-3:
The defensive linemen try to penetrate up the middle and block the kick.

© John Wiley and Sons, Inc.

In Figure 12-3, the three interior defensive linemen (LT, N, and RT) are over the two guards and the snapper. RT must align on the inside shoulder of the guard opposite him. N lines up directly across from the center. LT aligns on the inside shoulder of the guard opposite him. These linemen want to be able to gain an edge, an angle, on those blockers. Their attempts to block the kick won't work if the two tackles align squarely on top of the guards. They must pick a particular shoulder of the guard and attack to that side.

Both LG and RG (left and right guard) drive through the tackles' outside shoulders. Their objective is to apply enough individual pressure so as not to allow the tackle to slide down the line and help his buddies inside. Both players should attempt to block the kick if they break free. If not, they *contain* the opponent's linemen in case of a fake field goal attempt. Containing means to hold their ground and simply jostle with the players who are blocking them — all while keeping their eyes on the kicker and holder.

The only chance the middle block has of succeeding is if the pass-rush moves that the three interior defensive linemen make on the offensive linemen work. It's critical that all three players are isolated on one blocker. The defenders can decide to double-team a blocker, hoping one of them breaks free and penetrates the line.

Soccer-style kicking

One of the biggest developments in kicking came in the late 1950s, when soccer-style kickers began surfacing at U.S. colleges. Before the soccer style came into vogue, the straight-on method was the only way to kick a football. This American style of kicking is totally different from the soccer style. Straight-on kickers approached the ball from straight on, using their toes to strike the ball and lift it off the ground. A soccer-style kicker, on the other hand, approaches the ball from an angle, and the instep of the kicker's foot makes contact with the ball.

In 2010, not one NFL kicker used the straight-on method. For starters, the soccer style creates quicker lift off the ground. But basically, this method has simply stuck and become the pervasive kicking style. Mark Moseley, who retired from the Cleveland Browns in 1986, was the last straight-on kicker.

On other kick-block plays, teams attempt to break through from the outside, using two men on one blocker and hoping the single blocker makes the wrong choice and allows the inside rusher to get free.

Punting

Punting occurs when a team's offense is struggling, which means the offense is failing to generate positive yardage and is stuck on fourth down. Teams punt on fourth down when they're in their own territory or are barely across midfield. By punting, the team relinquishes possession of the ball.

One of the most difficult aspects of football to understand initially is why teams punt the ball. A team has four downs to gain 10 yards, and after accomplishing that, it receives a new set of downs. Why not gamble on fourth down to gain the necessary yardage to maintain possession of the football? Field position is the answer. Unless it's beyond the opponent's 40-yard line, a team would rather punt the ball on fourth down, hoping to keep the opponent as far from its end zone as possible (which, of course, stops the other team from scoring).

Teams punt routinely at the beginning of the game, especially when there's no score or the score is close. They rely on their defenses in such situations, believing that the benefits of field position outweigh any offensive risk-taking. Punting in these situations isn't a conservative tactic, but a smart one.

Punting is a critical part of football because some coaches believe it can change the course of a game. And no facet of the game alters field position more than punting. In the NFL, each punt is worth an average of 45 yards per exchange. However, some punters are capable of punting even farther than that, thus pinning opponents deep in their own end of the field and far, far away from a score.

The sections that follow get you acquainted with the punting process, the members of the punting team, the rules regarding punting, and more.

Setting up and kicking the ball

The punter stands about 15 yards behind the line of scrimmage and catches the ball after the snapper hikes it. The center's snap of the ball must reach the punter within 0.8 seconds. Every extra tenth of a second increases the risk that the punt may be blocked.

After receiving the ball, the punter takes two steps, drops the ball toward his kicking foot, and makes contact. This act requires a lot of practice and coordination because the velocity of the punter's leg prior to striking the ball, as well as the impact of his foot on the ball, is critical. The punter needs to strike the ball in the center to achieve maximum distance. When the punter strikes the ball off the side of his foot, the ball flies sideways (such a mistake is called a *shank*).

A punt, from the snap of the ball to the action of the punter, requires no more than 2 seconds. Most teams want the punter to catch, drop, and punt the ball in under 1.3 seconds.

Today's punters must be adept at kicking in all weather conditions and must strive for a hang time of 4.5 seconds. They must also boot the ball at least 45 yards away from the line of scrimmage. By the way, most punters also serve in a dual role as holder for the field goal kicker.

Meeting the key performers on the punt team

The punter isn't the only important player during a punt play — although it may seem like it sometimes, especially on a bad punt. Following are some of the other key performers:

- ✔ **Center or snapper:** This player must be accurate with his snap and deliver the ball to where the punter wants it. On most teams, he makes the blocking calls for the interior linemen, making sure no one breaks through to block the punt.

- ✔ **Wings:** The *wings* are the players on both ends of the line of scrimmage, and they're generally 1-yard deep behind the outside leg of the end or tackle. These players must block the outside rushers, but they worry more about any player breaking free inside of them.

- ✔ **Ends:** One *end* stands on each side of the line of scrimmage, and they're isolated outside the wings at least 10 to 12 yards. On some teams, these players are called *gunners.* Their job is to run downfield and tackle the punt returner. Often, two players block each end at the line of scrimmage in hopes of giving the punt returner more time to advance the ball.

- ✔ **Personal protector:** The *personal protector* is the last line of protection for the punter. This player usually lines up 5 yards behind the line of scrimmage. If five or more defensive players line up to one side of the snapper, the personal protector shifts his attention to that side and makes sure no one breaks through to block the punt.

  Most coaches prefer that a fullback or safety play this position because they want someone who's mobile enough to quickly move into a blocking position. Regardless, the personal protector must be a player who can react quickly to impending trouble and make adjustment calls for the ends and wings.

Figure 12-4 shows a basic punt formation involving these players against what coaches call *man coverage.* X is the center (or snapper); he stands over the ball. PP is the punter's personal protector, and P is the punter. The wings are labeled with Ws, and the Es (ends) are on the line of scrimmage about 10 to 12 yards away from the wings.

Figure 12-4:
A basic punt
formation.

Reviewing punt rules

As with everything else in football, punting has rules. Consider the following:

✔ In the pros, only the players lined up on the ends are permitted to cross the line of scrimmage after the ball is snapped to the punter and before the ball is punted. In college and high school, all players on the punting team may cross the line of scrimmage after the snap.

After the ball is punted, everyone on the punting team is allowed to cross the line of scrimmage with the intent of tackling the player fielding the punt (who's also known as the *punt returner*).

✔ Players aren't allowed to block below the waist on punt returns. Such an illegal block is a 15-yard penalty and is marked off from where the team returning the punt gained possession of the ball.

✔ If a punt doesn't cross the line of scrimmage, either team may pick up the ball and run toward its own end zone.

✔ A *touchback* occurs when a punt touches the end zone before the ball touches a player on either team, or when the punt returner catches the ball in the end zone and drops to one knee. The ball is then spotted on the receiving team's 20-yard line.

✔ Either team can *down* a punt after it hits the ground or after one of its players touches the ball past the line of scrimmage. To down the ball, a player must be in possession of the ball, stop his forward movement, and drop to one knee. Such action leads to an official blowing his whistle, signaling the end of action.

✔ A partially blocked punt that crosses the line of scrimmage is treated like a typical punt.

Several times during a game, you see the punt returner stand and simply catch the ball. He doesn't run. In this case, he's probably calling for a *fair catch*. To signal for a fair catch, the player who's preparing to receive the punt must clearly extend his arm over his head and then wave it from side to side to let the officials and the defensive players know that he doesn't plan to run with the ball after catching it. After signaling for a fair catch, the punt returner can't advance the ball. If the defenders tackle him after he signals a fair catch, the kicking team incurs a 15-yard penalty.

However, the player signaling for a fair catch isn't obligated to catch the ball. His only worry is not to touch the ball because if he does so without catching it, the loose ball is treated like a fumble, and the other team can recover it. After he touches it or loses control and the ball hits the ground, either team is allowed to recover the ball.

If the returner *muffs a kick,* or fails to gain possession, the punting team may not advance the ball if they recover it. If the returner gains possession and then fumbles, however, the punting team may advance the ball.

Punting out of trouble

A punter must remain calm and cool when punting out of trouble — that is, anywhere deep in his own territory. Any poor punt — a shank or a flat-out miss — can result in the opponent scoring an easy touchdown, especially if the other team gets the ball 40 yards away from its end zone. Poor punts inevitably mean an automatic three points via a field goal. A dropped snap can mean a defensive score; ditto for a blocked punt — and you'll see little sympathy when that punter returns to the sideline. In 2013, NFL teams averaged 4.9 punts per game, so coaches and players fully expect punts to happen without a hitch.

When I played with the Raiders in Super Bowl XVIII, our punter, Ray Guy, won the game for us. You may be thinking, "What role can a punter have when you beat the Washington Redskins 38–9?" Well, after a bad snap early in the game, Guy jumped as high as he could and grabbed the ball one-handed. When he landed, he boomed his punt way downfield. We were deep in our own territory, and if the ball had gone over Guy's head, the Redskins might have recovered it in our end zone for a touchdown. Who knows?

Guy was a fabulous athlete. He was a first-round draft choice (who ever heard of a punter being taken in the first round?) and a tremendous secondary performer at Southern Mississippi. All I remember about him was that he was like Cool Hand Luke, the role Paul Newman played in the 1967 movie of the same name. No matter the situation, even if he was punting from our own end zone, Guy never got frazzled. In all my years in the NFL, he was head and shoulders above every punter I saw. He was such an exceptional athlete that he served as the quarterback on the scout team in practices, but all he ever did for us in games was punt. Guy led the NFL in punting during three seasons and retired after 14 years with a 42.4-yard average.

Examining the dangerous art of punt returning

Punt returning isn't always as exciting as returning a kickoff because the distance between the team punting and the punt returner isn't as great. A punt returner needs either a line-drive punt or a long punt (45 yards or more from the line of scrimmage) with less than four seconds of hang time — or spectacular blocking by his teammates — to achieve significant positive return yards.

The quick kick

One of the most underutilized trick plays in football is the quick kick. The *quick kick* is when the offensive team surprises the defense by punting the ball on third or even second down, usually from the shotgun formation (described in Chapter 5), although sometimes the ball is pitched to a halfback who does the punting. Teams try the quick kick when they're deep in their own territory and want to get the heck out of there. A quick kick is a risky play because the kicker is closer to the line of scrimmage, which increases the chances of his kick being blocked, and most quarterbacks and halfbacks aren't capable of punting the ball well. Still, if the play works, the ball can travel many yards because no defender is lined up deep in the defensive backfield to catch the punted ball.

To produce positive return yards, the receiving team must concentrate on effectively blocking the outside pursuit men and the center — the players who have the most direct access to the punt returner. The rest of the unit must peel back and attempt to set up a wall or some interference for the returner. Whenever the return unit can hold up four or five players from the punting team, the returner has a chance.

A returner needs to be a fearless competitor and must be willing to catch a punt at or near full speed and continue his run forward. If the defense isn't blocked, the collisions between a returner and a tackler can be extremely violent, leading to injuries and concussions.

A returner's other necessary qualities are superior hands and tremendous concentration. Because of the closeness of the coverage and the bodies flying around, the returner usually catches the ball in traffic. Several players are generally within a yard of him, so the sounds of players blocking and running tend to surround him. He must close out these sounds in order to catch the ball and maintain his composure. To catch the ball and then run with it, under such conditions, takes guts. A returner's final fear is losing the ball via a fumble, thus putting his opponent in favorable field position.

Punt returns typically average around 8 or 9 yards. Great punt returners including Devin Hester and DeSean Jackson have seasons where they average more than 15 yards per return.

A special teams player who's truly special

In 1986, the NFL and its players began awarding Pro Bowl invitations to each conference's best special teams player. Mainly, the award winner is the player who's best at covering punts and kickoffs — the one who's a fearless open-field tackler. Steve Tasker of the Buffalo Bills was even named the MVP of the 1993 Pro Bowl for forcing a fumble and blocking a field goal attempt, thereby preserving a three-point victory for his AFC teammates.

Chapter 13

Coaches, General Managers, and Other Important Folks

In This Chapter

▶ Getting acquainted with the different types of coaches, their roles, and their styles

▶ Exploring the functions of owners and general managers

▶ Scouting opponents and college prospects

▶ Finding out how trainers take care of players

*D*epending on the football franchise, a coach, a general manager, or even an owner has the ability to put the team in the best possible position to win. Each person's primary function is to help the team win, assisting the players in any way possible.

I'm proud to say that I became an All-Pro player because of Earl Leggett, who coached the defensive linemen for the Raiders. I had quickness and strength, the skills that I needed to play in the National Football League, but Leggett was the one who taught me how to harness my ability. He showed me how to anticipate an offense's intentions and use my talents on every single play. He was my mentor.

Probably hundreds of coaches, maybe not as gifted as Leggett, have the same impact on players throughout high school, college, and pro football. If a player is willing to commit to a coach's system, a good coach can develop him into a very good player.

In this chapter, I explain how coaches, from the head coach to the strength coach, work together toward one goal: winning. And for NFL coaches to win, they need a personnel department that has the ability to find players and then sign them. Similarly, a college coach needs the support of the school's administration to be able to recruit good players. I guess I'm saying that there's more to playing football and winning than simply the players — coaches, general managers, scouts, and all the rest play important roles on winning teams.

A Team's Fearless Leaders: The Coaches

Every army has a general and a group of lieutenants; similarly, every football team has a head coach and a coaching staff. The coaches are the leaders of the team; they're the men who put the players in the position to win games. They decide what offenses and defenses the team will use, and good coaches devise these schemes to get the most out of their players' talent. In the NFL, the coach is highly visible because the television cameras show him on the sidelines every Sunday or Monday night.

Some coaches are stars, like the New Orleans Saints' Sean Payton. He has a perfect personality for coaching football because he's charismatic and emotional. Other coaches prefer a low-key, business-like approach, which can be equally successful. Bill Belichick of the New England Patriots and Mike Tomlin of the Pittsburgh Steelers have had great success holding their cards close to the chest.

I'm using NFL coaches as examples because covering them is part of my job, and I know these men personally. I can relate to their powerful impact on a football team. However, thousands of high school and college coaches have the same impact on their teams. Why? Because coaches are special. They devote countless hours to preparing practice schedules and game strategies, working with players in practice and in film sessions, and dealing with them one-on-one when necessary. In high school and college, a coach can be stern and fair like a father. And many coaches have earned players' respect because of their success and longevity — they're revered for being great for the game of football.

A good coach is a special man, one who's supremely confident in his ability to build, prepare, and focus a team on winning a championship. Because the season is long and the games are few in comparison to other sports, a football coach must cope with the mood swings of his players during the week and know when and how to be assertive and when to be relaxed. He sets the tone for his team.

The sections that follow give you a better idea of the coaching staff members and their roles, as well as various coaching styles and philosophies and the day-to-day tasks of coaches.

Discovering who does what on the coaching staff

Almost every football team has more than one coach. Some teams have two coaches monitoring special teams: One coach handles the punter and placekicker, and the other coach handles coverages and kick protection. Including strength and conditioning coaches, the typical NFL team averages 15 assistant coaches. (A college team generally has 9 full-time assistants and 2 graduate assistants, not including strength coaches.) Here's a common NFL coaching staff:

- **Head coach:** The head coach is the main man who gets most of the credit for winning — and most of the blame for losing. Most head coaches are more than 40 years old, have 20 or more seasons of playing and coaching experience, and are experts on one side of the ball or the other. Their styles of coaching vary. Some head coaches demand control over what alignments and plays the team uses on defense and offense. Others delegate one aspect of the game plan, preferring to focus on their particular expertise, whether it's defense or offense. Depending on the franchise's power structure and ownership, the head coach may have a lot of flexibility and control over personnel, or he may have a rather limited role.

- **Offensive coordinator:** The offensive coordinator is the coach in charge of the offensive players. He usually calls the plays and works directly with the quarterbacks. He's responsible for developing the offensive game plan (the plays he believes will be successful against the upcoming opponent) and works with the head coach on how practice is organized, especially if some of the plays are unusual or somewhat unfamiliar to the offensive personnel. Some coordinators do all the work and are almost as valuable as the head coach. On some NFL teams, the owner is as involved in the hiring of the offensive coordinator as in the hiring of the head coach.

- **Defensive coordinator:** The defensive coordinator is the coach in charge of the defensive players. He usually decides what defensive schemes to run. Like the offensive coordinator, the defensive coordinator meets with half the team on a typical practice day and prepares them for the upcoming opponent. I've always thought that a good defensive coordinator is one who can adapt his system to his players' talents rather than the other way around. But sometimes teams want to find players that fit their particular system. The best defensive coordinators are the ones who are really flexible and simply strive to put their players in the best possible situation to succeed.

- **Special teams coach:** The special teams coach supervises the kickers, punters, kick return team, field goal protection team, punt return team, and so on. Generally, he's coaching the younger players on a team, and he must find a way to motivate them to do their jobs. Many of the special teams' stars are backups and reserves — they're players who aren't yet talented enough to be offensive or defensive starters. On some units, the special teams coach may have starters mixed in with rookies, and so he must find a way to get these players to complement one another.

He must study the strengths and weaknesses of how teams return kicks and cover kicks. Also, he studies film to discover whether a team is particularly weak in kick protection so he can prepare his team to attempt a block in a specific game.

✔ **Quarterback coach:** A quarterback coach is an assistant coach who monitors the physical and mental aspects of a quarterback's game. He works on the quarterback's footwork, pass-drop technique, and throwing motion. He makes sure a quarterback doesn't fall into bad mental or physical habits. In training camp, if the starting quarterback is an experienced veteran, the quarterback coach may devote extra hours to the backup and third-string quarterback, hoping to develop them for the future and prepare them to play in an emergency. On some teams, the quarterback coach serves as a sounding board between the quarterback and the head coach. On NFL teams, the head coach and the quarterback are usually under the greatest scrutiny.

✔ **Offensive line coach:** An offensive line coach works with the offensive linemen and generally has a solid understanding of the team's running game. He and the offensive coordinator spend time discussing what running plays may work, depending on what the offensive line coach views as his unit's strengths and weaknesses against the upcoming opponent. He is also a key component in developing the offense's pass protection schemes. A good offensive line coach can mold five blockers, all with different or varied levels of skill, into a solid, efficient unit. On some teams, the line coach is more valuable than the offensive coordinator.

✔ **Defensive line coach:** A defensive line coach is the guy who works exclusively with the defensive linemen. He works on individual technique (run stopping, gap control, pass rushing, and so on) and whatever stunts the defensive coordinator wants from these players.

✔ **Linebacker coach:** A linebacker coach works with linebackers and, depending on the team's style of defense, ranks a step below the defensive coordinator. Defenses that exclusively use four linebackers need a coach who can teach all the variations necessary for this scheme to work. This coach must work on tackling, pass-rushing off the corner, and particular pass coverage drops.

✔ **Secondary coach:** A secondary coach is the coach who works with the defensive backs. He must have a total understanding of pass offenses. He works on all aspects of pass coverage, from footwork and deep zone drops to how to prepare players for the particular receivers they'll face.

✔ **Strength coach:** A strength coach specializes in weight training and conditioning. He makes sure the players are strong and in shape throughout the season, and he often coordinates off-season training programs. A strength coach also works with team doctors to prepare and monitor rehabilitation exercises following player surgeries.

A team may also have coaches for specific positions, such as a receiver or running backs coach, depending on how many coaches the team can afford to keep on staff. On smaller staffs, the head coach may also serve as the offensive coordinator, or the special teams coach may also be the strength coach. On some large NFL staffs, the head coach, not the offensive coordinator, calls the offensive plays.

Exploring the different coaching styles and philosophies

Without question, a coach can have a dramatic impact on a football team. Some coaches want to control the emotional pulse of their teams; others attempt to use their influence by establishing good rapport with selected team leaders. A coach needs to stand apart as an authority figure, especially if he coaches younger players. He makes the rules, and the players must follow his orders. Still, a coach can't be as demanding as an army sergeant because he wants his players to feel comfortable talking to him about any serious off-the-field problems they may be facing. A pro coach may even allow himself to become friendly with his players and treat them like the adults they are.

No one set standard for being a head coach exists, nor is there a particular philosophy that a coach should adhere to. Good head coaches learn from the men for whom they've worked, absorbing the good qualities and tossing out the bad ones that don't work with their personality. A coach needs to be himself and be true to how he would want to be treated. Players can spot a phony as soon as he walks into the team meeting room. The next sections run through the different types of coaching styles and philosophies.

The yell-your-head-off coach

Players don't like coaches who yell and scream all the time. But I've known some coaches who can communicate only by screaming. They aren't screaming because they're angry; they just know screaming is the only way their instructions are going to sink into their players' heads. (Granted, players can barely think on the practice field when their bodies are tired and aching from a long day.) The screamers are generally defensive coaches; offensive coaches tend to be calmer and more cerebral.

Many of these screamers are good coaches. When Steve Mariucci screamed at any of his Detroit Lions or San Francisco 49ers, everyone at practice knew he meant business. Mariucci wasn't a screamer by nature, but he, like many other coaches, yelled when a player or unit constantly repeated the same mistake. After all, a coach can be patient for only so long.

You can spot the yell-your-head-off coach anywhere. Here are some examples of that coaching style:

- ✔ Whenever these coaches believe their teams have been penalized unfairly, you can bet they're yelling at the referee or some official along the sidelines.

- ✔ Whenever a player misses an assignment and causes a critical play to fail, you may see these coaches actually grab the player and tell him, inches away from his face, how and why he screwed up.

- ✔ These coaches often grab a player's face mask and rattle his cage before telling him how poorly he's playing or practicing.

- ✔ These coaches throw things. Coaches who scream a lot love to toss their hats, clipboards, or whatever they're holding to get everyone's attention.

The kinder, gentler coach

Another kind of coach takes the kinder, gentler approach. These coaches rarely yell, and they believe that teaching good character to players can be as important as teaching physical skills. Tom Landry, revered coach of the Dallas Cowboys from 1960 through 1988, was known for his calm, stoic demeanor.

The smash-mouth football coach

Smash-mouth coaches love nothing more than to see a tremendous block by an offensive lineman and then watch their running back gain 10 yards while running over the opposition. Most of these coaches began as defensive coaches, and they believe in dominating the line of scrimmage and want their defense to decide the outcome of a game. On offense, they'd rather win by running the football. Bill Cowher (who won a Super Bowl with the Pittsburgh Steelers) and Bill Parcells (who won two Super Bowls with the New York Giants) are examples of the smash-mouth coach. They prepared their teams to be the stronger, dominant team in a matchup, and that's why they were successful.

So that you're sure to recognize this type of coach during a game, take a look at these examples of the smash-mouth coaching style:

- ✔ When the game is close and the offense needs to convert a play on fourth and 1, these coaches are likely to gamble, believing that their offensive line and running back can pick up the first down.

- ✔ These coaches are more apt to continue to run a successful play until the opposition stops it.

✔ These coaches' football teams usually focus on both the offensive and the defensive linemen. Their teams may not always win the game, but they plan on winning the war along the line of scrimmage.

✔ These coaches rarely waiver from their beliefs in how to approach a game or a particular opponent. They're very strong-minded coaches.

The offensive-genius coach

You see a lot of offensive-genius coaches in the NFL. Mike Shanahan, who directed the Denver Broncos to their 1998 and 1999 Super Bowl wins, typifies this type of coach. An offensive-genius is a coach who seems to have an unlimited ability to develop new plays; defensive coaches know that these coaches will try more than one new play or variation of an old play every week. Offensive-genius coaches aren't always viewed as tough guys because they're so cerebral. Nevertheless, although their minds may be working overtime on the sidelines, they don't tolerate a lack of discipline or shoddy play on the football field.

This kind of coach is constantly looking for an edge on the field. One example of Shanahan's genius took place in the 1997 season when the Broncos had to beat the Kansas City Chiefs to reach the Super Bowl. The Chiefs had a great pass-rusher in Derrick Thomas, and they preferred to line up Thomas on the weak side, away from the tight end. The Chiefs had a strong linebacker, Wayne Simmons, who demolished most tight ends. Prior to the snap, Shanahan would move his tight end off the line of scrimmage and motion him over until he was in front of Derrick Thomas. Then he'd call a running play directly at Thomas. That simple formation adjustment prior to the snap gave Shanahan's offense the matchups that he wanted on a running play. In such a short period of time, Thomas and Simmons couldn't switch sides before the ball was snapped. Denver had success running at Thomas while negating the Chiefs' greatest asset: Thomas's pass-rushing ability.

Here are some typical actions of the offensive-genius coach:

✔ These coaches generally wear headsets on the sidelines to communicate with their assistants upstairs in the press box, and they always have a *playsheet* (the game plan of offensive plays) in their hands. They're more involved with the offensive team than the defensive team during a game.

✔ These coaches tend to be more thoughtful and under control during sideline sessions with their players. They don't rattle easily.

✔ When they talk during practice, these coaches explain the whole play and show how a small aspect can lead to a gigantic reward. For example, each player's alignment dictates a defensive alignment response.

Anticipating the defense's alignment to a certain formation or pass route can lead to an opening to spring a big play.

✔ At the training facility, these coaches work alone most of the time. They have a daily staff meeting, but they like to think and tinker with the offense for hours on their own.

Looking into what coaches do when they're not yelling on the sidelines

Coaching a football team is a full-time job. While players rest during the off-season, coaches are busy planning for the season ahead. Following is a quick look at what coaches do during the season and in the offseason.

During the season

Coaches at all levels prepare playbooks that every player receives — and many of these playbooks include more than 200 plays for the offense alone. They meet with the general manager and other college and pro scouts regarding personnel — whom to trade for, whom to acquire, and whom to release.

With the head coach leading the way, the coaches meet during the players' day off. During this meeting, they prepare the game plan for the next week and review hours of film of their own players and the opposition, looking for tendencies, strengths, and weaknesses. During training camp, the coaching staff dissects what it wants to accomplish during the season in all phases of the game: offense, defense, and special teams. At the same time, the coaches test to see how the players are adapting to specific plays and strategies. From there, they refine their plan, tinkering with minute details in order to guarantee success.

In the NFL, every play is analyzed and dissected until the coaching staff knows exactly how it wants to instruct the players on the practice field. A coach can break down a single play on videotape to show a player taking the wrong first step, backing up too much, angling his shoulders improperly, or failing to read the other team's intentions.

College and high school coaches meet regularly with their school's athletic director and administrators regarding financial budgets and player eligibility status. They oversee travel schedules and are involved in picking hotels and meals for road trips. College and high school coaches usually work all day on Sunday, examining film of the weekend's game and preparing for the next week. They have staff meetings in preparation for meeting the players on Monday. And, of course, they devote a lot of time to motivating their players.

Coaches also deal with the media. In the NFL, coaches may have press briefings with newspaper, radio, and television reporters every day except Tuesday and Saturday. However, on Saturday, they must meet with network television producers and commentators to discuss their opinions of what may occur in Sunday's or Monday's game. College and high school coaches may also deal with local reporters, although on a smaller scale.

During the off-season

Although high school and college football teams are restricted to a certain number of off-season practice days, NFL coaching staffs work virtually year-round making free-agency decisions, scouting potential draft choices, monitoring selective *mini-camps* (three or four days of on-field practice), and attending countless organizational meetings. Most NFL coaches take their vacations in late June and early July, right before the opening of training camp.

An NFL head coach spends his days in the off-season preparing practice schedules for training camp and the regular season. The college coach devotes much of his off-season to *recruiting* high school players and hosting clinics for high school coaches. Recruiting means visiting a potential player in his hometown — which necessitates a lot of traveling — and meeting with his parents, guardians, and high school coaches.

Getting axed: The pressure of being a football coach

Coaches work long hours because they're usually under enormous pressure to win. If they don't win, even on the high school level, they get fired. As soon as an NFL season ends, several coaches are usually given the ax. Some teams seem to change coaches every year.

When a head coach is fired, usually his coaching staff of 10 to 15 assistants is also out of work. Or, sometimes, a head coach saves his job but is forced by management to fire some or all of his assistants. This situation doesn't happen a lot, but it does occur enough to make assistant coaches realize that coaching is more about business than it is about loyalty. Besides being fired, coaching staffs are constantly turning over as assistants move on to different teams and receive promotions. Changing teams creates a lot of upheaval for a coach's family, especially if he's married with children. Coaches who begin their careers dreaming of the NFL usually bounce around to several colleges, sometimes as many as eight different jobs, before landing a pro position. And I know good NFL assistant coaches who've worked for five different teams during their careers.

The Team's Public Face: The Owners

People buy teams for many different reasons, but most owners simply want to be public figures. The NFL is structured financially so that every club receives an equal share of television revenue and splits the ticket revenue — it's more or less a socialist system. The concept is that the weakest franchise can gross as much revenue as the strongest franchise. However, a team's revenue from local radio broadcasts, luxury boxes, parking, concessions, and private seat licenses (fans pay a fee for the right to own a season ticket) isn't totally shared with the other teams. But the revenue from NFL Properties (income generated from selling NFL logo clothing, hats, and so on) and the Super Bowl is shared. Therefore, you don't have to own a Super Bowl team to do well financially.

After the head coach and the star players on the team, the owner may be the next most visible person. Most football fans know, for example, that Jerry Jones owns the Dallas Cowboys. At one time Jones had his own television show in Dallas and also wrote a newspaper column. He's very visible in marketing his football team and is very active in network television negotiations. However, many franchise owners are rarely interviewed, choosing to remain behind the scenes, preferring that their coach and general manager speak for the franchise.

The NFL requires one person to own at least 30 percent of a particular franchise and prefers that this person has no financial interest in any other professional sports leagues. Some franchises, such as the Pittsburgh Steelers and Chicago Bears, have been owned for decades by members of one family. The New York Giants have two owners, each with a 50 percent stake in the franchise.

I don't think any owner in pro football knew more about the game than Al Davis of the Raiders, who passed away in 2011. In pure Xs and Os, the strategy of a game, Davis was like a coach. He actually started in football as a coach and was an excellent one. And in terms of making the financial commitment, Davis always brought in great players. He made every possible effort to improve his team. You can't say that about every NFL owner.

In its August 2014 annual listing of NFL franchise values, *Forbes* magazine placed the value of franchises between $930 million and $3.2 billion. You must be extremely wealthy to own an NFL franchise. Although the financial return is generous, many businesspeople would tell you that better ways exist to invest that amount of money. Many NFL owners are actually sports fans, people who love the game as much as their pursuit of financial success. Many of them contribute their time, energy, and financial resources to their respective communities, believing that football is part of their region's social fabric.

An Owner's Eyes and Ears: General Managers

On many NFL teams, general managers are the eyes and ears of the owner, and they oversee the day-to-day operation of the team. They must be cold and calculating people because they have to make a lot of difficult personnel decisions. They make the player trades and free agent acquisitions, decide salary levels, and ultimately determine which players to select in the NFL draft. General managers must be excellent judges of every player's ability because they're responsible for doing what's best for the organization. They must have a feel for what the team needs and be able to work in conjunction with the head coach and his needs.

The best possible scenario is to have a solid general manager and a great head coach, who can put their egos aside and work together. But this situation is very rare these days because head coaches usually want total control over personnel, like Pete Carroll has in Seattle.

General managers oversee a large front-office staff. Some teams have business, marketing, and public relations personnel. People reporting to the general manager include the following: *capologists* (who monitor a team's salary scale within the salary cap; more on the salary cap in Chapter 17), business managers, contract negotiators (also known as a club vice president), human resources directors, and public relations directors.

The People Responsible for Finding Talent: Scouts

Two basic kinds of scouts exist in the NFL: pro scouts and college scouts.

A team can have a great week practicing, but if the players don't know what to expect from their opponents, they may find themselves behind by 14 points or more in a hurry. *Pro scouts,* people who attend NFL games and study a team's opponents, exist so teams can anticipate what each opponent will do. These scouts attend the games of upcoming opponents and take copious notes, tracking every offensive and defensive tactic, keeping an eye on key players, noting who gets injured, and so on. Then they bring this information back to the coaches, who may devise parts of their game plans around the scouts' input.

A *college scout* examines a pro prospect's every move. He times the player in the 40-yard dash, studies his ability and decisions on every play, and monitors him off the field. NFL teams want to know whether a prospect has ever been arrested and, if so, for what crime. They're concerned about illegal drug use and also about how the player performs in the classroom. They want to know about his attitude, his personality, and his approach to football and to life in general. A good college scout watches the prospect in practice and games and also watches film of all his games. The scout then interviews the prospect and members of the college coaching staff. He may even interview opposing coaches to find out their views of the player, and athletic trainers to check on a player's past injuries or training room habits. When scouting the top 100 college players, teams often have two or more scouts examine a prospect.

Keeping Players Strong and Healthy: Trainers and Team Doctors

A team isn't very good if its players don't stay healthy or recover quickly if they get injured. Trainers and team doctors step in to help alleviate these concerns. Most teams have their own orthopedic surgeon and general practitioner. Unless these doctors have total autonomy, they're often put in really difficult positions because their job is to take care of the player, but their employer, who's the owner of the team, wants the player on the field all the time.

A trainer's job is to monitor every injury and then work with the doctor on the rehabilitation process. In some instances, players seek outside medical opinions, especially if the injury is considered serious or the team doctor prescribes surgery. The league monitors injuries and has several medical groups that assist on serious injuries, particularly injuries involving the head and neck.

A trainer also works with the strength trainer to make sure injured players aren't overextending themselves in the weight room or exercising too much. Most pro and college teams have at least two full-time trainers, and some have part-time assistants for training camps. Trainers are responsible for dispensing and monitoring all medicine prescribed by the doctors and all dietary supplements that players are taking. A trainer also inspects team meals to make sure they contain the proper proteins and carbohydrates.

The best trainer is trusted by both the players and the coaching staff. The worst thing a trainer can do is inform the head coach that a certain player isn't hurting as badly as he claims to be. If the trainer feels that way, he must confront the player as well. Players need to believe that the trainer is concerned about their welfare, regardless of how that concern (possibly in the form of keeping a player off the field) may affect the team's win-loss record.

Part V
Football for Everyone

Visit www.dummies.com/extras/football for an article on one of the great teams of all time, the 1970–1974 Miami Dolphins.

In this part . . .

- ✔ Follow youth, high school, and college football
- ✔ Understand how the NFL has become so successful
- ✔ Find out how to play fantasy football

Chapter 14

Armchair Quarterbacks and Other Fabulous Fans

In This Chapter

▶ Understanding football jargon

▶ Following a game on TV or the radio

▶ Watching a game in the stands

▶ Keeping up with the game in various ways

*F*ootball is a great sport because you don't have to play it to enjoy it. (In fact, after you watch a few of the hits football players take, you may decide you'd *rather* watch.) This chapter gives you tips for making the most of the viewing (or listening) experience, however you're following the game — on television, from the stands, through your browser or mobile device, or through the radio. I also tell you about all the ways you can keep up with your favorite teams when no games are being played — through newspapers, magazines, and the Internet. Finally, I let you know how to visit the College and Pro Football Halls of Fame.

Deciphering the Announcers' Slang

One of the most difficult and intimidating parts about following a football game is that the announcers sometimes seem to be speaking a foreign language known only to true football enthusiasts. But if you remember a few key terms, you'll be way ahead of the game. Here are some terms you may hear, along with their definitions (The Appendix defines a whole bunch of football terms as well):

✔ **Corner blitz:** A blitzing linebacker or defensive back rushes the quarterback from the outside edge of the offensive alignment or the *corner* of the offensive line.

- **Dime back:** When the defense has six players in the secondary, the sixth player is called a *dime back* because he's the second nickel back (two nickels equal a dime).

- **Forklift:** A defensive lineman lifts an offensive lineman off the ground, moving him aside as he rushes the quarterback.

- **Franchise player:** Commentators routinely refer to the most important player on a team as the *franchise*. In Indianapolis, for example, quarterback Andrew Luck is the franchise player; the Colts can't win without him.

- **Looking off a defensive back:** Commentators say this when a quarterback eyeballs a defensive back, giving the defensive player the impression that he's throwing the ball toward his area. In actuality, the quarterback intends to throw in a different direction. He fools the defensive back by *looking him off.*

- **Muscling his way through:** When a commentator says this, he means a player managed to gain a physical advantage over an opponent.

- **Nickel package:** The defensive team is using five defensive backs in the secondary to defend the pass.

- **Running to daylight:** The running back has found the soft spot in the defense and is running freely down the field toward the end zone.

- **Shooting a gap:** A defensive player somehow runs untouched through a space that should have been blocked by an offensive player. The gap is often between two offensive players or to the outside shoulder of one player.

- **Stretch the field:** An offense is employing three to five wide receivers in a formation that's spread out along the line of scrimmage. A defense has to stretch to cover all of the receivers.

- **Zeroing in on a receiver:** The quarterback is focused on throwing to one specific receiver. The quarterback watches the receiver while he's running his route and then releases the ball when he's open.

Following a Game on Television or Radio

If you can't be there in person, the next best thing is to watch the game on television or listen to it on the radio. Hey, don't knock the radio. Radio announcers add pizzazz to the game. They have to paint a picture of the game in words, so most of them have developed a colorful vocabulary and a delivery that makes a game more exciting. I know more than a few fans who get the video portion of the game through their television set and the audio portion from their favorite radio announcer. In the upcoming sections I share the fine points of following a game on television and the radio. (By the way, I realize you can now watch games online, but the stream is essentially the same as what's broadcast on television.)

Watching a game on television

In a way, television is the best way to watch a football game; you can see up close what's happening on the field, and you can watch replays of the big plays if you missed them the first time around. My innovative bosses at FOX Sports devised the scoreboard clock, which appears in the upper corner of your television screen and gives you a stadium feel. It gives you the score, the down and distance, and how much time is remaining in a particular quarter.

Excellent football analysts add humor and insight to the game. They're also good with a device known as a *telestrator,* which allows them to circle players on the screen or demonstrate how a certain play was successful by diagramming it on the screen.

I like to watch a game from the inside out; first I look at the quarterback and then I check out the action away from the ball. Because the networks use so many cameras, you can follow the entire game and not miss a play. What's great about television are the replays — you can watch a replay of a critical play from two or three different angles. These different views are often necessary to determine whether a player was in possession of the ball, especially on really close plays involving receptions and fumbles. Also, the different angles help fans interpret whether the officials called the correct penalty, especially on penalties like pass interference (I fill you in on penalties, including pass interference, in Chapter 3).

Here are some tips to help you become a more savvy and informed viewer when you're watching a game on television:

- ✔ **Start at the line of scrimmage.** Look wide to see how many receivers you spot and where they're located. Scan to see how many players are lined up on the defensive line and in the defensive backfield. Where and how the players line up gives you an indication of what the play may be.

- ✔ **Keep an eye on the game's progress.** In the upper corner of the television screen, check out what the down is, how far the offense needs to go for the first down, how much time is left on the clock, and what the score is. The score and the time left on the clock often dictate whether a team will run or pass.

✔ **Check the quarterback.** If he's positioned 5 yards behind the center, he's in the shotgun formation, meaning there's a 90 percent chance he'll pass the ball. The other 10 percent of the time, the quarterback drops back and then hands off the ball to a running back or runs on his own.

✔ **Look for movement among the linebackers and defensive backs.** If defenders appear to be creeping toward the line of scrimmage, they're probably going to either blitz the quarterback or fill all the running lanes to neutralize a run play.

✔ **Look at the defensive fronts, paying particular attention to the defensive tackles.** If only three linemen are lined up close to the line of scrimmage, the defense expects the offense to pass the ball. If the defense has four down linemen on the field and the linebackers are within a couple yards of the line of scrimmage, the defense expects the offense to try to run.

✔ **Count the number of defensive backs.** If more than four defensive backs are in the game, the defense is geared toward preventing a pass completion.

Listening to a game on the radio

Every NFL team and most major college teams have a local radio station that owns the rights to the teams' broadcasts. And because of the popularity of sports talk radio, many fans want to tune in to their favorite broadcasters.

Perhaps the best thing about listening to the radio is that you get the home-team announcers' insights into what strategy your team plans to use. These announcers know the players and can immediately tell you which player has the ball and who made the tackle. They also have access to the injury reports, so you can receive player updates throughout the broadcast. You also hear important statistics — such as how many total yards and first downs each team has collected — faster than most scoreboards can provide them.

The first time I saw a fan listening to a radio in a ballpark was during a Los Angeles Dodgers game. Although the fans were watching the action in person, they wanted to hear Vin Scully, the radio announcer, describe it. Just like these baseball fans, many football fans also enjoy listening to the radio when attending a game.

Talk radio: Getting the inside scoop

I enjoy being a guest on most sports talk shows. To me, talk radio is another way to get information about pro football. These shows discuss the inside scoop and address all the serious issues.

Sports talk radio has altered the landscape of sports journalism. Players and coaches listen to these shows. One season, Philadelphia's WIP radio station was so critical of the Philadelphia Eagles that the team declined to issue game credentials to some of the station's commentators. I know that coaches on the team quit listening to the morning shows because they would get too upset to go to work. This shows you the power of talk radio and how it can irritate people.

However, I recommend listening to the pro football reports in most NFL cities. If the talk radio show includes a lot of conversations about your team and regular player interviews, the program is probably worth listening to. Some talk radio hosts can be more insightful than some reporters; they do their homework on the team.

Other talk radio hosts allow callers to dominate their programs. This kind of interaction with the audience might make for great radio, but you rarely get much insight from local fans, whose commentary, let's face it, generally breaks down into these categories: calling for the quarterback to be benched after a loss, calling for the coach to be fired after a loss, complaining about the refs, or declaring their team an unbeatable playoff contender after any regular-season victory.

Attending a Game

To the die-hard football fan, nothing beats watching a football game live. You get caught up in the excitement of cheering for your team. You sometimes get the feeling that the outcome of the game is in your hands — and in a way it *is* in your hands because cheering loudly can disrupt the other team's offense and make it difficult for the other team to hear its quarterback barking plays. Most of all, attending a game is just plain fun. The following sections look into some of the nuances of watching a game in person.

Picking the best seats

The really good seats in every stadium are near the 50-yard line, 25 rows up, where you can scan the entire field. But those great seats usually belong to longtime season ticket holders. If you aren't a longtime season ticket holder or lucky enough to have an official sideline credential, the end zone can be a good place to watch a game. The best seat in the house, from my perspective, is in the end zone about 20 rows up. Of course, you need good binoculars. I like to see plays developing and watch the line play on both sides of the ball, and the end zone offers the best vantage point to see this action.

Sitting in the end zone, you can focus on a matchup of two linemen, like a defensive end battling an offensive tackle, and watch how they attack each other. Whoever wins this battle is going to win the war (the game). These individual battles can teach you a lot about football, even when the play or ball is going in the opposite direction. For a team to win, its players need to win these individual battles.

I love to watch a game from the sidelines. It's too bad more fans don't have that same opportunity at least once in their lives. Standing on the sidelines, you see firsthand the speed of the players and the ferocity of their hits. The contact occurs — and the overall game is played — at such a high speed. The players move like bullet trains plowing through a cornfield.

Wherever you sit, make sure you buy a program or check your local newspaper or team website for team depth charts and numbered rosters — these rosters are the only way to identify the many players on the field. A *depth chart* lists the starting lineups for both teams by their positions on offense and defense. It also lists the punter, placekicker, snapper for punts and kicks, and kickoff and punt return specialists. The reserves are listed alongside the starters on the depth chart, so when a player is injured, you can figure out who will replace him.

Knowing what to focus on

The beauty of watching a game in person is that you can see the entire play develop. As soon as the center snaps the ball, all 22 players on the field are moving. Television can't possibly capture that singular moment and every player, too. At the stadium, you can also watch what happens to a quarterback after the ball is released. On television, the camera follows the ball, but in person, you can see whether the quarterback is hit after he releases the ball. Occasionally, the quarterback and a pass-rusher exchange words (or even swings).

The special teams play, especially kickoffs and long punts, is exciting to watch in person because you can follow the flight of the ball and the coverage players running full speed toward the kick returner. Because kickoff and punt plays cover so much of the field, often 50 to 70 yards, television can't capture all the action.

During commercial timeouts, scan the sidelines with your binoculars. You can spot coaches talking strategy with players, and sometimes you can capture an animated conversation or debate. The more games you attend, the better able you'll be to follow the action and observe the sidelines. The pace is fast during plays, but there's enough down time between plays to check out what's happening on the sidelines and to figure out, by how teams are substituting, which play may be called next.

Enjoying the halftime show

Except for the elaborate halftime shows at the Super Bowl every year, halftime shows aren't televised anymore. To see a halftime show, you must attend a game in person.

College game halftime shows usually feature high-spirited bands, drill teams, and cheerleading squads doing their best to rally the fans. I remember when you used to see *card stunts* at college football games. To perform one, thousands of fans would hold up different-colored cards coordinated to display, for the entire stadium, a team name, mascot picture, or some other message for the faithful.

Some colleges are famous for their halftime performances. The Stanford band, for example, often puts on a comic show. At a show during Stanford's annual game against arch-rival California, the band dressed one member in a California band uniform and had him march around looking extremely confused during the Stanford performance.

Keeping Up with Your Favorite Teams

The fun of football doesn't end when the last seconds of the fourth quarter tick away. Diehard fans love to analyze the statistics of today's games and find out all about the upcoming ones. You can get this type of information from a wide variety of sources; I list some of my favorites in the next sections.

The NFL Network and the NFL Redzone Channel

The NFL Network offers non-stop, continuous coverage of professional football. It's available on most cable and satellite providers in the United States.

In addition to game highlights, in-depth analysis, and news coverage of teams and players, the NFL Network broadcasts half of the Thursday night games each season and also shows replays of the most interesting games from the previous weekend.

The NFL Redzone Channel broadcasts on Sundays during the regular season. Its goal is to provide instant coverage and highlights of every game taking place. If you're watching the Redzone Channel, you'll see every touchdown from every game. It's a great way to follow all the games every Sunday during the season.

Internet sports sites

You can find more football-related information on the Internet than you could read in a whole season — everything from who's being traded and who's injured to who's predicted to go to the playoffs and more. The following websites are great sources of up-to-the-minute football info:

- ✔ **CBS Sports** (`www.cbssports.com`): This site covers the NFL and college football. It's is an excellent source for information, such as team updates, schedules, injury reports, and statistics.

- ✔ **ESPN** (`espn.go.com`): This online version of ESPN offers in-depth information about the NFL and college football. At `espn3.com`, you can watch Web casts of college football games (if your Internet connection is good enough).

- ✔ **Deadspin** (`www.deadspin.com`): This popular site made a name for itself by breaking news on the more salacious and scandalous side of sports. Its columns and blog posts tend to be irreverent and humorous.

- ✔ **FOX Sports** (`www.foxsports.com`): This website covers college football and the NFL. If you're interested in knowing what's going on with your favorite NFL team during the off-season, check out the Teams area. You get full coverage of the signings, trades, and contract negotiations for each team.

- ✔ **NBC Sports** (`www.nbcsports.com`): This easy-to-navigate site covers both the NFL and college football.

- ✔ **NFL.com** (`www.nfl.com`): This is the official site of the NFL. In addition to scores, statistics, and news, it gives in-depth team coverage, including audio and video clips. The individual team pages offer links to your favorite teams' official websites.

- ✔ **Sports Illustrated** (`www.si.com`): This website includes comprehensive coverage of the NFL and college football.

✔ **Sporting News** (`www.sportingnews.com`): This site, which is the online version of the magazine, provides an abundance of information about NFL and college football. You can customize this site so that it displays your favorite sports and teams.

✔ **Yahoo Sports** (`sports.yahoo.com`): This sports site is one of the most visited on the Internet. In addition to football scores, news, and stats, it offers commentary from multiple columnists.

Fantasy football sites

Many of the major sports web sites listed in the preceding section (CBS, ESPN, FOX, NFL, Yahoo) offer free fantasy football leagues that you and your friends can join. They are all full-featured and provide up-to-date stats and scoring.

If you need advice on fantasy strategy, you're a simple web search away. Countless sites offer tips, stats, and picks for fantasy enthusiasts. If you're into fantasy football, you're probably visiting multiple sites per week looking for any tidbit of information that might give you an advantage over your opponent.

I offer some information on fantasy football in Chapter 18.

Twitter

It seems like everyone is tweeting these days, even if very few people have anything meaningful to say. Sports figures are no exception. Many football players in both the NFL and college tweet regularly. Sometimes they offer interesting observations; other times they accidentally send inappropriate pictures of themselves to thousands of fans. And a few players use their Twitter accounts to connect with fans and their community. Choose wisely when deciding whom to follow.

Sports columnists as well as radio and television personalities also use Twitter to communicate with fans. Many *live tweet* a game, meaning that they use their Twitter account to provide a running commentary during a live football game. Some of these tweeting marathons can be hilarious, and that's one of the reasons why so many people watch games with one eye on their phone, tablet, or laptop. In addition to following scores and fantasy stats, they're also reading Twitter and sending out tweets of their own. For some, this instant interactivity is a lot of fun. But it's also nice to occasionally put down all the gadgets and just watch the game. (I hope that doesn't make me sound too old.)

Mobile apps

Smartphones and tablets give football fans multiple tools for following their teams. NFL Mobile is a great app for checking scores and viewing highlights as the games are going on. You can also watch NFL games (after paying a subscription fee) using the NFL Sunday Ticket app. NFL Game Rewind, which also requires a paid subscription, gives you the ability to watch full replays of every NFL game.

Visiting the Football Halls of Fame

Visiting one of the football halls of fame — there's one for college and one for professional football — is a terrific way to find out more about how football became what it is today. Both are filled with memorabilia from players and teams from the turn of the 19th century to the present. The many exhibits include uniforms and pictures of Hall of Famers in action and screening rooms in which you can enjoy films of legendary players and teams. Following is the contact information for both halls of fame:

College Football Hall of Fame

250 Marietta Street NW
Atlanta, GA 30313
404-880-4800
www.cfbhall.com

Pro Football Hall of Fame

2121 George Halas Drive NW
Canton, OH
330-456-8207
www.profootballhof.com

Chapter 15

Youth Leagues and High School Football

In This Chapter

▶ Deciding when to let your child play football

▶ Understanding and succeeding in the high school game

On the youth level, football isn't like baseball or basketball. My experience with those sports is that not playing well is okay because you're not putting yourself in danger. With football, on the other hand, you can really get hurt if you're not physically and mentally equipped to handle the game — especially if you're a young kid.

But football can teach you a lot about life; it's a character-building sport. Young players can discover the rewards of hard work, dedication, teamwork, and discipline. Football, like a lot of sports, is a great way to bring families together.

In this chapter, I discuss the benefits of youth football, from Pop Warner and flag football to high school football. I offer my own thoughts on coaching, the father-son relationship, and the things that young players need to focus on to be successful with the game and with life. I also look at making the transition from high school to college football.

Determining When to Start Playing

 If your young son has the desire to play the game, let him play; just don't push him to play. Football either is or isn't the right sport for him, and everyone will know quickly whether he made a good choice.

I didn't start playing football until I was 15; my oldest son, Chris, played football for the first time when he was 12, and now he's a defensive end for the St. Louis Rams. Because he was bigger than most boys his age, he couldn't play with his friends and other 12-year-olds; he had to play on the junior varsity football team with boys who were 15 and 16. Because of age differences, he got physically whipped. But I tried to help and support him.

If you want your son to play at a young age, you must be committed to supporting and consoling him during the tough times. Young players — particularly those who have talent but haven't had a lot of success — need encouragement. However, fathers who care *too much* and try to live vicariously through their children often ruin the football experience for their children. Find a good balance.

Pop Warner Football and other local junior tackle programs have teams for 7-year-olds. I think starting football at age 7 is a little too young because kids that age are too small and may get hurt. But if your child is mature for his age he may have fun. With young kids, though, every parent should monitor practices and make sure the coach knows what he's doing and that he encourages the players to have fun.

Signing Up Your Kids for Youth Football

Depending on where you live in the United States, your child has multiple options for playing youth football. The following sections explain what these options are.

When you sign up your child for youth football, you need a copy of his birth certificate and a current report card. (Most leagues won't enroll students who are failing in school.) Also, examine your health insurance and make sure that your child is covered for all types of injury.

If you can't find sign-up information, check with your town or city's recreation department. Most know how to locate league officials and know where teams are practicing.

Pop Warner and similar programs

The nation's largest youth football organization is Pop Warner Little Scholars, Inc., which is the legal name for Pop Warner Football. Pop Warner has leagues in 42 states and several countries. More than 300,000 boys and girls (the girls take part in cheer and dance teams) participate in those programs.

Pop Warner has stringent safety rules, including an age-weight schematic. This system ensures maximum safety because players are evenly matched in size and physical maturity. Pop Warner also has a no-cut rule, which means players don't have to try out. "First come, first on" is how Pop Warner operates. Pop Warner has different age-group divisions for players ages 5 to 16. Players move up to different divisions until they reach the Bantam division in which the 16-year-olds play. In many parts of the country, school districts no longer have junior high/middle school football programs, and youth leagues fill that void.

To find a Pop Warner program in your area, check your local phone book; email the organization at football@popwarner.com; write to Pop Warner Little Scholars at 586 Middletown Blvd., Suite C-100, Langhorne, PA 19047; call 215-752-2691; or visit www.popwarner.com.

Punt, Pass & Kick

Every year, thousands of boys and girls ages 6 to 15 participate in the NFL Punt, Pass & Kick competition. Since this competition began in the early 1960s, numerous participants — including quarterbacks Dan Marino, Drew Bledsoe, Brett Favre, Troy Aikman, and Randall Cunningham — have gone on to play in the NFL.

Kids compete by age group in this competition, which is offered on the local level in every NFL city. The competition is then regionalized, and those winners compete at the end of the NFL season in a prearranged NFL city. Every young athlete is judged on how far he or she throws a pass, punts a football, and kicks a football off a tee. Points are awarded by distance and accuracy, and most winners have won one if not two of the three categories. For more information, visit www.nflppk.com.

Coaching a youth football team

To coach any youth team, you must be able to give your time freely and want to do it for the kids. You must be committed to making the game fun; to helping develop a player's physical, mental, and social skills; and to winning the game. There's nothing wrong with trying to win, as long as you encourage the team to play the game fairly and teach your players good sportsmanship. Nothing can be gained from whipping an opponent 40–0 in a league of 10-year-olds. Think of how those kids on the losing team would feel!

You must make sure that *every* child has an enjoyable and successful experience. You need a lot of patience because you have to play every child, and sometimes you have to play a child in a position he isn't very good at.

(continued)

(continued)

Your job is to make sure each player can cope with his limitations and be placed in a position where he can succeed. Try to get to know your players individually — every kid is different.

To be a coach, you must know the rules of the game and understand the tactics of the game. If you don't, you may want to buy some coaching books and attend coaching clinics, which are held in every state. Check with local high school coaches about available clinics. And consider reading *Coaching Football For Dummies* by the National Alliance for Youth Sports with Greg Bach (Wiley).

Your practices need to be well-organized, and you need to start the season with a set of rules that applies to every member of the team. One rule should be that if a player misses a certain number of practices, he has to sit out a certain number of minutes during the game, even if he's a star player. Rules about players being on time for practices and remembering their equipment teach players how to be responsible. In the end, football is about building character. Remember, too, that children view most adults' actions from a right-or-wrong perspective. They can tell when a coach is playing favorites; that's why your rules need to be uniform.

Realizing What Sets High School Football Apart

Some high school principals believe that football is the most important extra-curricular activity on campus. Football generally starts off the school year in September, and a winning football team can create a positive attitude on campus. The spirit and enthusiasm that a football program generates can form a building block for a positive school environment.

At most high schools, the number of students who participate in the sport (including student managers and cheerleaders) can amount to ten percent or more of the student body. For these youngsters, the football experience can create a special bond that lasts forever. Because of its physical and mental demands, football is a sport that can make men out of boys. Of course, it's essential that the young men have the proper role models and authority figures in the head coach and his assistants.

All across America, high school football teams are part of small towns' identities. The team can serve as a rallying point for the community, mainly because of family ties to the players. In small towns, most people know everyone else; consequently, a lot of people take pride in a successful high school team. Local businesses usually purchase advertising in the football program or donate services that help the program succeed financially.

Every state has its own high school federation or association that governs football and other sports. These federations oversee all-state awards, name district all-stars, and compile records of achievement. The following sections provide even more insight into the high school game, including the scoop on rule differences and how to use players who play both offense and defense..

Rule differences

Table 15-1 shows how the rules governing high school football differ from NFL rules.

Table 15-1	Comparing High School Rules to NFL Rules
High School Rule	*NFL Rule*
Any ball carrier who touches the ground with any part of his body except his hands or feet is ruled down; the ball is dead at that spot.	A ball carrier is considered down when he's touched by an opponent while on the ground. For example, if an NFL runner slips and inadvertently touches the ground, he can get up and keep moving forward.
The defense can't advance a fumble. The ball is ruled dead where the defensive player recovers it.	The offense and defense can return fumbles.
A player is considered inbounds on a pass reception if he catches the ball with one foot down inside the sideline.	A player must catch the ball with both feet down inside the sideline to be considered inbounds.
The goalposts are 23 feet, 4 inches wide, and they rise to 20 feet.	The goalpost width is 18 feet, 6 inches, and it rises to 35 feet.
The hash marks are 53 feet, 4 inches from each sideline. Because the hash marks are close to each sideline, high school offenses can attempt more running plays to the wide side of the field.	Hash marks are 70 feet, 9 inches from each sideline.
Games are 48 minutes long.	Games are 60 minutes long.

Style of play

With a few exceptions, high school offenses generally run the ball more often than they throw it. Developing a good running game is easier than finding a quarterback who's capable of accurately throwing 25-yard passes and finding receivers who are fast enough to get off the line of scrimmage to catch the ball. Limited practice time (most states allow only 14 days of practice prior to the first game) is another reason many high school teams opt for a run-oriented offense; they can develop this type of offense more quickly.

Offense seems to be the priority in high school football. Coaches gamble more often on fourth down, believing that they can easily gain a yard or two to get the first down and keep the ball. Unlike pro quarterbacks, most high school quarterbacks are good runners. You see more old-style offenses in high school, too: You see a *full-house backfield* (three running backs lined up straight across behind the quarterback) and double-wing formations as coaches attempt to use more blockers in the backfield to better the chances of a successful play. For the most part, high school teams concentrate more on offensive preparation than on defensive preparation unless they're facing an opponent that operates a formation that's totally unfamiliar to them.

High school teams don't kick as often as pro teams because finding an accurate high school field goal kicker can be difficult. Some high school teams can't find a player who can even convert an extra point, which is basically a 20-yard kick. Plus, they don't have the time to concentrate on special teams play because of the time constraints on high school athletes.

Player lineups

The players on a high school roster may not compare in size to those on an NFL team, but high school players are definitely getting bigger. Today, a high school offensive line averaging 260 pounds isn't uncommon, whereas 25 years ago that average may have been 220 pounds. In the last few years, more illegal use of steroids has been reported among boys 18 and under than among college and professional football players. Unlike college and the NFL, no mandatory testing system for steroids is in effect at the high school level. (Some schools do test for marijuana and other drugs, though.)

You find more two-way players at the high school level because most high school teams don't have enough quality players. A *two-way player* is one who plays both an offensive position and a defensive position. Here are some examples of the different combinations of positions: Receivers may also play defensive back, quarterbacks may lead the offense and spark the defense at safety, and blocking backs are also linebackers.

When a school is forced to use a lot of two-way players, you may see sloppy play in the fourth quarter when the young players tire and begin to lose their concentration, which may lead to injury. Although two-way players don't always run out of steam at the end of a game, an opponent that doesn't need to use two-way players may have an advantage.

Making the Most of the High School Game

The first thing parents and young men should realize about high school football is that players experience many ups and downs. You win a game against your rival and nothing feels better. Next week, you lose and you feel down. But you have to bounce back. Football teaches you to be humble about success because when games go badly, you have to work hard to battle back.

Losing a football game isn't unlike some experiences that you go through in other aspects of life. You have to learn to deal not only with success but also with failure. I think that football is a great teacher of those lessons — more so than any other sport. Unlike high school baseball and basketball teams that play multiple games every week, in football you play only one game, which heightens each game's importance. You focus all week on one game, and if you lose, the pain may linger for days before you get an opportunity to redeem yourself in the next one.

The next sections give some tips to help players, coaches, and parents keep the game in the proper perspective and enjoy football to the fullest.

Players

If you're interested in playing high school football, go to the school's main office and ask where and how to sign up. The employees in the main office can send you in the direction of the athletic director or head football coach.

As a player, you need to adhere to the team rules and most likely get involved in a weight-lifting program. Most schools have programs that are monitored by a coach or teacher. In most parts of the United States, football players have a few weeks in the spring in which they work out without equipment. To make the team, you must take advantage of these training opportunities. Coaches like to see athletes working year-round and attending every practice. If your coach recommends that you attend a football camp, ask your parents for permission and find a way to earn the money to pay your way.

Ultimately, you play football (or any sport, for that matter) to have fun. It should be a worthwhile experience, not drudgery. But if you possess special athletic ability and your goal is an athletic scholarship, remain focused and work as hard as you can. Good things come from hard work.

Coaches

Coaching is a demanding career. High schools are having more and more trouble finding quality coaches because coaching is a time-consuming, low-paying profession. High school head coaches are usually also teachers, and teachers aren't paid well. Still, regardless of the financial rewards (or lack thereof), a high school football coach's chief reward is the personal satisfaction of working with young people and watching them grow. And that satisfaction is so meaningful to many high school coaches that they would gladly work for minimum wage rather than give up coaching.

If you coach high school football, make a point of recruiting other teachers. Get them on your side so that they understand what your values are and how hard your athletes are working. Every week, invite one or two teachers to the pregame meal and ask them to ride the bus to away games. Doing so will make them feel like a part of your program. You must educate them about the game and about what's happening with your team. If they know how much time the kids and coaches spend practicing and working at football, and if they're aware of the discipline you're teaching, they may view your program more favorably. Remember, you're a teacher, too, not just some jock.

The other benefit of building a good relationship with other teachers is that you need to know when players are failing classes. You need to do grade checks every four to six weeks. Some schools don't allow students to play sports if they're flunking one or more classes. Developing a good relationship with the other faculty members helps everybody.

Parents

I think most fathers expect their sons to go out for football because they played the sport in high school. Often, football is a family tradition. The grandfather played, the father played, and the uncles and cousins played, so a boy grows up wanting to emulate his relatives, particularly his father. Kids quickly learn how tough playing football is. Going to football practice is like going to boot camp. It's much different from practicing baseball, where you play catch and run around and have fun, or basketball, where you're mostly playing the sport all the time. With football, you spend a great deal of practice time working on conditioning, as well as hitting — and two-to-three hours of practice a day is hardly fun.

 When your child asks you why he should bust his butt for three hours a day and have people hit him and yell at him when he can stay home and play video games, that's the time you can have some real influence. Preach the benefits of teamwork and of not quitting something you start. Remind your child how much pride he'll feel in being successful at such a difficult sport.

Judging high school players' talent

The average college football coach would give his right arm to know which high school players will become college football stars. How can you tell whether a high school football player will achieve on the college level? College football recruiters can study tapes of players. They can measure a player's speed (in the 40-yard dash, which is the benchmark for measuring speed in football) and strength (in the bench press and other weight-lifting tests), but being a college star requires an extra something that's hard to quantify. This extra something usually goes by the name "heart" or "desire," and no test has yet been devised for measuring those intangibles.

Still, a cottage industry for judging high school football players has grown up in the past ten years. Web sites such as Rivals (`www.rivals.com`), Scout (`recruiting.scout.com`), PrepStar (`www.prepstar.com`), and ESPN College Football Recruiting (`espn.go.com/college-football/recruiting`) rate high school players; each year these services rank colleges to determine which have the best recruiting classes. Looking at these services' rankings from past years is fascinating. You can see just how difficult it is to tell which players will succeed in the college game. Some players who are highly ranked never make it in college football; often a player with a low ranking turns into a bright blazing star. For example, Clay Matthews of the Green Bay Packers, runner-up for the 2010 Defensive Player of the Year award, was a walk-on at USC. A *walk-on* is someone who tries out for a college football team without first receiving a football scholarship.

Here are some other recommendations for parents:

- ✔ A football player has to make a lot of sacrifices, so try to give your son some slack with chores; he has made a huge commitment to the team.

- ✔ Encourage your son to have a good work ethic and to study hard and maintain good grades.

- ✔ If your son has the talent to earn an athletic scholarship, consider sending him to summer football camps during his high school career. Many colleges and universities offer these types of camps.

Thinking Ahead to a College Football Career

High school players have many opportunities to play college football and receive financial assistance. In fact, if you include the smaller division schools, I think that more colleges and universities are giving scholarships to play football today than 40 years ago. Just as many schools are recruiting high school players, and the entire recruitment process has really advanced.

Forty years ago, the University of Southern California (USC) could give as many football scholarships as it wanted. Now, all Division FBS schools are restricted to 85 scholarships. Although not as many players have the opportunity to earn football scholarships at big-time schools like USC and Notre Dame as in the past, other colleges are picking up the slack. Colleges like Boise State and Montana go to small suburbs in California to find good players. Long story short? Good athletes don't get overlooked anymore because colleges are on a mission to find them.

If you're a parent and you believe your son has the ability to play college football, meet with the high school's guidance counselor during your son's freshman year and find out what course work is required by colleges that your son may be interested in. Doing so is a must to ensure that he's eligible to play at the college level when he graduates from high school.

If you're a student, remember that you go to school to receive an education. Of the thousands of young men who play college football, fewer than 300 are drafted by the NFL each year. Because college players have only a one percent chance of having a professional football career, education should be the number-one priority.

If you're a parent or coach, prepare young athletes for the realities of college by stressing the importance of academics and keeping track of athletes' academic records. To find out about the eligibility requirements for your son, check with your high school guidance counselor or the NCAA Initial-Eligibility Clearinghouse (www.eligibilitycenter.org). And start your research in his junior year if you believe that he has the ability to play college football.

Chapter 16

College Football — Where It All Started

. . . .

In This Chapter

▶ Understanding why there are so many conferences

▶ Examining the College Football Playoff and how it works

▶ Looking at college trophies and awards

▶ Getting the basics on all-star games

. . . .

*E*ven though the National Football League is made up of pros, don't let that fool you: The NFL's rules, traditions, and growth were nurtured by college football. In fact, the sport itself began on the collegiate level. The first college football game was played in 1869 between Princeton and Rutgers, and it took professional football almost a century to match America's love affair with college football.

Although the NFL and college football attract many of the same fans today, some of the rules, as well as the levels of competition, are different. In this chapter, I clue you in to the different divisions of college football, shine a little light on the sometimes mysterious inner workings of the College Football Playoff, and reveal the powerful impact of college coaches, among other things.

Why People Love College Football

Fans are passionate about college football because of its local and regional flavor, and also because it's built on more than a century of tradition. A college football fan doesn't have to be an alumnus of a particular college to become a serious fan, either. For example, if you're raised in Ohio and your mother or father is passionate about football, you'll probably hear about Woody Hayes (a legendary coach) and root for Ohio State.

In every pocket of America, fans are loyal to their state universities, both big and small, and when two state schools collide, a rivalry emerges and fans go wild. Ohio State's major rival is the University of Michigan; in Alabama, nothing is bigger than the matchup between the University of Alabama and Auburn, the state's other college football team; and in Florida, life stops for three-plus hours when Florida State and the University of Florida play.

Another primary appeal of college football is its young, amateur players. Even in major college football, you see smaller-sized athletes (the ones who aren't big enough, strong enough, or fast enough to play in the NFL) performing at a high level. And the style of the college game generally isn't as structured as the NFL game. College teams are more open about their approach to the game; coaches will try anything new if they think it will work. They use offenses and defenses that NFL teams would never consider, such as the *wishbone,* which features three running backs and emphasizes the run by using a ball-handling running quarterback. Because not every college team is stacked with great players at every position, superior coaching decides a lot of outcomes with offensive and defensive game plans that exploit specific weaknesses.

Plus, the college game offers pageantry — the tailgate parties, the marching bands, and the Friday night pep rallies. In many cases, a college campus mushrooms to more than twice its normal population on a Saturday afternoon as thousands of adult fans join students at the game. Major college sights and sounds include

- **The Notre Dame Victory March ("Cheer, cheer for old Notre Dame . . ."):** This school song is one of the most famous songs in the United States, right up there with the national anthem, "God Bless America," and "White Christmas."

- **The Stanford and Yale bands:** These bands are known for their zaniness, wacky attire, and willingness to attempt any outlandish halftime show imaginable.

- **The Trojan Horse:** The symbol of Southern California (USC) football is the Trojan Horse — a white horse with a man dressed like a Trojan warrior riding him. The horse's name is Traveler.

- **Dotting the *i* in Ohio State:** The Buckeye band ends every home pregame performance by spelling out *Ohio* on the field, with the sousaphone player completing the spelling by running to dot the *i.*

- **Mascots:** Mascots are huge in college football. Some of the best include the Falcons at the Air Force Academy, which fly at halftime; the real-life Buffalo at Colorado; the ugly-faced bulldog at Georgia; and the little Irish leprechaun at Notre Dame.

Rule differences between college and NFL football

If you watch a lot of NFL games, you should know that pro and college rules differ in three important areas:

- In college football, the hash marks are 10 feet 9 inches closer to the sidelines than in the pros.

- In college football, a receiver is ruled inbounds when he has possession of the ball and has one foot inbounds. In the NFL, the receiver must have both feet inbounds.

- In the NFL, any offensive player in possession of the ball — whether a running back, a quarterback, or a kick returner — can fall down, get back on his feet, and continue running if he isn't touched by a defensive player. A college player is considered down whenever one knee touches the ground, whether or not another player has touched him. Consequently, you'd better not slip in college football.

- **Atmosphere:** Atmosphere is what a college football game is all about. Here are some fan favorites: Any night game at LSU; the Florida–Georgia game, usually played in Jacksonville; Ohio State versus Michigan before 110,000 in Ann Arbor; Florida–Florida State and Notre Dame–USC anywhere; and any home game at Tennessee.

- **Battle of the bands:** The Grambling–Southern University game offers the finest strutting, dancing, and rhythm halftime show in college football.

Big, Medium, and Small

The *National Collegiate Athletic Association* (NCAA), the governing body of college athletics, reports that more than 650 member colleges fielded football teams during the 2014 season. These colleges are divided into divisions based on enrollment, financial commitment, and the competitive level of the conference to which they belong. The NCAA doesn't want big-time powers like Nebraska and Penn State playing small schools like Union College and Wabash. It wants a level playing field to make for more competitive games.

Consequently, as shown in Table 16-1, the 650 plus colleges are divided into four divisions: Division I FBS (Football Bowl Subdivision), Division I FCS (Football Championship Subdivision), Division II, and Division III. Within each division, teams are members of conferences. A *conference* is similar to a league in professional sports (see "Examining College Conferences" later in this chapter for more on conferences).

How the NCAA got its start

Although it oversees every sport and both men's and women's teams, the NCAA got its start as a governing body for college football. In 1905, representatives of 13 colleges got together to establish playing rules, and in 1906, 49 schools joined the original 13 to form the precursor of the NCAA: the *Intercollegiate Athletic Association of the United States,* or IAAUS. The IAAUS became the NCAA in 1910.

Table 16-1	Division Breakdown for the 2014 Football Season	
Division	*Number of Schools*	*Number of Conferences*
I FBS	128	10
I FCS	124	14
II	159	15
III	240	29

Hundreds of junior colleges (two-year programs) also have football teams, as do *National Association of Intercollegiate Athletics* (NAIA) schools, a group of smaller four-year colleges not associated with the NCAA. Unable to qualify academically to receive a four-year scholarship to a four-year college, many athletes attend junior colleges and hope to land a scholarship to a four-year school. Many of the NAIA teams are based in Kansas, North and South Dakota, Pennsylvania, Ohio, Nebraska, and Oregon.

The following sections introduce you to some of the big-time and small-time schools to know.

Big-time schools

Although 120 colleges and universities played Division I FBS football in 2010, less than half of them had a realistic chance of finishing in the top ten or being voted the national champion by either the Associated Press poll (which consists of a national group of sportswriters and broadcasters) or the *USA Today* Coaches' Poll. These two polls are the most respected college football polls.

Traditionally, Alabama, Florida, Florida State, LSU, Miami, Michigan, Nebraska, Notre Dame, Ohio State, Oklahoma, Penn State, Texas, and USC have the best college programs in the country. I could name another dozen, but if you want to pick the national champion in any of the next five years, the winner will probably come from among the schools listed in Table 16-2, which highlights the schools boasting the greatest number of college-players-turned-pro.

Table 16-2	Where NFL Players Came From, 2014
College	*Number of Players*
USC	57
Miami (Florida)	56
LSU	54
Alabama	50
Florida State	50
Georgia	47
Ohio State	46
Florida	45
Oregon	42
Notre Dame	41
Tennessee	40
California	39
Oklahoma	39
South Carolina	39
Wisconsin	39
Texas	38
Stanford	37
Iowa	35
Texas A&M	35
Clemson	34
Michigan	34
Penn State	34

Notre Dame, a Roman Catholic university located in South Bend, Indiana, has historically been the most recognized college football power. It began its rise in the 1920s and has maintained a lofty hold on the college scene ever since. Notre Dame's support is nationwide — it recruits high school players from virtually every state — and all of its games are televised nationally. (The term *subway alumni* is used to describe the many fans who support Notre Dame football. These fans act very much like they attended or even graduated from the school.)

The reputations of big-time schools help with recruiting because many of the best high school players want to play for a school where they have a chance to compete for a national championship, possibly prepare for the NFL, and also receive a good education. Every one of the schools mentioned earlier in this section adheres to those criteria.

Small college powers

Although small schools may not achieve national prominence, they certainly play tough football. Some of the winningest teams and coaches aren't at giants like Florida and Nebraska but rather smaller colleges, such as the following:

- ✔ **Mount Union College:** Just 18 miles east of the Pro Football Hall of Fame is the small Ohio town of Alliance, home of Division III powerhouse Mount Union College, the winningest college football program since 1990. In 2012, Mount Union won its 11th Division III Football National Championship in the previous 19 years by defeating the University of St. Thomas (Minnesota) in the Stagg Bowl.

- ✔ **Grambling State University:** From 1941 through 1998 Grambling was led by the great Eddie Robinson, who became the second winningest coach in NCAA Division I history with 408 wins. Among predominantly black colleges, Grambling has been the best producer of NFL players, sending more than 100 to the pros. Robinson, who coached 55 seasons at Grambling, was inducted into the College Football Hall of Fame in 1998.

Two of the greatest players of all time, Walter Payton and Jerry Rice, were small-college players. Payton starred at Jackson State in Mississippi, and Rice, another first-round draft choice, played at Mississippi Valley State in Itta Bena, Mississippi. Bigger doesn't always mean better!

Examining College Conferences

College football teams play most of their games against schools in their own conferences. Some conferences, such as the Ivy League, formed because their members have a shared focus on academic excellence and don't award athletic scholarships. Brown, Columbia, Cornell, Dartmouth, Harvard, Penn,

Princeton, and Yale are in the Ivy League conference (these schools — particularly Harvard, Princeton, Columbia, and Yale — helped spawn football in America). However, most conferences are formed with the goal of bringing together teams on the same competitive level in the same geographical area.

The best-known Division I FBS conferences are the Big Ten, Pac-12, SEC (Southeastern Conference), ACC (Atlantic Coast Conference), Big 12, and the American Athletic Conference. These conferences supply more than 60 percent of the players on NFL rosters.

Here's the lowdown on these well-known college football conferences:

- **Big Ten:** This conference, which actually has 14 members, is located mostly in the Midwest. Its members are Illinois, Indiana, Iowa, Maryland, Michigan, Michigan State, Minnesota, Nebraska, Northwestern, Ohio State, Penn State, Purdue, Rutgers, and Wisconsin.

- **Pac-12 (formerly the Pac-10):** The Pac-12 is located in the western United States. In 2011, Colorado and Utah joined Arizona, Arizona State, Oregon, Oregon State, Stanford, UCLA, University of California at Berkeley, USC, Washington, and Washington State in this conference.

- **SEC:** The members of the SEC are situated mostly in the southeastern portion of the country. Its members are Alabama, Arkansas, Auburn, Florida, Georgia, Kentucky, LSU, Missouri, Mississippi (also known as Ole Miss), Mississippi State, South Carolina, Tennessee, Texas A&M, and Vanderbilt.

- **ACC:** The ACC schools are mostly in the Carolinas and along the East Coast. They include Boston College, Clemson, Duke, Florida State, Georgia Tech, Louisville, Miami, North Carolina, North Carolina State, Pittsburgh, Syracuse, Virginia, Virginia Tech, and Wake Forest.

- **Big 12:** The Big 12 is actually composed of ten teams. The current members are Baylor, Iowa State, Kansas, Kansas State, Missouri, Oklahoma, Oklahoma State, Texas, Texas Christian University (TCU), Texas Tech, and West Virginia.

- **American Athletic Conference:** This conference formed during a period of NCAA conference realignments from 2010 to 2013. Many of its members were part of the former Big East conference. It includes these football programs: Central Florida, Cincinnati, Connecticut, East Carolina, Houston, Memphis, South Florida, Southern Methodist, Temple, Tulane, and Tulsa.

The other Division I FBS conferences are Conference USA, Mid-American Conference, Mountain West Conference, and Sun Belt Conference.

The ever-shifting Division I FBS conferences

The year 2011 saw a drastic realignment of teams in Division I FBS conferences. Nebraska left the Big 12 Conference to join the Big Ten. Not to be outdone by its rival the Big Ten, the Pac-10 Conference successfully courted two new members, Utah (formerly in the Mountain West Conference) and Colorado (formerly in the Big 12), which necessitated a name change for the conference; it became the Pac-12 Conference. Then in 2013, the Big Ten added Rutgers and Maryland, for a total of 14 teams. Sounds like a name change is long overdue for that conference.

The Mountain West Conference, smarting from the loss of Utah, signed up three new members in Boise State, Nevada (Reno), and Fresno State — all formerly of the Western Athletic Conference. Not long after, however, the Mountain West Conference received some bad news: long-time member Brigham Young (BYU) had decided to go solo. The BYU Cougars left the Mountain West Conference to become an independent football team.

Why this game of musical chairs? Why are so many teams jumping to different conferences?

One reason is because the teams are seeking a competitive advantage in the College Football Playoff (CFP), the playoff system used in Division I FBS football that began in 2014. Teams move to different conferences or go independent with the hope of positioning themselves for a shot at one of the four playoff spots. The thinking is that being a top team in one of the major football conferences increases a team's chances of being one of the four playoff teams.

Not all football teams belong to a conference. Navy, Brigham Young, and Notre Dame head the group of football independents. These schools don't have any trouble scheduling games because of their excellent football heritage. Plus, Notre Dame has its own network television contract.

Although it isn't a national championship, winning a conference championship is a major accomplishment and assists in postseason honors and invitations to bowl games (in Division I FBS) or playoff games (in the other divisions).

The College Football Playoff

From 1998 to 2013, Division I FBS college football used the Bowl Championship Series (BCS) to determine a national champion. The BCS relied on polls and computer rankings to select two teams to play in a single BCS National Championship Game. The BCS was controversial since its inception with many fans arguing that the championship game rarely paired the two best teams in college football. So for 2014, a new system, the College Football Playoff (CFP) was devised.

The CFP is a four-team playoff. Two semifinal games are played first, followed a little over a week later (always on a Monday) by a championship game pitting the two semifinal winners against each other.

The selection process

A committee of 13 football experts selects the final four teams for the semifinal games. The committee members include athletic directors from the major football conferences along with former athletic directors, coaches, players, and administrators, and even a retired sports reporter.

The four final teams are major conference champions, but as you may know, there are more than four major conferences. So the selection committee has to weigh factors such as overall record, strength of schedule, and head-to-head results. Polls and computer rankings are not used in the selection process. Ultimately, some major conference champions are left out of the playoffs. Those teams play in other bowls instead.

The selection committee seeds the four final teams from 1 to 4, with teams 1 and 4 playing in one semifinal and teams 2 and 3 playing in the other.

The semifinals

The two semifinal games are hosted on a rotating basis by six bowl games: Rose Bowl, Sugar Bowl, Orange Bowl, Cotton Bowl, and Peach Bowl. The games are played on New Year's Day along with other major bowl games featuring teams that didn't make the CFP. For the 2014 season, Alabama and Ohio State played in the Sugar Bowl, with Ohio State coming out on top. In the other semifinal game, Florida State and Oregon played in the Rose Bowl, with Oregon advancing to the final game.

The national championship game

The championship game is played on the first Monday a week after the semifinal games. Cities around the United States bid to host the game, which is held at a different location every year. For the 2014 season, the game was played January 12, 2015, at AT&T Stadium in Arlington, Texas, home of the Dallas Cowboys. The winning team earns the College Football Playoff National Championship Trophy.

College football firsts

Here are some firsts in college football:

- White lines are placed on the field at 5-yard intervals in 1882. As a result of the pattern, the playing field is called a *gridiron*.

- A game is played on the West Coast between the University of California at Berkeley and Stanford in 1892.

- *Collier's* magazine publishes the first All-American team in 1898. *Collier's* remains the official selection holder of teams through 1924.

- The length of the football field is reduced from 110 yards to today's standard of 100 yards in 1912.

- The University of Wisconsin erects an electronic scoreboard in 1926, and first uses it in a game against Iowa.

- Although a Fordham practice was shown in the preceding year, the game between Maryland and the University of Pennsylvania on October 5, 1940, is television's first game. Saturday afternoon telecasts emerge nationwide in the 1951 season.

The Heisman and Other Trophies

The Heisman Trophy is awarded annually to America's most outstanding college football player. The trophy is named in honor of John W. Heisman, a legendary football coach. The first Heisman was given to halfback Jay Berwanger of the University of Chicago in 1935. Over the years, the award has traditionally gone to running backs and quarterbacks and some wide receivers. Two exceptions were Larry Kelley of Yale in 1936 and Leon Hart of Notre Dame in 1949, who were both *two-way players* (meaning they played both offense and defense). The third exception is Charles Woodson, a cornerback from Michigan who in 1997 became the first full-time defensive player to ever win the Heisman. (Woodson also returned kicks and occasionally played wide receiver on offense.)

More than 900 people (former winners and 870 college football broadcasters and sportswriters) vote every year for the Heisman winner, which is announced in mid-December. To vie for the award, some college sports information departments wage what's tantamount to a political campaign, producing tons of brochures, handbooks, and campaign literature on its star player. The campaign for the next year's Heisman winner actually begins during spring practice prior to the start of the football season.

Besides the Heisman, college football has other prestigious awards, including the

- ✔ **Outland Trophy:** This trophy has been awarded since 1946 to the nation's top interior lineman. Some notable recipients include Alex Karras, Orlando Pace, and Ron Yary.

- ✔ **Maxwell Award:** Two years younger than the Heisman, the Maxwell Award, which began in 1937, also goes to the top college player of the year. Often, the Maxwell and the Heisman don't agree.

- ✔ **Lombardi Award:** This award is given to the nation's top lineman. Recipients include Cornelius Bennett, Orlando Pace (a two-time winner), and Terrell Suggs.

- ✔ **Davey O'Brien Award:** This award is given to the best quarterback. Steve Young, Peyton Manning, Vince Young, and Tim Tebow have all received the Davey O'Brien Award.

HOWIE SAYS

Remembering my college days

I went to Villanova on a football scholarship, and we never played on television. Our home stadium's capacity was around 7,000. We took buses to a lot of our games and stayed three to a room at motor lodges with two beds a lot of the time. We didn't have the fancy training facilities, film rooms, or big weight-lifting rooms that a Nebraska, Penn State, or Florida team has. I was just happy to have hot water for my shower.

But we played some big games at Villanova. We played Boston College twice, and Clemson was in the top ten when we faced them. The Boston College game was a big game for me because I was from Boston and was supposed to play for them. I always had some animosity for that game because the day after I had originally signed with Boston College the head coach told me I was going to play offensive guard. I didn't want to play that position. That's how I ended up at Villanova, playing defense.

When we played Clemson, they had something like seven first-round draft choices on their roster, and they beat us 30–0 with their third team. Clemson had the Bostic brothers (Jeff and Joe) playing center and guard, and they simply wore me out. They didn't beat me with athletic ability; they just knew a whole lot more about playing than I did. But I got my revenge in the Super Bowl, playing against Jeff, who was with the Washington Redskins. And our previous matchup definitely was on my mind.

College football has become much bigger since I played — more television, more money, and more exposure. Villanova, though, hasn't changed much. It's still a small college program.

All-American and Other All-Star Teams

The Associated Press All-America team is the most prestigious All-America team, followed by the Walter Camp All-America team. The American Football Coaches' All-America Team, which is selected by the coaches for all NCAA divisions and the NAIA (National Association of Intercollegiate Athletics), is also considered a highly accurate gauge of the best college talent.

These teams are *all-star teams* that honor the best players at their respective positions on a national scale. The Associated Press lists first-, second-, and third-team All-Americans. The selections are subjective. Often, coaches and football writers vote for players they know personally. Voters have their favorites and also their prejudices. Consequently, some deserving players may be ignored or fail to receive the recognition they deserve. In many ways, it's a popularity contest.

Because many of these all-star teams include players who are flunking classes and who have no intention of ever graduating, Academic All-America teams have emerged to recognize student-athletes who've had great careers and been successful in the classroom.

Some all-star teams actually compete in all-star games. Exceptional college football players can look forward to playing in these games when their college careers come to an end:

- ✔ **East-West Shrine Game:** Pits players from the eastern United States against players from the West. The game is held in Orlando, Florida, with proceeds going to benefit the Shriners Hospitals for Children.

- ✔ **Senior Bowl:** Held in Mobile, Alabama, with players divided into North and South teams. The game is considered a venue for players to showcase their talents to NFL scouts and coaches.

My invite to the Blue-Gray all-star game

When I was at Villanova, I was fortunate to receive an invitation to a college all-star game called the Blue-Gray Football Classic held in Montgomery, Alabama (the game has since been discontinued). I think another player canceled out, and I got in, sort of as a novelty. I don't think that I projected very high in the NFL draft, maybe a tenth-round pick, until I played in this all-star game.

The week of practice and the game itself helped me a lot. It gave me the opportunity to compete with the top college prospects in America, something I couldn't do every weekend at a smaller school like Villanova. Every NFL team had scouts at this game; very few scouts came to my Villanova games. I ended up playing well against a guy from Texas A&M who was considered to be a high draft choice, a first- or second-round pick. Jimmy Johnson, whom I ended up working with at FOX, coached me in the game. During the game, I blocked a punt and scored a touchdown, and my team won.

I had the opportunity to run for a lot of pro scouts at that game. I was running 4.7s and 4.8s and doing all their little eraser drills where you run 10 yards, pick up an eraser, drop it in a basket, and do it again. Run 20 yards, and pick it up. . . . I was really good at those drills. My vertical jump was good. I had all the intangibles, but I wasn't a good football player. So someone had to take a chance, and the Raiders did, drafting me in the second round. All-star games give a lot of unknown players like me a chance to prove that they belong at the next level.

Chapter 17

Taking a Look at the NFL (And Other Professional Leagues)

In This Chapter

▶ Discovering the NFL's history and divisions

▶ Checking out the NFL's schedule

▶ Assembling a winning team

▶ Exploring the business side of professional football

▶ Surveying the other professional leagues out there

*T*he National Football League (NFL) is the pinnacle of football — it's the ultimate high and the purest acceptance of anyone's ability as a football player or coach.

When I was a young player in the NFL, I thought I would always enjoy team success. I thought my team, the Los Angeles (now Oakland) Raiders, would go to the Super Bowl every year because we had so much talent. But so many intangibles are involved in reaching that game — things you can't control, such as injuries, complacency, and the loss of talent to free agency. Looking back on my playing career, I now understand and appreciate how lucky I was to play in and win one Super Bowl.

Although regular-season games begin in September and end in December or January (followed by a month of playoffs), the NFL is active year-round. During the off-season, players usually continue working out to remain in condition. The league also experiences coaching changes, players switching teams via free agency, the drafting of college players, and various organized training sessions called *mini-camps,* which last three to four days. Teams report to training camps in late July or early August, where players practice twice a day in preparation for the long season ahead. Preseason games, generally four per team, are played in August, prior to the start of the regular season.

In this chapter, I explain how the NFL started, how it works, how teams reach the playoffs, and how the money filters down to the players. I also demystify the salary cap, player movements, practice schedules, and life in general in the greatest league on earth.

The Birth of Pro Football

In its early days, and I'm talking about the early 20th century, professional football was disorganized because it lacked a league-wide constitution and guidelines. Player movement was rampant, with teams routinely bidding on players. The contracts for star players generally ranged from $50 to $250 a game, which was a considerable amount of money for that time. Many college players assumed aliases so they could earn some of that money by playing on Sunday afternoons with pro teams.

The Ohio League had the strongest professional teams, featuring such legends as the Canton Bulldogs and Olympian Jim Thorpe, until 1920 when a group of seven Ohio League owners/players created the first national professional football league. This organization, known as the American Professional Football Association (APFA), consisted of 14 teams. After the 1921 season, the APFA officially changed its name to the National Football League, or NFL.

In the first few years of the NFL, the championship wasn't decided on the field. Instead, it was awarded based on a vote at league meetings. The league didn't have a playoff system to decide its champion until 1933, and it wasn't until 1936 that every team in the league played the same number of games. In 1933, the NFL divided into a two-division alignment, with the winners of each division meeting for the league championship at the end of the regular season.

In the first 13 years of the NFL, the league lacked franchise stability; numerous teams folded because of a lack of money or fan interest. Nineteen teams lasted only one year, and another 11 managed just two seasons. Only two of today's teams, the Chicago Bears (originally the Decatur Staleys) and the Chicago Cardinals (whose franchise today resides in Phoenix, Arizona) started with the league in 1920. The Green Bay Packers are the third oldest team, joining the league in 1921.

The AFL joins the NFL

The American Football League (AFL) started in 1960 with eight teams. The pursuit of the same players by both the AFL and the NFL led to escalating salaries, which was great for the players but not for the financial welfare of pro football team owners. The NFL wasn't used to this kind of competition over talent. When the AFL, strengthened by its own network television contract, considered signing away many of the NFL's top quarterbacks, it forced the more established NFL to make peace. A merger of the two leagues was the solution, so the AFL and NFL agreed to merge in 1966 under the umbrella of the NFL. The two leagues held a common draft in 1967 and began interleague play in the 1970 season. The first four Super Bowls were actually between the champions of the NFL and the AFL.

Dividing the Ranks: The NFL Conferences

Today, the NFL is divided into two conferences: the *American Football Conference* (AFC) and the *National Football Conference* (NFC). Each conference consists of 16 teams and is divided into four divisions — East, West, North, and South — of four teams each. These division titles don't necessarily correspond to geographic parts of the country, though. For example, the St. Louis Rams are in the NFC West, yet St. Louis is smack-dab in the middle of the United States. Here's the breakdown:

- ✔ **The American Football Conference:** Along with six other teams, this conference includes ten franchises (in bold) that were once part of the old AFL.

    - East Division: **Buffalo Bills, Miami Dolphins, New England Patriots, New York Jets**

    - West Division: **Denver Broncos, Kansas City Chiefs, Oakland Raiders, San Diego Chargers**

    - North Division: Baltimore Ravens, **Cincinnati Bengals,** Cleveland Browns, Pittsburgh Steelers

    - South Division: Houston Texans, Indianapolis Colts, Jacksonville Jaguars, **Tennessee Titans**

- ✔ **The National Football Conference:** Along with 13 others, this conference includes three franchises (in bold) that once formed the original NFL.

    - East Division: Dallas Cowboys, New York Giants, Philadelphia Eagles, Washington Redskins

- West Division: **Arizona Cardinals,** St. Louis Rams, San Francisco 49ers, Seattle Seahawks

- North Division: **Chicago Bears,** Detroit Lions, **Green Bay Packers,** Minnesota Vikings

- South Division: Atlanta Falcons, Carolina Panthers, New Orleans Saints, Tampa Bay Buccaneers

Getting to Know the Pro Football Schedule

The NFL schedule begins with what's called the *regular season.* In regular-season games, teams compete for the best win-loss records, and the teams with the best records advance to the playoffs. The playoffs, meanwhile, decide who goes on to the Super Bowl. The following sections look at the ins and outs of the NFL football schedule.

The regular-season games

As laid out in the annual *NFL Record and Fact Book,* the NFL follows a formula for devising each team's regular-season schedule. Each team plays 16 games in 17 weeks (the week a team doesn't play is called its *bye week*). In the formula, every team's schedule is as follows:

- ✔ Six games, three at home and three away, against the three other teams in the division.

- ✔ Four games against teams from a single division of the other conference; these divisions rotate on a four-year cycle.

- ✔ Four games against teams from a single division of the franchise's own conference; these divisions rotate on a three-year cycle.

- ✔ Two games against teams within the franchise's own conference, based on the team's finish in the preceding season. (For example, a team that finished second one year plays the two second-place teams in the three divisions of its conference that it is *not* scheduled to play the next year.)

The playoffs

The NFL schedules all those regular-season games — 256 in a typical season — to separate the good teams from the bad. On every level of sports, people want to declare a champion. In the NFL, a total of 12 teams qualify for what amounts to the road to the Super Bowl.

Six teams from each conference qualify for the playoffs, with the four division winners qualifying automatically. These winners are joined by two teams called *wildcard teams,* who qualify based on the win-loss records of the remaining teams in each conference that didn't finish first in their respective divisions. The two division winners with the highest winning percentages host second-round games, skipping the first round of competition. The third and fourth division winners host the wildcard teams in the first round.

The winners of the two wildcard games advance to the second round of contests, called Divisional Playoff games. The lowest-rated wildcard winner (the first-round winner with the worst record) plays the division winner with the best record, and the other wildcard winner plays the division winner with the second-best record. Both division winners enjoy *home field advantage,* meaning they host the games.

For the Conference Championship games (the third round), any surviving division champion automatically hosts the game. If two division winners survive, the team with the better winning percentage hosts the championship game. If the two surviving teams have identical records, home field is based first on how the two teams performed in head-to-head competition during the season, and then on who had the best winning percentage in conference games. The winner of each Conference Championship game goes on to the Super Bowl.

The Super Bowl

The Super Bowl is the NFL championship game. It pits the winner of the AFC against the champion of the NFC. The game was born out of the merger agreement between the former American Football League (AFL) and the National Football League (NFL) in 1966 (see the nearby related sidebar).

In the first two years of the pro football championship, the game was billed as the AFL-NFL World Championship Game. But not until the third championship meeting between the two leagues in 1969 did the name "Super Bowl" stick for good. Kansas City Chiefs owner Lamar Hunt coined the name after a toy with super bouncing abilities. That toy was called the Super Ball. He derived the name because the game itself was considered to be "super" (and any fan would agree with that!). The term "bowl" came from the college game, where bowl games remain common post-season rituals (I fill you in on these in Chapter 16).

The Super Bowl is such a huge television and fan attraction that cities routinely bid for the game, offering to defray many of the league's expenses for hotels and travel. In fact, the Super Bowl is so large that cities are selected to host three to four years in advance. This extra time gives the cities the necessary time to prepare.

In the two weeks between the two conference championship games and the Super Bowl, plenty of hype and hoopla about the game arises. The two teams usually arrive in the host city on the Sunday prior to the game, along with more than 2,500 members of the media. The event has a national flavor to it. Week-long events, such as the NFL Experience (an interactive theme park that features more than 50 attractions, including games like Quarterback Challenge, the Extra-Point Kick, and the Super Bowl Card Show) are planned for youngsters and older fans alike. Parties are held at hotels and venues throughout the host city.

With ticket prices ranging from $500 to $1,200, and most fans paying five times that amount thanks to ticket scalping, the Super Bowl has become more of a corporate event than a bastion for hard-core football fans. You almost have to be somebody important or know somebody important to attend.

Building a Team: It's More than Drawing Straws

As you can imagine, building an NFL team is no easy task. Most teams focus first on acquiring a solid quarterback and then making sure they have highly skilled players at the running back and wide receiver positions. The offensive line is generally built to suit the specific offensive strategy of the team. For example, if the team likes to pass, it pays a premium for linemen who are better pass-protectors than run-blockers. Having linemen equally suited to both styles is best, but sometimes that's a luxury when you're selecting your roster for today's game. Injuries are a factor when most teams have only eight linemen on their 45-player rosters.

In terms of the defense, teams need at least five star performers among the players on the defensive line, the linebacker corps, and secondary. Ideally, these players rank among the top ten players at their respective positions. Most NFL teams have a core of seven to ten potential-superstar players, an average of 6 to 12 rookies, and a group of *veterans* (players with at least one year of pro experience) to round out the roster. Many teams have at least 20 players with five or more years of NFL experience.

All teams acquire players through the draft, and their plan is to develop the players that they draft over a couple seasons. They also acquire players by making trades with other teams and getting players through free agency. The next sections explore how coaches and general managers build what they hope will be a winning team.

Drafting players out of school

The annual NFL draft of college players occurs in late April or early May. The three-day event begins on a Thursday in prime time with the first round. Rounds 2 and 3 are on Friday evening with Rounds 4–7 on Saturday. The draft, which is televised by ESPN, was traditionally held at Radio City Music Hall in New York City, but beginning in 2015, the draft will take place at different venues that will change from year to year. Some of the top college players are in attendance. If a college player wants to play in the NFL, he usually enters via the draft. In a typical year, more than 2,500 college athletes become eligible for the draft, but only about 260 players are selected.

If a high draft choice doesn't become a starter by his third season, he's generally considered a bust. The team then attempts to replace him with a veteran or another rookie and starts the process anew.

Who picks when

The draft consists of seven rounds, and each team is allotted one pick in each round. The team with the worst record in the preceding season selects first. The team with the second worst record selects second, and so on, with the Super Bowl champion picking last in the first round and the Super Bowl loser picking next to last. Teams are allowed 10 minutes to make their selections in the first round, 7 minutes to make their picks in the second round, and 5 minutes in rounds thereafter.

How picks are made

At the NFL Scouting Combine in Indianapolis, Indiana, in February, medical doctors and trainers examine prospective players who are hoping to be drafted. These players also submit to weight-lifting and running drills and perform position-specific drills, such as a throwing drill for quarterbacks and a running pattern drill for wide receivers. Players are also tested for illegal drug use and are given intelligence tests. They're measured and weighed and interviewed by countless coaches, scouts, and club officials. This information-gathering process is so thorough that a casual observer might think the teams are conducting research for some sort of science project.

On draft day, every team has a representative at the draft venue, but the teams' coaching, scouting, and executive staffs remain at the training facilities or team headquarters in their respective cities. Teams usually have one huge room called the *War Room* where staff members meet to discuss potential players and formulate their final decisions prior to announcing selections. Depending on the team, the general manager may consult with the owner, the head coach, the director of college scouting, and other club personnel before making a selection.

Usually, the team is in contact with the player on the telephone prior to making the choice in order to inform him of its decision or to ask any last-minute questions regarding health or personal issues. The NFL security department does background checks on all prospective draft candidates and reports its findings to the member clubs when asked.

A player who isn't selected has the option of signing a free-agent contract with any team that wants him. These players are the lowest-paid players on the rosters, and most are released during training camp. Teams sign many of these players simply to provide bodies for the veterans to practice against during training camp. Of course, some undrafted, free-agent rookies make the team because they have more ability than drafted players. This scenario just shows everyone that scouts, general managers, coaches, and other player-personnel department members can make mistakes when evaluating all the draft-eligible players.

Trading to get who you want

Many trades involve the simple exchange of draft choices as teams want to move either up or down from their assigned selecting spots. The most amazing example of trading for a draft pick occurred prior to the 1999 draft, when Coach Mike Ditka of the New Orleans Saints traded away every pick after his first one, as well as the first- and third-round picks for the following year, to the Washington Redskins to obtain Heisman Trophy winner Ricky Williams, whom he selected fifth overall. The San Diego Chargers, a team in desperate need of a quarterback in 1998, traded two veteran players (running back Eric Metcalf and linebacker Patrick Sapp) and three draft choices (their first-round picks in 1998 and 1999 and a 1998 second-round draft choice) simply to move into the Arizona Cardinals' position in the 1998 draft. This was a blockbuster trade, considering that the Chargers surrendered a lot for the rights to draft Washington State quarterback Ryan Leaf, a huge bust.

Going the free agent route

If a team doesn't want to wait for the draft or can't make a trade, it usually opts to find what it considers a star player by signing a *free agent,* a player who sells himself to the highest-bidding team. Considering the NFL's salary-cap restrictions, a team must be careful in how it pursues free agents because it may not be able to afford a particular player — that player's salary may jeopardize the team's salary scale with its current players (for more information on the salary cap, see the later "The salary cap levels the playing field" section). Players often become upset when a new player earns more than they do, especially if they're considered team leaders or stars.

The free-agent period begins in March. Most of the top players agree to new contract terms in the first six weeks of the negotiating session, which ends in mid-July (usually prior to the start of training camp). A top free agent usually decides on a few teams he'd like to play for, and then he visits each club's facility to meet the coaches and general manager. His agent then begins negotiations with the clubs that are interested. A free agent usually makes his decision based on money, but occasionally his choice is affected by the offensive or defensive system the team uses, how he fits in with the other players, his city preference for his family, or whether he likes the coach. Some players accept less money to play with a team they think has the potential to make the playoffs.

Status Is Everything: Determining Player Designations

While listening to commentary or reading about the NFL, you hear many terms that relate directly to a player's status, such as *franchise player* or *restricted free agent*. Hard-core fans frequently toss around these terms. Many of the terms were agreed on by the NFL owners and the *NFL Players Association* (the union that represents the interests of the players) as part of their collective bargaining agreement (more on that later in the chapter).

The following list explains some frequently heard words used to describe players (and the people who broker contract deals for them), as well as some terminology that relates to a player's experience or active status:

- **Accrued season:** An *accrued season* is a season when a player spends six or more regular-season games on a club's active/inactive list, injured reserve list, or "physically unable to perform" list.

- **Agent:** An *agent* is a person who represents a player during contract negotiations. Many agents are attorneys, and some are friends and relatives of the players they represent. Agents are banned from most college campuses.

✔ **First-year player:** A *first-year player* is either a player who has spent the preceding season on an NFL practice squad or a player who was injured and has never played in the NFL before.

✔ **Franchise player:** A team can designate only one of its players as a *franchise player*. This player may not apply to become a free agent and seek a higher salary from another team. In exchange for giving up this right, the franchise player is paid a minimum of the average of the top five salaries at his position or 120 percent of his previous salary, whichever is greater.

✔ **Injured reserve:** A team can place an injured player who's deemed a physical risk in the *injured reserve* category. Usually, these players require surgeries for their injuries. A player in this category can't return to the active roster (and play again) during that season.

✔ **Practice squad:** Each team can place eight players on the *practice squad*. These players, who are eligible only to practice, are paid $5,200 at minimum per week and are considered free agents. Teams routinely sign players from other teams' practice squads in order to complete their weekly 45-man active rosters when they lose players due to injury or release them due to poor performance.

✔ **Pro-Bowler:** A *Pro-Bowler* is a player who's selected by a vote of the fans, players, and coaching staffs to represent his conference in an all-star game that takes place the week before the Super Bowl. Any player chosen to play in the Pro Bowl is considered among the league's elite.

✔ **Restricted free agent:** A player who has completed three accrued seasons and now has an expired contract is considered a *restricted free agent*. Under the terms of the collective bargaining agreement, the club basically controls what he will be paid. Most teams attempt to sign this player to a long-term contract if he's deemed a valuable starter. This move prevents the player from being an unrestricted free agent in his fourth season.

✔ **Rookie:** A *rookie* is a player who's on an NFL roster for the first time. A player who has played in another league, such as the Canadian Football League or the Arena Football League, is still considered a rookie by the NFL.

✔ **Transition player:** A team can designate no more than two *transition players* in the same season (as long it doesn't also have a designated franchise player). This player's club must pay him the average of the prior season's top ten salaries of players at the same position or 120 percent of the player's previous year's salary, whichever is greater. A transition player can seek a contract from another team, but his current team has seven days to match the offer and thus retain his services.

✔ **Unrestricted free agent:** An *unrestricted free agent* is a player who has completed four or more accrued seasons and now has an expired contract. Such a player is free to negotiate and sign a new contract with any team.

✔ **Veteran:** A *veteran* has played at least one season in the NFL.

✔ **Waiver system:** The *waiver system* is a procedure by which a player's contract or NFL rights are made available by his current team to other teams in the league. Teams may waive a player if they no longer need him. During the procedure, the 31 other teams either file a claim to obtain the player or waive the opportunity to do so, thus the term *waiver*.

The Business of Professional Football

Besides being the greatest league in the greatest game on earth, the NFL is also a big business. How big? The 32 teams in the NFL rake in about $8 to $9 billion a year. The players, of course, want a piece of the action. After all, they're the ones the fans come to see.

Through collective bargaining agreements that players have had with team owners, the players have received a specific percentage of the gross revenue earned by NFL teams. The collective bargaining agreement also stipulates a maximum amount that teams may spend to compensate players, the so-called salary cap. Keep reading to find out about player salaries, the salary cap, and the NFL's collective bargaining agreement.

Show me the money: Player salaries

Salaries in the NFL have risen dramatically since the late 1980s. In 1988, the average salary of an NFL player was $250,000. It jumped to almost $800,000 in 1997, to $1.5 million in 2005, and to $1.9 million in 2014. These increases came about because of the financial impact of the league's television contract, which in the years 2006 to 2011 amounted to $3.1 billion per year (at more than 70 percent, television income is the largest portion of a team's revenue). And in 2014 alone, the major networks and DirecTV paid the NFL 5.5 billion dollars for broadcasting rights. As of 2012, the teams were required under the collective bargaining agreement to share 55 percent of national media revenue, 45 percent of NFL Ventures revenue (merchandising and licensing), and 40 percent of local club revenue with the players.

My only knock on the wage system is the inequity inside the locker room; a definite caste system exists. According to the way the free agency system has worked since 1993, 20 percent of players tend to receive 60 percent of a team's payroll, leaving 80 percent of the players with the remaining 40 percent share. To simplify this equation, say a team's total payroll is about $100 million for 50 players. In that scenario, the breakdown would be 10 players earning $6 million each and the other 40 players earning $1 million each. That breakdown of salaries creates a huge disparity, which is unfortunate considering football is such a team game. And a great, highly paid quarterback is nothing without a good offensive line and solid receivers.

The salary cap levels the playing field

To understand how an NFL team decides which players to draft, sign in free agency, or outright release, you must understand the salary cap. As determined by the collective bargaining agreement, the *salary cap* is a limit on the amount of money each team can spend for its players' salaries. When it was introduced in 1994, the salary cap was $34.6 million; by the 2014 season it had risen to $133 million. The cap is based on players receiving a certain percentage of the defined gross revenues of the NFL teams, which include revenue from network television contracts, ticket sales, and product sales.

The salary cap was designed to put all the NFL teams on equal footing when competing for free agents and signing their number-one draft choices. Teams that don't charge exorbitant ticket prices or whose stadium leases don't provide extra income from luxury suites, parking, and concessions receive funds from the richer teams to supplement their gross revenues in order to make the cap as equitable as possible.

Every team is allowed a maximum of 53 active players under its salary cap. If a player is injured and unable to play the rest of the season, his salary still counts toward the cap. So, teams do a lot of juggling during the season as players come and go — clubs rework contracts in order to fit an entire roster under the cap. Each team usually has one executive, called a *capologist,* crunching the salary numbers of the players and making sure everyone fits under the salary cap.

NFL teams actually spend more money on their players than the salary cap allows. Teams are also required to fund pension and health benefits. And some teams spend millions in signing bonuses in order to lure top-notch free agents. Teams have been known to give as much as $35 million in one season in signing bonuses alone. These benefits and bonuses are spread out over a period of years, which lessens the impact on the salary cap and makes these perks possible.

How television transformed the NFL

No professional sports league is more impressive or more powerful than the NFL. It's a multibillion-dollar empire. In fact, the NFL virtually transformed pro sports into a big business, marketing its on-field product through the magic of television. Walking down the street anywhere in the United States, you're likely to see a fan wearing a ball cap or jersey featuring his or her favorite player or team.

The NFL and television have grown and expanded together over the last 45 years. Television allows cities and states to close ranks; it brings Miami to tiny Green Bay, Wisconsin, and San Diego to New York. The immediacy of television is picture-perfect for a national league full of nationalized teams. For example, no matter where in the United States you live, you can follow the exploits of your favorite team on television. In the early 1990s, southern California was the site of one of the biggest fan clubs for the Cleveland Browns.

Television is a powerful medium that's perfectly suited to NFL football and its many lengthy time-outs and delays. The timeouts and commercials enable fans to discuss strategy with other fans. In fact, the fans watching at home actually have a better view of what's going on in a game than the fans sitting in the stands. Television allows fans to see clear replays and up-close shots of the action.

Collective bargaining agreements

A *collective bargaining agreement* is an agreement between employers and employees. Since 1993, team owners and the NFL Players Association have negotiated or agreed to extend their collective bargaining agreement five times. The agreement includes pension benefits and health coverage for retired players. It also dictates what percentage of the league's gross revenue goes to the players and the salary cap amount.

The current collective bargaining agreement runs from 2011 through the 2020 season and the 2021 NFL draft. Players now receive 55 percent of national media revenue, 45 percent of NFL Ventures revenue, and 40 percent of local club revenue.

Big business and the television connection

The best way to explain the popularity of the NFL is to study its network television contract. In 2011, the league signed a nine-year, $28 billion national television contract with CBS, NBC, and Fox. The total obligation of these three networks is about $3.1 billion annually. In addition, the NFL has a separate eight-year broadcasting agreement with ESPN that pays $1.9 billion annually. Now you can understand why Super Bowl commercials are priced at $2.5 to 2.8 million per 30 seconds.

Franchise movement

After the NFL lost an antitrust lawsuit in federal court, and thus lost the ability to prevent the Oakland Raiders from moving to Los Angeles in 1982, six franchises have left their home cities in search of better stadium deals.

I started with the Raiders in Oakland, and then played most of my career in Los Angeles. In 1995, unsatisfied with the stadium situation in Los Angeles, the Raiders returned to Oakland. That same season, the Rams vacated Orange County, California, for St. Louis, Missouri, which left the Los Angeles area without a pro football team. In the 1980s, the Colts left Baltimore, Maryland, for Indianapolis, Indiana, and the Cardinals left St. Louis for Phoenix, Arizona.

The biggest jolt to the NFL landscape occurred in 1996, when the Cleveland Browns left Ohio for Baltimore and changed their name to the Baltimore Ravens. A new Cleveland Browns franchise resumed play in 1999. The Houston Oilers became the Tennessee Oilers in 1997, settling in Nashville but playing their games in Memphis. In 1998, the renamed Tennessee Titans began playing home games at the newly built Coliseum in Nashville.

For NFL owners, these are pretty good times. Annual income from television networks (about $100 million per team) just about covers payments to players. And owners benefit from the revenue earned from ticket sales, luxury suites, local radio broadcast rights, concessions, and *NFL Properties* (the NFL's marketing arm for hats, T-shirts, company logos, sponsorships, and so on). Individual club revenue adds another $40 million to many teams' bank accounts.

In case you're wondering, *luxury suites* are the glass-enclosed private boxes within a stadium that seat as many as 22 fans and include private bars, restrooms, couches, and television sets. Some stadiums feature large VIP restaurants and bar lounges for high-roller fans. Some fans have to pay seat licensing fees simply to earn the right to purchase season tickets. These fees are similar to a surtax on each seat and cost fans, on average, between $500 and $2,500 per seat.

When the Carolina Panthers and the Jacksonville Jaguars joined the NFL, beginning play in 1995, the teams had to pay an entry fee of more than $200 million to the NFL. The Cleveland expansion team, which began playing in 1999, paid more than double that amount. And if the league ever expands to Los Angeles, the nation's number-two television market, the price will probably be even higher.

Making the Players' Health a Priority

In a sport revered for its hard-hitting play and fast action, making sure that football players are healthy has always been a challenge. As I explain in Chapter 1, the early days of football could be very brutal, and the game was almost banned in 1906 after nearly 20 deaths occurred on the football field. In the years since then, equipment innovations and new rules have been introduced to safeguard the players' health, but football remains a dangerous game.

In 2009, a study commissioned by the NFL determined that retired players were experiencing high rates of Alzheimer's disease, dementia, and memory-related diseases. The study concluded that ex-players had these diseases as a result of untreated concussions they experienced in their playing days. In the wake of the study, the league outlawed deliberate helmet-to-helmet hits, which are considered the chief cause of concussions on the football field. The league also instituted a policy whereby a player who shows symptoms of a concussion can't return to play and must stay off the field until the symptoms disappear.

The current collective bargaining agreement with players (signed in 2011) includes enhanced medical and injury protection benefits. And the NFL has committed to spending close to $1 billion on health insurance and pensions for retired NFL players.

Peeking at Other Pro Leagues

The NFL isn't the only professional football league. Diehard football fans can watch football games in the summer months, football's traditional offseason, and watch games in countries other than the United States. Here's a rundown of the NFL's sister leagues:

- ✔ **Arena Football:** Arena football is a fast-paced, offense-oriented, indoor sport played with only eight players per team on the field at a time. Six of those eight players must play both offense and defense. The field is 85 feet wide and 66 yards long. Kurt Warner, the MVP of Super Bowl XXXIV, began his professional career with an Arena Football team (the Iowa Barnstormers, to be exact). To find out more about Arena football, visit `www.arenafootball.com`.

- ✔ **Canadian Football League:** CFL play begins in June and ends in late November with the Grey Cup, its version of the Super Bowl. The field is 110 yards by 65 yards, bigger than the 100 yards by $53\frac{1}{3}$ yards of a U. S. football field, which gives offenses more room to maneuver and score points. Several former NFL stars, notably Warren Moon and Doug Flutie, got their start in the CFL. You can find out more about the CFL by visiting the league website at `www.cfl.ca`.

Chapter 18

Playing Fantasy Football

In This Chapter

▶ Getting to know the basics of fantasy football

▶ Putting together a team

▶ Discovering where to get the scoop on players' stats and injuries

▶ Outlining a basic strategy for fantasy football success

Have you ever watched a football game and said to yourself, "If I were an NFL team owner, I'd do things differently, and my team would make it to the Super Bowl"? Well, you can live your dream of becoming an NFL team owner by participating in a fantasy football league. These leagues give you the opportunity to put together a dream team of NFL players and pit your team against other fantasy football teams. And at the end of the season, you may even win prize money — and more importantly, bragging rights!

Fantasy football leagues are everywhere, and many types of leagues exist. I know a lot of fans are obsessed with these leagues because people ask me for advice all the time. Some of them would rather have me advise them on whom to trade for than ask for my autograph. For example, during the 1997 season when San Francisco 49ers receiver Jerry Rice suffered an injury that forced him to miss much of the season, fans were asking how they could replace him. But there's no way to replace a player like Rice, the NFL's all-time leading scorer and receiver.

In this chapter, I focus on the rules and method of play of the most popular type of fantasy football league: the head-to-head league. I also point out resources for you to use to investigate other types of leagues.

Exploring How Fantasy Football Leagues Work

In a head-to-head fantasy football league, you and your fellow owners draft teams of NFL players and compete against each other's teams each week.

Your fantasy team roster includes individual offensive players (quarterbacks, running backs, wide receivers, tight ends, and kickers) and may include defensive or special teams units, depending on the particular setup of the league.

Throughout the season, you track the performance of the players on your team and tally the points, yardage, and other statistics they accrue. You earn points based on those real-life statistics. For instance, if your team's defense or special teams unit scores a touchdown or records a safety, you get points. Table 18-1 lists the common scoring categories and the number of points awarded in most standard leagues.

Table 18-1	Typical Fantasy Football Scoring Categories
Category	*Points Awarded*
Touchdown	6 points
Field goal	3 points
Safety	2 points
Two-point conversion	2 points
Interception	2 points
Passing yards	1 point per 25 yards
Rushing yards	1 point per 10 yards
Receiving yards	1 point per 10 yards

If your team outscores your opponent's team for the week, you get a win. At the end of the season, you compare your win-loss record against those of the other teams to determine who makes the *playoffs* — the head-to-head competition of the top teams in the league, leading up to the Fantasy Super Bowl. The last team standing in the playoffs is the champion.

Figuring Out How to Play

Entire volumes have been written on playing fantasy football. I'll skip over most of the intricate details found in other books and instead try to give you the basics you need to get started. Refer to a good fantasy football reference, such as Martin Signore's *Fantasy Football For Dummies* (Wiley), to get detailed coverage of the nuances of fantasy football.

Starting a league

Starting a fantasy football league is easy. Here's how:

1. **Recruit enough friends, co-workers, or neighbors to have eight, ten, or twelve teams (each person fields one team).**

   Definitely go with an even number of teams. Scheduling is too difficult with an odd number of teams.

2. **Name your league and have each owner name his or her team.**

   Each owner must submit a team name. (Get creative!)

3. **Select a date for your annual player draft.**

   This date is when you choose the players for your team. The weekend before the start of the NFL regular season usually works best.

4. **Agree on an entry fee.**

   This dollar amount can be as high or low as you like. Pool the entry fees to form the *pot,* the cash paid out as prize money to the lucky winners. (Note that you can skip this step if you and your fellow team owners don't want to play for money.)

That's it! Grab your clipboard and start scouting players as you begin the countdown to the draft.

Choosing a fantasy football site

Your first order of business after forming your league is to appoint an almighty commissioner. The commish arbitrates any and all disputes that crop up (and trust me, controversy rears its ugly head in most leagues).

After a commissioner is in place, find an online fantasy league site to join. (References like *Fantasy Football For Dummies* can help you in this regard.) The sites offer articles, message boards, injury reports, and stats. These head-to-head online fantasy football leagues are the most popular:

- **CBS Sports Fantasy Football:** `www.cbssports.com/fantasyfootball`

- **ESPN:** `http://games.espn.go.com/frontpage/football`

- **Fleaflicker:** `www.fleaflicker.com/nfl`

- **Fox Sports Fantasy Football:** `www.foxsports.com/fantasy/football/commissioner`

    ✔ **NFL.com Fantasy:** `www.fantasy.nfl.com`

    ✔ **Yahoo:** `http://football.fantasysports.yahoo.com`

    ✔ **RT Sports:** `www.rtsports.com`

Drafting a team

The goal for each owner is to draft a team of 15 to 18 players. (Determine the roster limit for each team beforehand; see the next section for the breakdown of roster spots.) You generally draft offensive players from different teams along with the defense and special teams units from a single NFL team.

The number of players to draft at each position is up to you, but here's a safe combination for a 16-member team:

    ✔ Two quarterbacks

    ✔ Four running backs

    ✔ Four wide receivers

    ✔ Two tight ends

    ✔ Two kickers

    ✔ Two defense/special teams (punt and kickoff return) units

During the most common kind of draft, the *snake draft,* each owner selects one player at a time. Generally, the commissioner draws numbers out of a hat to determine the draft order. The owners make their picks in order for the first round. Then they reverse this order for the second round. For example, in an eight-team league, Owners 1 through 8 make the first eight selections in order. Then Owner 8 gets the ninth pick, Owner 7 gets the tenth pick, and so on down to Owner 1, who makes the 16th and 17th picks, and so on until all owners fill their rosters.

Before the draft, designate two people to record all the player selections. Accurate records can help resolve conflicts that may arise later.

Filling out your roster

Each week, you enter a starting lineup — in a standard league, that lineup is made up of a quarterback, two running backs, two wide receivers, a tight end, a kicker, and a defense/special teams (punt and kickoff return) unit.

The remaining players are *reserves*. These players' statistics don't count while the players sit on your reserve squad; instead, reserves serve as backups for your starting lineup. Here's why reserves are important:

- ✔ **They replace poor-performing starters.** If your quarterback, for example, plays poorly, you can replace him in your starting lineup the following week with your backup quarterback.

- ✔ **They replace injured starters.** If your star running back breaks his leg (gulp!), you simply start your backup running back the following week.

- ✔ **They replace players on bye weeks.** Each NFL team has one *bye week* (a week when they don't play). Because of bye weeks, you need to insert backup players for your starters whose teams aren't playing that week.

Managing your team after the draft

Fantasy football requires active weekly participation. You can't just kick back after the draft and expect your team to be successful. For starters, each week you must submit your starting lineup. At a minimum, you should

- ✔ **Monitor the schedule.** Don't start a player whose team isn't playing that weekend.

- ✔ **Check out the injury updates.** You obviously don't want to start an injured player.

Consider the following options to try to improve your team over the course of the season:

- ✔ **Free agent acquisitions:** Closely monitor the pool of undrafted players; you may be able to acquire a great player no one else drafted.

- ✔ **Trades:** As a general rule, you must trade equal numbers of players. For example, if you trade two players, you must get two players in return to keep your team whole.

Note: The rules for free agent acquisitions and trading vary widely. Consult *Fantasy Football For Dummies* or fantasy football Web sites to find out more about other leagues' policies regarding free agents.

Figuring your point total and winning

As long as you know how many points go with which actions (see the earlier "Exploring How Fantasy Football Leagues Work" section), scoring fantasy football just comes down to basic math. Table 18-2 shows you an abbreviated scoring example. Using this example, you pit your 69 points against your weekly opponent's total. If you outscore that opponent, you get a win; if he or she outscores you, you lose; if you score the same total, you get a tie. Simple, huh? As the season progresses, you can gauge how well (or how poorly) your team is doing by comparing your win-loss record with the other teams' records.

Table 18-2	A Scoring Example	
Player	*Scoring Play*	*Points Awarded*
Aaron Rogers, QB	1 touchdown pass 278 passing yards 24 rushing yards	6 11 (1 point per 25 yards passing) 2 (1 point per 10 yards rushing)
DeMarco Murray, RB	2 touchdown runs 149 yards rushing	12 14
Rob Gronkowski, TE	1 touchdown reception 99 receiving yards	6 9 (1 point per 10 yards receiving)
Sebastian Janikowski, K	1 field goal	3
Chicago Bears, defense/special teams	1 kickoff return touchdown	6
		69 (total)

At the end of the regular fantasy season, the teams with the best records make the playoffs. These high-powered playoff teams vie for the pinnacle of fantasy football — the Fantasy Super Bowl!

Of course, financial incentive exists for fielding a strong team (but feel free to eliminate entry fees and play for pride only). Here's one easy way to distribute prize money (dollar amounts will vary based on the number of teams in your league and the entry fee amount):

1. **Award a small amount ($1 or $2) for each win during the regular season.**
2. **Give 20 percent of the pot to the Super Bowl loser.**
3. **Give the remainder of the pot to the Super Bowl champ.**

Finding Information to Help Your Team

Prior to the draft and throughout the season, you need to stay informed about your players. You can stay up-to-date by searching the Internet.

Fantasy football Web sites abound. The following some sites offer player profiles, team stats, injury reports, lots of good insider information, and links to even more fantasy sites:

- **ESPN Fantasy Football** (`http://games.espn.go.com/frontpage/football`)

- **FOX Sports** (`www.foxsports.com/fantasy/football/commissioner`)

- **NFL.com** (`www.nfl.com/fantasyfootball`)

- **Sporting News** (`www.sportingnews.com/nfl`)

- **Sports Fanatics Player Drafts** (`www.sportsdrafts.com`)

- **Sports Illustrated** (`www.si.com/fantasy`)

- **USA Today** (`http://fantasy.usatoday.com/category/football`)

Considering Tips for Fantasy Football Success

Everyone who plays fantasy football will give you a different set of tips, but here are a few that should serve you well in any league:

- **Check out the prior year's stats.** Make sure you know who the best players are at each position. Pay special attention to touchdowns scored because that's the name of the game in fantasy football.

- **In the early rounds of the draft, take the best player available regardless of position.** For example, if most of the top-notch quarterbacks are taken by the time it's your turn to pick, snag the best available player, such as a running back or wide receiver. Remember, however, that you must fill in all the necessary positions to field a legal team.

- **Don't draft a kicker in the early rounds.** The NFL has plenty of decent kickers, so use your early draft picks to acquire players at other positions.

- **Consider a player's opponent for the week when selecting your starting lineup.** If one of your running backs is going up against the best run defense in the league, you may want to start another running back.

Part VI
The Part of Tens

the
part of
tens

Enjoy an additional Part of Tens chapter online at www.dummies.com/extras/football.

In this part . . .

- ✔ Get to know the greatest offensive and defensive players
- ✔ Read up on the best football coaches

Chapter 19

The Ten (Or So) Greatest Defensive Players of All Time

In This Chapter

▶ Great intimidators

▶ Defensive backs who played with grace, speed, and heart

▶ Pass-rushers who paved the way for today's heroes

▶ Safeties who hit like linebackers

*W*hen creating a top ten list, you're bound to exclude a number of players who could easily make someone else's top ten — it's a subjective, personal thing. Everyone has a top ten list of all-time defensive players, so here's mine (with a couple extra players for good measure). Some of these selections are predictable; others may raise an eyebrow or two.

Doug Atkins

Doug Atkins, a 6 foot 8 inch, 275 pounder from Humboldt, Tennessee, started his athletic career as a basketball player at the University of Tennessee, where he also ran track. One year, he finished second in the Southeastern Conference high jump competition. When the football coach heard of his feats, he asked him to try football and put him at defensive end. Atkins was a natural — he started hurdling offensive linemen like he did high jump bars. He became an All-American at Tennessee and is considered one of the toughest men to ever play football.

Atkins played for 17 years in the NFL, from 1953 to 1969, a total of 205 games, mostly for the Chicago Bears and the New Orleans Saints. He played in eight Pro Bowls. Atkins was a terror on the field, refusing to quit. To keep him from destroying their quarterbacks, most teams used two men to block him.

Atkins was every bit as funny as he was mean. One of the best anecdotes about Atkins is how he literally (and liberally) interpreted the words of the Bears' tough-guy head coach George Halas. During practice one day, Halas was unhappy with Atkins's practice habits and ordered him to take a lap around the field while wearing his helmet. Atkins took his lap with his helmet on — but that's all he wore. His teammates cracked up, and so did Halas.

Dick Butkus

Dick Butkus is arguably the most intimidating player to ever play defense. In fact, I think players were flat-out frightened of him. He was probably the first defensive player who really caught fans' attention. Kids growing up in the late 1960s wanted to hit and tackle like Butkus, the 6-foot-3-inch, 245-pound middle linebacker for the Chicago Bears.

Butkus was so good that he was All-Pro seven times. He had the speed and agility to make tackles from sideline to sideline and cover the best tight ends on pass plays. The NFL didn't officially begin recording quarterback sacks until 1982, but the Bears say Butkus had 18 in 1967, a huge number for a middle linebacker. He averaged 12.6 tackles per game — today's pro players think that 10 tackles is a great game. The growling man dominated games, finishing his career with 22 pass interceptions and 27 fumble recoveries.

Besides being a ferocious and violent player, Butkus was an intelligent line-backer. He studied game film and knew what the opposition liked to do on offense. At the snap of the ball, Butkus seemed to fly to wherever the play was headed. He had super instincts, which is something every player needs to be successful on defense. He played every game as though it were his last, and had he not suffered a serious knee injury in 1970, his career may have lasted a lot longer.

Kenny Easley

Okay, Ronnie Lott was the best safety, bar none. But Kenny Easley, who starred in college at UCLA (University of California, Los Angeles), across town from USC (University of Southern California) and Lott, wasn't too far behind. He was the first player in Pac-10 Conference history to be selected All-Conference all four years, and he was an All-American three times. Easley was a three-sport star at Oscar Smith High School in Chesapeake, Virginia, and was offered college basketball scholarships by ACC (Atlantic Coast Conference) and Big Ten colleges.

Easley played only seven years in the NFL, but he managed 32 interceptions during his career. He was named AFC Defensive Rookie of the Year in 1981 after the Seattle Seahawks drafted him in the first round. In 1984, Easley was voted NFL Defensive Player of the Year when he collected ten interceptions, returning two for touchdowns. He was the defensive heart of his team and a huge reason why the Seahawks finished 12-4 that season.

Easley was 6 feet 3 inches tall and 206 pounds, and he hit people like a freight train. He was a wild man on the field, playing with a total disregard for his body. His career was cut short by a serious kidney ailment and, believe me, our receivers had mixed feelings. They hated to see Easley retire in the prime of his career, but they sure didn't miss his heavy-handed greeting card when they crossed the middle of the field. As a defensive player, I didn't mind watching him while I rested on the sidelines.

Joe Greene

Most people, especially in Pittsburgh, remember Joe Greene as "Mean Joe Greene." He was the heart and soul of the great Pittsburgh Steelers defensive teams of the 1970s. Pittsburgh's defensive line was so immovable and suffocating that it earned the nickname "The Steel Curtain." In fact, during a stretch of nine games in 1976, Pittsburgh's defense allowed only 28 points while going 9-0.

However, Pittsburgh fans weren't convinced that Greene — a 6-foot-4-inch, 275-pound defensive tackle from unknown North Texas State — deserved to be the club's first-round draft choice in 1969. The team had suffered through five consecutive losing seasons and hadn't appeared in a playoff game since 1947. A quarterback or running back made more sense to fans. Going with his own instincts, Chuck Noll, the first-year Pittsburgh coach, ignored some of the scouting reports and built his team, one of the NFL's best ever, around Greene.

The imposing Greene made an immediate impact in the league and was named Defensive Rookie of the Year. He was named All-Pro five times in the 1970s, played in ten Pro Bowls, and was NFL Defensive Player of the Year in 1972 and 1974. In 1972, with the Steelers needing to beat Houston to clinch their first-ever division title, Greene had an amazing game — five sacks, a blocked field goal, and a fumble recovery — in a 9-3 Pittsburgh win. During Pittsburgh's first Super Bowl–winning season, Greene used a new stance, lining up almost sideways between the guard and center. He was able to neutralize those two linemen or shoot a gap from this stance because he had such an unusual combination of speed, quickness, and sheer power. I can't think of a player who was able to duplicate Greene's production from that stance.

Jack Ham and Ted Hendricks

I couldn't separate Jack Ham and Ted Hendricks; they were two of the best outside linebackers I ever saw play. Both had tremendous range and a rare instinct for the game. They saw offensive plays developing before the ball was snapped: They could interpret any running back's stance. And when an offensive player went in motion, it instantly triggered something in their brains.

Ham — a consensus All-American at Penn State, the school known as Linebacker U — was the first and only linebacker of the 1970s to be named to eight consecutive Pro Bowls. Ham started every game as a rookie and was a Pittsburgh regular until he retired after the 1982 season. He was a big-play performer, much like Hendricks, and was adept at shutting down the short passing game; there were few running backs he couldn't defend.

Besides being extremely quick, Ham was an intelligent player and usually knew his opponents' formations as well as they did. He finished his career with 21 fumble recoveries and 32 interceptions.

Hendricks fell a little short of Ham — 16 fumble recoveries and 26 interceptions — but he was a master when the opposition was pinned near its own goal line. He retired with a record-tying four safeties. Like Ham, Hendricks was a starter on four Super Bowl–champion teams. He won three Super Bowls with the Raiders and his first with the Baltimore Colts in Super Bowl V.

Hendricks and Ham opposed each other in the great Steeler-Raider rivalry of the 1970s. Off the field, the iconoclastic Hendricks was the opposite of Ham. Hendricks was a chain smoker and a Good-Time Charlie. Because he was 6 feet 7 inches tall and gangly looking, Hendricks was nicknamed "The Mad Stork" coming out of the University of Miami, where he was a three-time All-American. He played in 215 regular-season games and was selected to eight Pro Bowls.

Mike Haynes

Mike Haynes was probably the best bump-and-run cover cornerback in the history of the game; he could stick with any receiver. His coverage seemed so effortless because of his superior athletic ability and speed. Haynes was unusually tall (6 feet 2 inches) for the cornerback position, yet he was so graceful. I like to call him a "black hole player" — any player he covered seemed to go into a black hole, disappearing from the field.

Haynes finished his 14-year career in 1989 with 46 interceptions, which ranks low on the all-time list. But in Haynes's case, statistics don't tell the whole story. He was so good that opposing quarterbacks quit throwing in his direction — which is the highest compliment for a cornerback. In 1976, the New England Patriots drafted Haynes in the first round, and he finished his first season with eight interceptions, a 13.5-yard punt return average, and AFC Rookie of the Year honors.

Haynes joined me with the Raiders after seven seasons in New England. With the Raiders, Haynes and Lester Hayes formed one of the finest cornerback tandems in the history of the game. During those years, teams threw toward Hayes because they feared Haynes. And Hayes was a great cornerback in his own right; in 1980, he had 13 interceptions, just one shy of the NFL single-season record. You can't play pass defense without solid cornerbacks, and Haynes simply put on a clinic every game, teaching other cornerbacks how the game should be played.

Ken Houston

How great of a strong safety was Ken Houston? So good that Washington Redskins coach George Allen traded five veteran players to the Houston Oilers for him in 1973. Houston was a defensive back who tackled like a linebacker. For 12 consecutive seasons, between 1968 and 1979, Houston was selected to either the AFL All-Star game or the AFC-NFC Pro Bowl. Without question, Houston was the dominant player at his position in that era.

Houston (6 feet 3 inches, 198 pounds) was a long strider with exceptional quickness and strength. He would sit back from his viewpoint as a safety and attack the line of scrimmage. He had tremendous instincts and owned that proverbial "nose for the ball." With the Oilers, he returned nine interceptions for touchdowns, an NFL record at the time. During his career, he intercepted 49 passes and returned them for 898 yards. He also recovered 21 fumbles.

One of the most memorable instances of Houston's signature style of tackling occurred in one of the Redskins' great rivalry games against the Dallas Cowboys in 1973. With seconds remaining, Cowboys running back Walt Garrison caught a short pass and started heading toward the end zone. Houston met him at the 1-yard line, lifted Garrison off his feet (a hit called a *decleater*), and planted him in his tracks. The game ended, and Houston's tackle preserved Washington's victory. Throughout his career, the super-strong Houston repeated this style of bone-chilling tackle.

Sam Huff and Ray Nitschke

Dick Butkus stands alone as the game's best middle linebacker, but Sam Huff and Ray Nitschke stand right behind him in terms of how they tackled running backs from the middle linebacker position. During a 13-year pro career, Huff was a well-known player because his reign of terror emanated from New York City. He appeared on the cover of *Time* magazine when he was 24 and was even the subject of a television special, "The Violent World of Sam Huff." He played in six NFL championship games with the New York Giants before finishing his career with the Washington Redskins.

Both Huff and Nitschke had a nose for the football and were difficult to block from their 4-3 formations. And both seemed to love the violent aspects of the game; losing their helmets after a rousing tackle was a trademark. Both were instinctively tough players who enjoyed football's collisions and brutality.

They were smart players, too. Huff had 30 interceptions; Nitschke had 25. And when Nitschke's team, the Green Bay Packers, beat Huff's Giants for the 1962 NFL championship, Nitschke was named the game's Most Valuable Player. He was a soft-hearted man who was loved by many thousands of Packers fans. He kept a home in Green Bay, Wisconsin, until his death in 1998.

Deacon Jones and Merlin Olsen

Listing one of these great Los Angeles Rams defensive linemen without including the other is impossible. David (Deacon) Jones and Merlin Olsen were a dynamic duo for the Rams for ten seasons (1962 to 1971) until Jones was traded to the San Diego Chargers. Olsen joined the Rams as a first-round draft choice in 1962 after an All-American career at Utah State and was a mainstay on the team's defensive line for 15 seasons. Jones entered the NFL as an obscure 14th-round draft choice who had played at South Carolina State and Mississippi Vocational. But regardless of their backgrounds, these two players worked together to wreak havoc on opposing teams. Because of Jones and Olsen, who lined up side by side on the left, the Rams' defensive line (nicknamed "The Fearsome Foursome") was one of the most feared and successful units in the history of pro football.

Olsen, who was 6 feet 5 inches tall and 270 pounds, was named to the Pro Bowl team a record 14 consecutive times. He was very agile for a big man, and he clogged the middle of the line, enabling speed rushers like Jones to cause trouble from the outside. Jones, 6 feet 5 inches tall and 272 pounds used his speed, strength, and quickness to beat offensive tackles who attempted to block him. While he played, Jones coined the term *sack,* which is used today to define the tackling of a quarterback behind the line of scrimmage. Jones claims that he's the all-time sack leader. And arguing with him is difficult because the NFL didn't begin to include this defensive statistic officially until 1982 — two seasons after Jones was inducted into the Pro Football Hall of Fame. In 1967 and 1968, Jones was chosen as the NFL's best defensive player.

The Rams teams of his era were defense-oriented, and Olsen was their leader. Olsen was team MVP six consecutive seasons and in 1974 was named NFL Player of the Year by the Maxwell Club, an athletic club based in Philadelphia, Pennsylvania, that conducts an annual poll of the national media. In addition to acting on TV dramas such as *Little House on the Prairie,* Olsen was a football analyst on network television for many years after he retired from football.

Jack Lambert

The beauty of Jack Lambert's career is that he came from a small, non-football power (Kent State) and was rather small by NFL standards, only to rise and become a Hall of Famer. At 6 feet 4 inches and 220 pounds, Lambert was Defensive Rookie of the Year with the Pittsburgh Steelers in 1974 after being a second-round draft choice. He was Pittsburgh's defensive captain for eight years, and many people believe that his presence at middle linebacker solidified the Steelers as a great defensive team. (Lambert is one of three Pittsburgh players I mention in this chapter.)

Lambert had an 11-year career with the Steelers and starred in their four Super Bowl victories. He was known for his toothless glare and confident demeanor. He was both an intimidator and a tormentor. Unlike the prototypical middle linebacker — the big, huge run-stuffers — Lambert could drop 20 yards deep into pass coverage because he was so fast. He had exceptional range while still possessing the toughness to make rock-solid tackles. No one messed with Jack Lambert, including his teammates.

Lambert was All-Pro seven times and was twice named Defensive Player of the Year. He finished his career with 28 interceptions.

Dick "Night Train" Lane

Dick Lane's story is an improbable one. He played one season of junior college football and a few years on a military team at Fort Ord, California. In 1952, he was working at an aircraft factory in California, carrying oil-soaked sheet metal, when he showed up at the Los Angeles Rams offices looking for work.

Coach Joe Stydahar was impressed by his workout and signed him. Lane went on to intercept 14 passes in his 12-game rookie season, a league record that still stands.

Most secondary coverage in those days was man to man, and Lane was fast enough to stick with any receiver. Plus, he fully understood the passing game because he had been a receiver on his military team. (Lane shifted to cornerback because the Rams already had Tom Fears and Elroy "Crazy Legs" Hirsch, two future Hall of Fame receivers.) Lane also got his nickname via Fears, who was partial to Buddy Morrow music. "Night Train" was one of Morrow's favorite songs, and a teammate put the tag on Lane one night while he sat in Fears's room listening to Morrow's music.

Amazingly, the Rams kept Lane for only two seasons, trading him to the Chicago Cardinals, who later dealt him to the Detroit Lions. His best seasons were with the Lions, where he played the final six seasons of his 14-year career. Lane never won a championship, but he finished with 68 interceptions, which is fourth all-time behind Paul Krause of the Minnesota Vikings, Emlen Tunnell of the New York Giants, and Rod Woodson of the Pittsburgh Steelers, Baltimore Ravens, and a couple of other teams.

Bob Lilly

Bob Lilly was the first-round draft choice of the Dallas Cowboys in 1961 after being a consensus All-American at Texas Christian in nearby Fort Worth (in fact, Lilly was the *first ever* draft choice of the expansion Dallas Cowboys). He had such a legendary 14-year career that he earned the nickname "Mr. Cowboy." At 6 foot 5 inches tall and 260 pounds, Lilly was built like some of today's pass-rushing defensive ends. And he played outside for two seasons before coach Tom Landry moved him to tackle, where his cat-like speed and punishing style forced most opponents to double-team him. Ernie Stautner, his old line coach, remembers some teams putting three blockers in his way.

Lilly was selected to 11 Pro Bowls in his 14 NFL seasons and was so durable that he played in 196 consecutive games. In the early part of Lilly's career, the Cowboys kept winning regular-season games and making title game appearances but couldn't win the championship game. Dallas played in six NFL/NFC championship games in an eight-year period. When the team finally won a title, Super Bowl VI, Lilly sacked Miami quarterback Bob Griese for a record 29-yard loss.

Usually, defensive tackles fall down when they recover fumbles, but Lilly could run. He returned three fumbles for touchdowns and scored again on a 17-yard interception return.

Gino Marchetti

Big Gino Marchetti was to defensive ends what the Cleveland Browns' Jim Brown was to running backs; he was light-years ahead of his time. Marchetti played the run and the pass equally well — he did it all. And he did it with his hands. During his era (the 1950s), most defensive linemen used their forearms and shoulders a lot, but not Marchetti. He kept consistent separation with his hands, meaning he shed blockers instead of battering his way through them by lowering his shoulder or knocking them over with his forearm.

When I first came into the NFL, I studied four or five players, looking for technique and style. I looked at some of Marchetti's old NFL films, and I tried to play the run like he did. His technique and style would have fit in the 1980s or 1990s — he had all the right pass-rush moves, using his hands so well. Marchetti, who was 6 foot 4 inches tall and 245 pounds, used his long frame to hound opposing quarterbacks. If the NFL had monitored quarterback sacks when he played, he probably would have ranked ahead of great pass-rushers like Reggie White and Bruce Smith.

Marchetti was also a tough guy. In the great 1958 NFL championship game between Marchetti's Baltimore Colts and the New York Giants, Marchetti made a key tackle on Frank Gifford, stopping him short of a first down with two minutes left and forcing the Giants to punt. Marchetti broke his leg making that tackle. (The Colts rallied to win the game in overtime after Marchetti was carried to the locker room.) The injury forced Marchetti to miss the Pro Bowl game. Had he not missed this game, he could have claimed after he retired that he had made ten consecutive visits to that all-star game during his career — a benchmark for many Hall of Fame players.

Chapter 20

More Than Ten Top Non-Quarterback Offensive Players

In This Chapter

▶ Runners who combined power with speed and fancy moves

▶ Huge men who dominated defenses, opening up the passing game

▶ Receivers who could play in any era and who blocked, too

*W*ith a few exceptions, this chapter's main criterion was choosing talented offensive players who were also great champions. And because the NFL has become such a passing league, I decided to list the greatest quarterbacks separately (in Chapter 21).

One player who could have made this list but didn't is Bo Jackson, the most gifted physical specimen I ever played with. Bo won the Heisman Trophy at Auburn University as a running back. In the pros, he was a two-sport star, playing football with the Los Angeles Raiders and baseball with the Kansas City Royals, Chicago White Sox, and California Angels. A severe hip injury suffered in a football game ended his career prematurely. What a shame — he had the most incredible, natural, raw physical talent I've ever seen. I left Bo off this list only because his career was cut too short.

Choosing players for all-time teams is extremely difficult. I ended up with 13 players in this chapter. I just couldn't help myself.

Jim Brown

Jim Brown was light-years ahead of his time. He also played in an age (1957 to 1965) when the running game was a big part of the offense. Still, with every team geared to stop him, none of their efforts seemed to work. Brown was 6 feet 2 inches tall and weighed 232 pounds — 10 to 20 pounds heavier than most running backs today and huge for a player in his day. In nine pro seasons, Brown led the NFL in rushing eight times and totaled 12,312 yards, 106 rushing touchdowns, and 756 points. He was Rookie of the Year in 1957 and MVP three times, in 1957, 1958, and 1965.

What's even more amazing about Jim Brown is the fact that he retired from football at age 30. He decided to become an actor and retired during the shooting of probably his most memorable movie, *The Dirty Dozen*. Had he continued to play, Brown might still hold every rushing record, may have gained 20,000 yards, and may have scored 150 touchdowns. To this day, every great runner — from Barry Sanders to Emmitt Smith to Adrian Peterson — is judged by his standards.

Brown, a splendid all-around athlete, dominated his era with a rare combination of power, speed, and size. For such a huge man, his waist was only 32 inches around. He was durable, and his head coach, Paul Brown of the Cleveland Browns, never shied away from using him. At Syracuse University, he lettered in basketball and was an All-American in lacrosse as well as football. He competed in track for one year and finished fifth in the national decathlon championship.

When fans rank their top five players of all-time, Brown should be on everyone's list. Two statistics set him apart: He never missed a game in nine seasons, and his 5.22 yards-per-carry average remains number one.

Earl Campbell

Earl Campbell ran like an out-of-control bulldozer, but he had Ferrari speed after he broke into the open. Campbell was 5 feet 11 inches tall, weighed 233 pounds, and people said that his thighs were as big as tree trunks. If he couldn't run *around* you, he simply ran *over* you. A Texas native, he was given the gentle label "The Tyler Rose," although he simply wreaked havoc on defenses. He won the Heisman Trophy at the University of Texas in 1977 and was an instant superstar when he joined the Houston Oilers the following season.

In his first pro season, Campbell won the rushing title, was named Rookie of the Year, and was the NFL's Most Valuable Player. The highlight of his rookie season was a Monday night game against the Miami Dolphins in the Astrodome. Campbell rushed for 199 yards and four touchdowns to lead the Oilers (a franchise that has since moved to Tennessee and changed its name to the Titans) to a 35–30 victory.

Campbell was a repeat winner of the MVP award in 1979, but his best season was in 1980, when he rushed for 1,934 yards — at the time the second-best single-season mark ever, behind only O.J. Simpson. Campbell made my list because although he was a punishing runner, he missed only 6 games out of 121 due to injuries.

Dave Casper

I picked Dave Casper as my tight end because he started his college career at Notre Dame as an offensive tackle. Right off, playing that position at that school means that he was a tough, physical player. In 1972, when Casper switched to tight end in his junior season, he instantly became the best blocking tight end in college football. The only way defenders could stop him was to hold him when he tried to run a pass route. He was simply too big (6 feet 4 inches, 240 pounds), strong, and fast for the average college player.

For such a physical player, Casper had soft hands — an attribute associated with wide receivers and running backs. Most big, tough guys, which Casper was, have hands of stone. He was a very reliable underneath receiver when he joined the Oakland Raiders in 1974. Had Casper played in today's wide-open offenses, he probably would have caught 80 passes a season. In his only Super Bowl appearance, Casper caught four passes, including one for a touchdown. No tight end was more complete than Casper; he could block anyone and also find a *crease,* that tiniest of open spaces, in any defensive secondary. He was very smart. When I think of the term *wily veteran,* I think of Casper.

Mike Ditka and John Mackey

Among all the tight ends ever to play, Mike Ditka and John Mackey went into the Pro Football Hall of Fame, one-two. Fans' first impression of Iron Mike Ditka was his toughness, but he, like Mackey, had exceptional hands. Mackey was faster and more of a breakaway threat than Ditka, but both were head and shoulders above every tight end over a 20-year period. They were power-ful blockers and ultimate tough guys. Ditka didn't miss a start for the Chicago Bears in his first 84 games, while Mackey missed only one game in his nine seasons with the Baltimore Colts and one with the San Diego Chargers.

Ditka burst onto the pro scene with 56 catches for 1,076 yards and 12 touch-downs in his rookie season — staggering numbers for a tight end. He was a tremendous two-way player at the University of Pittsburgh, plus he was the regular punter. Ditka caught 75 passes in 1964, a season-high record for tight ends that stood until 1980 and the era of 16 games. Together, these two players caught 758 passes for 11,048 yards and scored 81 touchdowns. Mackey averaged 15.8 yards per catch during his career; as a rookie in 1963, he averaged 30 yards on nine kick returns. He was such a scoring threat that, in 1966, he scored six touchdowns of 50 yards or more.

These two tight ends were similar in size, with Mackey at 6 feet 2 inches, 224 pounds and Ditka at 6 feet 3 inches, 228 pounds. Both men were fierce competitors on and off the field. Ditka was "Papa Bear" George Halas's personal pick to coach his beloved Chicago Bears. The franchise won its only Super Bowl after the 1985 season with Ditka as head coach. Ditka returned to coaching for three years starting in 1997 with the New Orleans Saints. He has since returned to being a television commentator.

Mackey, who was one of quarterback Johnny Unitas's favorite targets, served as president of the NFL Players Association. Many in football believe his passionate pursuit of player rights as the union leader initially held back his selection to the Hall of Fame.

John Hannah

John Hannah was big, mean, athletic, and a steamroller — all perfect ingredients for one of the game's finest all-around offensive linemen. When he came into the NFL in 1973, a first-round draft choice of the New England Patriots from the University of Alabama, Hannah was the first guard of such size (6 feet 3 inches, 265 pounds) who could also run well; he was a devastating pulling guard.

Some people had doubts about Hannah's ability to adjust to the pro game because he was strictly a zone, straight-ahead blocker while playing at Alabama. At the time, Alabama ran a wishbone offense, which featured option running by the quarterback, who also pitched wide to running backs. A lineman didn't have to leave his stance and run wide to block or concentrate on pass-blocking techniques in the wishbone offense. But Hannah had football in his genes (Herb, his father, played pro football with the New York Giants), and he was an adaptable athlete, having won varsity letters in wrestling and track, as well as football, at Alabama.

During his career, the Patriots were a few players and a little luck away from being a championship team. Hannah played in only one Super Bowl (and lost), but he was named All-Pro for ten consecutive seasons (1976 to 1985) and Offensive Lineman of the Year by the Players Association four times. In 13 seasons, he missed only 5 of 188 games due to injury.

Don Hutson

Everyone knows that Jerry Rice of the San Francisco 49ers was the best receiver ever, but old-timers will tell you that Green Bay Packer Don Hutson was the best. From 1935 to 1945, Hutson's receptions and receiving totals were almost three times greater than his nearest competitor. Teams didn't throw a lot in those days, but the Packers did because they had "The Alabama Antelope," one of the fastest and most graceful men in football. In 1942, Hutson caught 74 passes, more than all receivers on the Detroit Lions combined; his 1,211 receiving yards were more than two NFL teams; and his 17 touchdown catches were more than six NFL teams. Hutson was the consummate deep-ball threat, leading the NFL in touchdown receptions in 9 of his 11 seasons. In his second game as a pro, he caught an 83-yard touchdown from quarterback Arnie Herber. Teams never double- and triple-teamed players until Hutson showed up on the scene.

In college at the University of Alabama, Hutson was an all-around jock. In fact, one day, he was playing outfield in a baseball game and left to compete in a track meet. He ran a 9.7-second 100-yard dash, winning the event, before hustling back to his baseball game.

Hutson, a charter inductee into the Pro Football Hall of Fame, was a two-way performer, playing at left end and in the secondary on defense. In his final four seasons, Hutson intercepted 23 passes. His record of 99 touchdown receptions stood for 44 seasons. And he was great until the bitter end, leading the NFL with 47 receptions in his final season.

Before he died, Hutson was asked about modern athletes and whether he could play with them. "How many catches would you have today?" the young reporter asked. "Oh, probably about 50," Hutson replied. "Fifty? That's not as many as you had in your prime," the reporter retorted. "Well," Hutson said, smiling, "I am 74, you know."

Hugh McElhenny

People referred to Hugh McElhenny as "The King." On his first play as a pro with the San Francisco 49ers, he ran 40 yards for a touchdown. Some say that McElhenny was the greatest running back to ever catch a screen pass. He was dangerous in the open field, owning the complete repertoire of moves: He could pivot, sidestep, spin, change his pace, and fake you out of your pants. McElhenny likened running in the open field to walking down a dark alley: He instinctively knew what was lurking in every dark corner — he knew where the 11 defenders were hiding to nab him.

More than 60 colleges offered McElhenny a scholarship, and when the University of Washington won his services, the college's football program was immediately investigated for recruiting violations. When McElhenny became a professional in 1952, his teammates laughed, saying that his $7,000 salary meant that he was taking a pay cut.

McElhenny played many of his 13 pro seasons in pain. He needed a steel plate in his shoe and pain-deadening shots in his right foot because of severed tendons that he had suffered as a child. When he retired after the 1964 season, he had played for four different teams and totaled 11,369 all-purpose yards. He was a true game-breaker; he could score from anywhere on the field via the run, the pass, or the kick return. He averaged 4.9 yards a carry in his first ten seasons, plus he had touchdowns of 94, 86, and 81 yards.

Jim Parker

Jim Parker was the first offensive lineman elected to the Pro Football Hall of Fame. A first-round draft choice from Ohio State, Parker played both ways — offensive and defensive tackle — but Baltimore Colts coach Weeb Ewbank changed all that by starting him at only offensive tackle in 1957. The plan was pretty simple: Parker, all 6 feet 3 inches and 273 pounds of him, was supposed to protect quarterback Johnny Unitas, one of the greatest passers of all time. Unitas attempted 47 passes in his very first game and wasn't sacked once. Parker was magnificent at his job.

Parker was the first huge man — who possessed the quickness of a man 60 pounds lighter — to emerge as an outstanding blocker. Until men like Parker arrived, defensive players generally dominated pro football's line of scrimmage; most athletic big men preferred playing defense to offense.

Parker's gifts were immeasurable. He was a Pro Bowl player at tackle for four years when Ewbank was forced to shift him to left guard because of injuries to other players. Parker fit perfectly in that role and was named All-Pro at guard for four consecutive seasons. A knee injury ended Parker's career in 1967.

Walter Payton

Mike Ditka, the great Chicago tight end and coach, called Walter Payton the most complete football player he had ever seen. Payton's nickname was "Sweetness," but maybe it should have been "Toughness." He missed only one game in 13 seasons with the Chicago Bears, and that was due to a coaching decision made by Jack Pardee in Payton's rookie season (1975).

Excluding his rookie year and his final season, when he no longer was the hub of Chicago's offense, Payton touched the ball an average of 24 times a game for 119 yards, combining rushing and receiving gains. Payton is the NFL's second-leading all-time rusher with 16,726 yards (Emmitt Smith is first).

Players marveled about Payton because he did whatever he needed to do to win, and he stood out because he spent more than half his career on non-playoff teams. In fact, in Payton's first eight seasons, Chicago was a dismal 61–70. His passion for the game ran deep. He enjoyed blocking and would run a dummy pass route like he was the intended receiver. Heck, he even passed for eight touchdowns. In 10 of 13 seasons, Payton rushed for at least 1,200 yards. He needed arthroscopic surgery on both knees after the 1983 season, in which he gained 1,421 yards on those two gimpy knees. Tragically, he died in 1999 at age 45.

Gale Sayers

Gale Sayers of the Chicago Bears was a speedster with shake-and-bake moves — a dazzler in football pads. The only sad thing about Sayers is that two knee injuries shortened his career. Still, in basically a five-season career, he accomplished enough to gain entry into the Pro Football Hall of Fame on the first ballot. Sayers enjoyed nothing more than returning punts and kicks. In his first preseason game, he raced 93 yards with a kickoff and 77 yards on a punt return, and he also threw a 25-yard touchdown pass with his left (non-dominant) hand.

In 1965, Bears coach George Halas, who coached more than 40 seasons, remarked after Sayers scored six touchdowns on a muddy Wrigley Field against the San Francisco 49ers that it was the greatest performance he'd ever seen. Sayers gained 336 yards that day, and some people say that he covered more than 130 yards while scoring on an 85-yard punt return in which he zigzagged all over the field.

In basically 12 full games that season, Sayers scored 22 touchdowns and averaged 31.4 yards on kick returns and 14.9 yards per punt return. His 2,272 combined yards by a rookie still ranks second in NFL history. Sayers had only two 1,000-yard rushing seasons, but he did average 5 yards per carry and scored a touchdown one out of every 23.7 times he touched the ball.

Art Shell

Art Shell arrived with the Oakland Raiders as a third-round draft choice from tiny Maryland State–Eastern Shore in 1968, a year after Gene Upshaw. However, the two players eventually united to form the best guard/tackle combination in the history of the NFL. Shell, who was 6 feet 5 inches tall and weighed 265 pounds, became the starting left tackle in 1970 and was named to eight Pro Bowls in the 1970s. He became the Jim Parker of his era. Shell and Upshaw worked as one, dominating their side of the offensive formation on run sweeps.

However, Shell also evolved into a picture-perfect pass-blocker. In Super Bowl XI, Shell virtually buried talented Minnesota defensive end Jim Marshall to help lead the Raiders to victory. Shell was a mammoth man with a dancer's feet. He could *slide-protect* (he had quick feet, which allowed him to shift his body easily in any direction when protecting his quarterback in passing situations), and he could also hammer defensive linemen with his brutish strength. Shell developed his agility while earning All-State honors in basketball at Bonds-Wilson High in North Charleston, South Carolina.

Shell later became one of the first African Americans to become an NFL head coach in the modern era. He owns a 56–52 record in his two stints as coach of the Raiders. He opened the door for other African American coaches like Tony Dungy, Marvin Lewis, and Lovie Smith.

Gene Upshaw

Before his untimely death in 2008, many fans knew Gene Upshaw as the executive director of the NFL Players Association, a title that translates into the leader of the players union. As leader of the union, he fought on the players' behalf for better free agency terms, more money, and stronger benefits. The former Oakland Raider seemed destined for such a role because he entered the league in 1967, when its popularity was mushrooming, and left in 1981, knowing that pro football had surpassed baseball as America's pastime. Also, he was a Raiders captain for eight seasons, which is the same number of years this left guard was named to All-AFC or All-Pro teams.

Upshaw was the first of the really tall (6 feet 5 inches) guards, and he was drafted in the first round to block a specific Oakland opponent: Hall of Fame tackle Buck Buchanan of the arch-rival Kansas City Chiefs. Upshaw had never played guard, but he won the starting job as a rookie and kept it for

15 seasons. Upshaw is the only player to start on championship teams in the old American Football League and in the NFL. The Raiders won the American Football League title in 1967 and then Super Bowls XI and XV, with Upshaw leading the way. Upshaw was a fierce competitor who was equally adept at run-blocking and pass-blocking. All told, he played in 307 preseason, regular-season, and postseason games with the Raiders, 24 of them playoff games.

Chapter 21

The Ten Greatest Quarterbacks of All Time

In This Chapter

▶ Team leaders who became champions

▶ Stars who excelled when the spotlight was on them

*N*FL quarterbacks hold the most highly regarded position in all of sports. When they're good, they're stars in the eyes of the media and the world. When they're great, their exploits become the stuff of legend. Most kids today would rather aspire to be a great NFL quarterback than the president of the United States.

The players in this chapter are listed in alphabetical order. I made no attempt to rank these ten great quarterbacks.

Terry Bradshaw

I had to pick Terry Bradshaw or working at FOX Sports would be unbearable; he's like the older brother I never wanted. But kidding aside, Terry was really something in big games. The bigger the game, the better he played. He and Joe Montana of the San Francisco 49ers are the only quarterbacks to have led their teams to four Super Bowl championships. Bradshaw was voted the Super Bowl MVP twice with the Pittsburgh Steelers.

Bradshaw is a great example of a player who refused to quit when his career didn't flourish immediately. Although he was the first player taken in the 1970 college draft, the Steelers didn't immediately turn over the offense and the team to him. But Bradshaw overcame his struggles and his benchings to become one of the all-time greats.

When the Steelers were ready to win, Bradshaw led them to an unprecedented four Super Bowl wins in a six-year period (1974 to 1979). In Pittsburgh's first title run, his touchdown pass to Lynn Swann in the fourth quarter beat the Oakland Raiders in the AFC championship game, and in the Super Bowl that followed, his fourth quarter touchdown pass to Larry Brown clinched the victory over the Minnesota Vikings.

When the NFL liberalized its pass-blocking rules and prevented defensive backs from touching receivers after they ran 5 yards, Bradshaw's throwing talents really blossomed. He had a great arm, and during the 1979 season, the Steelers rode it to the team's fourth championship. In his two championship MVP performances, Bradshaw threw for 627 yards and six touchdowns. Believe me, I know all his stats; I've heard about them enough. If he tells me about the "Immaculate Reception" that robbed my Raiders of a fourth championship one more time, I'll flip!

Tom Brady

Nobody thought Tom Brady would amount to much more than a backup quarterback in the NFL. After a moderately successful stint as the starting quarterback at the University of Michigan, Brady was selected by the New England Patriots as the 199th pick all the way down in the 6th round of the NFL draft in the year 2000. At the start of his rookie season with the Patriots, he was their fourth-string quarterback. By the end of the season, he was their backup behind Drew Bledsoe.

A serious injury to Bledsoe early in the 2001 season meant that Brady would fill in as the Patriot's starter, and the rest, as they say, is history. Brady led the team to a first place finish in the AFC East and a berth in the playoffs. The Patriots eventually won the Super Bowl in dramatic fashion over the heavily favored St. Louis Rams. At that point, Brady was a star, and his career as one of the NFL's premier quarterbacks would continue for more than a decade.

As of the 2014 season, Brady and the Patriots have appeared in seven Super Bowls, winning four. Season after season, he is consistently one of the top passers in the NFL. Most followers of the NFL consider either Brady or Peyton Manning to be the greatest quarterback of their generation. Brady is certainly one of the all-time greats, and he's bound for the Hall of Fame at the end of his career.

John Elway

The son of a college football coach, John Elway was known as a great athlete as early as his high school days. In college at Stanford University, he excelled at both football and baseball, and a professional career in either sport was an option for him.

Elway played his entire NFL career with the Denver Broncos (though he was initially drafted in 1983 by the Baltimore Colts, who subsequently traded him to Denver). His reputation as a great quarterback who could perform at clutch time was cemented in the 1986 playoffs. Down seven in the AFC championship game against the Cleveland Browns, Elway orchestrated a masterful 98-yard, game-tying drive late in the fourth quarter. His Broncos went on to win the game in overtime and go the Super Bowl, only to lose to the New York Giants.

Elway brought the Broncos to the Super Bowl again in the 1987 and 1989 seasons, but in both games, the Broncos suffered blowout defeats. After eight years of continued greatness, Elway led the Broncos to their first Super Bowl victory after the 1997 season. The Broncos won the Super Bowl the following season as well, after which Elway retired. The two championships at the end of his great career erased the sting of three earlier Super Bowl losses.

Otto Graham

Any debate over Otto Graham's selection should cease when you consider that he's the only professional quarterback to lead his team, the Cleveland Browns, to ten consecutive championship games. The Browns won seven of those games, and Graham's teams won more than 83 percent of their games during his career. What's also astounding about Graham is that he played tailback, not quarterback, at Northwestern University. And many people in his hometown of Waukegan, Illinois, believed that his best sport was basketball.

Browns coach Paul Brown chose Graham in 1946 for his poise, leadership, and ball-handling skills and believed that he would be a great T-formation quarterback, even though Graham had never played the position. (In the *T-formation,* the quarterback moved behind the center to take a direct snap, and three players — mostly running backs — were aligned behind him, three across.)

In the late 1940s, Graham, who finished his NFL career with a 55.7 completion percentage, excelled at throwing the deep sideline and crossing routes that are prevalent in pro football today. Brown also used receivers in the backfield and put these players in motion, knowing that Graham was smart enough to deal with an evolving offensive strategy. The only knock on Graham and his Browns was that they played in the All-America Football Conference for four years, a league considered inferior to the NFL.

But after Graham and the Browns joined the NFL, their successes continued. In the Browns' 30–28 victory over the Los Angeles Rams in the 1950 championship game, Graham passed for four touchdowns. In the 1954 title game against Detroit, Graham passed for three touchdowns and also ran for three touchdowns. In his final season, Graham led the Browns to another title, again beating the Rams. In this game, he passed for two touchdowns and ran for two more.

Peyton Manning

The son of NFL quarterback Archie Manning, Peyton Manning was destined for greatness. He led the University of Tennessee to the SEC championship during his senior season, and he was runner-up to win the Heisman Trophy, the most prestigious award in all of college football. He was drafted number one overall in the 1998 NFL draft by the Indianapolis Colts, and he immediately became their starting quarterback.

Even though the Colts had a record of 3–13 during his rookie season, Manning showed that he was a top NFL quarterback, setting several records for passing by a rookie. As Manning's career progressed with the Colts, the team became one of the best in the NFL. From 1998 to 2010, the Colts with Manning as quarterback won eight division champions and two AFC championships. Manning and the Colts appeared in two Super Bowls, winning one in 2007.

Manning's career took an abrupt turn in 2011. After a neck injury and multiple surgeries, he was unable to play for the Colts the entire 2011 season. Despite being the premier player of a successful franchise for over a decade, he and the Colts decided to part ways. Manning signed with the Denver Broncos in 2012 and led them to an AFC championship and a Super Bowl appearance in 2014.

Manning's consistently great play throughout his entire career puts him at or near the top of the list of all-time great quarterbacks. He and Tom Brady, who have played against each other numerous times, are considered the best of their generation.

Dan Marino

Dan Marino was the last quarterback selected in the first round of the great 1983 draft class that included John Elway, Jim Kelly, and Tony Eason. According to his Miami Dolphins coach, Don Shula, this perceived slight of being passed over in the draft helped motivate Marino to prove all the other teams wrong.

Marino became the Dolphin's starting quarterback midway through his rookie season. He became was known for his strong arm and quick release. Though he wasn't mobile, he was rarely sacked because he was able to get rid of the ball so quickly.

In just his second season, Marino set records for most yards and touchdowns thrown as he propelled the Dolphins to the Super Bowl, only to lose to the San Francisco 49ers. Marino would never return to the Super Bowl, but his 17-year career with the Dolphins was notable for his consistent excellence.

Joe Montana

With the game on the line or a championship to be won, Joe Montana is the quarterback I want running my team. When I played against Joe Montana, I was always impressed with his ability to remain calm and focused (after all, many manic things happen on the field during a close game). His composure was merely one characteristic that set him apart. He was also a tremendously accurate passer — his all-time passing accuracy was 63.2 percent, and he once completed 22 consecutive passes.

Montana is one of those great quarterbacks who was raised in and played high school ball in a relatively small corner of western Pennsylvania. Joe Namath, Dan Marino, Jim Kelly, and Montana all come from that part of the state (and all are Hall of Famers). Although he appeared thin in build, Montana was a tough quarterback. After major back surgery in 1986, he returned to perform some of his greatest feats. His most productive seasons were in 1987 and 1989, the latter of which culminated in a 92-yard scoring drive to win Super Bowl XXIII in the final seconds.

Montana was named the Super Bowl MVP a record three times, and in his last two playoff runs to Super Bowl titles, Montana passed for 19 touchdowns with just one interception. The beauty of Montana is that he won at every level — high school, college at Notre Dame, and the NFL — despite some coaches and NFL scouts doubting his abilities. San Francisco Coach Bill Walsh designed an exquisite pass-control offense, and Montana directed it with the passing precision of a surgeon. If he wasn't the best quarterback of all time, he surely was the most instinctive player ever to play this position.

Fran Tarkenton

Mobile quarterbacks are common in the NFL now, but the first great one was Fran Tarkenton, who played for the Minnesota Vikings and New York Giants. Drafted by the Vikings in 1961, Tarkenton play was characterized by his ability to evade pass rushers and extend plays, gaining yardage by both running and throwing.

Tarkenton earned the nickname "Scrambin' Fran" playing for the Vikings from 1961 to 1967 and again from 1972 to 1978 after a stint with the Giants. In the 1970s, he and the Vikings appeared in three Super Bowls but lost all three. When Tarkenton retired, he held the records for most throwing yards, most rushing yards, most completions, and most touchdowns by a quarterback. Almost 40 years later, his numbers in each of those categories are still in the top ten all time.

Johnny Unitas

Johnny Unitas wasn't the first great quarterback in the NFL, but he was arguably the first star. That's not to say he wasn't an amazing quarterback, because he was, but his play made him a popular figure in the media, paving the way for future stars of the NFL.

Unitas' career in the NFL began inauspiciously. He was drafted by the Pittsburgh Steelers in the ninth round in 1955, but he was never given a chance to play. He left pro football and worked construction, playing semi-professional football on weekends. In 1956, the Baltimore Colts gave Unitas a chance. He began as a backup but became a starter due to an injury to George Shaw. His first few games were shaky, but he came into his own by the end of the season. In 1957, Unitas led the NFL in passing yards and helped the Colts to their first-ever winning season.

Unitas and the Colts won NFL championships in 1958 and 1959. The attention his performances garnered in the championship games brought the NFL to a new era of popularity. Throughout the 1960s, the Colts with Unitas at the helm were consistently one of the top teams in NFL. Unitas and the Colts lost the Super Bowl after the 1968 season but rebounded to win the Super Bowl after the 1970 season. Unitas played with an injured arm during the later years of his career, which hampered his production. Nonetheless, he was inducted to the Hall of Fame in 1979.

Steve Young

Steve Young excelled as quarterback for Brigham Young University. He was an accurate passer and an elusive runner, but his professional career stumbled out of the gate. Young first signed with the now defunct USFL (United States Football League) after leaving college in 1984. In 1985, he joined the NFL's Tampa Bay Buccaneers, who won a total of four games in their two seasons with Young on their roster. In 1987, Young was traded to the San Francisco 49ers, which already had a great quarterback playing for them, Joe Montana, discussed earlier in this chapter. For a few years, Young was a backup while Montana flourished.

But injuries to Montana allowed Young opportunities to play, and he took advantage. After strong performances by Young in the early 1990s, the 49ers eventually decided to trade Joe Montana, and Young became their starter. Young showed great athletic prowess, throwing the ball with precision in the 49ers' West Coast offense, and he often stymied defenses with his evasiveness in the pocket and ability to run the ball. Young led the 49ers to a Super Bowl victory after the 1994 season. He holds the record for the highest career quarterback rating (96.8) and has the second most career yards rushing by a quarterback.

Chapter 22

The Ten Greatest Coaches in the History of the Game

In This Chapter

▶ Getting to know coaches who helped make football what it is today

▶ Appreciating coaches who devised the offenses that most teams now use

I don't like choosing sides or picking favorites, so know that I went with my gut (and it isn't that considerable, either) when picking the best football coaches of all time for this chapter. I'm not a big history buff, so I didn't consider all the old-timers like Pop Warner and Curly Lambeau. And I skipped over some terrific former college coaches like Ohio State's Woody Hayes, Nebraska's Tom Osborne, Paul "Bear" Bryant (who actually walked on water in Alabama, I hear), and the University of Southern California's Pete Carroll.

I spoke with many coaching friends to narrow my list to the following men. Most of them were innovators, and all of them were winners. Everyone speaks of playing hard, win or lose. But I know that a football coach is special when he molds 30 to 50 men into a championship team. All these men are champions. And many of these great coaches are connected to one another. For example, Don Shula worked under Paul Brown, and I know he credits Brown for how well-organized and prepared he was on game days.

Paul Brown

I loved playing pro football, but I don't know if I could have sat still in a Paul Brown classroom. This man turned football into a science class back in the late 1940s. He graded every player's performance from game film and sent plays in from the bench. Players were turned off by his classroom approach.

However, his revolutionary approach to practice sessions and his demands that players take notes and carry playbooks became commonplace and have remained so for decades, from high school ball to the NFL.

In 1956, Brown wired his quarterback's helmet in order to transmit instructions. Nearly 60 years later, the NFL allows every team to do so (although those transmitters don't always work).

The Cleveland Browns are the only team named after a head coach — which proves just how talented Paul Brown was. The Cincinnati Bengals' Paul Brown Stadium is named after Brown as well. After winning a national championship at Ohio State and coaching Washington High School in Massillon, Ohio, to six consecutive state championships, Brown was paid the princely sum of $20,000 to coach and build a professional team, called the Cleveland Browns, in 1945. The Browns won four consecutive championships, but the team's success (52–4–3 record) doomed the All-America Football Conference. But when the mighty NFL absorbed the Browns, the team didn't play like second-rate performers. In their first game in the new league, the Browns defeated the NFL champion Philadelphia Eagles. They won three more championships over the next six seasons.

Brown eventually left Cleveland, retiring with a 115–49–5 NFL record. He returned to football in 1968 as the owner and coach of the Cincinnati Bengals, an expansion team. After only three years, the Bengals made the playoffs. Brown died in 1991, and his family continues to have a controlling interest in Cincinnati's NFL franchise.

Joe Gibbs

Although my Raiders beat his Washington Redskins in Super Bowl XVIII, we also lost to Joe Gibbs's team a couple of times during my career. I never thought that its personnel matched up with ours, but Gibbs always had his team ready to play and exploit our weaknesses. From top to bottom, the Redskins were as well coached as any group I ever faced. His teams always played hard; they were physical as well as daring, and they played together as a team.

Players say that Gibbs was strict but fair. The biggest testament to his abilities is that he won three Super Bowls — and that he won with three different quarterbacks. He didn't need many stars or dominant players to win. He knew how to build on his players' strengths and minimize their weaknesses. Not only was he great with quarterbacks, but he won with big backs (such as John Riggins) and small receivers. His teams were able to play power football (running the ball) one week, and then the next week, he'd open it up and beat you throwing the ball. One of his power football tactics was the three-tight-end offense. Not only did this offense help his team's running game, but it also negated the strength of New York Giants linebacker Lawrence Taylor.

Gibbs, who won 17 of 24 playoff games, was a tireless worker. I heard he slept in his office two or three nights a week and often worked 20-hour days. I know a lot of people see Joe as a serious guy, but he can also be pretty funny. And I thought he did a great job as an analyst on NBC's pregame show.

George Halas

George Halas is my first real old-timer. But I probably wouldn't be writing this book or even have my job at FOX if it weren't for George Halas, the father of pro football. When you think of Chicago, the city of broad shoulders, you immediately think of bigger-than-life men like Mayor Richard J. Daley, Al Capone, and "Papa Bear" Halas. I can't think of another large American city that has a bigger connection with a football team than Chicago, and it's all due to George Halas.

Legend has it that Halas was cheap with a buck and was a strict disciplinarian, but he was also a showman. In 1920, in the Hupmobile showroom of a Canton, Ohio, car dealer, Halas represented one of the NFL's original teams, the Decatur (Illinois) Staleys. (Imagine playing for a team called the Staleys!) A year later, Coach Halas wised up and moved the team to Chicago. The next year, he changed the team's name to the Bears.

Halas realized the pro game wouldn't survive without stars, so he signed Illinois All-American Red Grange in 1925. At that time, Grange was the most exciting player in college football. The Bears went on a barnstorming tour and played in packed stadiums, showing thousands of fans how great the pro game was. Halas pioneered radio broadcasts of games, and he was also the first to use a public address system to describe to fans what was happening on the field: how many yards were gained, who made the tackle, and what the down and distance were.

Halas was associated with the Bears from the team's inception until his death in 1983. He stepped away from coaching three times, and each time a rejuvenated Halas returned to lead Chicago to an NFL championship. He believed in hiring the best assistant coaches, and he didn't mind sharing the credit. Clark Shaughnessy drastically altered the Bears' offense in 1940, and the result was a 73–0 victory over Washington in the NFL title game. The lopsided victory provided national attention for the publicity-starved professional game. Until Don Shula broke his record, Halas was the number one coach with 324 pro football victories.

Jimmy Johnson

Jimmy Johnson, like Bill Walsh (whom I tell you about later in this chapter), is a super builder and talent evaluator who also happens to be a great football coach. Nothing ever slips by this man. In his first stint as head coach in the NFL, he totally rebuilt the Dallas Cowboys when that great franchise was on the decline back in 1989. He won two Super Bowls with young, drafted talent (free agency didn't exist in the NFL when he started). Later his replacement, Barry Switzer, won another Super Bowl with players like Troy Aikman, Emmitt Smith, and Michael Irvin — players Jimmy Johnson drafted.

When he left Dallas, the Cowboys were the most talented team in the NFL. Their second-team players could have been starters on other teams — and eventually that's what happened. When free agency began in 1993, Dallas wasn't able to keep all its players, especially the talented reserves.

Jimmy struggled in his second NFL coaching gig with the Miami Dolphins because the NFL system had changed. He inherited someone else's team, and it came furnished, but because of salary cap restrictions and players' possessive contracts (see Chapter 17 for more details about the pro football draft), Johnson could replace only one or two players at a time. Building a franchise through the college draft takes a lot longer these days. Plus, Jimmy believes that you win with defense (so do I) and by running the football, but Miami's best chance to win was with its quarterback, Dan Marino.

Vince Lombardi

When pro football first started to become popular on television in the 1960s, Vince Lombardi was in the process of transforming tiny Green Bay, Wisconsin, into the biggest franchise in the NFL. The Packers were as popular as baseball's Yankees; they were a national team. And Lombardi was the game's most recognized coach. Like a story fresh off a movie lot, the Packers appealed to many blue-collar fans because they're owned by the Wisconsin fans and not by some giant corporation.

Lombardi wasn't an innovator; he honed and borrowed from other coaches' methods. He learned the passing game from Sid Gillman while the two were assistant coaches at the U.S. Military Academy. He was a lineman in college, so he knew the blocking techniques as a player. While coaching at Army, the great coach Earl "Red" Blaik showed him what organization and execution mean to a team.

Lombardi was a man of basics, and the Green Bay power sweep was one of his productions. On the power sweep, the two offensive guards would run around the end to block, with a fullback leading the way for the halfback carrying the ball. The fans, the opposition, and everyone knew that the play was coming, but the Packers ran it with such precision that few teams were able to stop it consistently.

Over a seven-year period, the Packers won five championships, including the first two Super Bowls. The only championship game Lombardi lost was his first, 17–13 to the Philadelphia Eagles in 1960.

So much about being a football coach is teaching, and Lombardi was one of the best. "They call it coaching, but it is teaching," Lombardi said of his craft. "You don't just tell them it is so. You show them the reasons why it is so, and then you repeat and repeat it until they are convinced, until they know." Lombardi, like George Halas, is one of the game's legendary heroes, and the Super Bowl trophy honors his accomplishments. After trying his hand at management with the Packers, Lombardi returned to coaching with the Washington Redskins in 1969. He led them to their first winning season in 14 years only to die of cancer the following year at age 57. This great man went too soon.

John Madden

For nearly 30 years, John Madden was a TV football analyst, but before he became a television star and commercial pitchman, he was one of the game's best coaches. His enthusiasm and love of the game were obvious from the very beginning. A knee injury derailed his professional football career. However, he hung around the Philadelphia Eagles for most of the year anyway, learning as much as possible from Eagles quarterback Norm Van Brocklin, a future Hall of Famer.

Madden likes to come across as a lighthearted statesman for the game of football — he loves to garrulously describe the play of the oversized linemen and never seems to take the game too seriously — but he's always been a clever, intuitive leader. Smart like a fox. When you have an opportunity to sit and talk to John, it's like having an audience with the Dalai Lama; you sit, listen, and learn.

Like a lot of famous coaches, Madden began his coaching career at the very bottom, with a small junior college team in rural California. In a few years, Madden moved up to San Diego State, studying under Don Coryell, a great passing coach. "John never let his players give up, even if it was in practice," Coryell remembers. "Our practices got heated because John didn't even like to lose a scrimmage." Eventually, Oakland Raiders owner Al Davis hired Madden as an assistant and two years later elevated him to head coach. Madden, only 32, became the youngest head coach in the American Football League.

If you ever watch NFL films on cable television, you may catch a glimpse of Madden during the Raiders' great glory run of the 1970s. A big man, Madden was an emotional coach. He was constantly on the officials, bemoaning calls, waving his arms, and exhorting his players to work harder. Madden coached for only ten years, but he won 100 games faster than any other NFL coach at that time and led the Raiders over Minnesota to win Super Bowl XI. He walked away from the game on top, after the 1978 season, at the age of 42. Many coaches don't even earn their first head-coaching position until they're older than that!

Madden never had a strong urge to return to coaching. He became an icon in sports television, remaining in the game by working as a television analyst. And *Madden NFL,* the video game series officially sanctioned by the NFL, has carried his name since 1990.

Bill Parcells

Bill Parcells was a throwback coach in many ways. By that, I mean he could have coached in any era. His greatest strength was his talent to relate to his players and figure out the best approach to use their skills and turn them into a winning team. He knew how to push a player's buttons, strike a nerve, and force him to dig deep for something extra — for whatever it takes to win. Parcells was a defensive coach, so his focus was on that side of the ball, supported by an offense that preferred to run first and pass second. If I were physically able, I'd love to turn back the clock and play for this man. He was a coach who appreciated toughness and personal sacrifice for the good of the team.

Parcells coached the New York Giants to Super Bowl victories in 1987 and 1991. He retired after the second Super Bowl, but returned in 1993 to coach the New England Patriots to the Super Bowl. The Patriots were 2–14 in 1992, but in Parcells' first season, the Patriots won five games, and then an amazing 10 in 1994, which is when he won his third Coach of the Year honor. The 1996 team went 13–6, losing to the Green Bay Packers in Super Bowl XXXII.

A New Jersey guy, Parcells abruptly returned to New York City the next season to coach the New York Jets. And in typical Parcells fashion, he made an immediate impact. The Jets, who'd had eight straight non-winning seasons, finished 9–7 in his first season; the year before, they'd won just 1 of 16 games. Parcells is an expert at turning perennial losers into perennial winners. His first such accomplishment was with the New York Giants. After one bad season, Parcells enjoyed a remarkable run with the Giants, winning 10, 11, 17, 6, 10, 12, and 16 games (including playoffs) between 1984 and 1990 with teams led by linebacker Lawrence Taylor and quarterback Phil Simms. Parcells was named Coach of the Year in 1986 and 1989.

Parcells surprised the football world by taking the Patriots to Super Bowl XXXII, knowing that their only chance to win rested with quarterback Drew Bledsoe. Parcells, who would have preferred to control the clock with a running game, proved to everyone that he could win with an offense that went against his basic beliefs and background. However, his finest coaching job was in the Giants' second Super Bowl run. His team was forced to play the end of the 1990 season without Simms, and they neutralized two great offensive teams, the San Francisco 49ers and the Buffalo Bills, with a stifling defense and a ball-control rushing attack. They beat the 49ers by two points and defeated the Bills 20–19 in Super Bowl XXV.

In 2003, Parcells headed south to coach the Dallas Cowboys, where he was modestly successful with a 34–30 record, making the playoffs twice in four years before he retired at the end of the 2006 season. Parcells is the ninth-winningest coach in the NFL, with an overall record of 183–138–1 (a 0.570 winning percentage). He returned to the NFL to become the Executive Vice President of Football Operations for the Miami Dolphins from 2008 to 2010. He was inducted into the Football Hall of Fame in 2013.

Knute Rockne

I'm sure many non-football fans have heard of the University of Notre Dame in South Bend, Indiana. Notre Dame is synonymous with college football. And Knute (pronounced *Newt*) Rockne was college football's greatest coach. And what a great name! The sound perfectly suits the image of football: You have to be rock hard and tough to play this game.

"The Rock," as Rockne was affectionately called, guided Notre Dame to six national championships and had a 0.881 winning percentage — the all-time best winning percentage, college or pro. He won 105 games and lost only 12, with 5 ties. In *Knute Rockne — All American,* a great old movie, actor Pat O'Brien immortalizes Rockne's famous "Win one for the Gipper" speech. (Former President Ronald Reagan, who was a Hollywood star before going into politics, plays the ill-fated George Gipp.)

Rockne was a master of the fiery pep talk, a type of speech that even Little League coaches give now and then. When his team was playing badly, he would sarcastically refer to his macho players as girls, which is the last thing tough guys want to hear. But after the game was over and his verbal berating finished, Rockne loved his young players like a father. The players knew Rockne's rough words weren't personal — even though he scared them at times by saying he might die if they didn't win.

Rockne was an inspirational speaker and traveled the country sharing his thoughts and opinions of life and football. He sold football across the land and made many Americans stand up and take notice of the sport.

Rockne was also influential on the field. In 1913, playing end for Notre Dame, he teamed with quarterback Gus Dorais to develop the use of the forward pass in a game against West Point. He was also the first to use *shock troops,* or second-team performers, to wear down the opposition's first string. He believed in playing the best teams every week, which is how Notre Dame became a national team.

Don Shula

I don't know if Don Shula is the best coach who ever walked a sideline, but he certainly is the most successful. After the 1995 season, Shula retired after 33 years of coaching in the NFL with more wins (347, including the postseason) than anybody. He also possesses the league's only perfect season: 17–0 in 1972, a season the Miami Dolphins capped off by winning Super Bowl VII. He was the first head coach to cost his owner a first-round draft choice, the price Miami had to pay Baltimore for hiring him away from that team in 1970. The beauty of Shula, NFL executive George Young said, is that "he was best at playing the cards he was dealt." Shula built his offensive and defensive systems around his players, not the other way around, which is more common in the coaching fraternity.

"We take a lot of pride in that," Shula said of his adaptability. "My philosophy was to get the most out of the talent you have, then design your system to best take advantage of that talent. I'd rather not tell a player, 'Hey, this is my system' and demand they either do it this way, or I'll find someone else."

Shula had tremendous success with three different styles of offenses: He played power football with Larry Csonka in the early 1970s, a more balanced scheme with the Colts back in the 1960s, and at the end of his career he pretty much turned the offense over to Dan Marino's big arm and allowed him to throw as much as he wanted. Players win championships, and Shula was fortunate to have quarterbacks such as Johnny Unitas, Earl Morrall, Bob Griese, and Marino, all Hall of Famers, guiding his teams.

Shula has always been respected by his peers and upper management. He was always at the forefront of advocating better rules, and he supported the instant replay system for rectifying an improperly made call on the field.

Bill Walsh

They don't call Bill Walsh "The Genius" for nothing. He built the San Francisco 49ers out of the ashes (they were a 2–14 team when he took over) and transformed them into the dominant franchise of the 1980s. To this day, his imprint on the game remains visible. For example, Walsh created the West Coast offense, and now many NFL teams use a version of it (see Chapter 8 for more on this offense).

In Walsh's third season, the 49ers won their first of his three Super Bowls. His first offensive team had an incredible lack of talent, but he designed a system that truly worked for them. The 49ers, unlike the Raiders, worked on throwing short, possession-type passes. To them, a 5-yard gain was a 5-yard gain, whether it was a pass or a run play. Walsh didn't care; he simply wanted to maintain possession and keep the ball moving.

In the process of devising this offensive system, Walsh developed one of the game's best quarterbacks, Joe Montana. Now, Montana didn't have the greatest arm, nor was he the biggest guy. But he was one of the toughest and definitely one of the greatest quarterbacks under pressure. In fact, Montana may be the best decision maker pro football has ever seen. Walsh deserves a lot of credit for Montana and for designing a passing offense that was an extension of the running game.

Although Walsh was a huge factor in developing quarterbacks like Dan Fouts, Montana, and Steve Young, he's also a great judge of talent at other positions. His drafts built the 49ers into champions, and I know he had to watch only five plays by Charles Haley in college to know that Haley would be a great pass-rusher in the NFL. Jerry Rice, probably the best receiver who has ever played, was another Walsh selection.

Even though many players benefited from his offensive system, Walsh was often quick to release or trade veteran players that he thought were expendable or were running out of time. This policy caused some animosity in the locker room, but Walsh believed teams needed a constant infusion of young talent. He always seemed to be ahead of the curve, allowing an experienced veteran to depart while grooming a faster, quicker rookie for the role. Walsh was criticized for being cold and calculating, but I know he had a soft spot for many of his players and simply was dealing with the extremely high expectations of pro football owners.

Walsh is another coach connected to Paul Brown's tree. He coached under Brown in Cincinnati, but when he wasn't named Brown's successor, Walsh moved on, thus becoming available to the 49ers.

Appendix

Football Speak

audible: When the quarterback changes the play at the line of scrimmage by calling out prescribed signals to his teammates.

backfield: The group of offensive players — the running backs and quarterback — who line up behind the line of scrimmage.

blitz: A defensive strategy in which a linebacker or defensive back vacates his customary position or responsibility in order to pressure the quarterback. The object of a blitz is to tackle the quarterback behind the line of scrimmage (also known as a sack) or force the quarterback to hurry his pass, thus disrupting the offensive play. (Prior to World War II, this defensive strategy was called a red-dog, but the name was changed to blitz after the German Army's blitzkrieg tactics.)

bomb: A long pass play in which the quarterback throws the ball to a receiver more than 35 yards past the line of scrimmage.

bump and run: A technique used by defensive backs to slow down receivers. The defender bumps the receiver at the start of the play and attempts to keep his hands on him, as rules permit within 5 yards of the line of scrimmage, before running downfield with him.

carry: The act of running with the ball. In statistical charts, a runner's rushing attempts are listed as carries.

center: The offensive player who hikes (or snaps) the ball to the quarterback at the start of each play. The term comes from the fact that this player is flanked on either side by a guard and a tackle; he's the middleman (or center) in a contingent of five offensive linemen or blockers. He handles the ball on every play and also snaps the ball to the punter and holder.

clipping: When a player throws his body across the back of the legs of an opponent or charges, falls, or rolls into the back of an opponent below the waist after approaching him from behind. It's a 15-yard penalty.

coffin corner: The area between the opponent's end zone and 5-yard line. Punters try to kick the ball into the coffin corner so that the offense takes over the ball deep in its own territory.

completion: A forward pass that's successfully caught by an eligible receiver.

cornerback: A defensive player who lines up on one of the wide sides of the field, usually opposite an offensive receiver. Called a cornerback because he's isolated on the "corner" edge of the defensive alignment.

count: The numbers or words that a quarterback shouts loudly while waiting for the ball to be snapped. The quarterback usually informs his teammates in the huddle that the ball will be snapped on a certain count.

counter: A running play designed to go against, or counter to, the expected direction of the defense's pursuit.

defensive back: A member of the defensive secondary. Defensive backs form the line of defense whose job is to prevent receivers from making catches and then gaining lots of yards after the catch. Safeties, cornerbacks, and nickel backs are defensive backs.

defensive end: A defensive player who lines up at an end of the defensive line. His job is to contain any run plays to his side and prevent the quarterback from getting past him. On passing plays, he rushes the quarterback.

defensive line: The defensive players who play opposite the offensive linemen. The defensive line is made up of ends, tackles, nose tackles, and under tackles. Defensive linemen disrupt the offense's blocking assignments and are responsible for clogging certain gaps along the line of scrimmage when they aren't in a position to make the tackle themselves.

defensive tackle: A defensive player who lines up on the interior of the defensive line. His job is to stop the run at the line, or to shoot through the offensive line and make a tackle in the backfield. If he can't make a play, he needs to prevent the opponent's center and guards from running out and blocking the linebackers.

dime formation: When the defense uses six defensive backs rather than the usual four. The dime formation is used in obvious passing situations.

double foul: A situation in which each team commits a foul during the same down.

down: A period of action that starts when the ball is put into play and ends when the ball is ruled dead (meaning the play is over). The offense gets four downs to advance the ball 10 yards. If it fails to do so, it must surrender the ball to the opponent, usually by punting on the fourth down.

down lineman: A defensive lineman.

draft: The selection of mostly collegiate players for entrance into the National Football League (NFL). The draft occurs in late April. The NFL team with the preceding season's worst record selects first, and the Super Bowl champion selects last. Each team is awarded one selection during each of the seven rounds.

draw: A disguised run that initially looks like a pass play. The offensive linemen retreat like they're going to pass-protect for the quarterback. The quarterback drops back and, instead of setting up to pass, he turns and hands the ball to a running back.

drive: The series of plays during which the offense has the football. A drive ends when the team punts or scores and the other team gets possession of the football.

encroachment: A penalty that occurs when a defensive player crosses the line of scrimmage and makes contact with an opponent before the ball is snapped. Encroachment is subject to a 5-yard penalty.

end zone: A 10-yard-long area at both ends of the field — the promised land for a football player. A player in possession of the football scores a touchdown when he crosses the plane of the goal line and enters the end zone. If you're tackled in your own end zone while in possession of the football, the defensive team gets a safety.

extra point: A kick, worth one point, typically attempted after every touchdown (it's also known as the point after touchdown, or PAT). The ball is placed on the 2-yard line in the NFL, or the 3-yard line in college and high school, and generally is kicked from the 10-yard line. It must sail between the uprights and above the crossbar of the goalpost to be considered good. See *two-point conversion*

face mask: The protective bars on the football helmet that cover a player's face. Also the name of the penalty for grabbing these bars when tackling a player. Grabbing the face mask is subject to a 15-yard penalty.

fair catch: When the player returning a punt waves his extended arm from side to side over his head. After signaling for a fair catch, a player can't run with the ball, and those attempting to tackle him can't touch him.

field goal: A kick, worth three points, that the offense can attempt from anywhere on the field (but most kickers attempt it within 40 yards of the goalpost). The kick must sail above the crossbar and between the uprights of the goalpost to be considered good.

first down: A team begins every possession of the ball with a first down. The offense must gain 10 yards or more (in four downs) to be awarded another first down. Teams want to earn lots of first downs because doing so means they're moving the ball toward the opponent's end zone. See *down*

flanker: A player who catches passes, also known in more general terms as a wide receiver. In an offensive formation, he usually lines up outside the tight end, off the line of scrimmage.

flat: The area of the field between the hash marks and the sideline and in close proximity to the line of scrimmage. A pass, usually to a running back, in this area is described as a flat pass.

formation: A predetermined setup (or alignment) employed by the offense or defense.

foul: Any violation of a playing rule.

franchise player: A player who's designated by his team and must be paid the average salary of the top five players at his position. Football reporters also use this term to describe a superstar player who's invaluable to his team.

free agency: An open signing period, usually beginning in late February, during which an NFL team can sign any unrestricted player who doesn't have a contract.

free safety: The defensive player who lines up deepest in the secondary. He defends the deep middle of the field and seldom has man-to-man responsibilities. A coach wants this player free to read the quarterback and take the proper angle to break up or intercept any forward pass thrown over the middle or deep to the sidelines.

fullback: A player who lines up in the offensive backfield and generally is responsible for blocking for the running back and pass-blocking to protect the quarterback. Fullbacks also serve as short-yardage runners.

fumble: When any offensive player loses possession of the football during a play. The ball can simply drop from his hands or be knocked free by the force of a tackle. Either the offense or the defense can recover the fumble.

gap: The open space (also called a split) between players aligned along the line of scrimmage. For example, there's a wide gap between the offensive guard and tackle.

goalpost: The poles constructed in a U-shape at the rear of each end zone through which teams score field goals and extra points.

guard: A member of the offensive line. There are two guards on every play, and they line up on either side of the offensive center. The guards protect the quarterback from an inside rusher; they block defenders immediately across from them and also swing out, or "pull," and run toward either end to block any defender when the ball carrier runs wide.

hail Mary: When the quarterback, usually in desperation at the end of a game, throws a long pass without targeting a receiver with the hope that a receiver will catch the ball and score a touchdown.

halfback: An offensive player who lines up in the backfield and generally is responsible for carrying the ball on run plays. Also known as a running back or tailback.

handoff: The act of giving the ball to another player. Handoffs usually occur between the quarterback and a running back.

hang time: The seconds during which a punted ball remains in the air. If the punt travels 50 yards and is in the air for more than four seconds, that's very good hang time.

hash marks: The two rows of lines near the center of the field that signify 1 yard on the field. Before every play, the ball is marked between or on the hash marks, depending on where the ball carrier was tackled on the preceding play.

holder: The player who catches the snap from the center and places it down for the placekicker to kick. A holder is used on field goal and extra point attempts.

hole number: The number the offensive coaching staff gives to each gap or space between the five offensive linemen and the tight end. The players, particularly the running backs, then know which hole they should attempt to run through.

huddle: When the 11 players on the field come together to discuss strategy between plays. On offense, the quarterback relays the plays in the huddle. On defense, the captain relays the coach's instructions for the proper alignment and how to defend the expected play.

hurry-up offense: An offensive strategy that's designed to gain as much yardage as possible and then stop the clock. It's generally used in the final two minutes of a half when time is running out on the offense. The offense breaks the huddle more quickly and runs to line up in the proper formation, hoping to get off as many plays as possible. (Sometimes teams don't huddle at all.) Offenses tend to pass in the hurry-up, and receivers are instructed to try to get out of bounds, thus stopping the clock.

I formation: An offensive formation that looks like an *I* because the two running backs line up directly behind the quarterback.

incompletion: A forward pass that falls to the ground because no receiver can catch it, or a pass that a receiver drops or catches out of bounds. After an incompletion, the clock stops, and the ball is returned to the line of scrimmage.

interception: A pass that's caught by a defensive player, and thus stolen from the offense.

key: Either a specific player or a shift in a particular offensive formation that serves as a clue to a defensive player. From studying a team's tendencies, the defensive player immediately knows which play the opponent will attempt to run and to what direction.

kickoff: A free kick that puts the ball into play at the start of the first and third quarters, and after every touchdown, field goal, and safety.

lateral: A backward or sideways pass thrown from one offensive player to another. A lateral isn't considered a forward pass, so players can lateral to one another beyond the line of scrimmage.

line of scrimmage: The imaginary boundary between the two teams prior to the snap of the ball. The offense's and defense's scrimmage lines are defined by the tip of the ball closest to them and stretch from sideline to sideline. The defensive team usually lines up less than a yard away from where the ball is placed.

linebacker: A defensive player who lines up behind or beside the defensive linemen and generally is regarded as one of the team's best tacklers. Depending on the formation, most teams employ either three or four linebackers on every play. In a three-linebacker defense, the linebackers are called the strong-side, middle, and weak-side linebacker.

long snap: When the quarterback or punter takes the snap while standing 6 to 15 feet behind the center. A long snap is used in punts, the shotgun formation, and the wildcat formation.

man-to-man coverage: Pass coverage in which every potential offensive receiver is assigned to a particular defender. Each defensive player must stick to his receiver like glue and make sure he doesn't catch a pass thrown in his direction.

motion: When an offensive receiver or running back begins to move laterally behind the line of scrimmage — after his teammates have assumed a ready stance and are considered set — he is in motion. This motion can't be forward, and only one player is allowed to move at a time.

neutral zone: The area between the two lines of scrimmage, stretching from sideline to sideline. The width of this area is defined by the length of the football. Other than the center, no player can be in the neutral zone prior to the snap; otherwise, the official calls an encroachment or violation of the neutral zone (offside) penalty.

nickel back: An extra defensive back used in some defensive formations.

no-huddle offense: When the offense for several plays in succession lines up and snaps the ball without first going into a huddle. The no-huddle offense is used when time is expiring in the first half of the game and the team with the ball doesn't want to use precious time in huddles. Sometimes offenses run a no-huddle offense to confuse the defense or catch it off guard.

nose tackle: The defensive player (also called a nose guard) who lines up directly across from the center, or "nose to nose" with him. His job is to defend the middle of the offense against a running play.

offensive line: The human wall of five men who block for and protect the quarterback and ball carriers. Every line has a center (who snaps the ball), two guards, and two tackles. Teams that run a lot may employ a blocking tight end, too, who's also considered part of the offensive line.

offensive pass interference: A penalty in which, in the judgment of the official, the intended receiver significantly hinders a defensive player's opportunity to intercept a forward pass.

officials: The men in the striped shirts who officiate the game and call the penalties. Their decisions are final, except when overturned by videotape review.

offside: A penalty caused when any part of a player's body is beyond his line of scrimmage or the free kick line when the ball is snapped.

off-tackle: A strong-side run, meaning the running back heads toward the end of the line where the tight end (the extra blocker) lines up. The runner wants to take advantage of the hole supplied by the tackle (the tight end) and his running mate (the fullback). He can take the ball either outside the tackle or around the tight end. He hopes that the fullback will block the outside linebacker, giving him room to run.

onside kick: When the kicking team attempts to get the ball back during a kickoff by kicking the ball so that it travels a relatively short distance (but more than 10 yards) and is recovered by the kicking team.

option: When a quarterback has the choice — the option — to either pass or run. The option is more common in high school and college football, where quarterbacks may be excellent runners.

overtime: Extra playing time tacked on to the end of the game to decide a game that's tied at the end of regulation play.

pass interference: A judgment call made by an official who sees a defensive player make contact with the intended receiver before the ball arrives, thus restricting his opportunity to catch the forward pass. The penalty awards the offensive team the ball at the spot of the foul with an automatic first down. (In college, pass interference is a 15-yard penalty and an automatic first down.) See *offensive pass interference*

PAT: See *extra point*

personal foul: An illegal, flagrant foul considered risky to the health of another player.

pick-six: When a defender intercepts, or picks off, a pass and runs it back for a touchdown, thereby scoring six points. See *interception*

pigskin: A slang term for the football, which is actually made of leather, not pigskin.

pitch: The act of the quarterback tossing the ball to a running back who's moving laterally away from him.

placekicker: The player who kicks the ball on kickoffs, extra point attempts, and field goal attempts. Unlike a punter, a placekicker kicks the ball either off a tee or while it's being held by a teammate.

play-action pass: A pass play that begins with the quarterback faking a hand-off to a running back while he's dropping back to pass. The quarterback hopes the defense falls for the fake and doesn't rush him.

pocket: The area where the quarterback stands when he drops back to throw the ball. This area extends from a point 2 yards outside of either offensive tackle and includes the tight end if he drops off the line of scrimmage to pass-protect. The pocket extends longitudinally behind the line back to the offensive team's own end line.

point after touchdown (PAT): See *extra point*

possession: When a player maintains control of the ball while clearly touching both feet, or any other part of his body other than his hand(s), to the ground inbounds. A team is also considered in possession of the ball whenever it has the ball on offense. A team's possession ends when it scores, turns over the ball, punts the ball, or when a half of the game ends.

post: A forward pass that the quarterback throws down the center of the field as the intended receiver attempts to line up with the goalpost.

punt: A kick made when a player (the punter) drops the ball and kicks it while it falls toward his foot. A team usually punts on a fourth down. The farther the ball flies from the line of scrimmage, the better.

punter: The lone player who stands 10 to 12 yards behind the line of scrimmage, catches the long snap from the center, and then kicks the ball after dropping it toward his foot.

quarterback: The offensive player who usually receives the ball from the center at the start of each play. He informs his teammates in the huddle of the play that will be run and then, after the center snaps the ball to him, either hands the ball to a running back or throws to a receiver.

receiver: See *wide receiver*

red zone: The unofficial area from inside the 20-yard line to the opponent's goal line. Holding an opponent to a field goal in this area is considered a victory by the defense.

redshirt: A college player who postpones a year of eligibility due to injury or academic trouble or in order to gain another year of physical maturity. For example, a redshirt freshman is a player who's in his second year of school but is playing his first season of football. Players have four years of eligibility and five years in which to use them, so they can be redshirted only once.

return: To catch the ball after a punt, kickoff, or interception (or pick it up after a fumble) and run it back toward your own end zone.

reverse: A play in which the running back receives a handoff from the quarterback then runs laterally behind the line of scrimmage before handing off to a receiver or flanker running toward him.

roll out: When the quarterback runs left or right away from the pocket before throwing the ball.

route: The prescribed direction and exact distance, coupled with specific physical movements, that a receiver follows when he runs from the line of scrimmage for a forward pass. Every receiver has a route that he must run on a particular play.

running back: An offensive player who runs with the football. Running backs are also referred to as tailbacks, halfbacks, and fullbacks, depending on their exact responsibilities and alignment.

rushing: To advance the ball by running, not passing. A running back is sometimes called a rusher.

sack: To tackle the quarterback behind the line of scrimmage, resulting in a loss of down and yardage.

safety: A two-point score by the defense that occurs when one of the defensive players tackles an opponent in possession of the ball in the offensive player's end zone. See also *free safety* and *strong safety*

salary cap: In the NFL, the maximum amount of money a team can spend on player salaries in a given year under a formula that includes base salaries, prorated portions of signing bonuses, and likely-to-be-earned incentives. The salary cap figure is a league-wide number that every team must adhere to.

scheme: A slang term used to describe offensive and defensive formations and the overall strategy for using such formations.

scramble: When the quarterback, to gain time for receivers to get open, moves behind the line of scrimmage, dodging the defense.

screen pass: A forward pass in which at least two offensive linemen run wide to a specific side of the field and then turn and block upfield for a running back who takes a short pass from the quarterback.

secondary: The defensive players who line up behind the linebackers and wide on the corners of the field opposite the receivers and defend the pass. These defensive players, who are called defensive backs, are separated into safeties, cornerbacks, and, occasionally, nickel backs.

shotgun: A passing formation in which the quarterback stands 5 to 7 yards behind the center before the snap. This setup enables the quarterback to scan the defense while standing back from the line of scrimmage.

sidelines: The sides of the field along its long part, where players, coaches, trainers, and the media stand. These areas aren't part of the actual playing field; they're considered out of bounds.

slant: A run play in which the runner slants his angle forward after receiving the ball instead of running straight toward the line of scrimmage. Or a pass route on which an outside or "wide" receiver "slants" toward the center of the field.

snap: The action in which the ball is handed or hiked by the center to the quarterback, to the holder on a kick attempt, or to the punter.

special teams: The 22 players who are on the field during kickoffs, field goals, extra points, and punts. These units have special players who return punts and kicks, in addition to players who are experts at covering kicks and punts.

spiral: The tight spin on the ball in flight after the quarterback releases it. The term "tight spiral" is often used to describe a solidly thrown football.

split end: A player who catches passes. This player is also known in more general terms as a wide receiver. In an offensive formation, the split end usually lines up on the line of scrimmage to the opposite side of the formation from the tight end.

spread: A type of offense designed to spread the defense on the field. The spread offense features play-action runs, option plays, and roll-out passing. In a spread offense, the quarterback runs as often or nearly as often as he passes.

stance: The position that any player assumes prior to the snap of the ball and after he's aligned.

strong safety: A defensive player who generally lines up in the secondary, but often aligns close to the line of scrimmage. In most defenses, this player lines up over the tight end and is responsible for both playing the pass and supporting the run.

strong side: The side of the offensive formation where the tight end aligns. With a right-handed quarterback, the strong side is usually to his right side.

stunt: A maneuver by two defensive linemen in which they alter their course to the quarterback, hoping to confuse the offensive linemen and maximize their strengths. In most stunts, one defensive lineman sacrifices himself in hopes of his teammate either going unblocked or gaining a physical advantage in his pursuit.

substitution: The act of a player (called a substitute) running onto the playing field, replacing another player.

sweep: A fairly common run in every team's playbook. It begins with two or more offensive linemen leaving their stances and running toward the outside of the line of scrimmage. The ball carrier takes a handoff from the quarterback and runs parallel to the line of scrimmage, waiting for his blockers to lead the way around the end.

tackle: To use your hands and arms or body to bring down an offensive player who has the ball. Tackle also refers to a position on both the defensive and offensive lines. Offensive tackles are outside blockers on the line of scrimmage; on defense, the tackles are in the inside position, generally opposite the offensive guards.

tailback: An offensive player whose primary role is to carry the ball. Also known as a running back or halfback.

takeaway: How a defense describes any possession in which it forces a fumble and recovers the ball or registers an interception. Any turnover that the defense collects is called a takeaway.

tight end: An offensive player who serves as a big receiver and also a blocker. Unlike a wide receiver, this player generally lines up beside the offensive tackle either to the right or to the left of the quarterback. See *strong side*

touchback: A situation in which the ball is ruled dead behind a team's own goal line, provided the impetus came from an opponent and provided it isn't a touchdown or a missed field goal. After a touchback, the ball is spotted on the offense's 20-yard line.

touchdown: A situation in which any part of the ball, while legally in the possession of a player who is inbounds, goes on or beyond the plane of the opponent's goal line. A touchdown is worth six points.

turnover: A loss of the ball via a fumble or an interception.

two-minute warning: The signal that two minutes remain in the half.

two-point conversion: After a touchdown, scoring two points with a pass or run into the end zone rather than kicking through the goalpost to score one point in an extra-point try.

veer: A quick-hitting run in which the ball is handed to either running back, whose routes are determined by the slant or charge of the defensive linemen.

weak side: The side of the offense opposite the side on which the tight end lines up.

wide receiver: An offensive player who uses speed and quickness to elude defenders and catch the football, but who isn't primarily a blocker. Wide receivers are also known as pass catchers. Also called a wideout.

wildcat formation: An offensive formation in which the quarterback doesn't play and the ball is snapped directly to a running back. The formation allows for an extra blocker on the field and permits offenses to strike quickly without taking time to hand off the ball.

zone coverage: Coverage in which the secondary and linebackers drop away from the line of scrimmage into specific areas when defending a pass play. Zone means that the players are defending areas, not specific offensive players.

Index

• *Numerics* •

2-minute warnings, 32, 42, 352
2-point conversions
  college overtime rules for, 33
  defense against, 203–204
  defined, 352
  NFL rules for, 37–38
  offensive plays for, 146–148
3-4 eagle defense, 193–194
3-4 front defense, 132, 157, 191–192
4-3 front defense
  defensive ends in, 156–157
  history of, 189
  overview, 133
  players needed for, 190
4-across defense, 134–135, 143
5-yard bump rule, 126
5-yard hitch, 140
5-yard penalties, 32, 49–52
10-yard penalties, 52–53
15-yard penalties, 54–56
25-second clock
  field judge responsibilities, 42–43
  penalties for, 32, 49
  referee signal to reset, 47
40-second clock
  field judge responsibilities, 42–43
  penalties for, 32, 49
  referee signal to reset, 47
46 defense, 198–200
50-yard line, 19

• *A* •

A gaps, 156
ACC (Atlantic Coast Conference), 269
accrued season, 285
AFC (American Football Conference), 279
AFL (American Football League), 279–280
agents, 285

Allen, Marcus, 91, 95
all-star games, 274–275
Alworth, Lance "Bambi", 89
American Athletic Conference, 269
American Football Conference (AFC), 279
American Football League (AFL), 279–280
Anderson, Willie "Flipper", 184
angle blocking, 117, 122
Arena Football, 291
artificial turf fields, 22
assistant coaches, 231, 237
assists, 167
Associated Press All-America team, 274
Atkins, Doug, 303–304
Atlantic Coast Conference (ACC), 269
attending games, 247–249
audibilizing, 62, 74, 341

• *B* •

back judges, 42
backfield, 341
backpedaling, 70
bailing out of the play, 67
ball boys, 36
ball control, 92
bang-bang play, 179
Banks, Carl, 164
baseball, popularity of, 9
BCS (Bowl Championship Series), 270–271
bench areas, 21
Big 12, 269
Big Ten, 269
blast or dive, 104, 204
The Blind Side: Evolution of a Game
    (Lewis), 113
The Blind Side (film), 113
blind-side tackles, 112–113
blitzing
  corner, 243
  defined, 70, 162, 180, 341

blitzing *(continued)*
  throwing the post versus, 138
  zone blitz, 137–138, 196–198
blocking
  angle blocking, 117, 122
  blocking wedge, 216
  chop blocks, 54, 121, 123
  crackback blocks, 45, 55
  cut blocks, 45, 122
  cut-off blocks, 122
  defined, 111, 114
  double-teaming, 123
  drive blocks, 123
  front seven, 73
  by guards, 114
  low blocks, 55
  man-on-man, 123
  penalties for, 54–55
  pulling, 116
  reach blocks, 123
  reading defense, 71
  by receivers, 79
  rule changes benefiting, 78
  by running backs, 97
  running start to attempt to block kicks, 55
  slide blocks, 123
  trap blocks, 123–124
  zone blocks, 124
blocking wedge, 216
Blount, Mel, 176
bomb, 127, 184, 341
bootleg, 129
Bowl Championship Series (BCS), 270–271
bowl games, 271
box, 182
boxmen, 36
Bradshaw, Terry, 62, 323–324
Brady, Tom, 324
breaking, 170
breaking the plane, 36
breaking up a pass, 178
Brodie, John, 88
Brown, Jim, 313–314
Brown, Paul, 331–332
bubble side, 133
bullet throw, 87
bump and run, 176, 341
burst, 170

burst off the line of scrimmage, 80
Butkus, Dick, 304
bye weeks, 280

• C •

cages. *See* face masks
calling plays, 62, 74–75
Camp, Walter, 10–11
Campbell, Earl, 314–315
Canadian Football League, 291
capologists, 288
captains, 33
card stunts, 249
carries, 341
Casper, Dave, 315
centers
  defined, 112, 341
  diagram symbol for, 2
  directing other linemen, 114
  importance of clean snap for, 114
  on punting teams, 224
  role of, 113–114
chain gangs (chain crews), 35–36, 41
chains, 24, 35
challenging calls, 57
check with me strategy, 75
chop blocks, 54, 121, 123
Clady, Ryan, 115
cleats, 29–30
clipping, 54, 121, 341
clocks. *See names of specific clocks*
coaches
  assistant, 231, 237
  high school football, 260
  jobs during season/off-season, 236–237
  plays called by, 62
  pressure felt by, 237
  professional, 230–233
  styles and philosophies of, 233–236
  as team leaders, 230
  types of, 208
  youth football, 255–256
codes. *See* rules and regulations
coffin corner, 342
coin tosses, 33–34, 211
collective bargaining agreements, 289

college football. *See also* National Collegiate Athletic Association
  all-star teams, 274
  appeal of, 264
  beginnings of, 263
  big-time schools, 266–267
  Bowl Championship Series, 270–272
  coach's job during off-season, 237
  fanbase for, 11, 15, 263–264
  firsts in, 272
  holiday traditions involving, 9
  NCAA divisions and conferences, 265–266
  NFL players coming from, 267
  overtime rules for, 33
  pageantry of, 15, 264–265
  popularity of pro football versus, 9, 11–12
  rules in NFL versus, 265
  rules to prevent injuries, 11
  season for, 14
  smaller colleges, 265, 268
  team doctors and trainers, 240
  trophies and awards, 272–273
College Football Hall of Fame, 13, 252
Collins, Mark, 184
combo man coverage, 180
comeback pass pattern, 85
completion percentage, 75
completions, 342
conferences, 265. *See also names of specific conferences*
contact, illegal, 45, 56, 179
containing, 155, 221
conversion attempts, 38
corner blitzes, 243
cornerbacks
  challenges faced by, 170
  defined, 342
  in man-to-man coverage, 171, 181
  pressure felt by, 184
  qualities necessary for, 170
  staying with receivers, 177
  in zone coverage, 172
corners, 243
count, 74, 342
counter, 104
counter plays, 342
cover one defense, 71

cover two defense, 72, 201–202
cover three defense, 72
cover four defense, 73
coverage, 180
coverage men, 216
crackback blocks, 45, 55
creases, 315
crossbar of goalposts, 23
crossing pass pattern, 86
crossing routes, 127
crowd noise, excessive, 50
Csonka, Larry, 94
curl pass pattern, 86
cut blocks, 45, 122
cut-back running, 97
cut-off blocks, 122

• D •

Dallas 4-3 defense, 194–195
Davey O'Brien Award, 273
Davis, Al, 238
Davis, Terrell, 120
decleater hits, 307
declined penalties, 32
defensive alignments, 165–166, 169
defensive backfield, 169
defensive backs
  cornerbacks, 170–172
  defined, 169, 342
  disrupting pass timing by, 176
  in man-to-man coverage, 180–181
  nickel and dime backs, 174–175
  numbers on jerseys, 26
  plays used by, 178
  safeties, 172–174
  staying with receivers, 177
defensive coordinators, 231
defensive ends, 156–157, 342
defensive fronts, 188
defensive line coaches, 232
defensive linemen
  diagram symbol for, 2
  numbers on jerseys, 27
  overview, 153–154
  penalties relating to, 179–180
  qualities of, 157–158

defensive linemen *(continued)*
  responsibilities during play, 160–161
  role of, 154–155
  stances of, 155
  terminology, 158–160, 166
  types of, 155–157
defensive lines, 342
defensive strategies
  3-4 eagle defense, 193–194
  3-4 front defense, 132, 191–192
  4-3 front defense, 133, 189–190
  46 defense, 198–200
  choosing base defenses, 187–189
  cover one defense, 71
  cover two defense, 72, 201–202
  cover three defense, 72
  cover four defense, 73
  Dallas 4-3 defense, 194–195
  eight men in the box, 182
  flex defense, 195–196
  four-across defense, 134–135, 145
  man-to-man coverage, 81–82, 180–181
  Nickel 40 defense, 183–184
  over/under 4-3 defense, 200–201
  press coverage, 71, 135
  quarterbacks reading, 71, 197
  reasons behind choosing, 189
  in short-yardage situations, 204
  against star players, 203
  stopping two-point conversions, 203–204
  zone blitz, 137–138, 196–198
  zone coverage, 135–137, 182
defensive tackles, 156, 342
deferring, 34, 210
deflection, 83
delay draw, 133–134
delay of game
  penalties for, 49, 54
  referee signal for, 44
  too much time before snap, 32
delay of kickoff, 49
depth, 164
depth charts, 248
diagrams, key to symbols in, 2
dime backs, 174–175, 244
dime formation, 342
dip and rip technique, 82
directional kicking, 213

Ditka, Mike, 315–316
Dorsett, Tony, 101
double fouls, 342
double pick, 147
double-team blocking, 123, 155
down a punt, 225
down linemen, 343
down markers, 24
down stance, 99
down system, 35–36. *See also* first downs
downs, defined, 342
draft
  defined, 343
  examining players, 283–284
  for fantasy football, 296
  schedule for, 283
  selection rounds in, 283
draws, 105, 129, 343
drive blocks, 123
drives, 36, 343
driving through, 55
drop into coverage, 190
drop-kicking, 219–222
dropping back, 63, 65, 69

Easley, Kenny, 304–305
East-West Shrine Game, 274
edge, 115
eight men in the box, 182–183
elephant ends, 160
Elway, John, 61, 120, 129, 325
encroachment, 44, 49, 121, 343
end lines, 19
end zones, 19, 343
ends, 224
escapability, 65
Everett, Jim, 184
extra points, 37–38, 343. *See also* points
    after touchdown

face masks
  defined, 343
  overview, 28–29

penalties relating to, 54
referee signal for grabbing, 44
fair catches
defined, 343
penalties relating to, 51, 55
by punters, 225
referee signals relating to, 46
fakes, 86
false starts, 44, 50, 121
fantasy football
advice for, 299
drafting teams in, 296
filling rosters in, 294, 296–297
managing teams in, 297
online resources for, 251, 295–296, 299
playoffs and winning, 298
scoring points in, 294, 297–298
starting leagues in, 295
field
dimensions of, 18–19
goalposts, 23
marks and lines on, 19–21
surface of, 21–22
terminology, 210
field goal kickers, 208
field goals
blocking, 219–222
college overtime rules for, 33
defined, 343
NFL scoring statistics, 217
penalties relating to, 54, 56
pivotal role of kickers, 217
players used for, 218
rules for, 38, 218–219
rulings for good, 218
field judges, 42–43
field of play, 19
field position pass, 139
first downs
defined, 35, 344
referee signal for, 44
on television screens, 36
yard lines for anticipating, 19
first-year players, 286
flagged, 179
flankers (Z receivers). *See also* receivers;
wide receivers
defined, 344

lining up, 81
role as receivers, 79
flat, 87, 198, 203, 344
flex defense, 195–196
flexes, 195
fly (streak) pass pattern, 87
flying wedge, 11
football halls of fame, 13, 252
football smart, 65
footballs
K-balls, 24–25
penalty for loose, 52
referee signal for illegally touching, 46
rules for, 24–25
forced fumbles, 178
Ford, Mariet, 215
forklifts, 244
formations
defined, 88, 102, 344
dime, 342
I formation, 100, 102, 346
offset I formation, 103
penalty for illegal, 51
pistol, 131
pro-set, 100, 102
referee signal for illegal, 44
shotgun, 88–90
single wing, 13, 104
split T formation, 100, 102
split-back, 100, 102
T-formation, 325
wildcat, 130, 352
forward passes, 45, 50
fouls, 344
four-across defense, 134–135, 145
four-point stance, 80, 209
fourth downs, 44, 140–142
franchise players, 244, 286, 344
franchises. *See* National Football
League
free agency
choice of, 284–285
defined, 344
restricted, 286
unrestricted, 287
free safeties, 71, 173–174, 344
front seven, 73, 182, 188
fullbacks, 94, 344. *See also* running backs

full-house backfield, 258
fumbles
  causes of, 114
  defined, 36, 344
  forced, 178

• *G* •

game clocks. *See also names of specific clocks*
  lengths of quarters/halftimes, 31
  official's responsibility if inoperative, 42
  reasons for stopping/restarting, 32
  referee signals for, 44, 48
gaps, 162, 344
Garner, Dwight, 215
general managers, 239
getting your eyes in line with the flight of the ball, 81
Gibbs, Joe, 332–333
Gilchrist, Cookie, 94
giving the defensive player different looks, 119
go for two. *See* 2-point conversions
goal lines, 19, 23
goalposts, 23–24, 344
Graham, Otto, 65, 325–326
Grange, Harold "Red", 11–12
grass field surfaces, 21–22
Greene, Joe, 305
gridiron, 272
grip for passing, 70
ground game. *See also* running backs
  against 3-4 front defense, 132
  against 4-3 front defense, 133
  ball control in, 92
  basic running plays, 104–109
  formations in, 102–104
  for fourth down, 140–142
  overview, 92
  quarterback sneak, 63, 142
  running back's role in, 93–94
groundhog hits, 178
grounding, intentional, 46, 56, 83–84
guards, 114, 345
Guy, Ray, 226

• *H* •

hail Mary, 345
Halas, Joe, 333–334
halfbacks, 93–94, 345. *See also* running backs
halftime, 31, 249
Ham, Jack, 306
handoffs, 70, 96, 345
hands, illegal use of, 46, 49, 53
hang time, 345
Hannah, John, 316
Harmon, Mark, 214–215
hash marks, 20–21, 345
Hayes, Lester, 172
Haynes, Mike, 172, 306–307
head coaches, 231
head linesman, 41
Heisman, John W., 13
Heisman Trophy, 13, 272
helmets, 28–29, 54
helping the runner, 53, 121
Hendricks, Ted, 306
Hickey, Red, 88
hidden yardage, 217
high school football
  advice for coaches, 260
  advice for parents, 260–261
  advice for players, 259
  earning scholarships, 261–262
  importance of, 256–257
  judging talent in, 261
  life lessons taught by, 259
  player lineups in, 258
  rule differences in, 257
  season for, 14
  style of play in, 257–258
history of football
  author of first rules, 10–11
  early great players in, 13
  evolving from other sports, 10
  first form of game, 10, 263
  popularity of early pro football, 11–12
holders, 345
holding
  by defensive linemen, 179
  defined, 83

by offensive linemen, 122
penalties for, 49, 53
referee signal for, 44
Holy Roller play, 53
home field advantage, 281
hook pass pattern, 86
Houston, Ken, 307
Howard, Desmond, 215
huddles, 50, 345
Huff, Sam, 190, 308
hurries, 167
hurry-up offense, 345
Hutson, Don, 317

● **I** ●

I formation, 100, 102–103, 346
incomplete passes, 46, 346
ineligible receiver downfield, 122
influence blocks, 123–124
Ingram, Mark, 93
injured reserve, 286
injuries, 11, 212
instant replay challenge system, 57
intentional grounding, 83–84
interceptions, 71, 84, 178, 346
interference. *See* pass interference
intersection point, 119
isolation, 204

● **J** ●

jerseys, 26–28
Johnson, Jimmy, 217, 334
Jones, Deacon, 166–167, 308–309
juggled pass, 47

● **K** ●

K-balls, 24–25
keys, 135, 160–161, 346
kicking. *See* field goals; kickoffs; points
    after touchdown; punting
kicking game, 207
kicking teams, 33. *See also* kickoffs
kickoff returns
  coverage for, 216–217

hidden yardage in, 217
penalties relating to fair catches, 51, 55
purpose of, 215
returner's abilities in, 215–216
rules for, 213, 216
kickoffs
clock restarting after return, 32
decisions made at coin toss, 33–34, 211
defined, 346
directional kicking in, 213–214
kicking team's objectives in, 212–213
penalties relating to, 49, 51
rules for, 34–35, 213
setting up for, 211–212
knockout tackles, 178

● **L** ●

Lambeau, Earl "Curly", 77, 89
Lambeau Field, 18
Lambert, Jack, 309
Lane, Dick "Night Train", 309–310
lateral passes, 50, 214, 346
leading the receiver, 138
LeBeau, Dick, 137
left guards, 112
left tackles, 112
leverage, 119
Lilly, Bob, 310
line judges, 41–42
line of scrimmage, 41, 51, 346
linebacker coaches, 232
linebackers
blitzing by, 70
defined, 346
job description of, 162
numbers on jerseys, 27
roles and responsibilities of, 161–162
senses used by, 163
types of, 164–165
lining up, 81
live action, 25
live tweets, 251
Lombardi, Vince, 334–335
Lombardi Award, 273
Long, Howie
on artificial turf, 22

Long, Howie *(continued)*
  Blue-Gray all-star experiences, 274–275
  college football experiences, 273
  effect of coaches on, 229
  effect of football on, 7
  first football game seen by, 7
  preparing for offense, 188
  on quarterback's qualities, 61
  on running backs, 91, 98
  special teams experiences, 209
  structure/discipline learned from
      football, 10, 253
  Super Bowl experiences, 16, 277
  on wage inequities, 288
  on when to start playing, 253–254
long snaps, 346
looking off a defensive back, 244
loose balls, 52
loss of down, 47
Lott, Ronnie, 173
low blocks, 55
luxury suites, 290

• M •

Mackey, John, 315–316
Madden, John, 335–336
man free coverage, 180
Manning, Peyton, 64, 75, 326
man-on-man blocking, 123
man-to-man coverage
  beating, 81–82
  cornerbacks in, 171, 181
  defined, 162, 180, 346
  types of, 180–181
Marchetti, Gino, 311
Marino, Dan, 327
Maxwell Award, 273
McElhenny, Hugh, 317–318
middle field goal blocks, 221
middle linebackers, 165
midfield territory, 210
Mike linebackers, 165
mini-camps, 237, 277
mobile apps, 252
Moen, Kevin, 215
Montana, Joe, 61, 327–328

motions
  defined, 346
  penalties relating to, 51–52
  referee signal for illegal, 45
Motley, Marion, 94
moving the pile, 104
muffing a kick, 226
Muñoz, Anthony, 111
muscling his way through, 244

• N •

Namath, Joe Willie "Broadway Joe", 89
National Association of Intercollegiate
      Athletics (NAIA), 265
National Collegiate Athletic Association
      (NCAA). *See also* college football
  divisions and conferences of, 265–266,
      268–270
  instant replay challenge system, 57
  reason for conference-shifting in, 270
  scholarship eligibility, 261
National Football Conference (NFC),
      279–280
National Football League (NFL). *See also*
      pro football
  club financial structure, 238
  coaching staff, 230–233
  collective bargaining agreements,
      289, 291
  colleges with most players turning
      pro, 267
  conferences, 279–280
  drafting players, 283–284
  early days of, 278
  franchise movement, 290
  instant replay challenge system, 57
  jersey specifications, 26–27
  overtime rules, 33
  passer rating formula, 76
  player designations, 285–287
  player salaries, 287–289
  playoff qualification process, 280–281
  playoff system, 8
  Punt, Pass, & Kick competition, 255
  regular season, 277–278, 280
  roster size, 25

rules for footballs, 24–25
scouts, 239–240
season for, 14
signing free agents, 284–285
Super Bowl, 16, 281–282
team doctors and trainers, 240
television contracts, 289–290
trading players, 284
two-point conversion rules, 37–38
uniform codes, 30
website for, 250
NCAA. *See* college football; National
    Collegiate Athletic Association
neutral zone, 52, 114, 347
NFC (National Football Conference),
    279–280
NFL. *See* National Football League; pro
    football
NFL Network, 249–250
NFL Properties, 238, 290
NFL Record and Fact Book, 280
NFL Redzone Channel, 250
Nickel 40 defense, 183–185
nickel backs, 25, 174–175, 347
nickel package, 244
Nitschke, Ray, 308
no-huddle offense, 138–139, 347
nonstarting players, 25
north/south runners, 95, 97
nose tackles (nose guards), 155–156, 347
Notre Dame, 15, 266–267
numbers on jerseys, 26–27

● *O* ●

offensive backfield, 93
offensive coordinators, 231
offensive line, 347
offensive line coaches, 232
offensive linemen. *See also names of
    specific positions*
  blocking terminology, 122–124
  critical traits of, 117–121
  job description of, 111–112
  liberalization of rules for, 78
  past and present physiques of,
    116–117
  penalties for, 121–122

positions of, 112–116
  sizes of, 116–117, 127
offensive pass interference, 53, 347
offensive players, 2, 27
offensive plays and strategies. *See also*
    ground game; passing game
  5-yard bump rule in, 126
  against 3-4 front defense, 132
  against 4-3 front defense, 133
  against press coverage, 135
  against zone blitz, 137–138
  against zone coverage, 135–137
  basic running plays, 104–109
  calling plays, 62, 74–75
  check with me strategy, 75
  disguising successful, 148–149
  failure of, 125
  flying wedge, 11
  formations in, 102–104
  against four-across defense, 134–135
  for fourth-and-1, 140–142
  gaining field position with, 139–140
  hidden ball/hunchback trick, 13
  "Holy Roller" play, 53
  inside opponent's 10-yard line, 145
  keys to successful, 117–121
  no huddle offense, 138–139
  pistol, 131
  player's role in, 126
  quarterback sneak, 63, 142
  shotgun offense, 128–129
  spread, 131
  "Statue of Liberty" play, 13
  triple or vertical stretch, 143–144
  for two-point conversions, 146–148
  West Coast offense, 78, 117, 127–128
  wildcat, 130
officials
  defined, 347
  employment/compensation of, 40
  instant replay challenge system, 57
  referee signals, 43–48
  referees, 40
  responsibilities of, 39–40
offset I formation, 103
offside, 52, 122, 347
off-tackle, 105, 116, 347
Olsen, Merlin, 308–309

online resources
  fantasy football sites, 295–296, 299
  for judging high school players, 261
  keeping up with teams with, 250–252
  pro league sites, 291
  for scholarship eligibilities, 261
  sports sites, 250–252
  viewing older games, 130
onside kicks, 347
open end side, 158–159, 166
open ends, 159
open side tackles, 200
options, 200, 347
out of bounds, 21, 50–52
Outland Trophy, 273
over-loaded defense, 137
overloading, 129
overs, 133
overtime, 33, 348
over/under 4-3 defense, 200–201
owners, 238

• P •

Pac-12, 269
pads, 29
Page, Alan, 167
Parcells, Bill, 336–337
Parker, Jim, 318
pass coverage, dropping into, 173
pass cut-up, 188
pass defensed, 178
pass drops, 164
pass interference
  by defensive linemen, 179
  defined, 348
  penalty for, 53
  referee signal for, 46
pass patterns/routes
  comeback, 85
  common patterns, 85–88
  complexity of, 78
  crossing, 86, 127
  curl, 86
  defined, 70
  dropping back for, 69
  hook, 86
  pick, 203

post, 69, 86, 138, 344
slant, 86
square-out, 87
streak (fly), 87
swing, 87
passer rating formula, 76
passes. *See also* forward passes
  5-yard hitch, 140
  bomb, 127, 341
  field position, 139
  incomplete, 21
  juggled, 348
  penalties for interference, 53, 56–57
  play-action, 140, 348
  possession, 139–140
  quick out, 145
  referee signals relating to, 46–48
  route tree for, 87–88
  screen, 350
  speed of fast, 64
  timing for successful, 78
  uncatchable, 48
  underneath passes, 72
passing game
  beating man-to-man coverage, 82
  against blitz defense, 137–138
  disguising successful plays, 148–149
  against four-across defense, 134–135
  gaining field position with, 139–140
  great players and coaches, 89
  inside opponent's 10-yard line, 145
  pass patterns, 78, 85–88
  popularity of, 77
  against press coverage, 135
  red gun offense, 129
  rule changes in favor of, 78
  shotgun formation of, 88–90
  shotgun offense, 128–129
  terminology, 83–85
  triple or vertical stretch, 143
  for two-point conversions, 146–148
  West Coast offense, 78, 117, 127–128
  against zone coverage, 135–137
passing progressions, 67–68
passing reads, 68
pass-rushing ends, 160
PATs. *See* points after touchdown
Payton, Walter, 268, 318–319

penalties
  5-yard, 32, 49–52
  10-yard, 52–53
  15-yard, 54–56
  defined, 49
  disputing calls about, 57
  for offensive linemen, 121–122
  pass-play, 56–57
  referee signals for, 44–48
percentage kicks, 214–215
personal fouls, 47, 348
personal protectors, 224
pick pass pattern, 203
picks, 147, 203
pick-six, 348
pigskin, 24, 348. *See also* footballs
piling on, 55
pirates, 175
pistol formation, 131
pitching, 106, 348
placekickers, 34, 208, 348
placekicking. *See* kickoffs; points after
  touchdown
The Play, 214–215
play-action pass, 140, 185, 348
players. *See also names of specific*
  positions
  drafting process for, 283–284
  as free agents, 284–285
  health and collective bargaining
    agreements, 289, 291
  maximum number on field, 25
  NFL designations, 285–287
  NFL salaries and caps, 287–289
  nonstarting, 25
  numbers per side, 25
  penalty for failure to report change
    of, 50
  penalty for too many on field, 51
  referee signal for ejected, 47
  referee signal for ineligible, 46
  roster sizes, 25
  sizes proportionate to positions, 9
  trading, 284
playoffs. *See also* Super Bowl
  Bowl Championship Series,
    270–271
  fantasy football, 294

  NFL, 280–281
  single-elimination tournament style, 8, 16
plays, 74
playsheets, 235
pocket, 56, 348
points after touchdown (PATs)
  blocking, 219–222
  college overtime rules for, 33
  defined, 210
  overview, 37
  penalties relating to, 54, 56
  players used for, 218
  rules for, 218–219
  rulings for good, 218
Pollard, Fritz, 13
poor reads, 177
Pop Warner Football, 254–255
possession, 348
post, 70, 86, 138, 348
pot, 295
power offense, 116
practice squads, 286
press coverage, 71, 135
pressing, 184
prevent defense, 143
pro football. *See also* National Football
    League
  arena, 291
  Canadian, 291
  early days of, 278
  Hall of Fame, 13
  holiday traditions involving, 9
  as part of Americana, 8
  playoff system unique to, 8, 16
  popularity of, 9, 12
Pro Football Hall of Fame, 13, 252
Pro-Bowlers, 286
prolate spheroids, 24
pro-set formation, 100, 102
protecting the football, 100–101
pulling, 108, 116
Punt, Pass, & Kick competition, 255
punt returners, 208, 225, 227
punters
  abilities of, 223, 226
  alignment of, 223
  defined, 349
  responsibilities of, 208

punting
   after three and out, 35
   art of, 226–227
   benefits of, 222–223
   consequences of poor, 226
   defined, 35, 349
   man coverage in, 224
   out of own territory, 226
   penalties relating to, 51–52, 54
   players used for, 223–224
   rules for, 225
   setting up and kicking, 223
punting teams, 208
pursuit and angles, 101
pushing, illegal, 45

• Q •

quarterback coaches, 232
quarterback sneak, 63, 142
quarterbacks
   audibilizing by, 62, 74–75
   bailing out of the play, 67
   blitzing, 70
   calling plays by, 62, 74
   defined, 349
   fundamental skills of, 68–71
   general discussion, 61–62
   as great passers, 89
   job description of, 61–63
   judging of, 75–76
   numbers on jerseys, 26
   pass routes of, 70
   reading defense by, 63, 71–73
   shotgun snap to, 63
   size of, 67
   staying in pocket position, 63
   traits of, 64–68
   uniforms protecting, 29
quarters, 31
quick feet, 65
quick kick, 227
quick out, 145

• R •

radio, 246–247
rainbow pass, 184

reach blocks, 123
receivers. *See also names of specific
      receivers*
   better rules for protection of, 78,
      179–180
   blocking by, 79
   face masks for, 29
   great receivers, 89
   line up for, 81
   numbers on jerseys, 27
   penalties for illegal contact, 56
   penalties for interference with, 53, 57
   penalties relating to ineligible, 50
   role of, 78–79
   running backs as, 78
   sizes of, 78–79
   stances for, 80
   teaching kids stances of, 80
   techniques of, 82–83
   terminology, 83–85
   X,Y, and Z, 79
receiving teams, 33, 213, 216
recovering, 64
recruiting, 237. *See also* scouts
red gun (run-and-shoot) offense, 129
red zones, 349
redshirts, 349
referees, 11, 40, 43–48
Reid, Mike, 168
release (quarterback), 66
release (tight end), 160
reserves, 297
restricted free agents, 286
retreating, 65
returners, 35
returns, 51, 349
reverses, 106, 349
Rice, Jerry, 82, 268
right guards, 112
right tackle, 112
Rockne, Knute, 337–338
Rodgers, Richard, 215
rodmen, 35
roll out, 349
rookies, 286
Roosevelt, Theodore, 11
rosters, 25, 296–297
roughing the kicker, 56, 218

roughing the passer, 55, 84
roughness, unnecessary, 56
route trees, 87–88
routes, 83, 349. *See also* pass patterns/
    routes
rugby, 10, 92
rules and regulations
    author of first, 10–11
    ball specifications, 24–25
    changes to passing game, 78
    coin toss and kickoff, 33–34, 212
    college football, 265
    down system, 35–36
    field goals and PATs, 218–219
    game clocks, 31–32
    high school football, 257
    instant replay challenge system, 57
    NFL uniforms, 30
    overtime and sudden death, 33
    penalties, 49–57
    punting, 225
    referee signals, 43–48
    role of officials, 39–43
    scoring points, 36–39
    violence and, 11
run cut-up, 188
run-and-shoot (red gun) offense, 129
running at the defense's weakest
    point, 134
running backs. *See also* receivers
    characteristics of, 91
    in college versus pro football, 99
    defined, 349
    fullback's role as, 94
    fundamental skills of, 95–97
    job description of, 97–98
    as main ball carrier, 93–94
    numbers on jerseys, 26
    priorities of, 100–101
    role as receivers, 78
    sizes of, 94–95
    stances of, 99–100
running into the kicker, 218
running to daylight, 244
rushing, 155, 349

• S •

sacks
    defined, 53, 67, 85, 155, 166, 308–309, 350
    NFL recording, 166–167
    rules for, 167
safeties (players), 172–174
safeties (score), 39, 47, 350
salary caps, 287–289, 350
Sam linebackers, 164
Sanchez, Mark, 66
Sayers, Gale, 319
schemes, 154, 350
Schmidt, Joe, 190
scoring points
    extra points, 37
    field goals, 38
    safeties, 39
    touchdowns, 36
    two-point conversions, 37–38
scouts
    college, 239–240
    online resources for, 261
    pro, 239
scrambles, 350
screen passes, 350
scrum, 10
sealing of the outside, 115
seam, 195
seasons
    for college, 14
    for high school, 14
    for National Football League, 14, 280
SEC (Southeastern Conference), 269
secondary
    defined, 71, 162, 169, 350
    players in, 169–175
    quarterbacks reading, 71, 197
    tricks and techniques of, 176–177
secondary coaches, 232
Senior Bowl, 274
Shanahan, Mike, 235
shanks, 223
shedding, 164
Shell, Art, 320

shifts, 45, 50, 52
shock troops, 338
shoes, 29–30
shooting a gap, 244
short zone coverage, 197
short-arming the ball, 114
short-deep areas, 162
short-yardage situations, 204
shotgun formation, 88–90
shotgun offense, 128–129
shotgun snap, 63, 88, 350
Shula, Don, 338–339
side judges, 43
sidelines, 19, 350
signal count, 113
single wing formation, 104
single-elimination tournaments, 8
six o'clock step, 70
size of players
  defensive backs, 170
  defensive linemen, 153, 157
  high school players, 258
  offensive linemen, 116–117
  proportionate to positions, 9
  quarterbacks, 67
  receivers, 78
  running backs, 94–95
  skilled players, 65
slant pass pattern, 86
slants, 107, 350
slide blocks, 123
slide-protect, 320
sling-shot goalposts, 23
snake drafts, 296
snap. *See also* wide receivers
  center's job during, 113–114
  defined, 350
  overview, 112
  penalties relating to, 32, 51–52
  shotgun or long, 63, 88, 350
soccer, 10
soccer-style kicking, 222
Southeastern Conference (SEC), 269
special teams. *See also* placekicking
  awards for, 228
  contribution to total points by, 209–210

defined, 207, 350
NFL scoring statistics for, 209
notability of, 207
players in, 208
units in, 208
special teams coaches, 208, 231–232
specialists, 208
spiking the ball, 84
spirals, 351
split ends (X receivers). *See also*
  receivers
  defined, 351
  lining up, 81
  role as receivers, 79
split T formation, 100, 102
split-back formation, 100, 102
splitting the uprights, 23
spotting the ball, 20–21
spread, 131, 351
square-out pass pattern, 87
stadiums, 17–18, 247–248
Stagg, Amos Alonzo, 13
stances
  of defensive linemen, 155
  defined, 351
  of offensive lineman, 117–118
  of quarterbacks, 69
  of receivers, 80
  of running backs, 96, 99–100
stand-up stance, 80
Statue of Liberty play, 13
Staubach, Roger, 65
stemming, 177
Stephenson, Dwight, 111
stiff arm, 101
straight man coverage, 180
streak (fly) pass pattern, 87
streak route, 70
strength coaches, 232
stretch, 108
stretch the defense, 143
stretch the field, 244
stringing out a play, 167
strong safeties, 173, 351
strong side, 173, 351
stunts, 156, 185, 204, 351

substitutions, 45, 51, 351
subway alumni, 267
sudden death, 33
Super Bowl
    birth of, 281
    intangibles in reaching for, 277
    popularity of commercials, 16
    preparations for, 282
    uniqueness and popularity of, 16
sweeps, 70, 107, 351
swim technique, 82–83
swing pass pattern, 87

● T ●

tackles
    blind-side, 112–113
    defined, 11, 351
    introduction of, 11
    knockout, 178
    overview, 167
    right, 112
    role during off-tackle runs, 116
    traits and job of, 115–116
tailbacks, 351. See also running backs
takeaways, 352
Tampa two defense, 202
Tarkenton, Fran, 66, 328
Tasker, Steve, 228
Taylor, Lawrence, 192
team doctors, 240
tees, 34, 211
telestrators, 245
television
    electronic first down lines on, 36
    football coverage on, 249–250
    increasing football popularity, 15
    NFL contracts and growth with,
        289–290
    Super Bowl's broadcast on, 16
    watching games on, 245–246
T-formation, 325
third-and-long, 139
Thorpe, Jim, 13
three-point stance, 80, 99, 118
throwback jerseys, 28

tight end side, 158
tight ends. See also wide receivers
    defined, 352
    line up for, 81
    receptions in NFL by, 78
    Y receiver replacing, 79
timeouts
    defined, 34
    penalty for excessive, 50
    referee signal for, 48
    two-minute warning for, 42
timing pass, 85
touch football, 9
touch passes, 87
touchbacks
    defined, 216, 352
    kickoff rules resulting in, 212
    punting rules for, 225
    referee signal for, 48
touchdowns
    defined, 36, 352
    methods of scoring, 36
    referee signal for, 48
trainers, 240
transition players, 286
trap blocks, 123–124
trapping when catching, 85
trenches, 9
tripping, 48, 53
true linebackers, 164
turf burn, 22
turnovers, 84, 188, 352
Twitter, 251
two-gap style, 192
two-gappers, 191
two-point stance, 96, 99
two-way players, 258, 272

● U ●

umbrella defense, 189
umpires, 41
under tackles, 159
underneath, 135
underneath passes, 72
unders, 133

uniforms
  helmets and facemasks, 28–29
  jerseys, 26–28
  necessity of, 26
  NFL codes for, 30
  pads, 29
  shoes and cleats, 29–30
Unitas, Johnny, 89, 328–329
unnecessary roughness, 56
unrestricted free agents, 287
unsportsmanlike conduct, 48, 56
up stance, 96, 99
uprights of goalposts, 23
Upshaw, Gene, 320–321

• *V* •

veering, 109, 352
veterans, 282, 287
Vick, Michael, 64, 66
violence in football, 10–11

• *W* •

waiver system, 287
walk-ons, 261
Walsh, Bill, 339–340
Walter Camp All-America Team, 274
War Room, 284
Warner, Pop, 13
weak side, 132, 352
weak-side lead, 132
weak-side linebackers, 164
websites. *See* online resources
wedge busters, 216
West Coast offense, 78, 117, 127–128
White, Randy "The Manster", 195
wide receivers. *See also* receivers
  defined, 352
  flankers, 79, 344

  line up for, 81
  receptions in NFL by, 78
  split ends, 79, 351
wildcard teams, 281
wildcat formation, 130, 352
Wilfork, Vince, 154
Willis, Patrick, 162–163
Willy linebackers, 164
wings, 224
wishbone, 264

• *X* •

X receivers. *See* receivers; split ends

• *Y* •

Y receivers, 79. *See also* receivers
yards after the catch, 75
Young, Steve, 65, 329
youth football
  advice for coaching, 255–256
  character-building aspects of, 253
  signing up for, 254–256
  when to start, 253–254

• *Z* •

Z receivers. *See* flankers; receivers; wide
   receivers
zeroing in on a receiver, 244
Zimmerman, Gary, 120
zone blitz defense, 137–138, 196–198
zone blocks, 124
zone coverage
  cornerbacks in, 172
  defensive backs in, 182
  defined, 352
  offensive plays against, 135–137

About the Authors

Howie Long is a former Oakland/Los Angeles Raider defensive end with eight Pro Bowl appearances, a Super Bowl XVIII victory over the Washington Redskins, and many other accolades to his credit. His size (6'5" 275 pounds), combined with his speed, strength, intensity, durability, and explosive quickness, set him apart. He retired from the NFL after the 1993 season.

Long is currently a commentator on the Emmy Award–winning *FOX NFL Sunday* program, which is the most-watched NFL pregame show in America. His previous television broadcasting credits include ESPN's *Up Close,* on which he had a regular segment discussing current sports issues, HBO's *Inside the NFL,* the weekly *NFL Diary,* NBC's *NFL Live* as a guest studio analyst, and *Costas Coast to Coast.* He also wrote the opening chapter to Bo Jackson's book, *Bo Knows Bo* (Jove).

Long is no stranger to the limelight, as he's been involved in many commercials and campaigns for Nike, Hanes, Coca-Cola, and Pizza Hut. He also made his big-screen debut in the action-adventure film *Broken Arrow* with John Travolta and Christian Slater and was featured in the 1998 film *Firestorm.*

At Villanova University, Long was a four-year letterman in football as a defensive lineman. He was All-East and honorable mention All-American as a senior, and was tabbed the Most Valuable Player in the 1980 Blue-Gray Game. He was also a champion boxer as an undergraduate, and graduated with a degree in communications in 1981.

John Czarnecki has reported on the NFL for 32 years. He has consulted for FOX NFL Sunday since the program began in 1994, and he previously consulted for NFL Today. A former newspaperman with such dailies as the Los Angeles Herald Examiner and the Dallas Morning News, Czarnecki is currently one of 44 selectors to the Pro Football Hall of Fame.

Dedication

For Paul Barnes (who taught me to be of service) and Helen Barnes (who loved it when I called her that). – Roy Barnes

Author's Acknowledgments

From Howie Long:

First, I'd like to thank my wife, Diane, and my three sons for their support. I'd also like to thank my former coach at the Los Angeles Raiders, Earl Leggett, who taught me not only how to be a great football player but also how to be a man. And I can't forget my coauthor, John Czarnecki, for all his hard work and dedication to this project. Thanks also to my friends around the NFL, Terry Robiskie, Hudson Houck, and Artie Gigantino, who contributed to this book. Finally, I'd like to thank all the people at John Wiley and Sons who participated in this project.

From John Czarnecki:

Thanks go to my proofreading wife, Vicki, and to my daughters for staying clear of me on my bad days. To my mom, who knew that I would do a book one day. To Ben, my computer expert, and Kathy, my transcriber, and John and Mike at Clone Copy. To the coaches, Earl Leggett, Terry Robiskie, Fritz Shurmur, Hudson Houck, and Ernie Zampese. To Barry Meier, my neighborly coaching expert. To Artie Gigantino, a special teams/television expert. To Garrett Giemont, a very special strength trainer. To two helpful workers, Don Seeholzer and Bryan Broaddhus. To Ron Wolf, for all his insightful football knowledge these past many years, and to my good friend, Peter King, for all his advice. And to my best friend, Pat, for not calling me for three months.

Publisher's Acknowledgments

Executive Editor: Lindsay Lefevere

Assistant Editor: David Lutton

Project Editor: Tracy Brown Hamilton

Copy Editor: Kathleen Dobie

Technical Editor: Michael Daniels

Art Coordinator: Alicia B. South

Production Editor: Kinson Raja

Cover Photos: ©iStock.com/Matt_Brown